Evil Necessity

Evil Necessity

Slavery and Political Culture
in Antebellum Kentucky

HAROLD D. TALLANT

THE UNIVERSITY PRESS OF KENTUCKY

Publication of this volume was made possible in part
by a grant from the National Endowment for the Humanities.

Editorial and Sales Offices: The University Press of Kentucky
663 South Limestone Street, Lexington, Kentucky 40508-4008

07 06 05 04 03   5 4 3 2 1

Library of Congress Cataloging-in-Publication Data

Tallant, Harold D., 1956-
  Evil necessity : slavery and political culture in antebellum Kentucky
/ Harold D. Tallant.
      p. cm.
Includes bibliographical references and index.
  ISBN 0-8131-2252-X (acid-free paper)
  1. Slavery—Kentucky. 2. Political culture—Kentucky. 3.
Kentucky—Politics and government—1792-1865. I. Title.
E445.K5 T35 2002
326'.09769—dc21   2002152767

This book is printed on acid-free recycled paper meeting
the requirements of the American National Standard
for Permanence of Paper for Printed Library Materials.

Manufactured in the United States of America

For Ann and Amanda

Contents

Preface

This book is a study of the slavery controversy in antebellum Kentucky, one of the few slave states where genuine debate about the benefits and existence of slavery continued right up to the Civil War. It looks especially at the influence of a distinctive ideology of slavery, the theory of slavery as a necessary evil, which ironically both promoted dissent against slavery in Kentucky and thwarted effective action against it. This study focuses on the years from the formation of the Kentucky Colonization Society in 1829 to John Brown's Raid in 1859, a period which begins with the necessary-evil theory at the height of its popularity and influence in Kentucky, and ends with the bitter and definitive southern reaction against all antislavery activity, just months before the Confederacy went to war to protect slavery.

A brief word is in order to explain the methods I have used in quoting other sources. I have changed ampersands in the original texts to the word *and,* and occasionally altered the initial capitalization and terminal punctuation of quotations in accordance with common scholarly practice. Otherwise, I have retained the original form of quoted material, including italics and other forms of emphasis.

During my work on this project, I have become indebted to a number of individuals and institutions who lent support to my work. Librarians at the following institutions greatly aided my research efforts: Duke University, the University of North Carolina at Chapel Hill, the Historical Society of Pennsylvania, Indiana University, Florida State University, Emory University, the Library of Congress, Fisk University, Vanderbilt University, Western Kentucky University, the Louisville Free Public Library, the University of Louisville, Southern Baptist Theological Seminary, the Filson Historical Society, the Kentucky Historical Society, the University of Kentucky, the Lexington Public Library, Lexington Theological Seminary, Morehead State University, Centre College, Berea College, the Scott County Public Library, and Georgetown College. The Lost Cause Press kindly provided me with microcard editions of several very rare pamphlets and books.

Several institutions gave me financial and material support for research and writing. The Department of History at Duke University provided financial support for this project, and Duke's Management Information Services gave me special access to computer equipment. Georgetown College supported this project by providing sabbatical leaves and by partially underwriting the costs of photocopying, travel, student help, and research materials.

I also owe thanks to several scholars. At various stages of the writing process, John F. Hoadley, Daniel Feller, Raymond Gavins, Michael Morrison, David E. Price, Richard L. Watson, and Major Wilson read and commented on portions of the manuscript. Clark R. Cahow gave a close reading to an early version of the manuscript and provided generous financial support during the years I assisted him with teaching and research. Robert F. Durden helped shape the formative stages of my thinking on slavery, directed the dissertation, and did more than any other person to improve my writing skills. William W. Freehling and Marion B. Lucas gave valuable advice which guided the final revisions to the manuscript. Special thanks go to Lindsey A. Apple and James C. Klotter. Lindsey, as department chair during most of my years at Georgetown College, provided constant support and encouragement for research and writing. Jim provided sound advice about writing and took time from his own book project to give the manuscript a thorough reading with the eyes of an experienced editor and master historian.

A project like this requires the support of friends and family, something I have had in abundance. Two friends, Tony and Bertha Busseni, took a special interest in this project and, probably without knowing it, prompted me to keep pressing toward the final goal. My in-laws, Wallace and Evelyn Boyd, have been constant encouragers, as have been my sister and her husband, Marilynn and Billie Friel, and my sister-in-law, Linda Root. It is impossible for me to number fully the many contributions to this book made by my parents and by my wife and daughter. No one believed in me more than my father, Harold D. Tallant Sr., whose hope for the completion of this project sustained me through the difficult early writing stages. My mother, Rhoda E. Tallant, also provided crucial assistance during the initial stages of research and suggested several changes that improved the final version of this work. My greatest debt of gratitude is to my wife Ann and my daughter Amanda. Both willingly sacrificed much so that this book could be completed. No one is prouder to see the book finally completed than Amanda. In addition to the emotional sustenance only a spouse can offer, Ann contributed to virtually every phase of this project in some way. Her many contributions to this book are beyond description. And without the loving support of Ann and Amanda, the writing of this work would have been a more arduous and less joyous endeavor.

1

The Necessary Evil

The final years of the 1790s found Kentuckians engaged in an earnest debate about what sort of government and society they should
have in the future, a debate occasioned by the efforts of many Kentuckians to revise the state's constitution, then less than a decade old.
Joining this debate was a young attorney who had recently arrived
from his native Virginia. Writing under the name "Scaevola," the
twenty-one-year-old lawyer penned a letter to a local newspaper urging Kentuckians to abolish slavery in their new constitution. "All
America acknowledges the existence of slavery to be an evil, . . ." he
wrote. "It deprives the slave of the best gift of heaven, [and] in the
end injures the master too, by laying waste his lands, enabling him
to live indolently, and thus contracting all the vices generated by a
state of idleness." Such talk deeply alarmed the friends of slavery.
Although most proslavery Kentuckians—if pressed on the point—
would have agreed with "Scaevola" that slavery was wrong in the
abstract, they greatly feared emancipation and charged that people
like "Scaevola" wanted to ruin the state by immediately turning loose
its entire population of slaves. For his part, "Scaevola" denied these
charges, writing in a second letter that he opposed immediate emancipation and supported only a gradual plan of emancipation in which
slaves would be trained for freedom. "Although [natural] rights are
immutable," he wrote, "cases may be conceived in which the enjoy-

ment of them is improper. That of the present race of negroes is one. Thirty thousand slaves without preparation for enjoying the rights of freemen, without property, without principle, let loose upon society would be wretched themselves, and render others miserable."[1]

Kentucky did not abolish slavery in its Constitution of 1799. And when Kentuckians prepared to hold a constitutional convention to revise that document half a century later, slavery was again the main topic of political discussion. Almost exactly fifty years after he had written his second letter in support of emancipation, "Scaevola" again took up his pen in support of freedom. No longer an inexperienced, unknown lawyer, he was now one of America's leading statesmen—a United States senator, former Speaker of the House of Representatives, former secretary of state, and five-time presidential candidate. This time, he abandoned his pen name and used his real name: Henry Clay. Although much had changed in Henry Clay's life, the position he took in 1849 was remarkably similar to what it had been half a century earlier. "A vast majority of the people of the United States, . . ." Clay wrote in 1849, "lament that a single slave treads our soil, deplore the necessity of the continuance of slavery in any of the States, regard the institution as a great evil to both races, and would rejoice in the adoption of any safe, just and practicable plan for the removal of all slaves from among us." Again Clay urged his fellow Kentuckians to place some plan of emancipation in the state constitution, and again he expressed hope that the plan would be a moderate one: "slow in its operation, cautious and gradual, so as to occasion no convulsion, nor any rash or sudden disturbance, in the existing habits of society."[2]

Some political commentators of Clay's time and some historians of the modern age have accused Clay of tailoring his public positions on slavery to suit the ever changing tide of national public opinion. Today, Clay's nickname, "the Great Compromiser," takes on a derogatory meaning entirely unintended by the adoring supporters who gave it to him. Yet, despite Clay's frequent vacillations on specific issues concerning slavery, throughout his career he displayed a remarkable consistency in asserting that slavery was an evil to master and slave alike—an evil, however, to be tolerated until individual states could devise gradual, cautious plans of emancipation that would prevent blacks from becoming a threat to the white population. Clay's consistency on this point was fitting for a man who so often sought the favor of the voters of Kentucky. Throughout most of the period before the Civil War, white Kentuckians generally viewed slavery much as Clay did. They thought of slavery as an evil to their state, but one whose burdens must be borne patiently until some safe and practical solution to the problem could be found. To them, slavery was a necessary evil.[3]

This book examines the political ramifications in Kentucky between 1829 and 1859 of the idea that slavery was a necessary evil. It will argue that during a period in which white residents of the Lower South were coming to idealize slavery as a positive good, Kentuckians continued to insist that slavery was a necessary evil. In Kentucky, at least, this was no mere rhetorical flourish; rather, it bespoke genuine—albeit ambivalent—opposition to the future of slavery in Kentucky. Even in the 1850s, when the views of white Kentuckians on slavery began to resemble those of people farther south, most Kentuckians remained doubtful that slavery was the unequivocal boon that proslavery ideologues of the Lower South claimed it to be. White Kentuckians' long history of moderation on the issue of slavery provided an atmosphere in which a genuine, native antislavery movement could operate throughout the years before the Civil War. Ironically, though, Kentucky's antislavery movement was hindered as well as helped by the nearly universal agreement among white Kentuckians that slavery was a necessary evil. Since even the state's antislavery advocates believed that slavery was, for the immediate future, a necessary instrument for controlling the state's black population, their willingness to take firm action against slavery was often inhibited. Moreover, the demonstrated unwillingness of most Kentuckians to take any definite action to abolish slavery—despite their professions that slavery was indeed an evil—often led to crippling disheartenment among the state's antislavery advocates. Kentucky's position on slavery could well be described with an analogy from the Bible often cited by northern antislavery writers. Those who held that slavery was a necessary evil were trying to serve two masters:

God and Mammon—their highest principles and the things of the world. As the New Testament warned, "No man can serve two masters: for either he will hate the one, and love the other; or else he will hold to the one, and despise the other. Ye cannot serve God and mammon." While professing to love freedom, Kentuckians held on to slavery until the bitter end of the American Civil War in 1865.[4]

Historians have long been aware that many southerners proclaimed slavery a necessary evil before the 1820s. It was not until later that southerners began using the militant, uncompromising proslavery argument familiar to the student of the antebellum sectional controversy. Indeed, before the 1820s the necessary-evil theory may have come closer to describing the national consensus on slavery than any other position advocated before the Civil War. Supporters of the theory described slavery as an accursed blight on the American nation, an embarrassing anomaly in a new republic founded on the ideals of freedom and equality. Believing that blacks were fully human and endowed with innate intellectual potential similar to that of whites, necessary-evil theorists argued that African Americans had the same natural rights to life, liberty, and property as white Americans. Proponents of the necessary-evil theory maintained that while blacks might be inferior to whites at the moment, it was the degrading conditions of slavery that caused this inferiority. Additionally, they argued that slavery was an inefficient form of labor that threatened the nation's wealth. Accepting the idea that a system of free labor was integral to national prosperity, necessary-evil theorists argued that laborers could not be compelled to work efficiently against their will. On the contrary, they would work slowly, do as little as possible, and perform the work poorly. In contrast, free laborers worked with maximum efficiency because they worked for their own self-interest to maximize profit. Slave states were sure to decline economically as they competed with more efficient free-labor societies in the modern world of capitalist markets. As a consequence, slavery was dying from economic causes.

Additionally, slavery forced whites into constant contact with a purportedly inferior, corrupting, and hostile race of people. Despite their statements about the innate potential of blacks, necessary-evil theorists did not dispute the current depravity of African Americans. Slavery degraded whites by exposing them to a people of supposedly loose morals and low intellect. Even worse, slavery endangered the safety of society by placing within it a potentially revolutionary force: vengeful black slaves. Necessary-evil theorists claimed that racial animosity was a natural condition of humanity, and that history showed that two races had never lived in the same society in peaceful harmony with each other. Examples of this tension and conflict were easy to find in places like Kentucky in the form of slave resistance and escapes. Every year that slavery continued to exist, they claimed, such animosity increased. Eventually the slaves would rise up in rebellion, just as whites would do were they held in bondage. Thus, the existence of slavery threatened the very safety of whites.

Slavery was so harmful to the future of the nation, the argument went, that only the far greater harms that would arise from a precipitate and premature emancipation of slaves—the abridgment of property rights, the unsettling of the labor supply, and the creation of an uncontrollable free black population—prevented white Americans from destroying the institution of slavery immediately. Necessary-evil theorists argued that if humans lived in the perfect world God designed, with blacks and whites living separately in Africa and Europe, there would be no racial competition and no reason to establish or maintain slavery. All of humanity would be free to enjoy its God-given natural rights. However, people currently inhabited an imperfect world corrupted by humanity through sin, greed, and immorality. With blacks and whites unnaturally mixed together, the result was racial hatreds and competition. Even if blacks were freed from slavery in places like Kentucky, the racial hatreds would remain. Acting on their prejudices, whites would deny blacks access to the avenues of advancement and reward that prompted people to conform to the values of society. Without these inducements to social conformity, free blacks would be prone to slothfulness, crime, and violence. Eventually, former slaves would rise in a racial war of retribution against whites for the injustices done to them both before and after slavery. This fact, said necessary-evil proponents, dictated that slavery was a necessary means for controlling the black race as long as it remained in America. While all people have an abstract right to life, liberty, and property, the most important is life, or the right to self-preservation. Accordingly, the Negro's right to liberty must be temporarily sacrificed in order to safeguard the Caucasian's right to self-preservation.

Slavery, then, was thought to be a *necessary* evil, one whose burdens would have to be borne until the slow workings of social, economic, and demographic trends made the problems of emancipation solvable. But slavery would die someday, if not at the hands of lawmakers, then by its own cancerous nature. Slavery had existed in all of the American colonies at the beginning of the Revolution, but by the turn of the nineteenth century the imperatives of liberty and the demands of economics had driven it from most of the northern states. The existence of slavery was being debated in the rest of the northern states and some of the states of the Upper South, and many expected that the states of the Lower South would eventually enter this debate.

During the 1820s and 1830s, however, this explanation for the existence of slavery began to lose favor throughout the United States. In the midst of a new and booming market for southern cotton, the people of the Lower South increasingly abandoned any thought that slavery was, in the main, a harmful, evil institution. By the late 1830s most whites in the Lower South would have agreed with John C. Calhoun's famous dictum that "where two races . . . are brought together, the relation now existing in the slaveholding States between the two, is, instead of an evil, a good—a positive good." In the North, the trend was more uncertain. As slavery continued to grow and expand into the new cotton-growing sections of the American southwest, many northerners began to question whether slavery was in fact hastening to a quick death caused by economic inefficiency. As southern politicians demanded increasing protection for slavery at the apparent expense of northern interests, people in the North rightly wondered what had happened to the enlightened southern politicians, represented in an earlier age by people like Thomas Jefferson and Patrick Henry, who had once seemed to be leading their section toward emancipation. Although many in the North showed little concern over slavery and proved more than willing to defer to the South on the issue, by the late 1840s some northerners grew impatient with the idea that slavery should be tolerated—and northern interests sacrificed—out of deference to property rights, federal amity, or racial control. Yet while northerners demonstrated a new resolve to limit the expansion of slavery into the western territories, there was little impetus in the North to strike down slavery in the southern states, except from a small group of northern abolitionists who insisted that slaveholding was morally wrong and should be abandoned immediately.[5]

Only in the Upper South, in states like Kentucky, did the idea that slavery was a necessary evil retain much currency during the antebellum era. The continuing allegiance of Kentuckians to this traditional idea was noted by a number of contemporary observers. One Pennsylvanian who immigrated to Kentucky in the 1830s, for instance, wrote home that "I have talked with rich and poor alike on the subject, and find them alike, would be glad if there was not a slave in the state." In fact, he encountered this sentiment often enough that he believed it "very probable that a few years will see K[entuck]y a free state." Indeed, nearly any public discussion of slavery in Kentucky provided ample evidence of the dogged tenacity with which Kentuckians insisted that slavery was a necessary evil. Until the 1850s, most discussion proceeded from the assumptions that slavery in Kentucky was harmful to the welfare of most whites and that the existence of African-American slavery was tolerated only out of deference to the property rights of slaveholders and out of concern for the alleged necessity of controlling the black race in Kentucky.[6]

Thus, in Kentucky and the other states of the Upper South there flourished a conception of slavery that differed sharply from views found in both the North and the Lower South. Important conceptual linkages, however, did remain between the ideologies of slavery embraced by the Upper South and those embraced by the other two sections. Both the theory of slavery as a necessary evil and the theory of slavery as a positive good were used to justify the existence of slavery, at least for the near future. In addition, the two theories shared many individual propositions about slavery and blacks. Both theories, for instance, incorporated the racist perspective that blacks were so degraded that slavery was the best condition for African Americans while they remained in America. Both denied that the Bible condemned slavery in the abstract and argued that slavery had the beneficial effect of exposing African slaves to Christianity in America. Both showed extraordinarily strong respect for the rights and prerogatives of slaveholders.

Despite these and many other points of agreement, there were significant differences between the necessary-evil theory and the positive-good theory in regard to the future viability of slavery. In fact, necessary-evil proponents shared interesting habits of thought with northerners, especially a tendency to let other issues, values, and concerns significantly shape their responses to the slavery issue, rather than letting slavery shape their responses to other issues. By the 1830s, positive-good theorists in the Lower South were much more likely than either Kentuckians or northerners to reorder their entire value systems around their positions on slavery. This may help explain the greater enthusiasm of the Lower South than the Upper South to fight a war to protect slavery in 1861, and the reluctance of northerners and the border slave states to involve slavery as an issue in the fighting.[7]

The willingness of Kentuckians throughout most of the antebellum period to concede that slavery harmed their state and to profess a desire to be rid of the peculiar institution can be partly attributed to the fact that much of the population had little direct connection with the institution of slavery. As in other parts of the South, ownership of slaves in Kentucky was confined to a small portion of the population. In 1850, nearly 77 percent of the state's adult white males owned no slaves, a figure close to the median for the South as a whole. Perhaps more important, the average size of the slaveholdings in Kentucky was the fourth smallest in the South. In addition, although slaves made up between 19 and 24 percent of Kentucky's population during the antebellum period, large portions of the state had almost no slaves at all. Slavery was mostly confined to the Bluegrass area in north central Kentucky and a few scattered regions along the Ohio River and the southwestern border with Tennessee. Few slaves lived in the mountainous eastern third of the state. By 1850, for instance, there were three thousand fewer slaves in the twenty-four counties of the eastern mountain region than there were in the single county of Fayette in the Bluegrass region, even though the combined white population of the mountain counties was twelve times the size of the white population of Fayette County.[8]

The continuing adherence of most Kentuckians to the doctrine of slavery as a necessary evil can also be partly attributed to the fact that, in a border state like Kentucky, economic forces did not seem to require the use of slave labor, but the existence of a significant black population did seem to dictate the racial controls of slavery. During the antebellum period, most parts of the state lacked the labor-intensive staple crops that most southerners believed were necessary to support slavery. Next to Virginia, Kentucky had perhaps the broadest economic base of any state in the South. The breadth of Kentucky's economy is demonstrated by the federal census of 1850, which measured the production of some forty-seven types of agricultural and manufactured goods. Among the fifteen slave states, Kentucky ranked either first or second in the production of well over half of these items. As these statistics suggest, by 1850 most of the state had turned to a diversified economic base of hemp and grain production, livestock breeding, and small-scale manufacturing. Even the slave-rich Bluegrass region, once an important center of tobacco production, had largely abandoned this staple for a mixture of cereals, hemp, and livestock, a transition that made slavery seem increasingly irrelevant as a form of labor. Only in the southwestern portion of the state, where tobacco remained an important cash crop, did slavery seem to Kentuckians to be an economic necessity. Although even nonslaveholding whites showed an easy familiarity with the economics of slavery, such as the fair market value of slaves based on their age, gender, and skills, Kentuckians overall had a more limited economic stake in slavery than most other white southerners.[9]

Thus, when Kentuckians thought about how slavery as an institution might benefit their state, they were inclined to dismiss economic factors. Indeed, it was almost a cliché in antebellum Kentucky to call slavery a drain on the state's economy and argue that Kentucky's overall economic condition could be improved by an exclusive reliance on free white labor. If white Kentuckians discussed slavery as a beneficial institution at all, they generally did so as a system of controlling the black population. There was, of course, an influential group of white Kentuckians whose personal stake in the future of slavery went far beyond the state's supposed need to control the black race. By 1850, nearly forty thousand people in Kentucky owned slaves, and many thousands more either lived in slaveholding families or aspired to own slaves themselves. Coming from a planter whose livelihood derived from holding other people in perpetual bondage, the argument that slavery was a necessary evil—the argument that despite the obvious wrongs of slavery, there was no ethical reason why he and his children should not enjoy the fruits of African-American labor for decades to come—was certainly no compelling indictment of the peculiar institution.[10]

This fact has given rise to questions among some historians about the sincerity of southerners who proclaimed slavery to be an evil, albeit a necessary one. The first historians of slavery tended to take southerners at their word when they called slavery an evil, and these early historians were more likely to blame northern abolitionists or the cotton boom of the antebellum years for the development of the positive-good doctrine. These historians argued that southern statesmen like Thomas Jefferson, Patrick Henry, and James Madison understood both the evils of slavery and the practical problems associated with emancipation, and that during the early years of the American republic such politicians worked to abolish slavery in a timely yet responsible manner. Only the emergence of northern fanatics whose self-righteous denunciation of slaveholding made southerners understandably defensive or, in some historical accounts, the discovery of an inexpensive method for ginning cotton which made the cultivation of cotton by slave labor profitable deterred southerners from the path to emancipation and encouraged them to defend their "peculiar institution" as an unmitigated "positive good."[11]

Historians writing since the 1950s, however, have modified this portrait. More sympathetic to northern abolitionists and more concerned over the persistence of racism in the contemporary United States, these historians have tended to minimize the significance of the antislavery professions of early southerners. Some historians—most notably William W. Freehling, Carl N. Degler, and Ira Berlin—have upheld the old idea that for many southerners, the necessary-evil doctrine bespoke genuine hostility to slavery. Yet these historians have also recognized that the necessary-evil doctrine represented an "ambiguous and ambivalent" statement of protest, which was rarely translated into effective action against slavery.[12]

Other historians have doubted that southerners meant what they said when they called slavery an evil, arguing that throughout the history of slavery, nearly all white southerners defended the institution. Although during the Revolutionary era southerners did acknowledge some of the real—but supposedly unconquerable—evils of African-American servitude, this acknowledgment was mere "lip service" paid to the liberal spirit of the age and had no real substance when set beside the obvious fact that southerners intended to keep their slaves. As historian Drew Gilpin Faust notes, the decline of the necessary-evil argument and the rise of the positive-good doctrine represented a change "more . . . of style and tone than of substance," as southerners purged from their vocabulary the rhetoric of liberty, which they had temporarily attached to their defense of slavery during the Revolutionary era. The change in southern thought about slavery in the 1820s and 1830s had less to do with determining "*whether* slavery was right"—something southerners had always believed—than it did with understanding "precisely *why* . . . [slavery] was right and how its justice could best be demonstrated."[13]

For those in the Deep South, the doctrine of slavery as a necessary evil may well have been primarily an exercise in understanding precisely why slavery was right. Even in a state of the Upper South like Kentucky, there were people who used the necessary-evil doctrine mostly to defend slavery and to explain to the world why it was right for whites in Kentucky to keep their slaves for generations to come. Yet, even in cases where the necessary-evil doctrine served mostly as an argument to defend slavery, it seems wrong to dismiss the significance of the declaration that slavery was somehow morally wrong or that it was harmful to society. The necessary-evil doctrine is perhaps best viewed as one of several possible strategies for resolving the conflict inherent in a national culture that valued freedom while supporting or tolerating slavery. It is instructive to remember the manner in which many white southerners resolved the conflict between slavery and republican liberty. Some who were enamored with slavery became ambivalent with, if not outwardly hostile to, the whole idea that freedom was the best condition for humanity in general. Other southerners retained an allegiance to the idea that all people deserved freedom, but they defined humanity in such a way as to exclude the African American and proclaimed that the Negro's bondage was the source of the Caucasian's freedom. In contrast, the proponents of the necessary-evil doctrine—no matter how strongly some of them may have hoped to maintain slavery indefinitely—consciously adhered to an ideology that constantly reminded them that freedom for all people, whether black or white, was a primary moral and civic value and that only "stern necessity" could justify its denial.[14]

Clearly, antebellum Kentuckians faced a conflict between two opposing and strongly held values: the hope of maintaining slavery for the immediate future and the belief that slavery should eventually be eliminated from the state. Seen in this way, the necessary-evil theory sheds light on the perennial question of whether southerners experienced guilt over slavery. After examining the professions of southerners that slavery was an evil, some historians have suggested that white southerners must have been filled with a deep sense of guilt for their enslavement of fellow human beings. Southern "guiltomania," to borrow Eugene D. Genovese's term, has been used to explain such phenomena as the overreaction of southerners to the threat of abolitionism, the decision to secede from the Union, and the failure of Confederate morale that undermined the Southern war effort during the final months of the Civil War. Of course, this argument has a noticeable flaw: historians have been able to find little evidence of guilt over slavery. Southerners seem rarely to have been bothered by the moral implications of their involvement with slavery. The evidence from Kentucky suggests that people who had misgivings about slavery experienced not guilt, but rather conflict or dissonance between two strongly held sets of values, neither of which they were ready to abandon. Kentuckians believed that slavery was wrong: it violated the natural rights of humans, hurt the economy of their state, and endangered the morals and safety of white Kentuckians. Yet they also found slavery useful: it enriched the pocketbooks of masters and provided a controlling mechanism for the state's substantial black population. White Kentuckians did not feel guilty for believing these things; rather, they felt discomfort or anxiety by being caught between the proverbial rock and hard place. The Virginian Thomas Jefferson best expressed what he and other whites of the Upper South felt. "I can say with conscious truth," he wrote, "that there is not a man on earth who would sacrifice more than I would to relieve us from . . . [slavery], in any *practicable* way. . . . But as it is, we have the wolf by the ears, and we can neither hold him, nor safely let him go. Justice is in the one scale, and self-preservation in the other."[15]

Believing slavery to be a necessity, at least for the time being, necessary-evil theorists argued that ownership of slaves was not immoral. It was immoral or sinful to deny liberty to a free person, Kentuckians often argued, and thus the English slave traders and others who originally captured the ancestors of the current slave population and sold them into slavery had acted immorally. However, the current generation merely continued the enslavement of a people who had never known freedom; slaveholders acted morally because their authority over slaves served the greater good of society by controlling the black race. Supporters of the theory of slavery as a necessary evil argued that under current conditions, God approved of American slavery. While God had originally intended for people to be free, in his mercy he had now provided the institution of slavery to take into account the practical aspects of living in a world his children had corrupted. Slavery, like governments and families, was an institution of authority given by God to his children to help restrain the sinful behavior of fallen humanity.

The necessary-evil theory allowed Kentuckians to construct a bridge between conflicting sets of values: they could simultaneously embrace both freedom and slavery without experiencing the psychological discomfort of holding obviously contradictory values. The necessary-evil doctrine never evolved into either a wholly antislavery or wholly proslavery stance: it simultaneously attacked the institution of slavery and defended it. That duality allowed Kentuckians to see the problem of slavery in a way that did not force them to choose between freedom and servitude. It is perhaps fitting that Thomas Jefferson is the American most often associated with the necessary-evil doctrine, for he was a man who was at home both in the world of the revolutionary democrat and in the world of the southern slaveholder. As in the case of Jefferson, who has often been criticized by historians for failing to take a more determined stand against the peculiar institution, the doctrine of slavery as a necessary evil worked in Kentucky to legitimize the status quo and to minimize direct political activity against slavery. Kentuckians could stop fretting over the problem of slavery and refuse to take any action to solve that problem, believing that the evils of slavery they saw around them were being worked out by the natural development of society.[16]

For Kentuckians and other southerners who owned slaves, the acknowledgment that slavery was an evil was a significant concession and, as positive-good theorists argued, a weak position from which to defend slavery. Yet, the doctrine of slavery as a necessary evil proved to be an even weaker position from which to attack slavery, a fact that had an important impact on the antislavery movement in Kentucky. The failure of necessary-evil theorists to act against slavery was, in the end, the great tragedy of the theory. Perhaps more than other southerners, Kentuckians continued after the 1820s to be burdened by the evil of slavery. They retained a belief that the best and strongest societies are democratic and committed to freedom and to the innate equality of all people. More than northerners, Kentuckians and others in the Upper South knew the wrongs of slavery firsthand. Slavery was not a distant abstraction nor a mere political question for them, but a living institution experienced in everyday life, an institution whose effects sometimes seemed to threaten their homes, their country, and their futures. Yet, Kentucky squandered this potential for antislavery action; proponents of the necessary-evil theory rarely took truly effective action against slavery. It is striking to observe how often necessary-evil theorists were genuinely good people, wanting and trying to do what was right about slavery amidst conflicting values and interests. In this struggle, they proved themselves to be inherent compromisers, driven to find the middle ground between opposing sides. While trying to give due regard to the complex issues and interests surrounding the slavery issue, proponents of the necessary-evil theory ironically developed a moral callus grown thick by constant rubbing against racism, economic and class interests, social pressures, and sectional interests. However much they might have believed that slavery was evil, they could not transcend their own beliefs on racial inferiority, their concern for the property rights of slave owners, their fear of offending their neighbors, and their loyalty both to the South and to the peace and harmony of the Union. In the end, they lacked the transforming moral vision that enables people to reorder their lives in accordance with an overriding principle and to act upon it.

The case of A.H. Triplett, a slaveholding Methodist minister from Daviess County, provides insight into the clouded moral vision and the limits on action imposed by the theory of slavery as a necessary evil. In the mid-1840s, as Methodists nationwide hotly debated the morality of ministers owning slaves, Triplett had a genuine crisis of conscience regarding slavery and his own involvement in it. After some time, Triplett embraced strong antislavery views, came to consider slaveholding a sin, and developed genuine guilt over his ownership of slaves. Wanting to do something to aid "all descendants of [the] unfortunate Africans" and hoping that "the sun may soon arise on a *free* America," Triplett became exceedingly "anxious to take some steps for liberating" his own slaves, a woman named Mary and a young boy. "I cannot conscientiously be a slaveholder," Triplett wrote, and he was not content to believe one thing and do another.[17]

Although he was close to the abolitionist position on many issues, Triplett rejected abolitionism as a solution to the problem of slavery, and turned instead to "the cause of colonization," which "I love." "I wish and pray for [the] success [of] the cause of colonization," wrote Triplett, "and that [it] may flourish until the last descendant of Africa shall be borne back to its native land." Even

though he was a slaveholder, Triplett was a man of modest means—
so short of funds, in fact, that he could not afford to subscribe to the
African Repository, the monthly periodical of the American Colonization Society (ACS). Yet Triplett favored the expensive method of
colonization to the nearly costless expedient of simply setting his
slaves free. Triplett was so anxious to get his slaves to Liberia that he
proposed to the ACS that it pay the expenses of his emigrants, with
Triplett reimbursing the ACS in sums of "10 or 15 dollars" over the
course of three years. Not satisfied merely to relieve himself of the
burden of his slaves by getting them to Liberia, Triplett informed the
ACS that he wished to take on the additional burden and costs of
"provid[ing] my slaves with some of the necessary conveniences of life"
after their arrival in Africa, namely "a quantity of land secured to them,
the necessary implements of husbandry, a year's provision[s]," "bed-
ding and clothing," and "livestock [and] seeds," if "advisable." Although the ACS agreed to Triplett's proposal, it mismanaged the
expedition on which Triplett's slaves were to sail to Liberia and,
through miscommunication, Triplett's slaves were left behind in
America. "I was never more mortified in my life," wrote Triplett
when he discovered the problem. "The agent has gone, and my servants are . . . left" behind. The incompetence of the ACS in this
affair left Triplett deeply troubled, for once again he was placed in
charge his slaves. "*I cannot be a slaveholder,*" Triplett complained to
the ACS. "I must get rid of my slaves in some way." In the hopes that
the ACS would simply remove from him the responsibility of acting
as master, Triplett wrote that "I will now offer them to you, to let
you have entire control over them" until it could send them to Africa. Fearing that the ACS would not do this, however, Triplett wrote
that he would find a way to free himself of his slaves. But "to set
them free in Kentucky I *cannot,* and will not. I fear I shall have to
adopt the *revolting* expedient of selling. I dread this: but I must do
something." Fortunately, Triplett's slaves were not sold but rather
taken to Liberia in 1847, after which Triplett continued to corre-
spond with them.[18]

In many ways, Triplett's position on slavery was atypical to that
of other Kentuckians. The depth and sincerity of his antislavery con-

victions shows that he embraced a view of the sin of slaveholding that few other Kentuckians and, for that matter, few other Americans had adopted by the 1840s. He did more than simply talk about the issue of slavery. He genuinely felt guilty about his involvement in slavery and acted upon that guilt by freeing his own slaves. And yet, Triplett never fully transcended the boundaries of the theory of slavery as a necessary evil. Despite his own yearning to free himself from the sin of slavery immediately, he feared the results of an abolitionist movement acting on this same impulse. Despite his obvious sympathy for blacks and his yearning to do something to help them, he was sufficiently racist that he refused to live among blacks who were not controlled by slavery and insisted that they be removed from the country. Perhaps most remarkably, he considered relieving his own guilt over slaveholding by selling his slaves to someone else.

This same clouded moral vision gave the necessary-evil doctrine a dynamic quality that often made its adherents, like Henry Clay, seem to change their position on slavery with each passing event. On one hand, because most Kentuckians genuinely thought that slavery harmed blacks and whites alike, Kentuckians sometimes proved surprisingly receptive to antislavery ideas. When events highlighted the deleterious effects of slavery on the state's economy or the supposed dangers posed by a large slave population, white Kentuckians willingly took moderate actions to limit the growth of slavery in their state. On the other hand, because most Kentuckians readily acknowledged that slavery served the useful function of controlling the black race, white Kentuckians often proved themselves receptive to the harangues of proslavery ideologues. When events promised to upset the allegedly tranquil disposition of the slave population or when northern criticism offended Kentuckians' southern sensibilities, the same people who criticized slavery often rallied to its defense.[19]

Usually, however, most Kentuckians firmly resisted any change in the relationship between master and slave, whether to make that relationship stronger, as proslavery supporters wanted, or to make it weaker, as antislavery supporters wanted. "There are three parties in this state," observed one antebellum Kentuckian, "the pro-slavery party—the emancipation party—and the party hostile to both and middle to both, favouring no increase of slavery and no measures to put it beyond future control—but hostile to every thing looking to present action, in the way of emancipation. This third party, is *perhaps*, the bulk of the state." The reluctance of most Kentuckians to act against slavery proved disheartening to antislavery activists. Aware of the numerous professions of Kentuckians that slavery was an evil, antislavery supporters often hoped for success, sometimes to the point of believing that Kentucky would be the first southern state to abolish slavery. This activism was encouraged by the belief that emancipation there would begin a domino effect leading to emancipation in the rest of the South. Some antislavery activists considered Kentucky to be the best place in America to work for the end of slavery. Yet the persistent unwillingness of Kentuckians to take definitive action to eliminate slavery repeatedly disappointed them. Wrote one antislavery man: "The very general confession of the evil of slavery, and the oft-repeated wish that we were clear of it, is often to be understood as we understand the drunkard, when he condemns drunkenness and wishes he were delivered from the habit, while he would quarrel with the man who would hide his bottle." Far from becoming the first southern state to abolish slavery, Kentucky actually ended up being one of the last. In fact, Kentucky was the only state in the Union to reject explicitly the Thirteenth, Fourteenth, and Fifteenth Amendments to the United States Constitution, which abolished slavery and provided for basic rights for blacks after the Civil War.[20]

In addition to providing Kentuckians with an explanation for slavery that quieted the conscience while justifying the institution itself, the doctrine of slavery as a necessary evil provided Kentuckians with a measure of unity and consensus during an age of increasing controversy over the issue of slavery. The popularity of the necessary-evil doctrine, for instance, ensured that certain conventions would be observed in the discussion of slavery. Most white Kentuckians could take some comfort in knowing that whatever happened, few of their neighbors would take rash or precipitate action against slavery or, on the other hand, make it impossible to rid the state of its slaves should circumstances warrant such an action. Most Kentuckians agreed that if the state were ever to abolish slavery, the best course would be through a scheme of gradual emancipation coupled with the resettlement or colonization of freedpeople outside Kentucky. The scheme of gradual emancipation most often mentioned was "*post nati*" emancipation. Under such a plan, the state would establish a date after which all children born to slave women would be freed once they reached a certain age—usually, an age near the onset of adulthood. Most such plans also proposed that after slaves had worked for their masters long enough to offset the expense of raising the slaves through childhood, they would be hired out for wages so that they could earn the money needed for migration to Africa.

Despite these areas of agreement, there were very real differences in how individual Kentuckians looked at the peculiar institution of the South. There were always small groups of people who viewed slavery either as a positive good or an unmitigated evil. As it turned out, Kentucky always had its own John C. Calhouns and William Lloyd Garrisons. But more significant were the varieties of emphasis that different necessary-evil advocates placed on the phrase "necessary evil." Some people viewed slavery as more necessary than evil. Arguing that contrary to conventional wisdom, slavery in Kentucky was not dying on its own and would be nearly impossible for others to kill, such people argued that white Kentuckians should understand the real and practical benefits that slavery provided to the state, rather than recoil in horror at the abstract evils inflicted on the African American by slavery. This side of the necessary-evil doctrine, with its emphasis on the benefits of slavery, was often a transitional argument between the conventional doctrine of slavery as a necessary evil and the subsequent argument of slavery as a positive good. Other Kentuckians, though, insisted that slavery was more evil than necessary. For them, the enormous wrongs of slavery outweighed the need for caution, and they urged their fellow Kentuckians to begin the process of emancipation rather than wait for the slow workings of nature to take their effect.[21]

The manner in which the necessary-evil doctrine attracted both supporters and opponents of slavery is suggested by the differing experiences of two men who played an important role in the history of slavery in Kentucky: James Gillespie Birney and Henry Bidleman

Bascom. The circumstances of their early lives could hardly have been more dissimilar. Birney—the son of a wealthy slaveholder of Danville, Kentucky—received all of the advantages that his father's fortune could bring him, including an expensive formal education at Transylvania University in Lexington and the College of New Jersey (later Princeton University). He returned home from school in 1811 to embark on a career in law and politics, and he soon enjoyed the success that comes to those with the advantages of great wealth, good schooling, and high social standing. Birney was elected to the town council of Danville at the age of nineteen and to the state legislature at the age of twenty-four. In 1818, Birney decided to seek even greener pastures in the Alabama Territory, and he quickly experienced even greater success there than he found in Kentucky. He took a leading role in the writing of Alabama's first state constitution in 1819 and was elected to that state's legislature later the same year. Birney also became quite wealthy. By 1820, James G. Birney—not yet thirty years old—owned twenty-eight slaves.[22]

Bascom, on the other hand, started life with few of Birney's advantages. Born in southern New York State, Bascom was the son of a poor family that moved frequently during his early life in search of a better means of living. Like many youths of his day, Bascom took a variety of odd jobs to help support his family and he received no formal education after his twelfth year. By the time he was fourteen, religion had come to play an important role in Bascom's life, and when he struck out on his own at age sixteen, it was to enter the Methodist ministry. For the next decade, he lived the arduous, impoverished life of an itinerant circuit rider, traveling hundreds of miles each year for an annual salary that sometimes totaled as little as twelve dollars. In pulpit oratory and the frontier camp meeting, however, Bascom had found his métier, and his fame as a preacher grew with every mile he traveled on horseback. By the mid-1820s, Henry B. Bascom was one of the best-known ministers in America, a fact demonstrated by his appointment as chaplain of the United States House of Representatives in 1823.[23]

Despite their differing backgrounds, both Birney and Bascom during the 1820s embraced a similar explanation for the existence of slavery in the United States. By the time the two men moved to Kentucky in the early 1830s—Birney, to be near his infirm father; Bascom, to accept a professorship at Augusta College—both men accepted a version of the doctrine that slavery was a necessary evil. While Bascom condemned slavery as "the most defacing stain" on the "country's reputation" and Birney worried about slavery's "corrupting influences" on young people, both men maintained that precipitate action to abolish the institution would abridge property rights and saddle the country with the corrupting influence of free blacks. Both men believed that these problems and the evils of slavery could be partially overcome by colonizing blacks outside the United States. As a reflection of their interest in colonization, both men served briefly as full-time agents of the ACS in the late 1820s and early 1830s.[24]

Yet, despite Birney and Bascom's mutual adherence to the necessary-evil doctrine and their mutual interest in colonization, by the early 1830s obvious differences in their approaches to the problem of slavery had emerged. Birney, who as late as 1824 had owned more than forty slaves, was becoming increasingly obsessed with the evils of slavery. Financial difficulties in the mid-1820s had forced Birney to sell off most of his large slave force. Then, in the late 1820s, Birney converted to Christianity, which caused him to question the morality of holding his fellow man in perpetual bondage and made him impatient with the thought that the problem of slavery was working out its own solution. By the early 1830s, the evil of slavery was, for Birney, coming to outweigh any argument for its necessity. Seeking peace with his own conscience, Birney corresponded frequently with the northern abolitionist Theodore Dwight Weld, and Birney himself become a convert to abolitionism during a dramatic meeting between the two men near Cincinnati in 1834. Soon Birney set out on a campaign to spread abolitionism in Kentucky, but by 1835 he became convinced that he could do little to bring about abolition while he lived in Kentucky—so he decided to leave his home state. Birney went on to become one of the most famous abolitionists in the nation, twice serving as the presidential candidate for the anti-slavery Liberty party.[25]

While Birney renounced his slaveholding past to become an abolitionist and surrendered his southern nativity to move north, Henry Bascom's life moved in an altogether different direction. Although he was born and grew to maturity in the North, Bascom ultimately cast his lot with the South and proved himself a better friend of slavery than the southern-born Birney. Bascom began his residence in Kentucky during the early 1830s much as Birney had, by denouncing the evils of slavery. Yet, even then his denunciations of slavery had a hollow ring to them—more platitude than heartfelt principle. In time, Bascom came to regard the evil of slavery as a matter of far less importance than the benefits it offered. In fact, by the time Bascom assumed the presidency of Transylvania University in 1842, he had become one of Kentucky's most ardent defenders of slavery. Bascom directed most of his efforts on behalf of slavery at the Methodist Church, relentlessly opposing the efforts of northern Methodists to secure the expulsion of slaveholders from the ministry. In the celebrated case of Bishop James O. Andrew, in which northern delegates to the Methodist General Conference of 1844 stripped Andrew of most of his episcopal authority because of his ownership of several slaves, dissenting southern delegates chose Bascom to write their official protest against the action of the General Conference. His book-length defense of the southern position, *Methodism and Slavery*, marked him as one of the leading proponents of the division of the Methodist Church along sectional lines. Indeed, in May 1845, when southern Methodists met in Louisville to form their own southern denomination, they chose Bascom to chair the committee that devised the organization of the new Methodist Episcopal Church, South. Later in the decade, Bascom was one of the primary movers in a lawsuit against the northern Methodists to obtain a division of church property more favorable to the southerners.[26]

Bascom's *Methodism and Slavery*—his most important contribution to the debate on slavery in Kentucky—was a long and rambling defense of slavery, filled with sharp invective against northerners and abolitionists. Yet Bascom did not adopt the new argument that slavery was an unmitigated, positive good. Instead, he defended the peculiar institution as a *necessary* evil. Bascom wrote that while slavery "was an outrage," a fact "felt and admitted by all," it was "so interwoven with the very existence and life blood of a large portion of society" that it was nearly impossible to devise a plan of emancipation which would not do more harm than good. Although the South had "always shown itself more ready than the North, to get rid of the negro by *removal* and *colonization* in Africa," the seeming impracticality of all known plans of emancipation dictated that southerners should not recklessly make war on an institution that provided the valuable function of controlling the black race. Southerners should instead work to ameliorate the harmful effects of slavery while leaving the ultimate fate of the peculiar institution in the hands of an almighty God. He wrote: "Were it in our power, without interfering with the rights of others, we would release [the slaves] from civil bondage; but as it is not, . . . we are content . . . to alleviate and render tolerable, a condition resulting from no act of ours, but having its origin in the organic arrangements of civil society." Bascom proclaimed that until the day when the abolition of slavery could be safely accomplished, southerners could rest easy in the knowledge that human bondage was in no way inconsistent with the teachings of the Bible, and that the "Prophets and Apostles, . . . have steadily and formally recognized . . . perpetual hereditary slavery, and have specifically . . . given direction . . . for the regulation of the duties and obligations arising out of such state and relations."[27]

Though Bascom's version of the doctrine of slavery as a necessary evil was basically a defense of slavery, there remained a significant difference between it and the increasingly popular idea in the South that slavery was a positive good. This distinction was recognized by some proslavery ideologues, who believed that the doctrine of slavery as a necessary evil—even when used to justify the existence of slavery—was uncertain ground from which to defend the South and southern institutions. These concerns were clearly evident in a fascinating exchange of letters between John C. Calhoun and his friend James Henry Hammond, the former governor of South Carolina—an exchange of letters sparked by the publication of Bascom's *Methodism and Slavery*. Soon after the initial appearance of Bascom's book, Calhoun had given it a cursory examination and found it to be "one of the fullest and most powerful vindications of the South and its institutions, which has yet appeared." He sent a copy of the book to Hammond and asked him, "as the defender of the institutions of the South against the assaults of the abolition[ists]," to write a favorable review of the book.[28]

Hammond read the book closely and was deeply concerned by Bascom's references to the evils of slavery and Bascom's professed hope for eventual emancipation. Hammond wrote to Calhoun that if Bascom's "book is noticed in *South Ca[rolina]:* such sentiments as these must be peremptorily denied and strongly rebuked." To do otherwise would be to throw a "damper" over the friends of slavery across the South, to encourage the growth of an antislavery movement in the South and the development of southern moderation on the issue of slavery in general, and "to give these *pseudo* friends of the Slaveholders an overwhelming domination over So[uthern] Methodism, which would soon become as dangerous to us as that of the North." In Hammond's opinion, Bascom's conception of slavery was "in principle" no different from Kentucky's antislavery reformers, and Hammond hoped that "all of that stamp will be put down completely and Kentucky redeemed." Chastened by Hammond's revelations about Bascom's book, Calhoun agreed that it should not receive a favorable notice from Hammond. But Calhoun warned Hammond to be temperate in his response to people like Bascom so as not to drive them away from the cause of the South: "We must not break with, or throw off those who are not yet prepared to come up to our standard, especially on the exterior limits of the Slave holding States. I look back with pleasure to the progress, which sound principles have made within the last 10 years [in the South] in respect to the relation between the two races. All, with a very few exceptions, defended it a short time since on the ground of a necessary evil, to be got rid of as soon as . . . [p]ossible. S[outh] C[arolina] was not much sounder 20 years ago, than Kentucky now is."[29]

Just as Calhoun hoped to proselytize southerners for his cause, Kentucky's antislavery activists hoped to win the allegiance of those who said that slavery was a necessary evil. Throughout the 1830s and 1840s, the supporters and opponents of slavery waged a pitched battle for the support of Kentuckians. This fight involved one of the most popular "benevolent" movements in antebellum Kentucky, a cause which was a logical outgrowth of the doctrine of slavery as a necessary evil: the organized removal of at least a portion of the Kentucky's black population to a location outside the state.

2

The Colonizationist Imperative

During the 1830s and 1840s, the Kentuckians who occupied center stage in the debate on slavery gave much of their attention to the issue of colonization. By nearly all accounts, the idea that at least a portion of the state's black population should be removed from the state proved very popular among white Kentuckians, receiving public endorsements from a wide variety of religious leaders, college presidents, and newspaper editors. Kentucky's politicians seemed especially drawn to the idea. At one time or another, people ranging from Robert Wickliffe, the state's largest slaveholder and most outspoken supporter of slavery, to Cassius M. Clay, Kentucky's most famous antislavery reformer, expressed support for colonization. Foremost among them was Henry Clay, the state's most prominent politician, who was president of the American Colonization Society from 1836 to 1852. Under the leadership of politicians like Clay, the state legislature endorsed colonization in 1827, 1828, and 1832, and it actually established a small fund to support colonization in 1833.[1]

Much of the popularity of colonizationism in antebellum Kentucky lay in the cause's congruence with the idea that slavery was a necessary evil: if whites believed that blacks corrupted society and

27

ruined the state's economy, it was easy for them to find merit in the
idea of removing blacks from the state. White opposition to colonization came from those at either end of the political spectrum who
rejected the whole notion of slavery as a necessary evil: abolitionists
like James G. Birney and John G. Fee, and militant supporters of the
positive-good theory. In rejecting colonization, then, both groups
were explicitly rejecting a central principle of the necessary-evil doctrine, that the best sort of society was racially homogeneous. To a
colonizationist like Robert J. Breckinridge, this signified the intellectual bankruptcy of both groups: "The abolitionist and the proslavery man, agree in nothing but the final result of their principles, .
. . that the black man and the white man ought to abide together
forever; whereas, if reason or experience teaches us any lesson, it is that
they ought not."[2]

But even as people worried about the Louisville society, interest
Yet for all of the popularity of colonization among white Kentuckians, there was a paradox central to this popularity, a paradox
often noted but rarely understood. At the same time that a wide range
of Kentuckians were giving verbal support to the cause, colonization
societies in the state were struggling to survive. As ACS agent Robert
S. Finley put it after a visit to Kentucky, "although there is a general
good feeling towards" colonizationism in Kentucky, "there is nobody
there active in our cause." Local auxiliaries of the ACS were often
formed in a flush of enthusiasm, only to wither away shortly afterward. The case of the Louisville Colonization Society illustrates this
process. The Louisville society was formed in 1829, during a two-
year period of enthusiasm in which some twenty-four local societies
and a statewide colonization society were formed in Kentucky under
the encouragement of ACS agents Benjamin Orr Peers and Henry B.
Bascom. After this initial push for colonization, however, interest
waned and the organization declined. The Louisville society was reorganized in 1833 but again so regressed that by 1836 some Louisvillians
were bemoaning the "languishing condition of the cause" in their
city and the "lethargy" into which "the citizens around us . . . seem
unfortunately to have fallen, upon the great subject of colonization."[3]

But even as people worried about the Louisville society, interest
in colonization was reviving there. In August 1836, Ralph R. Gurley,

secretary and general agent of the ACS, toured Kentucky and held "several Colonization meetings" in Louisville, enthusiastically promoted by editor George D. Prentice in the *Louisville Journal.* At the last of these meetings—"an overflowing assembly of the best people in the city," according to Unitarian minister James Freeman Clarke— the Louisville Colonization Society was again reorganized. This time the reorganization was more successful: when Gurley returned to Louisville to raise money three years later, he found the society flourishing. Despite the ongoing national depression, which had caused the receipts of the ACS to plummet in 1838, the Louisville society promised to raise four thousand dollars, a huge amount equivalent to nearly 40 percent of the income of the ACS the previous year, and within a month had secured pledges for most of the sum. However, this enthusiasm did not last. When the Louisville Society tried to collect the promised donations, it was met with indifference and raised less than half the money pledged. "I regret to say that our bright anticipations . . . have not been realized," wrote J.C. Talbot, an officer of the Louisville Society. "The spirit is completely down here."[4]

Even the Kentucky Colonization Society (KCS) found its support shallow and its existence tenuous. The KCS was established on January 14, 1829, in Frankfort, with high hopes for success. Colonizationists of all varieties—from proslavery Robert Wickliffe to antislavery Robert J. Breckinridge—joined together in the formation of the statewide society. "I am perfectly astonished at the ardour with which all men of all ranks enter into it," wrote ACS agent Benjamin O. Peers after the organizing meetings of the KCS. "If the proper exertions are used, we shall succeed far, far beyond the most extravagant dreams of the wildest enthusiast." Yet the state colonization society was so ineffective that it sent only 661 blacks to Africa during the entire antebellum period. Indeed, several times in the history of the KCS, including one three-year stretch in the early 1840s, there was so little interest in the work of the society that it did not even hold its annual meeting. Writing after the longest of these periods of inactivity, a new agent for the KCS, Alexander M. Cowan, wrote that "I have found the Kentucky State Col[onization] Soc[iety] defunct. . . .

The Auxiliary County or town Societies [are] in like state. . . . I have tried to get up a meeting of the friends here but so far [the prospect is] not very promising."[5]

Perhaps this paradox of Kentucky's colonization societies—struggling for survival at a moment when Kentucky's citizens were expressing support for colonization—has not been understood because the nature of colonizationism in Kentucky itself has not been well understood. Colonizationism in Kentucky was less a unified movement represented by organized colonization societies than it was an imperative shared by a wide range of Kentuckians: the belief that if blacks were to be free, they should be removed from the state. But no matter how popular the colonizationist imperative was, it was too ambiguous to serve as a basis for concerted political action for Kentuckians of widely varying interests. Colonizationism in Kentucky, then, needs to be approached differently from the way it has been approached in the past to determine what motivated individual colonizationists. Historians have not taken seriously enough the differences among proponents of black removal; they have tended to treat the most racist and proslavery avowals of certain colonizationists—or conversely, the most nonracist and antislavery avowals of certain other colonizationists—as the true measure of colonizationist attitudes. Further, historians have tended to define colonizationism by the activities of the American Colonization Society and its auxiliaries. In Kentucky, a variety of motives guided the colonizationists' actions; ultimately, the organized colonization societies did not fully represent the range of opinion on the subject.[6]

There were three major groupings of colonizationists in Kentucky; each saw in colonization a program for establishing its own version of race relations in the state. One group saw colonization as a means of strengthening slavery; the second group saw it as a way to facilitate emancipation; the third group saw it as one mechanism among many to bring about the simple removal of the hated black race from the state. These groups shared the aversion to free blacks that was at the core of the colonizationist imperative—the feeling that blacks must either be controlled by slavery or removed from the state—and the belief that colonization could help remove this hated class. For supporters of slavery, colonizing free blacks offered a chance to remove an element that seemed to threaten the very existence of slavery. Free blacks held out an example of freedom to slaves, they could provide aid and shelter to fugitives from slavery, and they might even lead slaves in an insurrection against white domination of society. For opponents of slavery, colonization of free blacks provided a means to remove what seemed to be the primary obstacle to the elimination of slavery: the public's fear of an uncontrolled black race. For the third group of colonizationists, perhaps more appropriately called separationists, colonization was a way to get rid of the most troublesome portion of a despised race.[7]

In the late 1820s, many Kentuckians hoped that colonizationists of all stripes could ignore their differences and work together. To conciliate the various groups attracted to colonization, the ACS and its Kentucky auxiliaries proposed a simple and specific plan. As described by the constitution of the Danville Colonization Society, the plan embraced "the Colonization on the coast of Africa with their own consent, [of] the free people of Colour of the United States." The plan made no reference to slavery, so that it could draw support from everyone who believed it would be beneficial to remove free blacks from the country, for whatever reason. Those associated with the colonization societies regarded colonization of free blacks as a worthwhile principle in itself; they had trouble understanding why everyone from abolitionists to proslavery advocates did not agree that the emigration of free blacks to Africa would be salutary, both for the emigrants and for the country they left behind. "If you wish to see the negro race rise to the rank which they are capable of sustaining," argued future congressman Joseph R. Underwood, "send those who are free to Africa. If you desire to get clear of [the] leaders and advisers of your slaves, . . . if you wish to benefit the laboring white man, [or] if you wish to exterminate slavery, send the free negroes to Africa."[8]

By concentrating on free blacks and remaining mute on the subject of slavery, colonization society officials hoped that people would read into colonization whatever they wanted. In the words of Presbyterian minister Robert J. Breckinridge, "The friends of Colonization north of us, may favor [colonization] for reasons which those south of us may entirely reject; and we in the centre may proceed on grounds quite different from those on either extreme." Yet such ambiguity imposed its own burdens. For colonizationism to retain its chameleonic quality, the societies not only would have to encourage people to define colonization as they pleased but also would have to discourage them from publicly proclaiming colonization to be anything but a plan to send free blacks to Africa. To do otherwise would wreck the fragile consensus that undergirded the societies.[9]

The desire to keep the program amorphous led to the now familiar spectacle of antislavery colonizationists proclaiming that colonization posed no threat to slavery and, likewise, of proslavery colonizationists arguing that colonization might facilitate emancipation. Ironically, the very efforts of the colonization societies to preserve the ambiguity of their program became a significant obstacle to garnering popular support. At a time when it was increasingly difficult to remain neutral on the issue of slavery, the ambiguity of organized colonizationism meant, in the words of one Kentuckian, that "in the slave States, . . . it involved the advocates of colonization in the same indiscriminate censure with rabid Abolitionists, whilst in the free States it presented them as the abettors of slavery, and the worst enemies of the African race."[10]

One reason that abolitionists were suspicious of this ambiguity was that it was unambiguously racist. As Kentucky abolitionist John G. Fee put it, "*Prejudice,* unholy prejudice is at the bottom of the whole of it." Although some historians have argued that "the Kentucky colonizationists cannot be called racists in any strict sense," colonizationism makes little sense unless understood in light of its supporters' racism. After all, what makes a person a racist? If racism is the belief that there are important differences between blacks and whites and that these differences make blacks less worthy than whites, then racism was certainly at the heart of the colonization movement in Kentucky. Proslavery colonizationists found merit in the subjugation of blacks in America and wanted to fortify white control over slaves by removing potentially rebellious free blacks. Separationists so disliked blacks in general that they simply wanted to remove them from Kentucky. Even antislavery colonizationists were guilty on this count. To Breckinridge, blacks were "persons, who from their physical organization create disgust." "Nature has made the distinction of color," claimed Joseph R. Underwood, "and in it has laid the foundation of the partialities which bind us to our own likeness, and of the repugnances which turn us from those who do not resemble ourselves."[11]

The belief in black inferiority led most antislavery colonizationists to adopt a denigrating paternalism toward African Americans. To colonizationists, blacks were simply incompetent to make basic decisions about their lives; while they dedicated themselves to helping blacks improve their lot in life, antislavery colonizationists in particular seemed always to take the attitude of a parent fending for a helpless child. For instance, colonizationists recognized the obvious reluctance of blacks to leave their native American soil, where many had lived for generations, for the faraway land of Africa. Antislavery colonizationists found this resistance astonishing, especially the opposition of slaves to colonization, since it seemed obvious to whites that colonization would infinitely improve blacks' condition in life. "Why should such an unfortunate class desire to remain among us?" asked Henry Clay. "Why should they not wish to go to the country of their forefathers, where . . . they should 'stand redeemed, regenerated and disenthralled by the mighty genius of universal emancipation'?"[12]

Although antislavery colonizationists observed blacks' opposition to emigration, they could not understand it. As white Americans who counted liberty highly and who lived in a nation of migrators, colonizationists found it hard to imagine that someone would not take a chance to improve his condition by moving to a new frontier, or even a new world. Indeed, antislavery colonizationists like Robert J. Breckinridge argued that the very fact that blacks preferred America, with its *oppression and contempt* for Negroes, to Africa, "simply because it is not his home," was a sure sign that blacks in America still needed the paternal guidance of whites and poor evidence that African Americans should "be admitted to the privileges of citizenship, among a people who love liberty with idolatrous devotion."[13]

The experience of Charles Wilkins Short highlights the paternalistic undertones of antislavery colonizationism. Professor of medicine at the Medical Institute of Louisville and one of the leading botanists of his age, Short wished "that every slave upon the American continent" could be "humanely rescued from perpetual slavery," but he accepted the colonizationist imperative that the "liberation" of slaves "while they remain among us is a serious evil to the country at large, and no good to them." In the late 1820s, Short obtained several slaves from his father's estate, as did his uncle, William Short of Philadelphia, who kept his slaves in Kentucky by hiring them out or lending them to relatives. As early as May 1830, Short broached with his uncle the possibility of colonizing these slaves in Africa. William Short was himself an active member of the Pennsylvania Colonization Society, and by 1837 he had agreed to pay for the colonization of several of his Kentucky slaves, with his nephew to act as his agent in the matter. By May 1838, two of William Short's slaves, David and Charles, "expressed the great willingness—indeed an earnest desire, to be allowed that priviledge [*sic*]" of going to Africa.[14]

Already the Shorts' paternalistic impulses were at work. Charles Short was well aware of the general reluctance of American blacks to migrate to Africa. Believing blacks to be "so ignorant as to be easily dissuaded from any object," Short worried about contacts that David and Charles might have with other blacks who would try to discourage them from migrating. Short's fears were confirmed in October 1838, when he learned that David had second thoughts about leaving his family in western Kentucky and wanted to be sold to a master in that part of the state. Short wrote to his uncle from Louisville that "the best way . . . to secure your benevolent designs . . . will doubtless be to get them here as soon as possible. . . . Perhaps after all the truest benevolence to them consists in acting for them, without reference to thier [*sic*] whims or caprices."[15]

Soon thereafter, Short brought David and Charles from western Kentucky to Louisville to watch over them and to get them ready to depart for Liberia. As so often happened with such colonization expeditions, innumerable delays occurred along the way. In the meantime, Short was determined to keep David and Charles "out of the way of the worst of all evils—idleness." He hired them out to white mechanics so that the waiting emigrants would learn a trade and earn money to support themselves in Africa. Short continued to worry that the men might change their minds now that they lived among Louisville's large black community, and he made it clear that the men's freedom was contingent on their emigration. According to Short, he also "told them most distinctly that in the event of their declin[ing]" to go to Africa "they would be sold as slaves for life," and he determined "to use every effort in my power to 'screw their courage to the sticking point.'" Short's desire to "hold" David and Charles to their earlier decision came perilously close to a violation of the colonization societies' principle that emigration be voluntary. Charles Short did "reason" with the men, pointing to the benefits of freedom in Liberia, but he believed ultimately that "those, who are entirely incapable of judging for themselves, should have others to do so for them."[16]

Short's continuing fears were partially realized when it was time for the men to embark for Africa in November 1839. Charles seemed "exceedingly anxious" to go, but Short was "mortified" that David now declined. Despite the months of what Short termed David's "shuffling and equivocating," Short was still astounded that David could "deliberately and willfully prefer . . . unconditional slavery, for the remainder of his [life] . . . to freedom and emigration!" According to Short, "He told me, indeed, that he had rather be sold to almost any master, than to be a free man and go." Short was so disappointed with David's decision that he now believed David lacked the character and intellect to make a successful colonist, and David was not forced to go to Africa against his will. Ironically, David was hired out to other masters, with his wages sent to Liberia to help support Charles.[17]

The contrast between the decisions made by David and Charles only heightened Short's estimation of Charles, who, Short noticed, now styled himself Charles Gist. "Should he carry with him to his new home, the same habits of industry, sobriety, and rectitude, which he has manifested here," Short wrote, "I doubt not that he will succeed to our fullest wishes." Short and his uncle took "a great interest in the success of Charles, at his new home." They carefully followed the publicity surrounding the departure of Gist's expedition; and when, after an initial letter announcing his arrival in Africa, the emigrant did not write the Shorts for another year, Charles Short brooded over the possibility that Gist had succumbed to the "acclimating fever." Needless to say, Gist's next letter was met with relief and not a little "regret," as Short put it, "that I had not made him devote more time to the acquirement of an elementary education." Soon after Gist had departed from Kentucky, Short rather sarcastically speculated that Gist "would certainly make in Liberia a very imposing 'Judge or General,'" but when Gist wrote that he had "been lately appointed constable for the county of Grand Bassa, and . . . is enabled to write so well as to discharge all his official duties satisfactorily," Short was genuinely pleased at Gist's success—not to mention his own.[18]

Perhaps nothing better illustrates the Shorts' continuing concern for Gist than their monetary gifts to the colonist. In the six years following Gist's migration, the Shorts sent him hundreds of dollars, both from David's wages and from their own pockets. At first Charles Short continued to express the same haughty appraisal of Gist's capacity to make decisions that Short had expressed when Gist was still just Charles the slave. When Gist complained that he had been given bad advice about buying supplies by Judge Samuel Wilkeson, president of the board of directors of the ACS, and by Governor Thomas Buchanan of Liberia, Short disdainfully wondered if "perhaps Charles may have thought that he could make a better disposition of his own money than either the Judge or the Governor" and attributed the complaint to "the inherent disposition" of blacks "to murmur and complain." But eventually Short developed a real respect for Gist, at one point acknowledging to Gist that "we cannot under take to advise you" on monetary matters. "You are now your own master, and are competent to judge and accede for yourself."[19]

Such recognition of black competence was unusual in Kentucky, even among antislavery colonizationists. Short's continuing concern for Gist after the former slave migrated was not so unusual, and a

similar concern for Liberia characterized most antislavery colonizationists. Unfortunately, this concern usually reflected only the most
benevolent manifestation of the same paternalistic prejudice that lay
at the heart of colonizationism. White colonizationists continued to
send help to black emigrants, in part for the same reason they would
not listen to black objections to migration to Africa: because the
colonizationists did not take seriously enough the ability of blacks to
make decisions for themselves. White colonizationists, even the antislavery variety, treated blacks as children ever in need of paternal
guidance and support.[20]

Antislavery colonizationists' view of black incompetence and
corruption made it impossible for them to imagine living among
numbers of free blacks. Their racism placed a conceptual straitjacket
on their antislavery practices: they never even considered the possibility of emancipation on the soil. While this racism was important,
there is a risk in overemphasizing it in explaining their actions. In a
nation where most people—including more than a few abolitionists—were racists, the fact that colonizationists also held such beliefs
does not tell us much about their behavior. As the cases of some
abolitionists demonstrate, racism does not always explain why some
people became abolitionists and others became coloniza-tionists.
Likewise, when one group of racists wanted to enlist the voluntary
cooperation of blacks in ending slavery through migration to Africa,
while another group of racists wanted to use colonization to rivet the
chains of the slave forever, while still another group of racists cared
little about the future destiny of slavery as long as blacks were removed from Kentucky, then racism offers only a partial explanation
of colonizationists' actions. The racism of colonizationists did not
exist in a vacuum—it was tempered and shaped by outside forces
and the colonizationists' other values.[21]

Foremost among these values was one's position on slavery. Observers of the colonization movement—from William Lloyd Garrison to modern historians—have had no problem accepting the fact
that a person's support for slavery might have influenced his position
on colonization, but the same observers have had trouble accepting
the converse proposition. The racist underpinnings of coloniza-

tionism and the ambiguous program of the colonization societies have made it hard for some observers to accept the idea that a person could genuinely oppose slavery and support colonization at the same time, much less that a person's antislavery position could influence the approach he took to colonization. In this, antislavery colonizationists often have not helped their own reputations. If they have seemed like clandestine supporters of slavery, it was because they cast themselves in the role of apologists for slavery. As gradual emancipationists who accepted the idea that slavery was a necessary evil, they ipso facto approved of at least a temporary preservation of slavery. And increasing calls for the immediate abolition of slavery often pushed them into a strident defense of the status quo as less dangerous than indiscriminate emancipation. Moreover, colonization was such an impracticable means of emancipation that supporting it seems at best naive, at worst disingenuous.[22]

The tendency of antislavery colonizationists to work through colonization societies still officially dedicated to the colonization of free blacks—but not slaves—heightened this appearance. Claiming that masters wanted to free their slaves but were hesitant to increase the number of free blacks, some antislavery colonizationists argued that the efforts of the KCS to remove free blacks would lead to ever-multiplying acts of emancipation and, hence, the end of slavery in Kentucky. This would certainly be a slow and ineffective process; abolitionist John G. Fee compared it to trying "'to ladle out one of'" the Great Lakes "'with a kitchen utensil,'" and James G. Birney likened it to moving the ocean "by the discharge of a popgun on the beach." A surprising number of antislavery colonizationists accepted the logic of Fee's and Birney's criticism. Some, like John C. Young, the president of Centre College in Danville, and John D. Paxton, a prominent Presbyterian minister, doubted that colonization would ever remove all blacks from the state and supported the KCS as a means of aiding free blacks and helping ease the process of abolition. "I believe they [the slaves] will be colonized when we construct a rail-road to the moon," admitted Young in a moment of candor. "Long before the public mind would be willing to begin the march in earnest . . . they will amount to a number which will bid defiance to all efforts of even a nation's wealth to transport and support."[23]

Other antislavery colonizationists continued to believe that colonization could be used to end slavery, but assumed that the efforts of the KCS and other societies to colonize free blacks would not significantly reduce the number of slaves. They argued that the most important way the colonization societies promoted emancipation was not in colonizing free blacks per se, but in demonstrating the efficacy of colonization itself. The society itself was not presumed to be able to end slavery; rather, its task was to demonstrate that for a minimal cost per person, blacks from the United States could be taken to Africa, where they could prosper and build a republic, even without the day-to-day governance of whites. Once the colonization societies had demonstrated the feasibility of this notion, state governments could apply it to the elimination of slavery. On this point, at least, the antislavery colonizationists were not duplicitous. Although they continued to work through a state colonization society dedicated only to the colonization of free blacks, they also worked outside the KCS to get the state government to adopt a plan of gradual emancipation that incorporated the principles of colonization demonstrated by the KCS.[24]

Even in the hands of these comparatively realistic people, colonization remained such an expensive and gradual method of emancipation that it is sometimes hard to believe that they sincerely thought colonization might lead to the end of slavery. Joseph R. Underwood was one such colonizationist who sought to devise "a system of colonization, which shall have for its object the extermination of slavery." His actions leave little reason to doubt the sincerity of his commitment to emancipation. During his long career in public office, Underwood took a number of controversial positions that underscored the sincerity of his opposition to slavery. As a congressman, he offered perhaps the most famous defense of John Quincy Adams in response to the attempt to censure the former president for presenting antislavery petitions to Congress. As a senator, he spoke out against the Mexican War and the acquisition of territory as a result of the conflict. And in the late 1840s he worked hard to get his home state to adopt a plan of emancipation, a stance that may have cost him re-election in 1852. Underwood's antislavery views extended to his private life too: unlike the mass of antislavery colonizationists who criticized slavery as a defective social and economic system but not slaveholding as an immoral action of individuals, Underwood developed moral concerns about slave ownership, and eventually he freed and colonized his slaves.[25]

Despite these views, Underwood devised a plan of colonization that was so expensive and gradualist that it strongly undercut his antislavery intentions. In an address before the KCS in 1835, Underwood proposed to end slavery in Kentucky by diminishing the reproductive capacity of the slave population. Believing that the typical slave woman began bearing children at the age of seventeen, Underwood recommended that slaves in Kentucky be sent to Liberia once they reached that age. As the existing adult slave population grew older and as those who were just reaching the age of fecundity were transported to Africa, in the course of two decades there would be few slaves in Kentucky capable of bearing children. As the remaining slaves began to die, slavery would be on the road to extinction; within fifty years of the first wave of colonization, there would be so few slaves left in Kentucky that the institution would be practically nonexistent.[26]

Underwood's plan had a number of advantages over most emancipation schemes based on colonization. His plan would begin freeing slaves immediately and offered freedom to about half of the existing slave population. But at best Underwood's plan was quite gradualistic, taking over fifty years to accomplish, and inordinately expensive, costing by Underwood's calculation $140,000 annually. James G. Birney, who heard Underwood's speech before the KCS, scoffed at the political feasibility of the program. "Have you . . . the most distant hope that, the people of Kentucky . . . will by their Representatives this year grant $140,000" for the colonization of slaves to Africa? Birney asked a northern friend. Birney believed such fantastic schemes and the "arithmetical benevolence" of such people as Underwood led only to the strengthening of slavery by "beguiling" those enlightened southerners who recognized the evil of slavery away from "that repentance which would save them." Likewise, abolitionist John G. Fee argued that colonization "perpetuates slavery by directing the sympathies, means, and activities of anti-slavery men in a wrong channel," and by acting as a "safety-valve through which to let off . . . [the] sense of natural justice which might burst out against the oppressor."[27]

In criticizing Underwood and like-minded colonizationists, Birney and Fee assumed that their opposition to slavery was sincere. "In stating the objections that exist in my mind to colonization," wrote Birney, "I wish it to be understood distinctly . . . that I do not, in the slightest degree, impute to . . . a large majority of those by whom it is . . . cherished, any unworthy motive as prompting their zeal." Perhaps Kentucky's abolitionists offered the best evaluation of antislavery colonizationists like Underwood: they were sincere but misguided opponents of slavery. There is ample evidence of antislavery sentiment in the private correspondence of Kentucky colonizationists. In addition, the fate of the KCS strongly suggests the authenticity of many colonizationists' opposition to slavery. During the early 1830s, an important segment of the KCS wanted the society to take a more radical position—if not to break with the ACS and its policy of colonizing free blacks, at least to acknowledge openly that many members of the Kentucky society wanted to see slavery ended by colonization.[28]

Most prominent among these was Robert J. Breckinridge, who was later to become a nationally famous Presbyterian minister. Son of John Breckinridge, Thomas Jefferson's attorney general, and uncle of John C. Breckinridge, James Buchanan's vice president, Robert Breckinridge had begun his public career as a lawyer-politician. In the 1820s, he served several terms in the Kentucky General Assembly, where he became known as an opponent of slavery—a reputation that eventually helped cost him re-election in 1830. Believing that "*ninety-nine in every hundred friends of colonization, who do any thing for the cause, are ardent friends of emancipation*," Breckinridge lamented that "there are very many who hope . . . to inveigle the friends of slavery into a short-lived friendship for [the] society; and that there are still more who are (I think) over-sedulous in avoiding all occasion of offence on the subject of slavery." To counteract the timidity of antislavery colonizationists, Breckinridge publicized the antislavery intentions of most of the active members of the KCS. "The political moral of the Colonization Society is strikingly plain," he wrote to the *Kentucky Gazette* in 1830. "It has taught us how we may be relieved of the curse of slavery in a manner cheap, certain and advantageous." "He who has considered the removal of our free blacks to Africa, as the ultimate point of this noble enterprise," Breckinridge argued before the KCS in 1831, "has taken a very inadequate view of a subject of . . . almost unlimited extent."[29]

Within a year of the formation of the KCS, antislavery colonizationists dominated the leadership of the society, making it one of the more radical of the state auxiliaries of the ACS. The KCS consistently chose antislavery colonizationists to deliver the annual address to the society; these speakers invariably expressed hope that the colonization society would facilitate emancipation. Occasionally, the annual report of the Kentucky society dared to break from the official line of the ACS that the societies wanted to colonize only free blacks. In 1831, for instance, the annual report of the KCS urged the federal government to provide funds for the colonization of "all free blacks, and all the slaves which . . . any of the State governments should determine to set at liberty."[30]

ACS agent Robert S. Finley, who wanted the national society to take a more definite antislavery position, was greatly heartened by the position of the KCS; after a visit to the Kentucky society in 1831, he reported that "public opinion is at least five years in advance of the *operations*" of the national society. But Kentucky's increasingly outspoken antislavery colonizationists did not please the national leaders of the ACS, who tried to quiet people like Breckinridge and Underwood. Breckinridge, who had sought ACS support for a speaking tour in the North to promote colonization, found his plans squelched by the cautious society. Afterward he complained to ACS secretary Ralph R. Gurley: "I apprehended that you and your board knew my views on these subjects—and considered me ultra—and feared to trust your cause in my hands."[31]

Nor were all colonizationists in the Kentucky society cheered by the course of reformers like Breckinridge. There were, Breckinridge noted to Gurley, "other friends" of the colonization societies who "have here in private, and before the nation in their public efforts . . . advocated your proceedings . . . [because] one effect of your Society might be to perpetuate slavery in this country. By all that class, . . . I had always been considered a most dangerous friend of your Society." If the goals of antislavery colonizationists have seemed unduly ambiguous to modern observers, they did not seem so to most Kentuckians of the antebellum period—within a year of the founding of the KCS, the growing resentment on the part of proslavery supporters toward antislavery activities was plain. Proslavery colonizationists took offense at a number of minor—often unintentional—indications that many members of the KCS saw colonization as something other than a plan to remove free blacks, and they seethed at the open proclamations by reformers like Breckinridge and Underwood that colonization could lead to emancipation. After 1830, proslavery advocates increasingly found themselves unable to cooperate with such people, and the Kentucky Colonization Society began holding less appeal for proslavery supporters.[32]

The tension between the pro- and antislavery members of the KCS was highlighted in the famous "slavery controversy" between Robert J. Breckinridge and Robert Wickliffe, the first president of the KCS. Wickliffe, known in Kentucky's political folklore as "Old Duke," was the leading figure of one of Kentucky's most prominent political families. He was also a gifted attorney, a man whose understanding of real estate law enabled him, by 1830, to become the state's wealthiest man and largest slaveholder. During the 1830s, Wickliffe became one of the state's most outspoken defenders of slavery and the leader of proslavery political forces in Kentucky.[33]

Believing that colonization "was not to be used to the destruction of the rights of property, nor in the slightest degree to interfere with the tenure of negro slavery," Wickliffe became a wholehearted supporter of the KCS. It did not take long, however, for Wickliffe to become disenchanted with the hidden agenda of antislavery colonizationists: they wanted to make the "object and tendency" of the KCS "general emancipation." Wickliffe's suspicion was confirmed during a speaking engagement before the Female Colonization Society of Lexington in 1830. During his speech, Wickliffe took the official position of the KCS, that the society had no intention to bring about emancipation and wanted only to remove free blacks from the state. Breckinridge followed Wickliffe on the program and promptly disagreed with "Old Duke," saying, as Wickliffe remembered it, "that if the object of the society was not to ultimately effect the emancipation of the negroes, he would not only wash his hands of it, but denounce it." Wickliffe soon came to believe that most members of the KCS shared Breckinridge's goal, and deciding that he had no taste for cooperating with antislavery activists, Wickliffe resigned his position as president of the KCS and withdrew from the society. "This ended my connection with the colonization society *forever,*" wrote Wickliffe. "I considered it in the hands of abolitionists."[34]

Significantly, as late as 1843 Wickliffe still claimed to support the principle of colonization. He objected only to the existing colonization society and to "its ultimate object in the hands of its present rulers." As far as he was concerned, colonization still had benefits to the slaveholder, but the colonization society had become harmful to the slaveholder's interests. Other proslavery advocates went further, though, and rejected the entire concept of colonization. At a time when advocates of slavery embraced an increasingly ardent defense of the peculiar institution, they inextricably linked colonization to a weakening of slavery. An editorial in the *Louisville Public Advertiser* written shortly after Wickliffe's withdrawal from the KCS spoke for this new feeling: "Under pretense of raising funds to transport the free people of colour to Liberia, hundreds of associations have been formed and appeal after appeal has been made to the sympathies of the public, the real object of which was . . . to induce the Kentuckians to undertake the great work of emancipation. We have always viewed the project of colonizing the people of colour in Liberia as deceptive and pernicious and only intended to cover the real designs of its leading advocates—that of emancipating slaves and leaving them among us." By the 1840s, the growth of such sentiments was responsible for making proslavery advocates—especially those who defended slavery as a positive good—Kentucky's most prominent opponents of colonization.[35]

The alienation of proslavery forces from the KCS neither transformed the society into an outright antislavery society nor entirely
resolved the ambiguity of its message. Like all auxiliaries of the ACS,
the KCS remained officially dedicated to the colonization of free
blacks. But the virtual absence of ardent proslavery supporters from
the society after the mid-1830s meant that the values of antislavery
colonizationists would shape the unwritten agenda of the KCS in
significant ways, making the society seem so antislavery in tone that
it would not attract significant support in Kentucky. For instance,
there was a subtle shift away from the argument that colonization
would strengthen slavery to one that the KCS could carry out its
plan without interfering with the rights of slaveholders. When this
theme was coupled with the argument that colonization would promote emancipation, the result was the assertion that colonization
was, as newspaper editor George D. Prentice put it, "the only plan
consistent with individual rights . . . which has been or can be devised, for the abrogation of slavery in the southern states." This was
still an appeal to slaveholders—indeed, most antislavery colonizationists were themselves slave owners—but it was an argument directed less to ardent defenders of slavery like Wickliffe than toward
slaveholders who felt that, as a social and economic system, slavery
was harmful to Kentucky.[36]

The argument that colonization could promote emancipation
without interfering with property rights eventually became one of
the most common themes used by the KCS. Of course, the matter of
how the society could accomplish this goal was somewhat problematic. For some, this was a question of style: slaveholders did not have
to fear colonization societies because they did not act like abolition
societies, which most southerners regarded as mean-spirited, dishon-
orable, and reckless organizations. In contrast to abolition societies,
noted Judge William F. Bullock of Jefferson County, "no vindictive
and persecuting spirit has marked the annals" of the colonization
society. "No incendiary spirit . . . fan[s] the flame of civil discord."
For others, like Henry Clay, the argument that the colonization societies did not intend to interfere with the rights of slaveholders
amounted to an assurance that the societies wanted to leave the fate

of slavery in the hands of southerners. This argument, though, was not designed to assure proslavery advocates that, if left in the hands of southerners, slavery would be secure forever; rather, it was intended to reassure slaveholders that when emancipation came it would be carried out by slave owners with due regard for their own sensibilities and property rights.[37]

Still other members of the KCS argued that the organization did not threaten the rights of slaveholders because it depended on the voluntary cooperation of slave owners. "It has never been disguised that [the KCS] regards slavery as an evil [nor] . . . that it does contemplate the eventual extinction of that evil," argued James T. Morehead, but "not by any process of constraint or coercion nor by the interposition of laws exerted, over an unwilling people." Instead, the colonization society would depend on the flowering of "enlightened views of public policy and self-preservation" to convince slaveholders to emancipate their slaves. But by the 1840s, antislavery colonizationists had fewer reasons to hope that voluntary emancipation would supply colonists, and they hoped to use the power of the state to free Kentucky's slaves while still respecting property rights. By some interpretations of the Kentucky constitution, the General Assembly could free the state's slaves by compensating slaveholders for their lost property, a remedy that might go against the slaveholders' wishes but did seem consistent with the guarantee in the United States Constitution that property would not be taken for public use without compensation. Similar concerns drew antislavery colonizationists to *post nati* emancipation schemes. They argued that a master had no property rights over the unborn children of slave mothers; hence the state could free these persons at their birth, without infringing on property rights.[38]

Nothing, though, illustrates the extent to which antislavery values had colored the approach of the KCS to colonization than its failure to win the approval of separationists, who were perhaps the largest potential source of support for the KCS. As their name implies, the separationists' principal goal was the separation of the white and black races; more than any other group in Kentucky, they rejected the idea that a biracial society had benefits for either whites or blacks, a stance that made them more explicitly racist than the anti-slavery colonizationists. Where antislavery colonizationists were moved by opposition to slavery but allowed racism to shape their reform activities, the separationists were moved from the beginning by a racist desire to remove blacks from Kentucky. And while the separationists usually gave at least nominal support to the idea of colonization, they usually favored more practical and certain methods of African-American removal. They saw the KCS version of colonization as particularly extravagant, for it seemed to be more expensive than some plans for removing blacks, and it also seemed to incorporate values which went beyond black resettlement. The KCS responded to these criticisms not by designing a simple and cheap alternative to biracialism, but by doggedly defending their plan in a manner that revealed them to be less racist and more committed to antislavery than these critics.[39]

The most widely shared objection to the KCS scheme was that it was impractical. This seemingly simple accusation actually involved a number of related criticisms of the plan. The most common objection pointed to monetary and logistical problems. Estimates of the expense needed to destroy slavery in Kentucky through colonization varied wildly, although by almost any calculation, colonization of even a portion of the state's slaves would be inordinately expensive, a charge leveled not only by abolitionists like Birney, but also by separationists and proslavery advocates. Beyond monetary constraints was the matter of logistics. For colonization to succeed, some system would be needed to gather large numbers of emigrants from around the state, transport them to the nation's seaports, and house them until they could be sent to Africa. Organizers would have to secure large numbers of ships to transport the emigrants across the ocean and keep the emigrants supplied with the necessities of life until they were established in their new homeland. In short, it would require central planning on a scale both unpopular and unknown at that time in the United States. And given the colonization societies' notable lack of success in dealing with the relatively small-scale emigration they had already sponsored, few were sanguine about their ability to manage such an operation.[40]

Opponents of the colonization societies' plan believed that the location of the Liberian colony in Africa was central to the monetary and logistical problems. They often suggested a more convenient destination for the colonists, such as Central America, the islands of the Caribbean or the Pacific, or even the western portion of North America. Even some antislavery colonizationists, like Presbyterian minister John D. Paxton, called for a more practical location. Paxton lamented the fact that the colonization societies' energies were "directed abroad" and "feared" that "their efforts . . . will . . . fail to save the south, unless other measures, not embraced in their plan, be set in operation." Paxton was particularly enamored with the notion of establishing a colony in the western United States—Arkansas or Texas, perhaps—which he believed was an eminently more practical location than faraway Africa.[41]

Members of the KCS generally reacted coolly to these criticisms of African colonization, persistently defending the location of the Liberian colony. Kentucky colonizationists claimed that the other suggested locations for the colony offered greater economic and logistical difficulties than Liberia did. To counter reports about poor living conditions in Liberia, the KCS appointed several agents to visit Liberia and then return to Kentucky to report on the colony. Many of these agents were free blacks chosen specifically because potential emigrants could trust them. To demonstrate the economic potential of Liberia, Kentucky colonizationists sought to display Liberian exports such as coffee and palm oil publicly; these displays "excite[d] great interest" in Kentucky, according to ACS agent Robert S. Finley.[42]

In the 1840s, however, the KCS faced a greater challenge from deportation schemes than from rival colonization plans. Separationists and some proslavery advocates believed that the monetary and logistical problems presented by colonization schemes—especially any that depended on the voluntary cooperation of reluctant black migrants—were so great that it was more practical to remove free blacks by simply banishing them from the state. For proslavery forces, deportation provided the benefits of colonization—the removal of a troublesome free black population—without the antislavery tendencies of colonization. And this new method of African-American removal promoted the interests of the white race in a manner consistent with the desire for small, cheap government.[43]

Former Democratic State Senator Thomas James, for instance, criticized the state government for establishing a small fund to colonize "free persons of color" and "the slaves that might be extorted from the good people of the state" instead of using the money to "pay the interest on the state debt" or "defray the expenses of your courts of justice." Squire Turner thought that the expense of colonization made the issue one of deciding whether the state government existed to help whites or blacks. If the state burdened the white taxpayers with the costs of colonization, it would be "setting at liberty the slaves of the country" by "enslaving the white race." A more workable solution, both men agreed, was "to prohibit the emancipation of slaves" by individual masters "without a provision for their deportation when emancipated." Such sentiments were becoming increasingly popular in Kentucky during the 1840s, and by 1851 they had resulted in the passage of tough new laws designed to limit the number of free blacks living in Kentucky. Slaves could be manumitted only "upon condition of their being removed from, and [their] continued residence out of, the state of Kentucky," and it became a felony punishable by five years imprisonment for free blacks to move into the state.[44]

Despite the monetary and logistical problems identified by proslavery and deportationist critics, antislavery colonizationists like Henry Clay and Joseph R. Underwood continued to regard colonization as a goal worth pursuing, and they pointed out how easily many of the problems of colonization could be overcome. Clay argued that the nation already had the financial resources to colonize slaves. If the United States were to divert one-tenth of the funds it was spending to repay the national debt into paying for colonization, the entire annual increase of the slave population could be removed from the country "without feeling it." It was in this vein that Clay proposed his famous land distribution bill, which would have applied part of the proceeds from the sale of federal lands to pay for the building of roads and canals, the education of children, and the colonization of blacks—funds that Jacksonian Democrats usually wanted to apply toward decreasing the national debt and providing cheap government. Likewise, Underwood claimed that the funds needed for his colonization plan could be raised by an annual "poll tax" of seventy cents per free person. During the Mexican War, which Underwood opposed as a war to obtain more slave territory, he complained bitterly that "one-half the expenses of the Mexican War invested in a six per cent. stock" would raise enough money to "extirpate slavery in the United States" through colonization. The willingness of the country to spend large sums of money for purposes other than colonization convinced Underwood that "our purses are not the cause of the failure" to colonize slaves.[45]

The charge that colonization was impractical, Underwood perceived, went far beyond mere monetary considerations. African colonization often seemed impractically expensive not because governments lacked the means of raising the necessary funds, but because it embraced visionary goals of "the glory and welfare of mankind" that sapped the will of governments to spend funds. It has not been fully appreciated that when critics of the KCS called colonization impractical, they often meant not so much that it was "impracticable in its means" but that it was "Utopian in its end," as Henry Clay put it. Colonizationists repeatedly defended themselves against the charge that their scheme was a "fond enthusiasm" or "one too visionary to merit serious consideration." But in truth the colonizationists' own appeals did nothing to allay the utopian image of their plan, for they could not refrain from using grandiloquent language to describe colonization as precisely such a visionary enterprise. Underwood regarded the advent of colonizationism as a sign that "the glory of the Millennium has dawned" and that there was a "new order of things in man's destiny on earth." Stuart Robinson, a Presbyterian minister, spoke of colonization as a visionary scheme of "grandeur and magnitude" comparable to the discovery of the New World and the invention of the steamboat and telegraph. "So is this scheme visionary," he argued, "visionary for the same reason that great minds ever seem to smaller minds visionary."[46]

Robinson's comparison of colonization to some of the greatest products of human imagination was apt, for the colonizationists embraced a vision of humanity's ability to control its environment and fate that contrasted starkly with the fatalism of many southerners. An antislavery colonizationist like John C. Young might argue that it was not "strange, considering the enlargement of human power, that we should view as practicable a project, which ruder and poorer ages would have pronounced visionary; that we should possess the courage to grapple with an evil, at the magnitude of which they would have stood appalled; and that we should with confidence undertake to avert a catastrophe which they would have deemed inevitable." It is not surprising that a scheme which was admittedly "vast in its conception" would be opposed by someone like David Meriwether, state legislator and future United States senator, who believed that "whatever man can do, Kentuckians can do; but he who accomplishes this, is either more or less than man. It is not within the grasp of man to do it."[47]

The most common criticism of the allegedly utopian vision of the KCS, however, stemmed from the fact that the unofficial goal of its colonization scheme went beyond the immediate and "practical" objective of eliminating free blacks from Kentucky: the society also wanted to transform the African continent and cleanse America's soul. The KCS believed that the establishment of a self-governing republic of American blacks in Africa would spread American culture and Christian religion to the "dark continent," saving Africa, in the words of James T. Morehead, "from the dominion of ignorance and barbarism and superstition and sin." In the colonizationists' imagery, a colony of American blacks in Africa would tame a physical and cultural wilderness: "It will open forests, build towns, erect temples of public worship, and practically exhibit to the native[s] . . . of Africa . . . the superior advantages of our religious and social systems," argued Henry Clay.[48]

Moreover, members of the KCS insisted that the return of some of Africa's lost children would help not only reform a continent, but remove the dark stain of slavery and the slave trade from America's past. "It will be the melancholy task of the future annalist of our country," lamented James T. Morehead, to record that "the American people, justly claiming to be a nation of free men, swayed the sceptre of dominion over a nation of slaves." The United States owed a special debt of atonement to Africa and the descendants of Africans for "the dark atrocity of the slave trade, and the long bondage of the deadly rice swamp." "May we not hope that America will extinguish a great portion of that moral debt which she has contracted to that unfortunate continent" of Africa, asked Henry Clay, "if, instead of the evils and sufferings which we had been . . . inflicting upon the inhabitants of Africa, we can transmit to her the blessings of our arts, our civilization, and our religion?"[49]

The colonizationists of the KCS embraced Africa with an ardor born of true emotional attachment for the place and the crusade it represented. Their motives may have involved racism and a self-interested antislavery, but they also genuinely desired to do good—while pursuing self-interest. If a colonization scheme could be designed that would end slavery and remove blacks while redeeming a continent and cleansing America's soul, so much the better. There are several reasons to believe that the colonizationists' desire to reform Africa was not simply a subterfuge designed to help make black removal palatable but a genuine motive in itself. First, this was an age that took missionary activity seriously. At a time when American religious denominations spent thousands of dollars every year to send missionaries all over the globe, there is little reason to doubt that colonizationists might sincerely regard the "Christianization" of Africa as an important goal in itself. Even an ardent anticolonizationist like John G. Fee believed that "good is growing out of the colony at Liberia," while still maintaining that the conversion of Africa to Christianity could be accomplished more efficiently by sending to Africa trained missionaries instead of free blacks. Although James G. Birney went so far as to argue that colonization might be counterproductive to the conversion of Africa, he still thought that many people sincerely believed that colonization would be the mode by which the "Christianization of A[frica] may be carried on."[50]

Second, colonization societies in the United States were patriotic organizations; indeed, according to one historian, the ACS "was probably the nation's most influential patriotic organization in the two decades that followed the War of 1812." Embracing a "spread-eagle patriotism" and wanting "to cleanse America and restore the assumed purity and . . . stability of her Revolutionary beginnings," the colonization societies tried to remove the allegedly corrupting influence of free blacks on the nation's welfare and to allay sectional differences by taking a middle ground on slavery issues. Members of the KCS certainly shared these goals. As patriots, they sensed that slavery was wrong, that it was damaging "our national character," threatening "our republican form of government," and bringing the nation into disrepute by contradicting "those principles promulgated to the world in our Declaration of Independence." Not surprisingly, colonizationists enthusiastically embraced a scheme that seemed to atone for the past wrongs of the nation. In fact, the patriotism of Kentucky's colonizationists turned the program of Liberian settlement into a form of national self-congratulation: Liberia was to become a new America in the African wilderness, with its success replicating the American experience. Like the earlier American colonists, Liberian colonists would be drawn from the ranks of the oppressed. Armed with the genius of American institutions, the settlers would conquer a continent, producing a land in which any American—were he or she black—could feel at home. "We hear every where the familiar accents of our own language, and see every where the evidences of that all-pervading commercial activity which democratic institutions . . . never fail to engender, . . ." imagined John A. McClung. "Everything displays the bustle and activity of a young and growing people." Robert J. Breckinridge echoed this thought: "Yes, it is a child of our country!—outcast it may be—but still a child!"[51]

Breckinridge's image suggests a third reason to think that the colonizationists' enthusiasm for the redemption of Africa was genuine. The colonizationists were obviously interested in something more than the removal of blacks from America. They showed a real—albeit paternalistic—interest in the success of America's "child," the Liberian colony. Just as individuals like Charles W. Short often continued to send money and supplies to their former bondsmen for years after they had left the United States, the membership of the

KCS often showed continuing support for Liberia's progress. The KCS sometimes spent money to improve the quality of life in Liberia, money that could have been used to send more blacks to Africa. In the early 1850s, for example, it sent funds to help build a high school in Monrovia. Indeed, in the mid-1840s, the KCS nearly seceded from the national society, in part because the ACS was not doing enough to provide support for emigrants from Kentucky after their arrival in Africa. And colonizationists exhibited an obvious pride in Liberia's accomplishments, boasting of the establishment of schools, libraries, newspapers, churches, and democratic government in the colony.[52]

Most importantly, the redemption of Africa must have been important to the members of the KCS, for they tenaciously held to their original plan of colonization despite the criticisms of it as utopian. At a time when a variety of "practical" schemes for black removal—ranging from colonization within the Western Hemisphere to simple banishment—were proposed for public consideration, the dedication of the KCS to the redemption of Africa prompted the society to oppose other plans and kept the society committed to its original plan of action. The single-minded dedication of the society to the redemption of Africa caused John D. Paxton to charge bitterly that the society was so interested in seeing "Africa . . . become regenerated and made to share the blessings of the gospel and civilization" that it was willing to sacrifice the efficient removal of the slave population and risk a slave rebellion in order to colonize Africa.[53]

Indeed, the strength of the society's devotion to African colonization is even more striking when one realizes that its plan of redeeming Africa stood in direct opposition to the increasingly popular southern image of the innate inferiority of African Americans and the positive good of slavery. For all the colonizationists' racism and their nagging doubts about blacks' ability to run their own lives, their scheme of colonization depended on notions of black capabilities that more virulent racists regarded as laughably out of touch with reality. The conception of a self-governing black republic redeeming an entire continent rested fundamentally on what many Kentuckians considered the "doubtful" question of "whether the African race can govern themselves." Deportationists and proslavery ideologues scoffed at the idea. After considering the question, Democratic politician James Guthrie had "satisfied my own mind and judgment that it is impossible to send them" to Africa. "There is no country" of white men "to receive them—they have not the wisdom to govern themselves." Instead of emigrants taming a wilderness, as the colonizationists would have it, blacks would be destroyed by it, destined to meet, as one skeptic put it, "starvation, ruin, [and] desolation" without the help of whites. To the colonizationists, though, the very existence of Liberia, in the words of George D. Prentice, "proves beyond all question that colored persons are fully competent to take care of themselves. . . . They are not under the superintendence of masters or friends, and the consequence is that they conduct the affairs of the Republic successfully."[54]

Further, anticolonizationists in Kentucky argued that even if it could be proved that blacks were capable of self-government, the state's resources should not be wasted in an effort to redeem Africa. Where the state's colonizationists thought that some kind of "great debt of national regeneration was due" to Africa and the black race, those who found African colonization to be unduly visionary usually denied that America owed any sort of special debt to Africa. Most opponents of the KCS plan clearly believed that the descendants of Africans had benefited from their enslavement in "civilized" America. Declaring slavery to have "been a great blessing to the negro," Baptist minister John L. Waller asked Kentuckians to "compare the condition of that race here with their condition in Africa." On that continent, Waller claimed, blacks were "dwarfish in stature, ungainly in person, . . . [and] but a remove above the ourang-outang" in intellect. They lacked law and "social comforts," lived as "cannibals," and supported a religion that, he believed, had "sunk below idolatry into absolute fetic[h]ism." Waller argued that in the United States blacks "have been improved, physically and intellectually; all of them have been taught the true religion, and many of them are among the most pious christians in the land." In contrast to this, colonizationists maintained that the Negro's primary problem—in both Africa and America—was the Caucasian. Most colonizationists argued that "African degradation" was caused by the debilitating effects of the slave trade and that the seeming inferiority of American blacks "has been brought upon them, chiefly if not entirely by our own policy and social state." The easiest way to "improve" the black man was to get him clear of the white man by sending him to Africa.[55]

The colonizationist argument for the redemption of Africa embraced controversial positions on two of the day's most divisive issues: the innate capacity of blacks and the morality and general benefits of slavery. By opposing the emerging southern consensus on these issues and giving shape to the amorphous program that it inherited from the ACS, the Kentucky society alienated those who might otherwise have supported it. Most Kentuckians remained nominal colonizationists—sympathetic to the imperative that freed slaves should be removed from the state—but the Kentucky Colonization Society did not speak for them. The Kentucky experience demonstrates the importance of colonizationist diversity and reveals the limits of the influence of the ACS on colonizationism. It also demonstrates the remarkable persistence of colonization. The colonizationist impulse was important fifty years before the ACS was organized, and it lasted for years after the society ceased to be a major force in black migration. Colonizationism thrived for such a long time in part because it embodied a goal—the organized resettlement of blacks—that could be incorporated into a wide range of ideologies, from ardent support of slavery to militant black nationalism. The ACS tried to organize and absorb the popularity of colonization by separating the goal of black emigration from the variety of ideologies that impelled people to support it, but its success was both incomplete and fleeting.

The issues that caused organized colonization societies in Kentucky to founder formed part of a debate about human progress and the prerequisites for a good society. In this debate, members of the KCS joined a larger group of antislavery conservatives whose critique of slavery was shaped by their day-to-day participation in the slave system. Though they were members of the master class, the conservatives proved to be surprisingly perceptive analysts of race relations in the state. Conscious of the fact that white racism could have harmful effects on blacks, they blamed white racism for most of the inferiority attributed to blacks. Conservatives feared that blacks would not docilely accept the degradation they suffered at white hands forever and that the result would be an understandable and violent reaction by blacks against their white oppressors. Yet the conservative vision was tragically limited by the mores of their society and by their own racism, and these limitations would ultimately impede the effectiveness of their antislavery activities.

3

The Dilemma of
Conservative Reform

The debate over slavery and race in the 1830s and 1840s perplexed
few Kentuckians more than it did John Clarke Young of Danville.
Young, a native of Pennsylvania, moved to Kentucky after his gradu-
ation from Princeton Theological Seminary in 1828 to become pastor of a Presbyterian church in Lexington, and he quickly found a
place among the state's elites. He married a member of Kentucky's
illustrious Breckinridge family, became master of his wife's slaves,
and assumed—at the age of twenty-seven—the presidency of Centre
College in Danville. Young also quickly became part of a class of
people familiar to anyone conversant with southern antislavery: slaveholders who denounced slavery. Indeed, Young went further in his
critique of slavery than most: he was very nearly an abolitionist.
Young believed that "the system of slavery . . . is sinful" and that it
was the "duty" of all Christians "to rid ourselves of all participation
in the sin which it involves" by taking "vigorous and immediate measures for the destruction of this whole system." This included the
duty of slaveholders to make "conscientious efforts to qualify . . .
slaves for freedom," and, true to his word, Young not only educated—and later freed—the slaves he obtained through marriage, but

he also purchased other slaves in order to free them. Young railed against those who said that the Bible approved slaveholding as practiced in the South, calling their arguments an "insult [to] the God of heaven." He argued that the oft-cited reciprocal duties of masters and slaves as outlined in the scriptures had been intended primarily to restrain masters from "the exercise of injustice and oppression." If masters seriously followed the biblical commandment to give their slaves "'that which is just and equal'"—interpreted by Young to mean not only providing food, clothing, and shelter, but also paying a slave what he or she could earn as a hired laborer—it "would be at once an end of all that is properly called slavery."[1]

What aroused Young's perplexity was northern reaction to his views on slavery, views which before the 1830s would have been considered radical. It is a measure of just how far antislavery thought had come that, in the middle of the 1830s, Young found himself publicly denounced by abolitionists as an "apologist for slavery" whose declaration that slavery was "sinful" had "some deceit about it" and was "worth nothing." The source of the abolitionists' ire was Young's widely republished letter to the *Cincinnati Journal* defending the Presbyterian Synod of Kentucky, which in October 1834 passed a series of resolutions proclaiming slavery to be sinful and urging slaveholders to emancipate their bondsmen—but only after the slaves had been made fit for freedom. Young argued that religious duty required masters to "execut[e] deeds of emancipation for [their] slaves, to take effect at a certain fixed period hereafter" and to make "vigorous and conscientious efforts to qualify [their] slaves for freedom." Moreover, he continued that "it is sinful in any individual to delay . . . unnecessarily the day of complete emancipation." But to begin the arduous task of preparing slaves for freedom was to change the very nature of the master-slave relationship, transforming slavery "into a kind of apprenticeship," and Young wrote that under these circumstances "it is not sinful in an individual to retain his legal authority over those of his servants" he is "preparing . . . for the right and beneficial enjoyment of liberty." This letter, with its assertion that slaveholding could be justified in certain limited circumstances, immediately became a cause célèbre in abolitionist circles and was denounced by such notables as Theodore Dwight Weld, Samuel Crothers, Charles Stuart, and even Young's close friend James G. Birney.[2]

Young was hurt by such criticism, much of which was couched in what he considered to be "harsh and vituperative language." His distress over the incident was perhaps augmented by the fact that while he understood the nature of his differences with the abolitionists, he could never fathom the vitriol of their response to his letter. He thought he agreed with them about "the criminal nature of slavery" and "the duty of immediate action on this subject," and, as he understood it, they disagreed with him only about "the best mode of getting rid of this evil." Indeed, Young was close enough to the abolitionist position that, once the controversy over his letter had died down, he toyed with the idea of proclaiming himself an abolitionist. In the end, however, the small differences that Young believed lay between the abolitionists and himself proved decisive. Young could abandon neither his distaste for "sudden revolutions in society" nor his fear of "the *sudden* elevation of an immense, uneducated, and degraded mass of human beings from their low condition to a full equality with the rest of the citizens." In Young's opinion, the safety of society demanded that slaves be restrained until they had been trained for freedom.[3]

John Young was not typical of antislavery reformers in Kentucky: he went further toward abolitionism than most Kentuckians dared. However, he shared with the leadership of the state's antislavery movement a conservative fear of disorder that ultimately prevented him from following people like James G. Birney into full-blown abolitionism. In fact, it was this concern for disorder that marked the leaders of Kentucky's antislavery movement as conservatives. Kentucky's antislavery conservatives neither blindly worshiped the preservation of the status quo nor wanted to return America to some bygone, golden age. The conservatives thought they were "progressive" because they looked forward to changes that heralded a future of human advancement. But their overriding concern was that change should be orderly and that it should produce a stable, harmonious society in the future. The fact that such people dominated the state's antislavery movement ultimately proved to be its great strength as well as its great weakness, for while conservatism moved easily into a potent critique of slavery, its very nature limited its effectiveness. The conservatives would never endorse a truly effective program of emancipation for fear that it would destroy everything they were trying to accomplish. They were trapped by the dilemma of conservative reform: the problem of eliminating one source of disorder without creating another one in the process.

The conservative worldview was not, of course, peculiar to Kentucky or to the South; rather, it was shared by Americans of all sections, and particularly by members of the Whig party, the political home of most of Kentucky's antislavery conservatives. One reason so many northerners—like Young—could come to Kentucky and fit easily into the ranks of antislavery conservatives was that the outline of Kentucky conservatism had much in common with the northern variety. But the antislavery conservatives had a heightened fear of imminent disorder shaped by a purely southern influence: their relationship with the state's slave population. The conservatives knew that slaves made up the state's largest antislavery group and that their opposition to enslavement represented an important source of disorder in Kentucky.[4]

Before the 1950s, most historians disputed the proposition that American slaves actively fought the depredations of bondage. Slavery was thought to have been either so benevolent an institution that few slaves resisted their masters' control, or conversely, so brutally oppressive that it reduced adult slaves to a childlike, psychological dependence on their masters. In regard to Kentucky, numerous observers regarded slavery there as comparatively benevolent; as historian J. Winston Coleman, Jr., put it, "slavery [existed] in Kentucky in its mildest form, better than in any other slave state, with the possible exception of Maryland or Virginia." Several accounts by former slaves also made the claim that slavery in Kentucky was somehow less severe than in the Lower South. From a certain perspective, such observations were correct: slavery in Kentucky probably was milder than it was in the cotton belt of the Lower South. Working in a region with a shorter growing season, on farms that rarely depended on a single cash crop, slaves in Kentucky experienced less monotonous work routines and less sunup-to-sundown gang labor than slaves on Lower South plantations. Many Kentucky masters appear sometimes to have used the task system of labor, in which slaves were assigned jobs to complete and allowed to use the time left over as their own. Living on small farms with few other slaves and, hence, fewer potential mates, most slaves were forced by circumstances to find spouses on other farms and to maintain their families across farm boundaries. This fact, and the greater variety of jobs assigned to slaves meant that Kentucky slaves probably experienced greater mobility than slaves of the Lower South. Certainly slaves sold south from Kentucky and the Upper South found their work suddenly harder in the cotton and sugar belts. They faced unfamiliar work routines and their new masters' unrealistic expectations for performance.[5]

However, the claim that slavery in Kentucky was milder than it was in the Lower South depends largely on restricting the discussion of slavery to the narrow field of labor conditions. In other regards, slavery in Kentucky and the Upper South actually appears to have been harsher than slavery in the Lower South. The principal reason for this was also the smaller size of Kentucky farms. Slaves on small farms experienced a greater degree of contact with the masters than slaves on large plantations. While in some cases intimate contact probably humanized the master-slave relationship, in more cases it appears that it simply exposed slaves to the constant demands of petty, racist tyrants. Evidence suggests that the greater degree of contact between masters and slaves on small farms also increased the likelihood of the sexual abuse of slave women by their masters. Unlike slaves on the large plantations of the Lower South, where an individual plantation might be the home of dozens of slaves, slaves on the small farms of Kentucky had greater difficulty making contact with and experiencing the comforting fellowship of a larger black community. Likewise, the small size of Kentucky farms and the consequentially high number of interfarm slave marriages placed enormous burdens on black family life. Not only was it hard for families divided across farm borders to spend time together as a family, but having two masters rather than one made it twice as likely that slave families would be divided by sale. To make matters worse, Kentucky's small farmers, having fewer economic resources to carry them through hard times, were more likely to be forced by economic circumstances to sell their slaves than large planters in the Lower South. Additionally, the transition of the slave-rich Bluegrass region to mixed crops and widespread cultivation of hemp, with its highly seasonal labor demands, meant that farmers often believed they had an oversupply of slaves, which also increased the likelihood of slave sales. According to the calculations of the historian Michael Tadman, a slave child born in Kentucky in 1820 had about a one out of three chance of being sold out of the state before his death.[6]

Quite apart from the living conditions of slaves, it should be noted that whether Kentucky slavery was milder or harsher than slavery in the Lower South, the principle of slavery in Kentucky was identical to that of the Lower South. Humans were still held in bondage as masters tried to make slaves into little more than extensions of their wills. Certainly no claim for the mildness of slavery can be used as an apology for its existence in Kentucky. It should not be surprising that slaves in Kentucky disliked slavery and, as Charles W. Short put it in 1837, they "look[ed] . . . forward to unconditional emancipation as the greatest of all earthly boons." The accounts of former Kentucky slaves tell of a nearly universal dislike for slavery among bondsmen. Even those who expressed a lingering affection for their former masters often did so with a wry sarcasm that denigrated slavery. George Scruggs, for instance, recalled that "my Old Boss wuz sho good to me. . . . I sho do luv im yet. Wy, he neva wood [al]low me to go barfooted, cause he was afraid I'd stick thorns in my feet, an if he eva caut me barfooted he sho wod make my back tell it." By the 1840s, the prospect of freedom appears to have been a much-discussed topic among slaves and, indeed, some former slaves reported that the very hope of emancipation in itself made their lives more bearable. White colonizationists affirmed these reports, noting that the slaves' hope of emancipation in Kentucky made African colonization seem far less desirable. Perhaps the clearest indicator of the slaves' true feelings about their bondage was the spontaneous outpouring of joy and hope that followed emancipation at the end of the Civil War. Freedmen organized celebrations of freedom across the state, such as the one in Louisville on January 1, 1866, at which five thousand blacks gathered to commemorate emancipation and the recent passage of the Thirteenth Amendment.[7]

The slaves' disdain for slavery did not translate into an insurrectionary force nor—usually—escape attempts. In a state where whites outnumbered slaves nearly four to one, the prospect of success for either option was so slim—and the penalty for failure so high—that even the boldest of slaves hesitated before seeking freedom through escape or insurrection. Out of necessity, then, the slaves channeled their opposition to slavery into the more practical form of resisting the depredations of bondage. Their goal was to soften the impact of slavery on their lives and resist becoming mere extensions of their masters' wills. Their resulting actions convinced a fair number of white Kentuckians that slaves were a peculiarly vexing form of property.[8]

Kentucky slaves tried to make their bondage more bearable in a variety of ways, most of them troublesome to whites. Kentucky slaves, for instance, engaged in practices referred to by some as "the slaves' economy." In hemp-producing counties, slaves engaged in a thriving trade in hemp tow—the short, broken fibers left over from the process of breaking hemp. These fibers could be sold or bartered to the makers of paper and twine, thereby earning a small income. Especially where the task system was used, slaves found opportunities to raise garden plots or even keep small livestock and sell what they did not consume. To obtain additional goods for sale, slaves sometimes stole items from their masters. Slave owners were often bothered by these aspects of autonomous slave life—they disliked the degree of independence that trading conferred on slaves, the theft it sometimes involved, and the allegedly corrupting contacts produced by trading between slaves, free blacks, and poor whites.[9]

Slaves found that one of the easiest ways to seek a measure of freedom in slavery was simply to ignore their masters' wishes and instead do what they wanted, covering the omission with a deception. Some bondsmen secretly used a name of their choosing after being renamed by their masters. Others provided food and shelter to runaway slaves. Sometimes, slaves who lived near the Ohio River built rafts to help runaway slaves cross the river or even ferried fugitives across in their masters' boats. More often, though, the slaves' deception of their masters took the more practical form of disobeying the rules of plantation discipline. At night, Kentucky slaves persistently left their masters' farms without permission. During the day, slaves intentionally slowed the pace of work or performed their tasks carelessly. Former slave Robert Anderson remembered that "I would often use every plan I could think of to get a few moments rest" from the "back breaking work" of weeding the garden:

> One scheme I worked more often than any other was to run to my Missis pretending that I heard her calling me. Sometimes when I would be awful thirsty, I used to answer her: "Comin', Missis. I's comin'," and run to her . . . altho[ugh] I knew she had not called me. All the time I would be running toward her, she would be telling me to get back to work or she would skin me alive. I pretended that I tho[ugh]t she was telling me to hurry.[10]

When Anderson finally reached his mistress and she demanded to know how he could have been so stupid to come to her when he had not been called, Anderson remembered that "I would hang my head and stammer that I tho[ugh]t she called me to come and get her a drink of cool water from the spring." Anderson had resorted to a ruse often used by slaves: when caught in a deception, they played to the master's racism by putting on a studied "Sambo act," appealing simultaneously to the master's feeling that slaves were incompetent to do what they were told and his desire for the slave's loyalty and affection. Former bondsmen like Anderson took great pride in such deceptions—in proving themselves "altogether too keen and shrewd for the best of" white people—so much so that some slaves preferred the challenge of traveling at night without a pass, even though their masters would have readily given them one.[11]

One area in which slaves seemed especially proud of their deception was the stealing of food. By all accounts, Kentucky slaves commonly took food without their master's permission. Former bondsmen claimed that slaves stole food because they were hungry or lacked variety in their diets. Although few Kentucky slaves appear to have been kept on starvation diets, it is also apparent that many masters, in the words of one bondsman, were "very careful not to let any of us over eat, and for fear we would, we were kept largely on a diet that left us hungry most of the time." But, there was another dimension to the slaves' expropriation of food: they clearly enjoyed the task of getting the upper hand on those who, as one slave put it, "watch us narrowly" for signs of stealing. Former bondsmen exulted over their ingenuity in obtaining extra food. Slaves dug up potatoes and then drove hogs into the field to make it look like the animals had rooted up the potatoes. They stole chickens and left "their feathers so scattered around as to indicate the havoc of Foxes." They butchered pigs and hid the meat under the skin of freshly killed opossums. Such activities required cunning and skill, and slaves took pride in those who mastered the craft. Lewis Clarke remembered one such woman who lived on his master's farm: "She would go out to the corn crib, with her basket, watch [for] her opportunity, with one effective blow pop over a little pig, slip him into her basket and put the [corn] cobs on top, trudge off to her cabin, and look just as innocent as though she had a right to eat the work of her own hands." Clarke's story points to one reason that so many slaves found the stealing of food such a satisfying form of deception: they were not just pulling the wool over the eyes of "ole massa," they were appropriating the fruits of their labor, which they felt had been extorted from them. So strong was this feeling that slaves reported that they rarely questioned the morality of taking food without the master's permission. "The only question, . . ." wrote Clarke, "was *how* and *when* to do it."[12]

Such actions sometimes made slaves seem ungovernable. A surprising number of slaves resisted punishment or openly broke their masters' rules, even though their behavior would probably mean harsher treatment. Kentucky bondsmen especially disobeyed or resisted punishment in matters that affected their families, whose emotional support made slavery more bearable. Lewis Clarke, who had been separated from his family when he was a child, thought that his master's oppression would have been "comparatively tolerable" with his family "near to sympathize with me, [and] to hear my story of sorrow." Slaves, then, were often willing to go to great lengths—even to the point of challenging their masters—to maintain their families. Slave husbands broke their masters' rule against leaving farms to see their wives, even though it could mean punishment or sale to the Lower South. Slave parents pleaded with their masters not to punish their children even though it could mean punishment for the parent.[13]

Often enough, such actions were not effective, and some Kentucky slaves reported that they developed a sense of helplessness about their condition. For example, Henry Bibb was greatly pleased when he was sold to the owner of his wife, but Bibb soon found himself "dissatisfied" with having to watch the daily "insults, scourgings and abuses" inflicted on his wife and child. "Who can imagine what could be the feelings of a father and mother," asked Bibb, "when looking upon their infant child whipped and tortured with impunity, and they placed in a situation where they could afford no protection?" These feelings of helplessness sometimes drove slaves to commit extraordinary acts beyond the typical acts of slave resistance. For instance, in a now-celebrated case from 1856, the runaway slave Margaret Garner killed her infant daughter when they were both captured by slave hunters from Kentucky, rather than see the child returned to slavery. The inability of other slaves to exert control over their lives drove some to commit the extraordinary act of retaliating directly and sometimes openly against whites. They might kill the master's favorite pet. They might burn down the barn of a white person who had mistreated them. Or they might physically attack offending white people. Former bondsman Harry Smith remembered that one night after the slave patrollers in his area had been particularly abusive, he and several other slaves stretched vines "across the road where they knew the patrollers were sure to come." When the patrollers appeared in the area, Smith and his friends sang loudly to attract the attention of the inquisitive patrollers and lure them into the trap, where they were knocked off their horses. Occasionally slaves took the most fateful step of all: they killed their masters. Harry

Smith told the story of a master who was attacked by three of his slaves after "he had made it a practice for years" to sexually assault "the wife of one of the slaves, compelling her at any time he saw fit to submit to his passions, and compelled her husband not to mention it under fear of death." The husband killed his master with a pitchfork, and then the three assailants turned themselves into the local authorities, who subsequently executed the slaves.[14]

In Kentucky and other southern states, such direct, retaliatory action against whites was comparatively rare, but the overall pattern of slave resistance troubled white people throughout the South. Surrounded by a people who seemed either unwilling or unable to conform to the mores of white society, in a system predicated on maintaining white supremacy, masters and overseers sometimes had to moderate their demands on slaves lest they provoke open acts of defiance. Except in isolated cases after slave insurrections, however, these circumstances did little to decrease the general support for slavery among whites. Indeed, slave resistance may only have reinforced the ideological attachment of white southerners to the peculiar institution. Some southerners believed that theft and haphazard work by slaves demonstrated that allegedly inferior black laborers needed more discipline and white supervision, and they consequently recommended the strengthening of slavery as a system of racial control.[15]

Like other southerners, Kentucky's antislavery conservatives were well aware that slave resistance could strain the patience of slave masters. As Joseph R. Underwood put it, "the faults of the slave will make you angry; his untruths and evasions will make you suspicious; his sloth and crimes . . . will rivet upon you a vexed life." Unlike proslavery ideologues, however, Kentucky's antislavery conservatives did not consider slave resistance a sign that slave tenure should be perpetuated. While antislavery conservatives as a group renounced neither the principle of slaveholding nor its current usefulness, they nevertheless shared a social vision in which slavery played only a transient role. The conservatives wanted to foster progress through the maintenance of order and social harmony. Slave resistance awakened in conservatives a profound fear that this goal would crumble. In other places or at other times, maintained conservatives, slavery might be an effective agency for organizing society, but its condition in Kentucky now seemed anomalous: it placed "Kentucky . . . in an unnatural or false position" in the course of history, as one group of conservatives put it, and it seemed an unconquerable source of turbulence and social tension that threatened to pull society apart.[16]

One reason that slave resistance aroused conservatives so effectively was that it confirmed their existing conception of the world. For instance, the theme of social harmony pervaded conservative thought in areas beyond the slavery issue. In the political realm, the quest for social harmony helped feed the antiparty strain in conservative political thought. Kentucky Whigs like Underwood often denounced professional politicians who sought "political elevation . . . [by getting] up an excitement about something. . . . Excitement, passion, [and] impulse are the rounds in the ladder which elevate some men to distinction." They called instead for the election of "men of all parties, who love the State more than they love their party or even their personal interests."[17]

Such arguments were a little disingenuous, of course, in that those who accused their political opponents of wrecking social tranquillity for personal advantage often explained their own partisan activities as simple patriotism. Nonetheless, conservatives sometimes placed social harmony above partisanship in ways that lent credence to their appeals. Antislavery conservatives like Underwood and Henry Clay sometimes argued that in order to preserve social tranquillity, the will of the majority—even one that included the conservatives—might have to yield to the needs of a passionately aroused minority. This was Henry Clay's argument in opposing the annexation of Texas. As early as 1837, Clay argued that "should there be a decided opposition by a large portion of the U.S. to the admission of Texas into our National family, that fact ought to have great, if not conclusive influence in the determination of the question." Even during his campaign for the presidency in 1844, when southern hostility to his position on Texas caused Clay to moderate his Texas policy, Clay refused to depart completely from his long-standing deference to the "decided opposition" of many in the North "to the admission of Texas." Even though in Clay's famous Alabama Letters of July 1844 he claimed that "far from having any personal objection to the annexation of Texas, I should be glad to see it," he maintained that "I . . . still believe, that national dishonor, foreign war, and distraction and division at home were too great sacrifices to make for the acquisition of Texas."[18]

It is easy to understand how a group of slaveholders worried about social harmony would be alarmed about slave resistance, which seemed to them no more conducive to tranquillity than the "eternal agitations" of partisan politicians. It is not as easy to understand why slaveholding Kentuckians like Underwood urged masters to promote "your own happiness . . . by ridding yourself of the cause of ill-temper, suspicion, and endless vexation." After all, other southerners valued harmony and order but believed slavery was the best institution to provide that order. Antislavery conservatives did recognize the value of slavery as an instrument of social control. In fact, most conservatives firmly argued that blacks should remain controlled by slavery as long as they remained in the state, and some of them were not above advocating that, until the day when slavery could be abolished, its control mechanisms should even be strengthened. But antislavery conservatives also believed that these mechanisms were at best ephemeral, because even when slave resistance involved nothing more than what Henry Clay called "crimes . . . of a petty description," it seemed to portend forces at work that threatened to overwhelm slavery's ability to control the black race.[19]

At the heart of this analysis was a profound belief in human interdependence. Believing that the fortunes of any individual were inextricably tied to his relationship with others and, hence, to the fortunes of society as a whole, antislavery conservatives sought to strengthen the links that bound people together and, in so doing, to increase the fortunes of the American nation. This attitude strongly influenced conservative politics. Most conservatives enthusiastically embraced Henry Clay's "American System," a program designed to strengthen American commerce and industry through the maintenance of a national banking system, the protection of American-made products through tariffs, and the enactment of federally subsidized road, canal, and harbor improvement projects. Such a program, the conservatives thought, would strengthen the nation not only by making it economically self-sufficient, but also by increasing the interdependence of the nation's various interests. As one group of conservatives described this interdependence: "Every person and everything perform a part toward the grand result; and the whole land is covered with fertile fields, with manufactories and canals, and railroads and edifices and towns and cities. . . . Modes of expeditious intercommunication knit the whole country into a closely compacted mass, . . . while the close intercourse of business and travel makes all neighbors, and promotes a common interest and common sympathy."[20]

Kentucky's antislavery conservatives sought to promote those factors that, as Underwood put it, caused Americans "to hang together as one nation and one people," including "a common language," a common history, and the interdependence of the nation's various economic interests. It is significant that Underwood also included among these factors such elements as "the ties of consanguinity" and "the delights of social intercourse," for these were links that excluded black Americans. After 1830, Kentucky's antislavery conservatives increasingly conceived of the United States as a white nation whose social system had no place for racial minorities. Unlike one developing line of proslavery thought that maintained that slavery not only controlled the black race but also integrated it into the social structure, conservative antislavery thought ultimately held blacks to be an anomalous group in the American nation. They were, argued United States Senator James T. Morehead, "a people between whom and ourselves there never can, in the nature of things, be any possible affiliation—a people, cut off as well by the distinction of color, as by the immutable laws of social order, from all connexion or fellowship with ourselves." In this context, slave resistance became especially disturbing to antislavery conservatives: for a group who believed that the very foundation of human progress was built on social interdependence, slave resistance was a continuing indication that blacks in the United States constituted an element which the nation "cannot trust in peace, or rely on in war," as Robert J. Breckinridge argued, a population "hostile by its nature, its position, its injuries and its utter hopelessness" to the white race.[21]

This avowedly racist argument rested on the conservative acceptance of a natural and justifiable animosity between the races, an animosity rooted in the simple physical differences between the races. Conservatives like Breckinridge argued that blacks constituted an immiscible, "hostile ingredient" in society because whites—"even . . . those who most deeply feel for the condition of the blacks"—"shrink with aversion" from people so different from themselves and that blacks responded in kind. The conservatives' ready acceptance of racial antipathy, despite its disrupting effect on social harmony and on the interdependence of all members of society, is striking. Racial antipathy, argued Presbyterian minister Stuart Robinson, was one of the "deep . . . mysteries of human nature. It exists—has always existed, and some very sensible people imagine it ever will exist." This conception of the immutability of racial enmity is especially remarkable when compared with the views of other southern conservatives who also valued order and social harmony, but believed that the reciprocal obligations of masters and slaves would build an affectionate relationship between the races. Underwood, for instance, considered that "the difference in color and our prejudices against the African race, constitute insuperable barriers" to such feelings. "I . . . look upon a close and intimate friendship on the part of the negroes towards us, as a thing in name, but without any real existence; distrust, envy, and hatred occupy the place of friendship."[22]

Antislavery conservatives argued that such animosity made slavery a necessary, short-term mechanism for controlling a hostile black race, but that ultimately even this mode of racial control would fail. The conservatives believed that racial enmity led to a natural rivalry between the races, and without slavery to regulate the relations of "two rival species of the family of man," as Underwood put it, society would be convulsed by "a state of perpetual warfare" between blacks and whites for control of the state. "No single fact has proved in all ages more dangerous to States than the existence of distinct races of men in their bosom," argued Breckinridge. "A harmonious residence together on equal terms has never occurred in any civilized State, . . . and never can occur while human nature remains unchanged." Breckinridge further asserted that "there is an utter impossibility of keeping" two races of people "united in the same community, except upon conditions highly injurious to both, or fatal to one." As proof of their argument, conservatives offered the example of relations between Indians and whites, two peoples who, according to Underwood, "have never harmonized in promoting each other[']s welfare." Indeed, Underwood claimed that from the beginning of European colonization, the Indian had been "jealous" of the white man because of "the distinction of color and the superior knowledge of the European." When these two distinct and free races became rivals for ascendancy on the North American continent, "whole nations" of Indians had been "annihilated" "in less than two hundred years," a fact that meant that Indians now harbored "unspeakable hatred towards the whites and their institutions." Whites were right "in the adoption of the severest treatment towards them, as the only sure means of keeping them in peace after open hostilities shall have ceased."[23]

The idea that racial enmity occurred as a natural part of the human character prompted conservatives to argue that such feelings were morally correct. In fact, the existence of racial hatreds as a permanent part of the human condition served as virtually the only argument conservatives offered in support of slavery. They rejected nearly every other argument used in the South to justify the long-term perpetuation of slavery. This is ironic, for while the conservatives built their theory of slavery around distaste toward the African American, in other respects the conservatives' views about racial differences were quite enlightened. For instance, they firmly rejected the idea popularized in the 1840s and 1850s by such writers as Josiah C. Nott, John H. Van Evrie, and Samuel A. Cartwright that the Negro was of a different and lower species than the Caucasian—that the "Ostrich, . . . the Camel, . . . and the Lions" of Africa were more comparable with "the miserable, naked and brutal negro, than he with the intellectual, improved and civilised white man," as one Kentucky politician put it—and, it followed, that like other subhuman species was properly subject to fully human, white masters. A number of conservatives echoed Attorney John A. McClung's reminder to God-fearing Kentuckians "that the negro belongs to the race of

Adam." White Kentuckians needed reminding that "in everything essential to his identification with human nature," the black man "is like yourself." "Every one of these human beings," argued Robert J. Breckinridge, "was, like us, created in the image of God; has, like us, an immortal soul; is, like us, capable of joy and sorrow; will, like us, lie down in the grave; and at the great day, stand with us before the throne of God. They are property; but still they are our fellow-men, our fellow-sinners, many of them our fellow-christians."[24]

Additionally, a number of conservatives would have agreed with Henry Clay that although the "two races of men" were "distinct in many important respects, . . . they alike possessed the gift of reason." In arguing that blacks and whites were somehow alike in their intellectual capacities, Clay and his fellow conservatives seemed to be disputing evidence to the contrary that most southerners—and, indeed, most white Americans—thought should be decisively obvious to any objective observer. Of course, antislavery conservatives were quick to add that they were referring to the innate abilities of most American blacks, not to their current intellectual state. Most Kentuckians would have agreed with John C. Young that American blacks were, in general, "ignorant and depraved beings." Most blacks, wrote Young, were "mere children in understanding and knowledge. The white youth at eighteen usually far surpasses the great mass of our slaves, in intelligence and capacity of managing successfully his own affairs." Yet for all their disparagement of the intellectual development of the slave population, antislavery conservatives tended to give more credit to blacks than the white population as a whole did. For example, Young claimed that the depravity of slaves had "been much overrated," that blacks were educable above the elementary level, and that it was a master's religious duty to educate his slaves. Robert Breckinridge added that while he believed "the manners, the habits, the wants, and the attainments" of American blacks fell below the white race, he considered their achievements "respectable as compared with the average of the human race."[25]

The argument that the intellectual development of blacks compared favorably to that of at least some whites did not, however, lead Kentucky's antislavery conservatives to adopt the logic of some southern conservatives: that slavery was a beneficial method of organizing the relationship of lower orders of humanity—both white and black—to the "better" class of people. Although antislavery conservatives were by no means ready to urge immediate freedom for unlettered blacks, they condemned the idea that the lack of intellectual attainments was, in the abstract, a proper justification for the permanent continuance of slavery. "If this argument be founded in fact, . . ." wrote Henry Clay, "it would prove that any white nation, which had made greater advances in civilization, knowledge, and wisdom than another white nation, would have a right to reduce the latter to a state of bondage, . . . [and] the wisest man in the world would have a right to make slaves of all the rest of mankind!"[26]

All the conservatives' talk about the essential humanity and innate intellectual capacity of blacks points to the fact that in the 1830s and 1840s Kentucky's antislavery conservatives clung tenaciously to an explanation of racial differences that was coming under increasing assault by scientists and proslavery ideologues. The conservatives argued that racial differences were determined by the environments in which people lived. If whites perceived that blacks in Kentucky were inferior to themselves, it was not the result of any inherent racial depravity, but rather of what John C. Young called "degrading bondage" and ruinous competition with more numerous and hostile white people who thwarted black achievement. "God has [not] so created a whole race, that it is better for them to remain in perpetual bondage, . . ." Young wrote. "God created all men capable of freedom—if, then, they have become unfit for this condition, it is by our fault they have become so." "Place ourselves, place any men, in . . . like predicament," echoed Henry Clay, "and similar effects would follow."[27]

Indeed, the conservatives believed that history was filled with the examples of different races whose fortunes and attainments had varied with the conditions in which they found themselves. "The sceptre of civilization and power has been successively wielded by many different races, from all of whom in turn it has been wrestled by another race," wrote attorney John A. McClung; each has "successively passed through extremes of power and degradation, of refinement and barbarism." Joseph R. Underwood cited the achievements of modern Germans and noted the irony that "the Germans in the days of Caesar were regarded by the Romans as barbarians; and so they were." An editorial in the *Louisville Journal* also noted the crudeness of medieval Anglo-Saxons: "And yet the Anglo-Saxons [have] now . . . surpassed all other races in those qualities that confer on nations eminent prosperity and undying glory."[28]

For modern Kentuckians who believed that the existing state of black attainments was a sign that African Americans were inherently and unconquerably depraved, antislavery conservatives offered the example of ancient Africa, which had given the world science through Egypt and Carthage, they claimed. "But for Africa, and African genius and talent, . . ." argued former state legislator Daniel Mayes, "the world we inhabit might yet be as dark as Egypt's darkest night." Were the world to examine those portions of modern Africa which had been untouched by the "baleful influence" of the slave trade and the dominion of white people, wrote Young, it would find that blacks could still be "lively, intelligent, and courageous," "not the stupid, dull, and ignorant race, which our imaginations have painted them."[29]

Antislavery conservatives believed that black degradation in the United States and in those areas of Africa under the dominion of whites ultimately grew out of the competition for power among antagonistic races and demonstrated the impossibility of bringing different races together on terms of equality. As the *Louisville Journal* argued:

There is no instance in ancient or modern times of two separate distinct races of men living together, in which one or the other has not become inferior, and in no one case have the members of the inferior race been able to show themselves as capable as the superior race of getting along. But when the races have been separated, the inferior race has been able to display quite as much aptitude in all that is essential to the growth and support of society as any other races of men have done. Such was the experience of our Anglo-Saxon forefathers, and such has been the experience of all subject races.

In the *Journal's* usage, the words "inferior" and "inferior race" denoted both the position in the power structure of a society and the capabilities and attainments of a race of people; in many ways, the conservatives' concept of environmentalism rested on a merger of these two themes. Races that held an inferior position in society became inferior; slaves became slavish. Remove people from this degraded condition and they would, in the words of the *Annual Report* of the Kentucky Colonization Society, be "elevated to the dignity originally assigned them by their Maker, that of intelligent and virtuous freemen."[30]

In this vein, antislavery conservatives expressed optimism about the fruits of Liberian colonization and about the colony's potential for success: "So soon as the African touches the land of his forefathers, and breathes an atmosphere in which he may be free indeed," argued Daniel Mayes, "we find in his constitution there yet remains a restorative principle, a recuperative energy, which . . . bursts . . . the bonds which bound down his faculties. . . . He no longer is the wretched, outcast African of the United States, but appears a being of a different order." Given this environmentalist perspective, antislavery conservatives were not being inconsistent, as contemporary anticolonizationists and later historians charged, when they maintained that blacks in the United States were, at one and the same time, degraded beings who could build a civilized Africa. While some conservatives believed it might take generations of living in this different environment before blacks, as a race, would be the equals of whites, compared to other white Kentuckians the conservatives were more optimistic about the potential of blacks for "improvement."[31]

Ironically, this very faith in the intellectual potential and essential humanity of blacks helped make conservatives fearful of the results of racial competition and anxious to end slavery and colonize blacks in Africa. Some conservatives were so confident of the intellectual capacity of blacks that they affirmed that, even under the degrading conditions of slavery, blacks would show intellectual improvement. Even now, Daniel Mayes argued, "so ardent is their desire of mental improvement, . . . it is necessary to arm the law with . . . [the] severest pains to repress their zeal for knowledge and bind them down in ignorance." Antislavery conservatives believed that the innate intellectual potential of African Americans put Kentucky in a dangerous position. As John C. Young explained, "We may as soon expect to fetter the winds, . . . as to prevent enlightened minds from recovering their natural condition of freedom." Yet at a time when most Kentuckians thought that keeping slaves ignorant was a key to controlling them, some antislavery conservatives doubted that slaves could be kept ignorant and worried about the day when blacks fully realized the injuries inflicted upon them by whites. The existence of slave resistance signified that blacks already felt the call of liberty, and unless slavery was ended and blacks were removed from the state, conservatives like Joseph R. Underwood argued, slaves "will rebel against the authority of their masters." Nor would it help simply to free the slaves while leaving them in the state, antislavery conservatives thought, because removing blacks from slavery would not remove them from the effects of white prejudice. Indeed, the conservatives thought that freeing slaves without removing them would only make matters worse, since as freemen, blacks would rightly expect to enjoy the privileges of that status, something to which whites would never assent. The result would be "bitter heart-burnings," as Underwood put it, and eventually, racial warfare.[32]

Thus, the conservatives believed it was the refusal of whites to allow blacks to live among them except in a state of subjection and the natural reaction of blacks to such degradation that made African Americans an alien and potentially insurrectionary force in Kentucky. This analysis owed much to the conservatives' concern about the seemingly inevitable consequences of maintaining a biracial society, but it also owed much to their conviction that slavery was at odds with "the advancing spirit of the age" and their general desire to establish a harmonious and well-ordered society.[33]

This is not to say that the conservatives rejected the need for institutions to provide order and structure to society. Indeed, in contrast to the general American emphasis on the primacy of natural rights and the inability of governments to remove those rights, conservatives emphasized the need for governments to remain ever-vigilant in maintaining the public order, an imperative embodied in the con-

cept of ordered liberty. This concept revolved around a central paradox: governments must have the power to take away some liberties
in order to secure the power to protect the larger body of liberties. As
Underwood argued, "All human government is but an infringement
on, and curtailment of, natural rights and privileges." Of course, this
rationale could result in a significant reduction of freedom in the name
of protecting liberty, a proposition antislavery conservatives readily accepted. "It is an undeniable truth," wrote Robert J. Breckinridge, "that
society has the right of restraining the liberty, and taking away the life
of any citizen for the public good."[34]

The primacy of the public good over individual rights, in fact,
formed the very basis for maintaining slavery. The rights of some
people—in this case, a seemingly hostile, insurrectionary race of
people—must yield to ensure the security of the majority. Ironically,
though, conservatives believed that this rationale could also serve as
the foundation for the *abolition* of slavery. The conservative argument that the state must necessarily restrict some natural rights to
protect others gave them a basis for fighting the slaveholders' increasingly militant insistence that the security of their property rights
should come before all other considerations. Just as a black minority
might have to forfeit its rights to the need for white security, so might
slaveholders, "who constitute so small a minority," as one group of
conservatives argued, have to forfeit their rights to own "a species of
property which is so greatly detrimental to a large majority of the
people of the State." Even though conservatives wanted to end slavery within the framework of law—either through compensation or
post nati emancipation—they usually acknowledged that slaveholders
might be compelled by the state to give up their slaves.[35]

For all their talk about the necessity of restricting natural rights
to provide a necessary degree of social order, antislavery conservatives loved liberty. Indeed, they ebulliently celebrated the American
system of government because it provided for both of these concerns:
it fostered liberty while substituting subtle mechanisms of order and
stability for anachronistic and harshly restrictive mechanisms. "The
genius of our republic," argued Underwood, "has opened the avenues of honor and distinction to every citizen alike. A noble emula-

tion, and the cultivation of those virtues which will bring man into public notice and esteem are the consequences." These virtues, "the love of praise, the deathless thirst for renown, the ambition that impels, the hope that cheers, the desire to be loved, to be admired, [and] to live in the memory of his fellows," echoed John A. McClung, cultivated in humanity "all that is lofty and ennobling" in human nature, overriding "the base emotion of *fear*, and the low passion for the gratification of . . . animal appetites" which threatened society.[36]

These subtle and, as the conservatives argued, benign forms of control depended on people wanting to yield to them and allowing others to do the same. Yet, because of the bitter rivalry between the races, whites refused to allow blacks admission into the arena of public renown. As Henry Clay argued, "No talents however great, no piety however pure and devoted, no patriotism however ardent, can secure their admission," a fact demonstrated by the experience of free blacks in the United States. With blacks cut off from those benign instruments of social control, Kentucky must temporarily resort to the more restrictive form of control offered by slavery, a system that, ironically, only further isolated blacks from the more subtle forms of social control. The conservatives argued that because slaves had "no other incentive to work than the fear of the lash," they would never internalize a work ethic or other values necessary to propel a society to greatness in modern times. Fear of the whip was an unnatural incentive for good behavior, one that would ultimately prove to be inadequate for controlling blacks—and ruinous to the prosperity of society. Antislavery conservatives claimed that biracial societies—even those that tried to maintain order through slavery—were destined to fall into anarchy.[37]

Antislavery conservatives feared the effects of this unnatural system of controlling human behavior: just as one class of people was corrupted by being slaves, so another class of people was corrupted by being masters. In contrast to proslavery ideologues who thought that slavery enhanced the morals of the master race and, indeed, created the highest stage of human civilization, antislavery conservatives worried that slavery in Kentucky partially removed whites from the operation of the subtle mechanisms of social control that promoted civilization. Conservatives believed that slavery discouraged the building of churches and schools, for example. Unlike wealthy northerners, southern slaveholders had little interest in providing funds to educate and improve the morals of white workers, the reason being that slaveholders drew their work force from coerced black labor. As a result, argued one conservative pamphlet, a "cloud of ignorance . . . now wraps our State, in common with the other slave States, as with a pall." Additionally, slavery seemed to suppress in whites—just as it did in blacks—the salutary desire to advance themselves through hard work. In a state where labor was associated with black skin and the whip and chain, white workingmen feared becoming "white slaves" or "white negroes," as proslavery advocates like Robert Wickliffe contemptuously labeled them, and "every man shuns labor as an evil." Under these circumstances, claimed a group of Louisville conservatives, "necessity alone can compel a man to toil by the side of his neighbor's slave, and under this compulsion the freeman becomes discontented with his social rank."[38]

Conservatives believed that the peculiar institution caused even slave owners to view "labor with contempt." Joseph R. Underwood noted that the children of slaveholders "learn, at a very early period, to expect the performance of every work by a slave. . . . The child grows up to manhood, accustomed to order a slave instead of waiting on himself." As adults, they remained little more than "consuming drones," refusing to become "diligently employed in the practice of some art, or business, which creates property" and increases the general prosperity of society. Further, masters developed what slave owner John C. Young called "the habit of regarding ourselves as born to command, and others as born to obey." Slaveholders became tyrants who "disregard[ed] . . . the rights and interests of others," a tendency which led to their own "moral injury." Antislavery conservatives, thus, boldly claimed that slavery "demoralized" the state's entire population, white as well as black.[39]

To the conservatives, it seemed clear that slavery diminished in Kentuckians those values needed to undergird social and economic progress in the modern world. As one group of conservatives argued, "If . . . we are not progressing as the world around us, there is but one cause for it all—slavery." Despite sometimes equating progress strictly with industrial and commercial growth, antislavery conservatives usually defined this issue in the grander arena of human evolution itself. They saw history as the gradual evolution of human society in increasingly advanced stages, a particularly Whiggish view of the world. Underwood ridiculed Democratic politicians who "detected . . . diseases which were rapidly hastening our hitherto pure government to the last stages of decay," a view of history which stood in stark contrast to his own belief that "the world at this day is better and wiser than in any past age," and that it would continue to progress as "the pulpit and schoolhouse . . . enlighten our race by the diffusion of religion, morals and general intelligence." It was in part a similar confidence in the ability of humanity to improve itself that gave antislavery conservatives confidence in their ability to carry out a project as massive as African colonization and in the ability of black Americans to tame the African wilderness.[40]

If the conservatives' faith in human progress and romantic conception of the coming industrial order seem misplaced by today's standards, even by the standards of their day there was visionary quality to these hopes. Given to grandiose schemes to implement progress and suitably grandiloquent language to describe it—just as they had been in promoting African colonization—they spoke glowingly of "the power of ceaseless progress" and the "onward march of Christian civilization." They extolled "the new order of things introduced by modern inventions" as a sign of "the immense progress in improvement which the world has made and is making." And they were sure that slavery was incongruous with the advancing "spirit of the age"; it was an outmoded institution akin to feudalism, monarchy, and other authoritarian institutions now being "obliterated by the advance of freedom and truth." If the advance of modern liberty were not enough to doom slavery, then the fruits of an industrializing national economy, an increased labor supply, and improved "labor-saving machinery" would surely kill it.[41]

Joseph R. Underwood took the imperatives of the new age more seriously than most conservatives. Not content to confine his activities on behalf of industrialization to the halls of Congress, Underwood spent his spare time studying those "labor-saving devices" that he thought were furthering progress. Fancying himself to be "an inventor" who "might astonish the world some day" by discovering "the power by which the affairs of the world are to be revolutionized," for years Underwood tinkered with devices that he hoped would "supercede horsepower[,] water power[,] steam power[,] and *slave* power." By 1852 he believed he was on the verge of perfecting a machine utilizing a form of power that had eluded inventors for centuries: perpetual motion. Underwood was quite serious about his device: he commissioned a local artist to draw up diagrams of his machine, discussed with the United States Commissioner of Patents the possibility of patenting his invention, and apparently fashioned models of the device. Underwood also sought the advice of James Pollard Espy, the internationally renowned physicist and meteorologist working at the Smithsonian Institute when Underwood was a member of the Senate. So confident was Underwood in his invention that when Espy tried to deter the distinguished senator and would-be inventor from embarrassment, Underwood feared that Espy only wanted to steal his ideas.[42]

Underwood's quixotic pursuit of laborsaving inventions reflected both the conservatives' penchant for visionary, even utopian, schemes of social development and their general fascination with the mechanization and industrialization they saw taking place in the North. Kentucky's antislavery conservatives constantly looked northward to assess social and economic developments in the free states, an exercise that proved truly sobering to southerners who measured human progress by technological change and the ability to tame the wilderness. Conservatives assiduously gathered statistics comparing slave states and free states, concluding that every statistic measuring the progress of civilization suggested that states using slave labor had fallen behind states using exclusively free labor. Conservatives claimed that the South's population growth was slower than the North's, that the total value of its agricultural and industrial products were less than the North's, and that it had fewer churches, fewer students in school, fewer people engaged in the "learned professions" than the North—but more criminals and illiterates. Conservatives believed that the conclusion Kentucky should draw from this "pain-fully humiliating contrast" between slave states and free states was clear: as one group of conservatives in Louisville wrote, "The institu-tion [of slavery] has thus far been a curse, a withering blight on [Kentucky's] growth and prosperity and must so continue as long as the institution is kept up in the state."[43]

In comparing Kentucky with free states, most conservatives ar-gued that "the climate and agriculture of Kentucky are not suited to negro slavery, and . . . they prevent her from prospering as a slave State," a belief that implied that black slave labor might be perfectly viable in the Deep South. Conservatives like John A. McClung some-times avoided the question of what "may be the future destiny of African slavery in the region of the cotton plant and the sugar cane," while insisting that "in the Northern slave States, . . . it is not a per-manent, but merely a temporary institution, which is now slowly receding in a southern direction."[44]

Few conservatives left it at this, however. The geographical forces working against Kentucky's prosperity as a slave state were magnified by the necessity of competing in an economic system that included free states. Conservatives imagined Kentucky and other southern states competing with the North in a "race of prosperity" in which the unflinching advance of the free states would eventually compel all slave states to adopt free labor exclusively in order to survive. The course of human development seemed to conservatives to have changed the preconditions for success; the North had understood this, it had adapted its economy accordingly, and it had prospered as a result. There were a few conservatives like Presbyterian minister Stuart Robinson who grew nostalgic about the diminishing viability of slavery but saw its demise as inevitable. However, most conserva-tives were like Underwood and Breckinridge: enthusiastic, even ec-static, about the coming order and eager to promote it. All were interested in making the demise of slavery as painless as possible: they tried to mitigate the problems arising from Kentucky's anoma-lous condition in a nation increasingly devoted to free labor.[45]

To antislavery conservatives, slavery in Kentucky represented the remnant of a once useful institution for providing labor, one that had now been surpassed by forms of labor more in keeping with the current state of human development. Conservatives claimed that population density was the key to determining the economic viability of slavery and, indeed, to determining the general level of civilization and progress in any society: as the ratio of people to productive land increased, slavery became less profitable and society more civilized. In the American context, conservatives believed, slavery was most profitable in frontier areas, where population density was generally the lowest. It seemed to antislavery conservatives that under such circumstances, people who were bent on carving farms out of the forest felt compelled to secure less efficient, but cheaper and more easily obtainable slave labor.[46]

The problem was that in nineteenth-century America, few places remained frontiers for very long. As antislavery conservatives saw it, the inevitable growth of population, the maturation of society, and the progress of humanity set in motion complex economic trends that undid whatever advantages slave labor had once offered, especially when it was forced to compete with free labor. As population density in newly settled states began to increase, conservatives argued, the scarcity of labor began to decrease as well; consequently wages for free labor would fall until they were competitive with the costs of slave labor. Conservatives also claimed that slavery-induced indolence among white laborers had made free labor artificially scarce, which kept free-labor wages artificially high in Kentucky, while in neighboring free states like Indiana and Ohio wages for white labor had actually fallen below the cost of maintaining slaves in Kentucky. And, given the greater efficiency of free labor, producers of agricultural and manufactured goods in Kentucky seemed at a true disadvantage to their northern competitors.[47]

Antislavery conservatives believed that the apparently high cost of agricultural and manufactured products made in slave states had dire consequences for Kentucky. Since cheaper free-state products lured Kentucky consumers away from their own state's products, Kentuckians were sending money elsewhere rather than keeping it in the state. Antislavery conservatives bemoaned this trade deficit because it sapped the state of capital for investment: because Kentucky capitalists were not reaping due profit from consumption within their own state, potential investors lacked the resources to develop Kentucky's manufacturing base. Conservatives claimed that this circumstance had woefully diminished the growth of industry in Kentucky, isolating it from developments that seemed to epitomize the course of progress in the nineteenth century. Moreover, Kentucky's stagnant industrial development seemed to exacerbate the drain on the state's capital resources, as Kentuckians who needed manufactured goods were increasingly unable to buy them from other Kentuckians and were increasingly obliged to buy them from northern industrialists.[48]

To antislavery conservatives, Kentucky's failure to develop a home market for its own goods represented a major failing of a slave economy, for in the home market lay the preconditions for economic success. The consequence, argued conservatives like Underwood, was that "slave-holding states, will forever remain dependant [*sic*] upon the non-slaveholding states, or on foreign nations . . . for every costly article of necessity. The slaveholding states are, therefore, exactly suited to occupy a colonial condition, looking to the mother country for supplies. True independence they cannot feel because of their incapacity to supply their own reasonable wants." Yet the very nature of slavery in a modern economy seemed to prevent the growth of that domestic economic interdependence so vital to a state's progress. If slavery had any economic viability, it lay in the fact that it delivered workers who labored "for a bare subsistence," as one group of antislavery conservatives put it. According to conservatives, this fact alone forestalled the growth of southern manufacturing. What slaveholder whose profit came from obtaining labor at subsistence levels could be counted on to spend the same amount of money provisioning his black labor force with manufactured goods as a free white labor force of the same size would spend on itself? "Every slave that is brought here," argued Robert J. Breckinridge, reduces the opportunities "of some poor white man, to make a comfortable living by honest industry."[49]

Kentucky's use of slave labor prevented the development of a sizable market for goods produced by the state's own workers. Antislavery conservatives argued that this circumstance forced Kentucky laborers to migrate from the state, or as Breckinridge put it, "to seek in some freer land, . . . that protection to their toil and that encouragement to their efforts, which . . . under the dictation of a few thousand misguided masters, Kentucky denied to the great mass of her people." This argument was crucial to the conservative critique of slavery and, indeed, constituted a major theme in the writings of antislavery conservatives. As a theory, conservatives believed it was confirmed by census figures showing that Kentucky's population was not growing as fast as the states around it. Extrapolating from the growth rates of nearby states and from Kentucky's own earlier growth rates, conservatives calculated that by 1850, the state would suffer a net loss of nearly half a million people through migration. This figure, conservatives pointed out, was nearly double the number of slaves in Kentucky, clear proof to the conservatives that had Kentucky ended slavery earlier, it could easily have supplied its labor needs from white workers who, were it not for slavery, would have had no reason to emigrate. To conservatives, the net loss of population due to emigration provided significant evidence of the poor economic condition in which white workingmen in Kentucky found themselves. Even worse, the apparent flood of emigration was a cause as well as a consequence of Kentucky's economic problems, as migration to the free states kept the state's population density unnaturally low, reinforcing the high cost of labor in Kentucky.[50]

This portrait of Kentucky's economic decline, along with concerns that the state was failing to keep pace in the race of progress, fueled the conservatives' overriding fear of disorder. To them, it seemed not only that Kentucky's lack of progress was rooted in the chaos of failed social controls—the confusion engendered by a subversive, alien race of workers and an indolent, slovenly race of masters—but also that the state's stymied progress itself contributed to disorder. In the imagery evoked by conservatives, the state's failure to advance at the same pace as its northern neighbors represented not stasis, but decay. "Slavery . . . is no longer compatible with progress," warned one group of conservatives. "It is a deadweight and worse; it has become a wasting disease" in the body politic. The conservatives filled their writings with such references to social decay. They spoke of the "halting, if not deteriorating condition of Kentucky," of lands "smitten with premature barrenness" and of other "marks of premature decay." Hostile, unwilling slave laborers provided individual slaveholders with a very personal acquaintance with decaying fortunes: as Underwood noted, "the slave is neglectful and inattentive to feeding and sheltering livestock. He is careless of the implements, fences, houses, and land of the farmer. The eye of the master must superintend all things, otherwise they will be found out of order and in a rapid state of decay." Antislavery conservatives argued, however, that few masters diligently "superintended" the operations of their farms, for the masters' own improvidence and slothfulness spread disorganization throughout the slave states. In a society dominated by slaveholders, there were "no neat cottages with gardens and flowers giving life to the landscape," observed one group of conservatives, "no beautiful villages where cultivated taste blends with rustic simplicity; . . . no flourishing towns alive with the bustle of industry; . . . [and no] well cultivated farms with their substantial homesteads and capacious barns." Instead, "Neglect, the harbinger of decay, . . . has stamped her impress everywhere."[51]

In a particularly striking image, conservatives argued that such occurrences marked slavery as a sort of social "leprosy," with all of the connotations of living decomposition that that word has traditionally evoked. This portrait of impending decay, with its portents of economic and social disaster, joined with the conservative fear of racial warfare to produce a compelling indictment of the slave system. To the conservatives, it seemed as though slavery was causing their world to disintegrate before their very eyes. While slave owners feared the imminent loss of their property and happiness, white Kentuckians of all stripes worried about losing wealth and power to areas with a free-labor force. Overall, the state seemed to be falling into a decaying and less civilized condition. And conservatives feared that the very existence of society was being threatened by the hostility of an alien and subversive race of people. Yet the same worldview that produced such a potent critique of slavery trapped many of Kentucky's antislavery activists in the dilemma of conservative reform. Antislavery conservatives believed that however pernicious slavery would ultimately prove to Kentucky, it remained a fundamental institution for ordering society, and they were determined to be cautious about removing it—lest they create more disorder than had slavery itself.[52]

4

The Limits of
Political Action

Although abolitionists and other radical antislavery activists worked in Kentucky throughout the 1830s and 1840s, during this period antislavery conservatives dominated the state's antislavery movement. The conservatives proved to be decidedly cautious reformers, prompting the state's antislavery movement to support political policies that offered little hope for implementing a truly effective scheme of emancipation. Although much of the conservatives' caution was rooted in their image of blacks as a permanently hostile race that had to be controlled, the conservatives' caution also resulted from their conception of how social change occurs. The conservatives' glorification of progress indicates that they did not oppose social change per se, but they stressed that true progress came only through a gradual and orderly process, in which small changes over a period of years led to a fundamental transformation in society.[1]

Likewise, fundamental social reforms could be achieved only through slow but steady growth. Though people might see social ills which cried for immediate reform, argued Breckinridge, "it is one of the sad conditions of all that is evil on earth, that when we have once done wrong, we cannot fully and immediately undo it." Conservatives like Breckinridge and John C. Young claimed that there were few problems so pressing that society should correct them at the expense of public order or the risk of "dangerous convulsion." When it came to the timetable required to effect significant change without risking revolution, conservatives were decidedly patient. Changing complex and fundamental institutions like slavery throughout the United States might take decades or even centuries.[2]

The conservatives' political activities on behalf of emancipation reflected their desire to effect fundamental change through cautious and gradual programs of reform. They most often sought to reduce the growth of the slave population in proportion to the growth of the white population, thus letting the inexorable workings of slow demographic trends abolish slavery. This goal reinforced the conservatives' support for colonization and *post nati* emancipation plans, which together allowed emigration and death to reduce the number of slaves in Kentucky gradually, until there were none left in the state. Similar goals lay behind the main focus of the conservatives' antislavery political activities from the late 1820s to the late 1840s: securing—and then maintaining—a legislative prohibition of the importation of slaves into Kentucky.

In seeking to limit the number of slaves imported into Kentucky, antislavery conservatives were addressing one of the oldest political issues in the state's history, an issue on which the General Assembly had spoken several times, most notably in 1815 with legislation imposing mild restrictions on the importation of slaves. While controversial in the usual political sense, the effort to limit slave importation was not—at first—a cause that struck fear in the hearts of slaveholders. And strictures against slave importation were not unique to Kentucky. Between the Revolution and the Civil War, only four southern states failed to enact similar laws, although the strictness and longevity of Kentucky's laws on the subject proved to be unusual. As the existence of interest in nonimportation throughout the South implies, friends of slavery found several features of nonimportation unobjectionable or even attractive. For instance, some Kentuckians linked the domestic slave trade with the foreign slave trade, comparing the importation of slaves into Kentucky to the traffic in native-born Africans that, as one antislavery conservative argued, "the united suffrage of Christendom has declared piracy . . . justly punishable with death." Before the late 1840s, there was very little disagreement in Kentucky that the domestic slave trade should be discouraged, although people differed about what constituted the slave trade and sometimes violated their own scruples on this subject. But it was not hard to rally legislative majorities against slave importation, as symbolized by disreputable slave traders and chained coffles of blacks moving along the commonwealth's roads and highways. Even during the late 1830s and 1840s, when bills intended to ease restrictions on the importation of slaves by citizens of the state and immigrants to Kentucky had their greatest support in the legislature, few such bills proposed to eliminate restrictions on slaves brought into the state as "merchandise"; some actually contained provisions intended to tighten restrictions on the importation of slaves for resale.[3]

Although nonimportation limited an activity that even many slaveholders found reprehensible, several features of nonimportation actually strengthened the slaveholder's hand, a fact that antislavery conservatives noted. Kentuckians knew from their own practice that the bondsmen sold to the slave trader were often those who were least manageable—the "troublemakers" and "refuse slaves," as many Kentuckians termed them—and some slaveholders worried that these imported bondsmen would disturb the good order and tranquillity of the native slave population. Further, in the parts of Kentucky with diverse economies that did not depend upon highly labor-intensive staple crops—notably the Bluegrass region around Lexington and the counties bordering the Ohio River—many slaveholders believed that the children born to their own slaves would more than supply their future labor needs. In this circumstance, restricting the importation of slaves seemed to secure a monopoly on such labor for existing slave owners, thereby enhancing their competitive position in relation to other farmers by raising the monetary value of their own slave property and promising a higher profit should they decide to sell some of their slaves. There was nothing about the restriction of slave imports that was necessarily incompatible with support for slavery or the welfare of existing slaveholders, although during the 1840s the supporters of unlimited slave importation began to regard proslavery supporters of nonimportation as dangerously timid allies in the defense of slavery.[4]

Antislavery conservatives made their arguments in favor of non-importation much more than a simple appeal to the interests of slaveholders. If they stated that limiting slave importation upheld public order by keeping out "refuse slaves" or that it raised the value of the slaveholder's property, they also explained that the state had no more urgent need than to increase the ratio of whites to blacks through nonimportation. If Kentucky was already in an anomalous position because of its reliance on slave labor and if the state was isolated from the progressive currents of the age or threatened with internal violence and insurrection because of slavery, then bringing more bondsmen into Kentucky would be foolish. "We have already as many slaves in Kentucky as is consistent with any possible view that can be taken of the subject," argued Robert Breckinridge, "unless we are prepared to say that slavery is, in itself, a blessing, and that it is good to increase it by all possible means. . . . [But,] if slavery is ever to cease here, it is mere folly to augment the number of slaves by artificial means."[5]

Given such attitudes, conservatives and other opponents of slave importation were distressed when the state's nonimportation law of 1815 proved ineffective. It was inherently difficult to police slave importation in a region in which illegal transactions in the slave trade might take place on farms far from the eyes of the nearest neighbor and in which illegally imported slaves could often be camouflaged in a sea of anonymous black faces. In addition, the legislature of 1815 compounded these problems by packing the law with light penalties, ambiguous language, and numerous loopholes. According to Robert J. Breckinridge, by 1830 the law had become "a dead letter on the statute book, . . . [and] the shocking and disgraceful traffic which it was designed to put an end to, is regularly and openly carried on." Thus, during the late 1820s and early 1830s, conservatives like Breckinridge and Judge John Green led an invigorated effort to toughen the state's slave importation laws. Antislavery conservatives produced a flurry of newspaper articles urging the enactment of tougher nonimportation laws for the general good of the common-wealth and as a first step toward emancipation. Green was instru-mental in the introduction of nonimportation bills into the state Senate sessions of 1827–28 and 1828–29; although neither bill was successful, a similar bill came one vote short of passing the House in the next session of the General Assembly. One political weakness of these early bills was that they would have granted freedom to ille-gally imported slaves, and a number of legislators apparently feared that not only would the proposed bill increase the state's free black population, but it would also make Kentucky a haven for runaway slaves from other states seeking freedom as illegally "imported" slaves. When this provision was dropped from nonimportation bills in the next two sessions of the legislature (1830–31 and 1831–32), both proposed bills passed the House only to fail in the state Senate. Fi-nally, in the next session of the General Assembly, a similar bill passed both houses of the legislature and became law on February 2, 1833.[6]

The Nonimportation Act of 1833, or the "Law of 1833," as it would soon become labeled, tightened the restrictions on slave im-portation in three significant ways. First, the law increased the penal-ties for participating in the illicit slave traffic, allowing the arrest of alleged violators of the law and tripling the fine for selling or buying illegally imported slaves. Second, the Law of 1833 attempted to im-prove the enforcement of nonimportation by stating in stronger lan-guage the duties of prosecuting attorneys, grand juries, and judges in enforcing the law. As an added incentive for the commonwealth's attorneys to do their duty, the law granted them a payment of 20 percent of the fines collected in successful prosecutions. Third—and what would ultimately prove to be the most controversial of all—the Law of 1833 significantly redefined illegal slave importation. Ken-tuckians would no longer be able to "hire" any slave from outside the state for more than one year, and the state's citizens were forbid-den to purchase and import into Kentucky slaves for their own use.[7]

This latter restriction was really quite remarkable: as historian Frederic Bancroft noted, it was "wholly exceptional" in the antebel-lum South. Ironically, the deciding voice in approving this "wholly exceptional" restriction came from militant proslavery advocates, among them Robert Wickliffe, who had previously opposed further restrictions on slave importation. By 1833, such people were becoming increasingly alarmed by the nascent abolitionist movement in the North and its apparent extensions into Kentucky: the increased activity of antislavery supporters in the state, their growing influence in the state colonization society, and, in 1831, the appearance in Lexington—the heart and soul of Kentucky's slave district—of a society of slave owners whose members promised to free their future born slaves "at the age of twenty-one." To the supporters of slavery, nonimportation became what one observer called "a black flag of truce held out to abolitionists and emancipationists"—the peace ransomed from a murderous pirate. Nonimportation came to be viewed by the supporters of slavery as a measure that might placate antislavery forces and defuse the slavery issue. Proslavery forces would soon regret the enactment of the Law of 1833. By the mid-1830s, it increasingly seemed to militant defenders of slavery that, in dealing with antislavery forces, no "flag of truce" was the right color. They were joined by farmers from the booming Green River country in southwestern Kentucky, that underdeveloped portion of the state seemingly most suited to slave-based agriculture and most ravenous for additional slaves. The Green River country never liked the Law of 1833, and its residents resented buying slaves at inflated prices from Bluegrass planters when just a few miles away, across the Tennessee border, lived farmers eager to sell their excess chattel at reasonable prices to their Kentucky neighbors. In the legislative session of 1833–34—the very next session of the General Assembly following the passage of the Law of 1833—a bill was introduced for the repeal of nonimportation, and similar repeal measures would be debated in every session of the legislature until 1849.[8]

But to a large extent the original assessment of the friends of slavery had been correct. Although the Law of 1833 did nothing to allay northern abolitionism and antislavery advocates continued to make their presence felt in Kentucky, the passage of the Law of 1833 very nearly accomplished the whole of the conservatives' immediate political program. As previously noted, they continued to lobby loudly for colonization and *post nati* emancipation schemes, but before the late 1840s antislavery conservatives saw these as long-range goals rather than imminent and enactable political programs, and they reacted accordingly. Indeed, confronted with proslavery opposition to nonimportation, conservatives spent most of the 1830s and 1840s simply trying to protect what they had won in 1833. Throughout the fifteen years of legislative debate that followed the enactment of the Law of 1833, antislavery conservatives—among them James T. Morehead; William F. Bullock; Ira Root of Campbell County; and William P. Thomasson, William E. Glover, and James Speed of Jefferson County—played a prominent role in trying to save nonimportation. They were joined by Cassius M. Clay, the person who eventually became the most visible symbol of antislavery in Kentucky. He cut his political teeth on the politics of nonimportation as a twenty-five-year-old legislator in 1836. Clay, Breckinridge, and others employed the whole range of conservative arguments against slavery to remind voters and legislators of the evils of slavery, and they claimed that the Law of 1833 was helping deflect the worst effects of the peculiar institution. "If slavery be a 'blessing,'" argued Clay, "by all means repeal this law. But, if it be an evil, as I hold, . . . then you dare not touch that law, which stands like a wall of adamant, shielding our homes . . . [from] calamities." Such appeals and the support of Clay and other conservatives helped keep the Nonimportation Act on the state's books until 1849, when it was finally repealed.[9]

Throughout the 1830s and 1840s, antislavery conservatives found themselves fighting a holding action politically, neither advancing nor retreating. Much of the conservatives' failure to push for stronger measures was by design. Having secured a law that promised to increase the proportion of whites to blacks slowly—a law whose "influence, though silent and perhaps not considerable, yet throws the force of time, for the white and not for the black race, for liberty and not for slavery," as Breckinridge put it—most conservatives were content to defend the law and to advocate colonization, and hope that the public would someday be ready to support stronger measures.[10]

Such a gradual approach to antislavery was weak on several points, not the least of which was that it ensured that thousands would go to their graves as slaves. Beyond this, though, the conservatives' gradualism, their willingness to tolerate—even embrace—slaveholding during the period of gradual emancipation, proved to be a serious ideological and tactical handicap in an age of sectional controversy. The conservatives' seeming inability to condemn slaveholding became a serious weakness in their ability to fight slavery, for it kept them in thrall to the mores of their society and directed their political activities into ineffective channels of reform. It also reflected their overriding concern for maintaining order. If slavery increasingly served as a source of disorder, as conservatives believed, it still performed the useful function of preventing anarchy. And, in providing order through coercive relationships based on the unequal distribution of power among individuals, conservatives argued, slavery did not differ in principle from the power exercised over the insane, criminals, paupers, soldiers, children, and women. On this basis, conservatives refused to join abolitionists in proclaiming the act of slaveholding itself to be a sin against God. Using the familial imagery of southern patriarchs, antislavery conservatives joined proslavery politicians in arguing that power relationships like slavery, government, and marriage had been given to humanity by God to provide order and stability to society—"to bind the wild, the erring, and aggressive will and freedom of fallen man," as Underwood put it—and were not inherently sinful. These power relationships became sinful only when those to whom God had granted authority over others abused their authority. Governments could tyrannize their subjects; fathers could abuse their wives and children; and slave masters could mistreat their slaves. Sinful abuse would include failing to provide adequate food, clothing, and shelter; overworking or severely punishing slaves; separating families through sale; or denying to slaves religious instruction.[11]

Unlike proslavery ideologues, however, antislavery conservatives viewed this supposedly divine grant of authority over blacks as an explicitly temporary authorization of slavery that would ensure order and stability while two mutually hostile races lived with each other, a dispensation that would vanish once the reasons for its existence disappeared. Further, conservatives differed from proslavery advocates in their readiness to acknowledge that while slavery and slaveholding might not be inherently sinful, masters often acted sinfully toward their slaves. Conservatives argued that such sinful abuse had become so widespread and so thoroughly sanctioned and encouraged by law that the slave system in America, taken as a whole, constituted a national moral evil. In the United States, noted John C. Young, the law of slavery gave to the master "more power than natural justice warrants him using," thus encouraging abuses of the master's power. Young argued that "our slave system is . . . sinful . . . because by . . . [it] powers were conferred on a man over his fellows which no one could *exercise* without deep injustice." Antislavery conservatives worried that this national evil might well result in divine retribution, which might take the form of the slave rebellion that the conservatives so confidently expected. The prospect of divine retribution in no way implied that individual masters were necessarily threatened with perdition simply because they owned slaves; as Underwood claimed, slavery was a "sin of the State, . . . but no individual sin." A moral man who could resist the temptation to abuse his power as master might continue to own slaves with a clear conscience as long as the conditions that required the African American's enslavement continued. Indeed, if the state granted powers to the master that might be abused, argued Young, "certain *other* powers were conferred which were proper—which could not only be exercised without sin, but the exercise of which was a duty" required of the master by God. The religious duty to control people who, if left unsupervised, would bring "mischief to others around him, . . . almost certain destruction to himself and misery to his offspring," as Young put it, *required* God-fearing people to retain control over their slaves—at least for the immediate future. "The master who should turn loose uneducated, improvident slaves, . . . who would become a prey to sharpers, or be again reduced to slavery under the vagrant laws," claimed Underwood, "deserves the same respect and treatment that the father should receive who abandons his own offspring in helpless infancy."[12]

The conservatives' philosophy provided little impetus for them to abjure slaveholding—and among the leadership of the conservatives, slaveholding appears to have been fairly widespread. For instance, one contemporary estimate suggests that of the one hundred fifty delegates to the Frankfort Emancipation Convention in 1849—the most significant gathering of antislavery forces in the state's history—over half were slaveholders, who together owned nearly three thousand blacks. Conservatives took great pride in their ownership of slaves, citing it as evidence of their disinterested statesmanship, and they reassured their fellow Kentuckians that they could be trusted to handle the slavery issue with due regard for the concerns of white southerners.[13]

Historians have made much of the fact that conservative critics of slavery in the Upper South often owned slaves, citing it as evidence that southern antislavery advocates were either hypocrites who ignored the truth of their own arguments for the sake of their pocketbooks or covert supporters of slavery whose antislavery rhetoric was meant only as a subterfuge to deflect abolition by convincing the North that southerners were dealing with the slavery issue in a responsible manner. Although the conservatives' ownership of slaves did pose a number of obstacles to effective antislavery action, these criticisms seem misdirected, at least as they concern Kentucky's antislavery activists. As facile as the conservatives' explanation of their slave ownership might appear, their distress at the ruinous effects of slavery was too deeply held and their defense of slave ownership too logically consistent with their worldview for them to have been mere hypocrites or dissemblers.[14]

Likewise, the conservatives were not moved by a straightforward concern for financial gain. Although antislavery conservatives openly acknowledged that those who used slave labor could make a profit—arguing that, as long as the existence of slavery made white labor prohibitively expensive, the fiscally responsible were compelled to use slave labor—the main thrust of the conservatives' arguments was that everyone, including the current owners of slaves, would make more money if the state abandoned slavery. Indeed, the antislavery conservatives were so certain that their financial interests lay with the state's adoption of a free-labor system that they argued that even if they or other slaveholders initially lost money or property from statewide emancipation, this loss would be more than offset by the increased profitability of free labor. Robert J. Breckinridge claimed that "this State would gain many times the entire value of all her slaves, by the proposed change, and . . . the slave holders themselves would be amongst the largest gainers by the event." So strong was the impression among Kentuckians that antislavery conservatives were sincere in this belief that some supporters of slavery charged that to conservatives, emancipation was, in the words of Baptist minister John L. Waller, "a mere matter of political economy—a cold and heartless calculation of profit and loss. . . . The rich champion of emancipation would convert his slaves into cash." Given the conservatives' doubts about the profitability of slave labor, they often found the most compelling, self-interested argument in favor of becoming slave owners or retaining their own slaves to be one of status: in a society that treated ownership of slaves as a mark of exalted status, any family that forfeited its slaves declassed itself. "While their neighbors retain slaves," argued Joseph Underwood, the emancipators "cannot associate upon terms of equality, with their former slaveholding associates, who retain their slaves."[15]

If the conservatives' ownership of slaves did not necessarily make them hypocrites or dissemblers, neither did it make them effective agents of emancipation. Their explanation for their own slaveholding points to several ideological factors that weakened their ability to combat slavery effectively. In this, as in other questions, conservatives tended to look beyond the individual and to emphasize the well-being of society as a whole. In the conservatives' rhetoric, the moral evil of slavery threatened the state with divine retribution, without necessarily making individual slaveholders complicit. Slavery could be solved on a large scale by Kentuckians acting as a unit; the deeds of individuals acting by themselves counted for little. Indeed, the individual slaveholder might be morally and financially compelled to own slaves until the state acted to eliminate slavery as a system.

Northern abolitionists have often been criticized by historians for taking the opposite tack, for concentrating so exclusively on the individual's involvement in slavery that they failed to offer a program that could have ended the system of slavery. Whatever the inadequacy of the abolitionists' cure for slavery, though, antislavery conservatives could have used a dose of their medicine. Abolitionists were, in the conservatives' parlance, "monomaniacs," persons whose single-minded concern about the evils of slavery overwhelmed all other considerations. As newspaper editor George D. Prentice noted with unwitting praise, "the abolitionist marches straight onward to his purpose. He listens to no compromise, brooks no delay, accepts no conditions, regards no surrounding circumstances." Prentice's description suggests a mode of thought that helped sustain abolitionists through years of turmoil. Waging an unpopular crusade against a deeply embedded and far-reaching institution like slavery, the abolitionists' overwhelming concern for each individual's complicity in slavery proved to be a strong antidote to the pressures of public opposition and to the appeals of proslavery and racist values. In contrast, conservatives proved to be extremely timid reformers. During the 1830s, abolitionists in Kentucky who worked with antislavery conservatives were often amazed at this timidity, especially the conservatives' willingness to remain silent in the face of public opposition to antislavery.[16]

Further, the abolitionists' overriding concern with individual involvement in slavery encouraged them to subordinate other values to their antislavery principles. An abolitionist like John G. Fee might begin with the premise that complicity in slaveholding was sinful and, from there, re-examine his views about the proper form of ecclesiastical organization, the relationship between church and state in a democracy, and the meaning and use of violence to effect social change. Without a similar habit of thought and with little motivation to abjure slaveholding, Kentucky's antislavery conservatives did not critically re-examine the mores of their society and of the slaveholding class of which they were a part.

The appeal of southern values often had debilitating effects on the conservatives' activities, especially in periods of intense sectional discord, when every event seemed to conscript all people into a rhetorical defense of their state or section. Despite being ardent nationalists who truly regretted sectional animosity, Kentucky's antislavery conservatives also felt a strong sense of loyalty to their own state and section, a fact suggested by their critique of slavery. In their own way, as Eugene Genovese has suggested, Kentucky's antislavery conservatives were trying to promote their state's best interests by removing those slavery-induced impediments that prevented their state from occupying first place among the states of the Union. Although this variety of southern "patriotism" served antislavery conservatives well in decrying the malignant effects of slavery upon Kentucky's social and economic system, it also made them deeply resentful of similar talk when it came from the North, especially when it suggested that slaveholders were immoral or that slaveholders should be prevented from sharing equally in the benefits of the American Union.[17]

This prickly sensitivity to northern criticism was quite infectious. Harriet L. Smith, whose husband Benjamin Bosworth Smith was the Episcopal bishop of Kentucky and a leading antislavery conservative, visited her native state of New York in 1838 and was surprised to learn how defensive she had become about the South's peculiar institution. While visiting New York City, she attended a meeting of the American Anti-Slavery Society, where she heard speeches by abolitionist stalwarts like Gerrit Smith, Edmund Quincy, and Kentucky expatriate James G. Birney. There she thrilled to the eloquence of black abolitionist James McCune Smith, who she thought could easily be mistaken for "a graceful, intelligent highly educated Southerner" "had it not been for his *skin.*" Yet this woman, who grew to maturity in the North, thought nothing of attending a meeting of the nation's leading abolitionist organization, and observed "much . . . philanthropy among the crowded assembly" of abolitionists, found that "if a word is said in disparagement of Kentucky, I feel the warm blood [rush] to my cheek, and impatient words to my lips, as if I were a native Kentuckian. . . . I did long to be a man, that I might rise and reply to some of their most exaggerated statements."[18]

Obviously, the appeal of southern loyalty could be strong, as the indignation of Harriet Smith shows. Robert Breckinridge also succumbed to its power in 1855 when Breckinridge participated in an angry exchange of public letters and speeches with two leaders of the newly formed Republican party, Charles Sumner and William H. Seward. Deeply resentful of Sumner's and Seward's "insulting" attacks on the South, Breckinridge wrote to Seward:

> It is not possible for us to separate ourselves completely from immense and durable influences which surround us. . . . I have differed often—sometimes fiercely—with [Kentuckians]: . . . about many aspects of this very question of domestic Slavery. But, Sir, what is Slavery to me, compared with the lives, the fortunes, the honor, the safety of these men? . . . Since the world began[,] no bond ever existed, save amongst God's ancient people, which bound every man to his fellow, every State to all the rest, . . . like the bond which pervades these fifteen Slave States.

According to Breckinridge, the willingness of southerners to stand together in times of crisis meant that "if the North wants to settle the slavery question by the edge of the Sword, the North is in a very fair way to be perfectly gratified." Breckinridge warned Sumner that "a million . . . armed men will be ready to receive you and your followers, . . . [and] the North will see reason to change her mind very materially as to the wisdom of that method of settling the question." One would hardly suppose from such blustering rhetoric that the same man would, during the Civil War, become the temporary chairman of the Republican National Convention and the leading Unionist in Kentucky—a man whose promotion of wartime emancipation and relentless persecution of Confederate sympathizers in the state would cause many Kentuckians to view him as practically the Republican dictator of Kentucky.[19]

Breckinridge's position revealed him to be not only a man who stood for the Union and opposed slavery, but also one who loved the South. In the years before the war, conservatives like Breckinridge reconciled these seemingly disparate positions by attacking those apparently responsible for creating a conflict between love of nation and love of state: northern abolitionists. To antislavery conservatives, it seemed that abolitionists were planting seeds of discord throughout the nation, in the process demonstrating the worst possible mode of reforming society. Under the leadership of southern statesmen, conservatives liked to claim, the South had been proceeding along a safe but steady path to ultimate emancipation. The advent of abolitionism, though, had upset this course of events by arousing the ire of slaveholders, who now resisted any effort for emancipation, even one led by other slaveholders. Antislavery conservatives argued that since no one would accept emancipation on the abolitionists' terms, and since abolitionists had made it less likely that slaveholders would accept it on the conservatives' terms, the abolitionists, as Henry Clay put it, had only strengthened "the fetters of the slave, and subjected him to more rigorous penalties and more oppressive laws." Perhaps even worse, talk of immediate abolition made slaves restive and excited sectional passions, creating "animosity and strife, when a good fellowship should prevail."[20]

Together, the conservatives' gradualism, their consuming fear of discord, their hostility to abolitionists, and their willingness to defend the South against northern reproach weakened their fight against slavery. During most of the 1830s and 1840s, this nexus of attitudes prevented antislavery conservatives from using the one legal mechanism that offered any hope of implementing a formal plan of emancipation in Kentucky: the constitutional convention. Practical politics and constitutional interpretation required a constitutional convention to effect any formal, statewide plan of emancipation. In theory, any session of the General Assembly had the requisite constitutional authority to end slavery in Kentucky. The state's Second Constitution, written in 1799, limited the legislature's power only by specifying that "the General Assembly shall have no power to pass laws for the emancipation of slaves, without the consent of their owners, or without paying the owners, previous to such emancipation, a full equivalent in money for the slaves so emancipated." Of course, this statement implied that the state legislature could free the state's slaves—provided it was willing to compensate masters for their lost property, much as New York and New Jersey had done in 1799 and 1804, respectively, and as Great Britain had done in 1833. Although such an action *might* have been politically feasible in 1799, when Kentucky implemented its Second Constitution and the state had only 40,000 slaves, it was hardly thinkable by 1830, when the state had over 165,000 bondsmen. So remote was the possibility of a legislative scheme of compensated emancipation that antislavery conservatives hardly considered it.[21]

For all practical purposes, emancipation would have to be accomplished at the constitutional rather than the statutory level. And the Second Constitution dictated that changing the organic law of the state required the long and uncertain procedure of calling a constitutional convention. Kentucky's fundamental law made no provision for changing the constitution through specific, individual amendments. If the legislature or the voters of the state sought to change any individual provision of the Kentucky Constitution, they had to submit the entire structure of government for review by a constitutional convention. The procedure for calling a convention required the legislature to approve the idea of a convention and to authorize a popular referendum on the subject. If a majority of all eligible voters (not simply a majority of those who chose to vote at the referendum) approved the calling of a convention, a second referendum would occur the following year. If a majority of all eligible voters again supported the calling of a convention, then the selection of the convention's members would take place at the next general election. The convention could "readopt, amend, or change" the state's constitution as it saw fit and was not obligated to submit its handiwork either to the legislature or to the voters of the state for approval. This rather cumbersome procedure required a minimum of three years to complete. And since such a convention could change the constitution at will without having to seek popular or legislative ratification of its actions, it would be answerable to no one but itself—there was no guarantee that it would even implement the changes it was brought into existence to make.[22]

Nevertheless, throughout the 1830s and 1840s various reform groups occasionally joined together to exploit widespread dissatisfaction with Kentucky's Constitution of 1799. Some Kentuckians believed that the state's constitution established a chaotic and undemocratic form of government, which placed most of the effective, day-to-day powers of government into the hands of semiautonomous county courts, powers that extended into the executive, legislative, and judicial functions of government. The range of the county courts' formal powers was indeed enormous: they built roads and bridges within the counties, granted franchises for ferry operators, authorized the construction of milldams, assessed individuals' property for the state property tax, collected that tax, and prosecuted tax evaders. They were also responsible for "probating wills," "overseeing the administration of estates," "appointing guardians" for orphans, and administering the poor laws. Courts appointed most county officials as well.[23]

With this authority came vast financial and political power within the counties: the courts could make or break a man's fortune by choosing the location of roads, bridges, dams, and ferries; they could help or hinder a politician's career by influencing voters in Kentucky's viva voce electoral system. Voters could be intimidated by threats of higher property tax assessments and the prosecution of minor legal offenses or cajoled with promises of patronage jobs. What made this structure particularly grievous was that county courts were appointive and self-perpetuating. Individual members of the courts— the justices of the peace—were appointed for life by the governor from a list of two names submitted by the county court in question; under legal obligation to choose from this list, the governor usually picked the court's first choice. Few mechanisms in the county court system held the justices of the peace accountable for their actions by the people they served.[24]

A second source of dissatisfaction with the state constitution was its failure to provide for a more certain mode of emancipation. Slavery had been a central issue in Kentucky's first two constitutional conventions. At the first convention in 1792, slavery was the only issue before the convention divisive enough to require a roll-call vote. During the election of delegates to the second convention in 1799, slavery was the principal issue debated by the candidates in a campaign notable, among other things, for introducing the young antislavery politician Henry Clay to the voters of the state. Although both conventions resulted in discouraging failure for the state's antislavery movement, the revision of the constitution remained one of its principal goals. Following the passage of the Law of 1833, antislavery forces pursued the campaign for constitutional reform so relentlessly that politicians on both sides of the slavery issue assumed that if a constitutional convention were approved, emancipation would be the leading issue before the convention. Many were certain of the result of such a constitutional debate: "It is well understood here that when a convention is called," asserted Unitarian minister James Freeman Clarke in the mid-1830s, "slavery is gone in this state; and it is also known that a vast majority of the people are in favor of calling a convention."[25]

Clarke's observation, however, proved overly optimistic. After the emancipationists' convention bill failed by only three votes in the House and one vote in the Senate during the legislative session of 1834–35, the constitutional reform effort stalled. It was not until antislavery supporters made common cause with those seeking reform of the county court system during the session of 1837–38 that the legislature finally authorized a referendum on the convention. During this legislative battle, emancipationists had ample reason to be distressed by the actions of many antislavery conservatives. A few prominent conservatives gave their warm support to the convention movement, including James Freeman Clarke, Benjamin Bosworth Smith, and Francis Marion Bristow, a thirty-year-old legislator just embarking on a career that would eventually lead to the United States Congress and the Republican party. But most antislavery conservatives supporting the convention bill in the legislature were obscure people like Moses F. Glenn of Nicholas County and Robert Browder of Logan County, both of whom were first-term legislators during the crucial session of 1837–38. Throughout the 1830s and most of the 1840s, the real luminaries in the conservative constellation were cool and, in some cases, even hostile to the very idea of calling a constitutional convention to effect emancipation, for the proposal to call a convention tapped into some of the conservatives' deepest fears of impending chaos.[26]

Such fears arose largely out of the intellectual legacy of the

American Revolution. For the generation that fought the Revolution and lived to see a new government established by the United States Constitution, the centerpiece of a decade's worth of experimentation with republican self-government was in many ways the conceptualization of the constitutional convention. To many of these early Americans, as well as to their children and grandchildren in antebellum Kentucky, the constitutional convention represented the nation's most direct link to pure democracy, a clear proof that the people, not the government, were the source of sovereign authority in the United States. Governments established by constitutions had, by definition, only limited authority, and elected officials of those governments, intentionally removed somewhat from the excitable currents of public opinion, were thought to speak with something less than the perfect voice of the people. But unlike the powers of a legislative body, a constitutional convention wielded unlimited authority: it could design any sort of government it wanted. Moreover, unlike the members of a legislature, the delegates to a convention literally spoke with the "sovereign authority" of the people they represented. Thus, to call a constitutional convention was to suspend the rules of society, or as Robert J. Breckinridge put it, to place again "the people in the same condition they occupied before they made the constitution," to examine "the whole order of society," and to lay "the foundations of the State . . . afresh." It was, as antislavery conservatives saw it, to plunge society into a literal Lockean state of nature, or as Cassius Clay put it, to "dissolve" the "elements of society."[27]

This was heady stuff to those who feared disorder above almost all else. By including a provision for constitutional conventions in fundamental law, noted Breckinridge, "we have incorporated in that instrument the right of revolution," and although a constitutional convention was preferable to revolution by "rebellion, insurrection or civil war," it was revolution nonetheless. Suspending the rules of society and re-establishing the foundation of government was not something to be approached lightly; it was, reminded Breckinridge, "the greatest matter about which . . . [we] can be engaged." Although they truly valued the ability for peaceful change afforded by American constitutions, during the 1830s and indeed through much of the

1840s, antislavery conservatives remained steadfastly reluctant to resort to so momentous a device as the constitutional convention to achieve statewide emancipation.[28]

The immense authority of constitutional conventions almost overwhelmed some conservatives. Henry Clay—who by the 1830s did not usually involve himself in the issues of state politics—"felt constrained to take immediate, bold, and decided ground against" the calling of a convention, explaining to the abolitionist James G. Birney, an enthusiastic lobbyist for the convention, that "I was unwilling to hazard all the good, in our excellent Constitution" for the slim chance that a convention would approve an emancipation scheme. In truth, many of the changes that Clay and other conservatives were unwilling to hazard were ones advocated by those seeking to reform the system of county courts and other features of the constitution thought to be undemocratic. Antislavery conservatives opposed reforms of this nature, in some cases because the existing constitution promoted Whig ascendancy in Kentucky, and in other cases because the constitution distanced government officials from the mercurial passions of the people. Justices of the peace were, after all, judges, and to many conservatives it seemed that efforts to make members of the county courts subject to election, in the words of Cassius M. Clay, threatened to destroy "the independence of the judiciary" and to place "property, life, reputation and liberty . . . at the mercy of an excited multitude."[29]

Furthermore, these proponents of social harmony were not anxious to increase the sources of strife within the state. With the stakes so high, attempts to call a constitutional convention would bring out "demagogues," argued Cassius Clay, politicians "who appeal to the worst passions, who excite the 'poor' against the 'rich,' the 'mountains' against the 'valleys,' who are for ever flattering the people for their own aggrandizement, and watching the tide of human misfortunes, distress, and confusion, for the purpose of running into power." Conservatives like Breckinridge claimed that in such a state of affairs, "no state . . . could . . . form any scheme of fundamental law, which would be the most acceptable to itself in the ordinary condition of its affairs. Hence it has grown into a maxim, that a period of public excitement is not the best time for amending the constitutions of states."[30]

Breckinridge's rationale was also applied by conservatives to the tension engendered by the slavery controversy. By 1835, it seemed to many Kentuckians that in the short span of time since the passage of the Law of 1833, the state had been infected by the contagion of abolitionism. The year 1834 had witnessed the famous Lane Seminary debates across the river from Kentucky in Cincinnati, which converted several Kentucky students to abolitionism, most notably James A. Thome of Augusta. Around the time of the Lane debates, the Presbyterian and Methodist colleges of Kentucky—Centre College and Augusta College, respectively—were the sites of similar, albeit less momentous, debates; in both cases abolitionism won strong support among the students. The same year, Birney publicly announced that he had become an abolitionist and began touring the state to advocate radical antislavery. In 1835, Birney and some forty other Kentuckians established a state chapter of the American Anti-Slavery Society, and Birney announced plans to establish an abolitionist newspaper, the *Philanthropist,* in his hometown of Danville. Later that year, the American Anti-Slavery Society began its famous postal campaign, an ingenious and ambitious plan to "invade" the South through the mails by sending one million pieces of abolitionist literature to unexpecting southerners. More than any previous incident, the postal campaign alerted southerners to the threat of abolitionism, and the postmasters of Lexington and Danville were just two of many such officials across the South who refused to deliver the abolitionists' mailings.[31]

When compared to other southerners, antislavery conservatives were not unusually sensitive to the actions of abolitionists, but their hostility to the abolitionists did turn them decisively against the convention in the mid-1830s. Some conservatives explained their opposition to calling a convention in terms of practical politics: given the widespread public opposition to abolitionism in Kentucky, it was unlikely that a constitutional convention would approve any scheme of emancipation, and it might even make slavery more secure. Other conservatives were more blunt. With abolitionism abroad in the land, was it safe even to discuss the slavery issue, especially when doing so involved the use of a constitutional mechanism that would "disturb the very elements of society"? "Is this a time, . . ." asked Cassius Clay, "when a horde of fanatical incendiaries are springing up in the North, threatening to spread fire and blood through our once secure and happy homes?—I ask, is this a time to deliberately dispose of a question which involves the political rights of master and slave—the liberties—it may be the lives of one or both parties?" Under the influence of such feelings, when the legislature finally approved the convention bill in 1838, many antislavery conservatives who were members voted against the measure, including William F. Bullock, John A. McClung, Samuel S. Nicholas, James T. Morehead, and Cassius M. Clay.[32]

It is difficult to assess the influence that the conservatives had on the convention referendum, but surely the outspoken opposition of prominent politicians like Henry Clay and former Governor Morehead to the calling of a convention had an impact. In the August 1838 referendum, fewer than 27 percent of the state's eligible voters expressed support for a convention. Thereafter, legislative interest in a constitutional convention declined until the session of 1843–44, when proponents of the convention began to meet with more success in the General Assembly. By the session of 1846–47, only nine years after the voters of the state had first rejected the calling of a convention, supporters of the measure again convinced the General Assembly to submit the issue to the voters in a referendum, thereby beginning a process which three years later begat Kentucky's Third Constitution.

Through much of the 1840s, a number of the state's antislavery advocates would continue to be trapped by the dilemma of conservative reform, opposing the calling of a convention, warning that Kentucky was still not ready for emancipation, and lamenting that this premature effort at reform would only bring more strife and disorder than slavery itself. Though convinced that slavery threatened the state with economic ruin, moral corruption, and bloody rebellion, these conservatives could offer no better solutions than African colonization, nonimportation, and voluntary manumission.

Working within the parameters set by the necessary-evil ideology, they could not escape its limitations.

Interestingly, by the early 1840s a growing number of conservatives found their way out of this dilemma. By the end of that decade, these conservatives forced a showdown with the militant supporters of slavery, a showdown that resulted in a decisive victory for pro-slavery forces. Ironically, the person who most symbolized that shift in conservative thought and its increasing support for a constitutional convention was one of the leading opponents of the convention movement of the 1830s: Cassius M. Clay.[33]

5

The Crisis at the Door

If modern psychoanalysts were able to treat the leaders of Kentucky's antislavery movement for the chronic ailment that so debilitated them, the most likely diagnosis would be manic depression. The historian would readily concur with this diagnosis, for Kentucky's emancipationists experienced recurring swings of emotion throughout the state's history. Exultation over apparent advances for antislavery in the state was regularly followed by disheartenment over the stubborn refusal of Kentuckians to take any firm action against slavery. For every sign of success—the passage of the Law of 1833, for instance—there always seemed to be a corresponding sign of failure—like the defeat of the convention movement in 1838.

The history of the slavery issue during the 1840s continued this pattern. During the decade, a noticeable increase in opposition to slavery in Kentucky occurred. More Kentuckians counted themselves as committed emancipationists than ever had before, and many long-time antislavery advocates abandoned their old caution and worked wholeheartedly to bring about an end to slavery. This development cheered antislavery forces in the state and alarmed proslavery advocates throughout the South. This alarm was understandable. Under the leadership of a new breed of antislavery conservatives who had shed much of their predecessors' debilitating concern about racial competition and social order, the newly invigorated antislavery movement pushed the state into the most serious and wide-ranging debate about slavery in Kentucky's history, a debate that was ultimately settled by the promulgation of a new state constitution. When the state's antislavery forces lost this battle, they experienced a crippling disheartenment, which significantly diminished the fortunes of emancipation in Kentucky.

The person who most clearly exemplified this new activism and who, in the 1840s, led many of the early battles to secure the calling of a constitutional convention was Cassius Marcellus Clay of Madison County. The son of Green Clay, a longtime politician from Madison County and reputedly the largest slaveholder in Kentucky, Cassius Clay rose to prominence fairly early in life. In 1828—when Clay was eighteen—he joined the ranks of the Bluegrass planters when his father died, leaving him the family's 2,000–acre estate in Madison County, a one-sixth share of the father's 50,000–acre landholdings in western Kentucky, and seventeen slaves. At only twenty-five years of age, Clay entered the state House of Representatives, where he served three terms as a Whig during the late 1830s and early 1840s. In the legislature, Clay fell in with the loose antislavery coalition that battled annually to save the Law of 1833 from the assaults of proslavery legislators. Like many respectable slaveholders in Kentucky who criticized slavery, Clay initially espoused gradualism, denounced abolitionists, and advised caution in revising the state constitution. Even later, when Clay cast himself as a radical, his antislavery argument followed the general outline of the antislavery conservatives' critique of slavery.[1]

But by the time Clay turned thirty in 1840, it was apparent that there was something unusual about this opponent of slavery. Clay emphasized the economic analysis of slavery, arguing with depth and fervor that slavery was harming the state's economy. His original interest in such matters arose out of his sympathy for the Whig party, which prompted him to support both his cousin Henry's American System and state-sponsored commercial development. Clay's three terms in the legislature gave him ample opportunity to discover that the most vociferous opposition to such programs came from Kentucky's strongest proslavery advocates, a fact which encouraged

Clay to believe that support for slavery was antithetical to support for sound economic policies.[2]

This conviction deepened during the financial depression that followed the Panic of 1837. In Kentucky, the economic downturn continued well into 1843, and even after the economy began to turn around in that year, the recovery was slow and gradual. Clay had a very personal reason to become interested in the causes of Kentucky's financial woes: he lost most of his inherited wealth after several investments went sour and his brother-in-law, for whom Clay had pledged his own assets as security for debts, went bankrupt in the financial panic.[3]

The ongoing battle in the General Assembly to repeal nonimportation gave Clay the opportunity to explore the economic forces behind the financial difficulties of men like himself. As Clay prepared speeches and pamphlets in support of the Law of 1833, he developed an economic critique of slavery, which set the tone for the reformist career that would soon make him famous outside Kentucky. Clay believed that the depression had been caused by the economic policies of national politicians beholden to the interests of southern planters as well as by the inherent instability of the slave economy of the South. Not a particularly original argument, it strikingly resembled the analysis many northern antislavery advocates offered as an explanation of the depression. Indeed, Clay's main point—that slave labor damaged the economy of southern states and the livelihood of white workingmen by drying up the home market and by driving out capital for investment—had often been made by Kentucky's antislavery conservatives. But Clay approached these problems with a depth and sophistication rarely seen before, and according to historian Eugene D. Genovese, Clay's speeches and writings proved him to be "one of the most penetrating commentators on the economics of slavery" ever to study the issue.[4]

Moreover, the emphasis Clay placed on economic issues had a crucial effect on his willingness to seek reform of the peculiar institution. Unlike earlier conservatives, who had been so overwhelmingly concerned with racial competition and social harmony that they failed to take strong actions against slavery, Clay's interest in economics had a liberating effect on his antislavery thought. It was as though Clay, in his consuming interest in the debilitating economic effects of slavery, had finally found an effective counterbalance to whatever concerns he, as a conservative, might have had about the disorder that could be caused by emancipation.[5]

Clay's overriding concern for the economics of slavery was but one of several differences between his evolving brand of opposition to slavery and that of more traditional antislavery conservatives. Perhaps the most obvious of these differences was Clay's abandonment of colonization as a necessary component of any plan of emancipation. In the early 1840s, Clay began to claim that the impracticality of colonization had caused Kentuckians to abandon antislavery as a hopeless cause. To regain this waning support, Clay argued that antislavery forces should abandon their insistence that emancipation must be accompanied by the hopelessly impractical scheme of African colonization.[6]

This appeal to practical politics was not the principled, moral objection to colonization offered by abolitionists like Birney and Fee. Clay did not dispute the proposition that blacks and whites would mutually benefit from separation. He still hoped that slaves would be freed by some gradual *post nati* emancipation plan, and the specific plan favored by Clay envisioned a significant separation of the two races then residing in Kentucky. Making a point that many antislavery conservatives would adopt during the late 1840s, Clay argued that if the state enacted a plan of gradual emancipation, a master who wanted to protect his investment would be able either to remove his slaves from Kentucky or to sell them out of the state before the impending date of manumission. Such actions, Clay argued, would remove a large portion of Kentucky's black population without resorting to colonization. Further, Clay did not completely reject the idea that African colonization could help bring about a partial separation of the races. Clay stated that he would have no objections if the state, after agreeing on a plan of abolition, wanted to append to it a scheme of *voluntary* colonization. Indeed, in the mid-1840s Clay signaled that he was flexible about the mode of emancipation that should be adopted in Kentucky by enrolling himself as a lifetime member in the American Colonization Society.[7]

Historians have made much of Clay's lingering willingness to separate the races, citing it as prime evidence that Clay's brand of antislavery was merely another version of the sort of racially motivated antislavery that characterized many northern Free-Soilers and southern antislavery advocates. Clay himself freely admitted that "whilst I am not insensible to the injuries inflicted on the African race . . . I am mainly actuated by a still higher motive—the greater motive of achieving the complete independence and liberty of my own [people], the white Anglo-Saxon race of America." To make matters worse, Clay sometimes exhibited his racism in coarse language that would have made many older conservatives cringe. Clay's oft-quoted remark that he had "studied the Negro character" and decided that "we can make nothing out of them" because "God has made them for the sun and the banana" was probably the worst example of the sort of denigrating language Clay sometimes used in referring to blacks.[8]

Yet to see only Clay's racism or his toleration of colonization schemes in the 1840s is to see only part of the man's character and almost none of his achievement. In reality, Clay's views on colonization belied the racism that seemed often to undergird his antislavery sentiments. Clay understood that under the scheme of gradual emancipation without colonization that he hoped the state would adopt, a significant free black population would remain in Kentucky, even if large numbers of masters were to sell or remove their slaves from the state. Much of the novelty of Clay's argument arose from the fact that he neither objected to the existence of this population nor considered it a hindrance to a plan of emancipation. In fact, Clay was willing to forgo the period of training for prospective freedpeople that some conservatives, like John C. Young, insisted must be a part of any emancipation scheme that left significant numbers of free blacks in Kentucky. Given Clay's willingness to permit a significant number of black laborers to remain in the state, it seems wrong to conclude that Clay's only motive in proposing emancipation was to remove black workers whose competitive position in the marketplace was taking bread out of the mouths of white laborers. Finally, Clay insisted with a vehemence almost unheard of among Kentucky's antislavery conservatives that, no matter how much whites like himself might find it distasteful to live among free blacks, the African American had a natural right to freedom and that his claim to freedom and even political equality with the Caucasian could not be denied forever.[9]

Ironically, Clay's lingering toleration for colonization schemes during the 1840s partly reflected a new determination to see Kentucky embark on the work of emancipation soon. Although he feared that the impracticality of colonization would permanently forestall the enactment of emancipation, Clay also recognized that a significant portion of the state's most dedicated antislavery advocates had a long and seemingly unshakable attachment to colonization, and he did not want to exclude such people from the antislavery coalition he hoped to build. Clay hoped that antislavery activists could put aside their differences and castigate the evils of slavery—however those evils were defined—and agree to work together for the election of antislavery politicians to public office, no matter what approach those candidates took to antislavery. Once antislavery groups had gained the voters' confidence through such actions, Clay argued, it would become much easier for antislavery forces to unite on a program of emancipation.[10]

If this approach seems to have conceded too much to the colonizationists, it would be well to remember that Clay took the same approach to the abolitionists in the 1840s. One of the most significant changes in Clay's thought after 1840 was his new toleration for northern abolitionists. In fact, Clay proved eager to build channels of communication and bonds of affection between southern emancipationists and northern abolitionists. In Kentucky, Clay defended the radical followers of William Lloyd Garrison as people of good conscience, despite what he regarded as their fanaticism, and he could not say enough good things about the leaders of the Liberty party. Although in the early 1840s Clay hoped that the Whig party would be transformed into the agent of abolition in the United States, and although he initially refused to join a separate antislavery party, Clay believed that the leaders of the Liberty party were closer to his own views on slavery than most of the leaders of his own party.[11]

One result of Clay's desire to link all types of antislavery groups into a broadly based political coalition was a de-emphasis of policy considerations. Because he feared driving away potential political allies in the 1840s, Clay talked a great deal more about why slavery should be eliminated than he did about *how* it could be eliminated. When pressed to offer a plan, though, Clay favored the traditional *post nati* scheme. To implement this plan, Clay argued—in sharp contrast to his position in the late 1830s—that all varieties of antislavery activists should work together in Kentucky to promote the calling of a constitutional convention. Not surprisingly, Clay was not a stickler for the details of his program, and he considered most of the details open for negotiation if compromise would assure the implementation of some definite program for emancipation.[12]

It was, perhaps, Clay's overriding determination to see a definite program of emancipation enacted at an early date that most distinguished him from earlier conservatives. Unlike most conservatives who came before him, Clay was increasingly unwilling in the 1840s to let concerns about social stability sidetrack the process of emancipation. Although Clay's ideology remained largely conservative, he ultimately proved to have the heart of a radical. Clay's unflagging zeal for emancipation, his unwillingness to give up that cause without a fight, his readiness to use physical force to defend himself and his civil rights, and his open affinity for northern abolitionists caused proslavery forces in Kentucky to view Clay as an unusually dangerous man. This image was promoted by his several well-publicized and sometimes violent confrontations with proslavery advocates in the first half of the 1840s.[13]

The most famous and important of these confrontations involved Clay's establishment of an antislavery newspaper, the *True American*, in Lexington in 1845. The publication of an antislavery paper in a slave state was a bold move, as Clay well knew from Birney's abortive effort to establish such a paper in Danville ten years earlier, not to mention the death threats he himself received after announcing his intention to start the *True American*. However, threats seldom—if ever—scared Clay. He inaugurated the first issue of the *True American* in June 1845 with a belligerent editorial, defiantly proclaiming that "we are not to be deterred by vague threats or real dangers, coming from any man or set of men," and Clay maintained this defiant tone throughout the first two months of the paper's existence. Clay's bold rhetoric eventually got him and his paper in trouble, though. Clay was acutely ill with typhoid fever most of that summer and was barely able to scratch out his own editorials. During the second week of August, Clay—delirious with fever, as he later claimed—wrote an inflammatory editorial for the paper that included a dark prophecy for the fate of slaveholders. "But remember, you who dwell in marble palaces," wrote Clay, "that there are strong arms and fiery hearts and iron pikes in the streets, and panes of glass only between them and the silver plate on the board, and the smooth skinned woman on the ottoman. When you have mocked at virtue, denied the agency of God in the affairs of men, and made rapine your honeyed faith, tremble! for the day of retribution is at hand, and the masses will be avenged."[14]

This editorial, coming after several months of resentment against Clay for his intention to publish an antislavery newspaper in Lexington, proved almost too much for the city's civic leaders to bear. During the third week of August, a number of prominent Lexingtonians organized meetings to arrange for the suppression of the *True American*. Clay had made a number of enemies during his already stormy career, and several of the people clamoring for the suppression of Clay's paper seem to have been either old political rivals or estranged relatives. Others were concerned that violent confrontations involving Clay would result in "bloodshed and disgrace" upon the city of Lexington, and they joined the movement against Clay to provide it with a sense of order and an eye toward the law. Many slaveholders who opposed Clay were apparently concerned that he was undermining the support of white nonslaveholders for the peculiar institution. All seem to have been genuinely concerned that Clay's paper was promoting unrest among the state's slave population. On August 18, a committee entered Clay's printing office and—true to their desire for public order—carefully disassembled Clay's press under the direction of professional printers, packed it up in a crate, and shipped it to Cincinnati in care of a commission firm.[15]

Two months later, in October 1845, Clay resumed publication of the *True American*. The paper was now published in Cincinnati, where the committee had deposited his printing press, but Clay still edited the paper from Lexington and it carried a Lexington dateline. By resuming publication, Clay had again demonstrated that he would not be easily deterred from his battle for emancipation. In the North, Clay's resolute determination to continue the struggle against slavery won him the plaudits of antislavery activists. In Kentucky, however, Clay's efforts only added to his image as a dangerously reckless man, an image that would be a serious impediment to Clay's ability to win support for emancipation. By the summer of 1846, Clay himself realized that he had become so unpopular in Kentucky that few people would listen to what he had to say about slavery. In June 1846, Clay saw a chance to repair his public image and, he claimed, to aid the cause of emancipation in Kentucky. The state militia was recruiting troops to fight in the Mexican War, and Clay believed that if he enlisted and risked his life in defense of other Kentuckians, he could "*prove* to the *people* of the South that I warred not upon *them,* but upon *Slavery*—that a man might hate slavery and denounce tyrants without being the *enemy of his country.*" Clay explained to dubious northern antislavery reformers that "if I gained fame in arms it would enable me 'to overthrow slavery on my return'" to Kentucky.[16]

Clay's enlistment in the army did help to strengthen the antislavery movement in Kentucky—but not for the reasons he predicted. The Mexican War took Clay out of the state at a crucial moment in the history of Kentucky's antislavery movement. Opposition to slavery was on the rise in Kentucky: for the first time in many years, the various elements of the state's antislavery movement were beginning to coalesce, and the movement was beginning to test its new political strength. Clay's absence, therefore, removed from the antislavery movement the burden of daily association with his unpopularity. Clay's absence also served the useful function of causing the transfer of control of the *True American* from Clay to a group of ardent anti-slavery supporters in Louisville. This transfer of control, in turn, changed the *True American* from Cassius Clay's personal mouthpiece into the organ of a statewide antislavery movement.

The person most responsible for the transformation of the *True American* was perhaps John Champion Vaughan of Cincinnati, Ohio. Now almost forgotten by history, Vaughan was a former slaveholder from South Carolina who became convinced that slavery was wrong, freed his slaves, and moved to Cincinnati in 1837. After moving north, Vaughan became involved in many of the day's reform movements, including those to promote public education, poor relief, and pacifism. The movement that most concerned Vaughan, however, was the one that most directly affected his native South: antislavery. As early as 1838—only a few months after his move from South Carolina—Vaughan demonstrated his interest in the cause of the slave by traveling to Mason County, Kentucky, to act as defense attorney in the celebrated trial of John B. Mahan, an Ohio abolitionist who had been extradited to Kentucky from Ohio for allegedly helping several fugitive slaves from Kentucky make their way to Canada.[17]

Nearly two years before Clay began publishing the *True American,* Vaughan had been the prime mover in an effort by certain Ohio antislavery activists, including Salmon P. Chase, to establish an antislavery newspaper in Kentucky. These opponents of slavery had high hopes that an indigenous southern antislavery movement represented by people like Clay could be created, perhaps through the agency of antislavery newspapers located in southern cities. Chase, who regularly corresponded with Clay, tried to enlist him in the effort to establish Vaughan's proposed paper in Kentucky. At first, Clay doubted that the paper could be established in the commonwealth, but he later warmly supported the idea. After Vaughan did not follow through with his plans, Clay took up the idea of a southern antislavery newspaper, establishing the *True American* in the summer of 1845.[18]

When the removal of his press to Cincinnati forced Clay to publish the paper from there, however, Vaughan again became involved with the effort to publish an antislavery newspaper in Kentucky. In the fall of 1845, Clay hired Vaughan an associate editor in Cincinnati to facilitate the new long-distance editorial arrangement of the paper. Vaughan was still serving as associate editor when Clay marched off to war the next year. Before Clay left for Mexico, he installed Vaughan as the acting editor of the *True American* and brought three others into the management of the paper: Paul Seymour, Clay's business agent in Cincinnati, who was to handle the paper's finances; Clay's wife Mary Jane, who was to have final word concerning the operations of the paper; and Clay's older brother Brutus, who was to advise Mary Jane and to exercise Clay's power of attorney in matters concerning the paper.[19]

As the four of them were soon to discover, Clay had left them in charge of a rapidly declining enterprise. Incensed at Clay's decision to fight in a war that they saw as being waged solely to gain new territory for the expansion of slavery, many northern antislavery advocates canceled their subscriptions to the *True American* in protest. Since nearly three-fourths of the subscribers to the *True American* were northerners, they could inflict much financial damage to the paper. In October 1846, Paul Seymour estimated that over the next few months, subscriptions would decline by 40 percent. The added expense of Vaughan's and Seymour's salaries also increased the financial burden of the paper to the point that by the autumn of 1846, it was not paying one-quarter of its expenses. Clay had always paid the difference between the paper's expenses and its revenues, but by the fall of 1846, his personal finances were not in much better shape than the paper's.[20]

Vaughan and Seymour feared that Brutus and Mary Jane Clay, struggling to keep Clay's estate solvent, might withdraw their financial support from the *True American.* By the beginning of September 1846, Vaughan and Seymour had been in contact with several antislavery activists in Louisville about the possibility of moving the paper's operations there under the financial sponsorship of its emancipationists. The two men spent most of September and October of 1846 trying to convince the Clays to stand behind the paper until the beginning of the next year, by which time Vaughan hoped to find a new source of funding and to take over the paper "himself and place it in Louisville." The Clays, however, were unwilling to spend any more money on the *True American,* and on October 9, 1846, Mary Jane Clay told Vaughan and Seymour to close the paper with its next issue.[21]

The *True American,* however, was not dead yet. Vaughan and Seymour were determined to resume publication, as were a number of Kentucky antislavery reformers who wrote Vaughan, urging him to continue the paper. Vaughan also met with a committee of antislavery supporters in Louisville who, in the words of Salmon Chase, had "resolved that the paper shall go on under the charge of Mr. Vaughan, provided the necessary assistance can be had." Given the previous predilections of Kentucky's antislavery forces, what took place next was quite remarkable. The Louisvillians decided to sponsor Vaughan on a trip to the East, where he would attempt to raise funds for the paper from the abolitionists and antislavery reformers of New York and Boston. This was one of the most significant developments in the antislavery movement in Kentucky during the 1840s. For years antislavery forces in Kentucky had castigated northern antislavery activists, avoiding contact with abolitionists as if they carried the plague. Now, in the late autumn of 1846, southern antislavery reformers were sending an emissary to request financial support from these same northern antislavery groups.[22]

The Louisvillians who sponsored Vaughan's trip were quite aware of the sensitive nature of this mission. Indeed, the Louisvillians apparently hoped to keep their entire efforts to save the *True American* secret in Kentucky until they were ready to resume publication of the paper. Yet despite these and other signs throughout the late 1840s that Kentucky's antislavery advocates were cautious in their dealings with abolitionists, the efforts to solicit funds from northern antislavery activists represented a new openness on the part of many antislavery reformers in Kentucky to cooperation with abolitionists, both at home and in the North.[23]

In the months that followed, this new attitude blossomed, as the efforts of emancipationists in Louisville to secure funding for the *True American* placed them at the receiving end of an antislavery fund-raising network that extended from Louisville through New York to Boston and even Great Britain. Within their own state, the Louisvillians not only accepted with gratitude the offer of assistance made by an abolitionist like Fee, they also confided in him some of the most sensitive details concerning the paper and later even offered to sponsor him on a fund-raising trip to the North. For his part, Fee solicited aid from several northern abolitionists, including the famous northern philanthropist Lewis Tappan, who responded by publishing Fee's appeal for aid in the religious magazine Tappan edited, the *American Missionary,* by contributing funds himself, and by soliciting aid for the paper from the British and Foreign Anti-Slavery Society in London.[24]

The Ohio Libertyman Salmon P. Chase also served as a conduit for funds and aid to the *True American.* Chase, who had a strong interest in seeing the paper survive because of his friendship with both Vaughan and Clay and his long-standing desire to establish an antislavery paper in the South, had promised Clay that he would keep watch over the affairs of the paper during Clay's sojourn in Mexico. True to his word, Chase wrote to the wealthy abolitionist Gerrit Smith asking Smith to contribute to the *True American,* to "write a few lines in its behalf for one or more of the Liberty [party] Papers," and to send "a letter of encouragement to Mr. Vaughan." Smith responded by contributing one hundred dollars to the paper. Chase also wrote to the Conscience Whig Charles Sumner, asking him to aid Vaughan's fund-raising efforts in Boston. Chase wrote that "the importance of this paper . . . cannot well be overestimated. . . . It is the link between the Antislavery sentiment of the North and South. It cannot be lost without great detriment to the cause both North and South." Sumner, in turn, promised to introduce Vaughan to the "regular Whigs in Boston" and "to enable Mr[.] Vaughan to lay his case before them."[25]

With antislavery activists like Salmon Chase, Charles Sumner, Lewis Tappan, and Gerrit Smith supporting his efforts, Vaughan's trip to the East in the winter of 1846–47 proved successful. Within a period of six weeks, Vaughan raised four thousand dollars in New York and Boston, nearly enough to resume publication on a firm footing. Meanwhile, Vaughan's sponsors in Louisville began to set the direction the paper would take once it did resume publication. A financial committee would be established in Louisville to help the paper remain solvent. In addition, by January 1846 the leadership of the Louisville emancipationists agreed to change the name of the *True American*. According to Vaughan, Louisvillians refused "to have any thing to do with the old name" because of its close association with Clay and the enmity directed toward him, both by northern antislavery advocates who resented his participation in the war and by Kentuckians who resented Clay's seemingly reckless approach to antislavery. "'Let us start afresh' said they; 'not with different principles, but with those principles freed from the taint of war, and of the personal prejudice, which their defender had excited." These details were formalized "at a very full private meeting of the friends of emancipation at Louisville" in late March or early April of 1847. On June 19, 1847, the *True American*—now rechristened the *Examiner*—resumed publication in Louisville with John C. Vaughan as editor and Paul Seymour as publisher.[26]

The rescue of Cassius Clay's paper by an alliance of northern abolitionists and Louisville emancipationists was an apt development. Although other antislavery conservatives—John C. Young and Joseph R. Underwood among them—had friendly relationships with individual abolitionists, Clay was the first conservative in Kentucky who sought a cordial and mutually beneficial relationship with the abolitionist movement. By accepting the help of northern abolitionists, the Louisville emancipationists demonstrated that they were suitable heirs to Clay's brand of antislavery conservatism. The Louisvillians proved to be fitting successors of Clay in other ways as well. Like Clay, many of Louisville's antislavery reformers were rethinking the role that colonization should play in the emancipation movement. These emancipationists agreed with Clay that the apparent impracticality of colonization undercut support for emancipation among the state's voters. Some opponents of slavery in Louisville wanted to jettison colonization altogether, believing that doing so would promote emancipation. A larger number remained committed to the idea of a substantial separation of the races then residing in Kentucky. These antislavery advocates, however, argued that in emancipating the state's slaves, Kentuckians would have to rely on a variety of mechanisms—African colonization being only one—to achieve a satisfactory degree of racial separation. As their impatience with colonization indicated, many of Louisville's emancipationists had, like Clay, become convinced of the necessity of taking definite, formal steps to implement a plan of emancipation, and they hoped that such a plan could be secured through a revision of Kentucky's state constitution.[27]

Also like Clay, the emancipationists in Louisville were inordinately interested in the economic problems of slavery. By the late 1840s, the leadership of the antislavery movement in the city included some of its leading civic and financial figures, including the presidents and directors of banks, insurance companies, and turnpike companies; members of the boards of trustees of educational, charitable, and religious organizations; and several of the city's leading merchants, journalists, manufacturers, and professionals. In the aftermath of the depression of 1837–43, these community leaders viewed slavery as inimical to their own economic well-being and the progress and prosperity of their city. Like Clay, they downplayed the concerns of earlier conservatives about social order, instead emphasizing the inefficiency and low profitability of slave labor. Accustomed to competing with nearby Cincinnati for population, commerce, and renown, these boosters blushed at the frequent invidious comparisons made between the free state of Ohio and slaveholding Kentucky. Being "interest[ed] in everything tending to improve the city," as one of their number was described, these civic-minded Louisvillians tackled the problem of slavery with the same farsighted vision and reforming zeal with which they might organize a turnpike company or build an orphanage.[28]

The economic critique of slavery put forward by these reformers, like that of Cassius Clay, forcefully emphasized the traditional conservative belief in the superiority of free labor over slave labor. The Louisvillians extolled the dignity of manual labor, railed against the unfair competition of slave labor with whites of small means, urged the creation of jobs for white workingmen, and, in general, made the protection of white laborers a political priority. This tack helped forge an alliance between the antislavery conservatives of Louisville and the many white mechanics and laborers of that city who were beginning to complain about the competition they faced from slave labor.

The political advantage that could be reaped from such a coalition was potentially quite substantial. Among the ten largest cities of the South in 1850, Louisville had the highest proportion of workingmen and laborers in its male population. In addition, by the late 1840s many of these workers in Louisville were openly critical of slavery. During the late 1830s and 1840s, there had been several labor strikes in the city by journeymen carpenters, bricklayers, painters, and stonecutters seeking to limit the workday to ten hours. At least three of these strikes were broken up by employers using slave laborers to replace striking white mechanics. By the end of the 1840s, a number of white workingmen in Louisville had grown bitter over the failure of these strikes and over the disadvantages they faced when forced to compete with slave labor.[29]

A meeting of workingmen in April 1849, for instance, issued an address complaining that the low cost of slave labor made it hard for white laborers to find work. When white workingmen were able to find employment, they encountered employers who insisted on paying them the same low wages paid to hired slaves and demanded they work the same long hours as the slave laborers. But, the address continued, low wages, long hours, and high unemployment were not the only problems encountered by white workers. African-American slavery had so diminished the dignity of manual labor that many southerners openly declared their contempt for white workers, calling them "white negroes" and proclaiming that the "*menial labor*" of a workingman was not a suitable occupation for a white man. The address urged white laborers to stand up for their rights and dignity by working to abolish slavery in Kentucky. "A great deal has been said and written . . . respecting the rights of property," proclaimed the address. "We think it high time something should be spoken and written, touching THE RIGHTS OF LABOR." It continued: "*Negro slavery should cease in Kentucky,* at the earliest possible period consistent with the interests of all the parties to be affected by the change."[30]

Not surprisingly, this opposition to slavery among many of Louisville's mechanics and laborers proved to be important in the success of antislavery politics in the city. Antislavery workers voted for a loose coalition of antislavery conservatives and workers, which emerged in the city during the 1840s. This coalition enjoyed considerable success at the polls in Louisville during the 1840s; by the end of the decade, some people were calling the slate of candidates supported by the antislavery coalition the Free White Laborers' ticket. In the ten elections for the state House of Representatives held during the 1840s, only twice did the voters of the city fail to elect at least one antislavery advocate to the General Assembly. In the early part of the decade, the city's voters thrice elected as mayor one of the city's most active antislavery supporters, David L. Beatty. And in 1843 and 1845, Louisville helped elect to Congress William P. Thomasson, an ardent antislavery activist. In 1846, Thomasson was one of only three southern congressmen who voted for the Wilmot Proviso, the controversial proposal to ban slavery from the western territories.[31]

In addition, during the 1840s antislavery politicians filled a host of less visible public offices in Louisville, both elective and appointive. In the year 1848 alone, for instance, antislavery supporters occupied three of the eight seats on the Louisville City Council. They were represented on the judicial bench by the judge of the criminal and circuit courts of Jefferson County, by the chancellor of the Louisville Chancery Court, and by one of the city magistrates. In addition, they held a number of minor appointive positions, including town marshal and coroner, tax assessor, street inspector, and constable. Given the number of public positions held by antislavery advocates in Louisville, it is no wonder that proslavery activist Elijah F. Nuttall, the Democratic politician who was defeated by Thomasson for Congress in 1845, looked on the success of the emancipationists in Louisville as proof that the city "care[d] nothing about your slave property" and that it was the "headquarters of abolitionism and emancipation" in Kentucky.[32]

However, during the late 1840s the growth of antislavery activity was not confined to Louisville. The free-labor arguments in vogue in Louisville held increasing appeal to many Kentuckians. John C. Young noticed this trend, observing in 1847 that "there seems to be an increase in disposition to emancipation on the ground of the superiority of free labor, and there is a real increase of light on that subject." The growth of antislavery would prove to be especially noticeable in the towns and cities of the commonwealth, where antislavery forces were guided by the same impulses as the Louisville emancipationists; in the mountain counties of the east, where support for slavery had never been strong; and in certain parts of the Bluegrass area, where slavery seemed to be increasingly irrelevant to the region's economy. Indeed, from the late 1840s to the late 1850s, antislavery ultimately proved itself to be stronger in the twin cities of Newport and Covington, located just across the Ohio River from Cincinnati, and in several mountain counties of the east, than it was in Louisville. Before the 1850s, however, emancipationists in Newport and Covington and in the mountains lacked the organizational and financial resources to compete with Louisville for the leadership of the antislavery movement in Kentucky.[33]

In view of the marked increase in opposition to slavery across the state, it is no wonder that many proslavery Kentuckians like Richard French, a longtime congressman from Clark County and a former Democratic candidate for governor, worried that "the slave question in K[entuck]y has taken deeper hold and awakens more concern than usual." Indeed, when observing the rising fortunes of the antislavery movement in Kentucky and the increased debate on slavery in the state, many believed that the day was not far off when Kentuckians would determine, once and for all, whether their state was going to follow the path to freedom or the road to perpetual slavery. As French put it, "Many . . . regard the crisis as at the door." This observation was truer than most people would have dared imagine.[34]

6

The Crossroads

The second half of the 1840s was a period of crisis in American politics. In 1846, the Mexican War introduced the most sectionally divisive issue since the Missouri crisis of 1819–1820: the question of whether slavery should exist in the southwestern territories that the United States hoped to win from Mexico. The issue quickly cut across the traditional partisan rivalries of Whigs and Democrats to call forth uncompromising sectional responses from virtually all politicians. In the North, many leaders urged their section to resist the imperious demands of southern politicians, who had long dominated the nation's political life. In the South, some whites began to talk seriously about the secession of the slaveholding states from the Union.

Amid this crisis, Kentuckians began an unusual odyssey. For a brief moment at the end of the decade, Kentuckians took time out from the national debate to talk, not about slavery in the territories or the secession of the South, but about the existence of slavery in their own state. Southerners had, on occasion, talked seriously about this subject before. Virginians had earnestly discussed the topic in the late 1820s and early 1830s, but since then genuine debate about the abolition of slavery had rarely been heard in the South. Certainly the topic had not again been discussed in the South with the intensity and the resolution that marked the debate in Kentucky during the late 1840s; nor, as it turned out, would southerners again seriously consider the topic until the last days of the Southern Confederacy during the Civil War.

The debate over slavery in Kentucky proved to be wide-ranging, not only as Kentuckians argued about whether slavery should be abolished, but also as the supporters and opponents of slavery debated among themselves how best to accomplish their differing purposes. In the end, proslavery forces won a significant victory, and the debate of the late 1840s proved to be a crossroads for the slavery controversy in Kentucky. The result of this debate made it clear to most white Kentuckians that increasing numbers of their fellow citizens either stood foursquare behind the peculiar institution or gave it their tentative support in view of mounting evidence that slavery in Kentucky was not declining in strength. Subsequently, the type of antislavery activity Kentuckians had known throughout the 1830s and 1840s virtually disappeared.

The occasion for this debate was the renewed effort to revise the state constitution. After a period of quiescence following the defeat of the convention question in 1838, the supporters of constitutional revision renewed their efforts. In the legislative session of 1845–46, a convention bill supported by antislavery legislators like Ira Root of Newport, David Brooks of Bracken County, and William E. Glover of Louisville passed the House by a large majority, only to fail by two votes after its second reading in the Senate. Finally, in the session of 1846–47, nine years after the constitutional referendum of 1838, both houses of the General Assembly passed a new convention bill by large majorities.[1]

Unlike the abortive effort nine years earlier, however, the idea of calling a constitutional convention had now become very popular in Kentucky, a fact demonstrated by the large majorities that approved it in two successive referenda in 1847 and 1848. In the referendum of 1847, 67.7 percent of the state's eligible voters cast their oral ballots in favor of a constitutional convention. When, as required by law, a second referendum on the convention issue was held in 1848, 72.8 percent of the voters expressed support for the convention. After fifty years of government under the Second Constitution, Kentuckians were again ready to revise the state's fundamental law.[2]

The question of what prompted Kentuckians to support constitutional reform in such large numbers troubled contemporaries and continues to vex historians. Some contemporary observers and modern historians have attributed the success of the convention movement in the 1840s to the renaissance of the state's antislavery movement. Walter N. Haldeman, the emancipationist editor of the *Louisville Courier,* exulted over the results of the election: "What great evil did the people feel pressing upon them to require the immense vote of 101,828 in favor of remodeling the Constitution, . . . if it was not the principle of Emancipation?" asked Haldeman. "Scarcely a solitary friend of the perpetuation of slavery can be found among the 101,828 votes in favor of a Convention. . . . There can be, and should be no mistake as to the sentiments of Kentucky." Some proslavery activists agreed with Haldeman's assessment. opposing the convention movement out of fear that a constitutional convention would abolish the peculiar institution.[3]

If such observations suggest that opposition to slavery was the primary factor promoting the convention movement, other evidence demonstrates additional forces at work. Having learned from defeat in the referendum of 1838, a number of leading antislavery reformers apparently believed that their cause should maintain a low profile during the initial stages of revising the constitution. Although antislavery supporters took an active role in promoting the cause of constitutional reform in the 1840s, many emancipationists—though not all—intentionally de-emphasized the slavery issue when they urged the legislature to approve the convention bill. As Cassius Clay explained to Salmon Chase in 1845, "We are willing to see the dissatisfaction with the present constitution on other grounds increase" until the time "when we [can] *array* our strength in favour of liberty." At that point, the emancipationists would "go in" to the convention "and carry it at once." Additionally, a sizable contingent of antislavery conservatives remained unconvinced that the state should revise its constitution and did not contribute their voice to the movement for constitutional reform. Among them were such antislavery stalwarts as John C. Young and Joseph R. Underwood, who believed that Kentuckians were not yet ready to enact a plan of emancipation and genuinely feared that a convention might make emancipation more difficult. This perception of public opinion was shared by many, if not most, of the state's ardent supporters of slavery: some proslavery supporters joined the convention movement in the late 1840s precisely because they believed that public opinion stood so firmly behind slavery that a popularly elected constitutional convention would enact tough new guarantees for the preservation of slavery.[4]

A number of other issues also encouraged Kentuckians to support constitutional reform. As had been the case in the late 1830s, much of the support for constitutional revision came from those who believed that the state's existing government was undemocratic, particularly the county court system. Moreover, events of the late 1830s and 1840s had prompted many Kentuckians to condemn certain other constitutional structures that seemed to make their state government undemocratic and unresponsive to the voters of the state. Many Kentuckians complained that the Second Constitution did not contain sufficient checks to curb the supposed fiscal irresponsibility of the state legislature. During the depression of 1837–43, the General Assembly had refused the demands of many Kentuckians for debtor relief and had insisted that Kentuckians tighten their belts and live within their means. At the same time, however, the legislature had seemingly indulged a passion for spendthrift appropriations bills, thereby greatly increasing the state's public debt and, in the opinion of many, hypocritically passing on the burden of its own fiscal irresponsibility to the taxpayers. By the late 1840s, many wanted to place some constitutional limitation on the ability of the legislature to increase the public debt. Others wanted to enact some constitutional protection for the state's common school fund, which the legislature had regularly expropriated during the depression as a source of funds for internal improvement projects.[5]

In addition, many Kentuckians believed that defects in the Second Constitution had created a system in which the distribution of public offices did not accurately reflect the political loyalties of the voters. Democratic politicians in particular were most insistent on this point. By 1849—the year when Kentucky's constitution would be rewritten—it had been fourteen years since the Democratic party had won a statewide election of any kind in Kentucky. Democrats loudly complained that much of their failure in Kentucky politics had been caused by defects in the state's constitutional system. The Second Constitution, they claimed, gave the General Assembly too much leeway in making up electoral districts for the General Assembly and for Congress, allowing Whigs to gerrymander Democrats out of their fair share of representation. Moreover, Democrats complained that under the Second Constitution, most public officials came to office by the appointment of the governor, many of whom enjoyed life tenure of office. These facts, Democrats charged, allowed the dominant Whig party to monopolize public office unfairly.[6]

It seems clear that a variety of forces impelled Kentuckians to support constitutional reform. But after the state's voters gave their final approval to the constitutional convention in August 1848, the issue of slavery quickly overshadowed most other issues as the state prepared to select delegates to the constitutional convention in an election scheduled for August 1849. During the fall of 1848, antislavery forces abandoned their earlier silence on the issue of slavery and openly came out in favor of taking some formal step toward emancipation in the new constitution. Now that it was certain that a constitutional convention would be held, some antislavery conservatives who had opposed the convention movement, like John C. Young, began speaking out on behalf of emancipation so that the right kind of candidates would be elected as delegates to the convention. And, as was so often the case in southern politics, the slightest hint of antislavery activity brought out proslavery advocates in droves to denounce the emancipationists. By the beginning of 1849, the issue of slavery had become so important in the campaign to elect delegates to the constitutional convention that the issue was causing a breakdown of the traditional Democratic and Whig party alignments in some parts of Kentucky, as antislavery and proslavery political organizations replaced the regular parties in many electoral contests.[7]

The supporters of slavery moved first to establish a separate political organization, holding a convention of the "Friends of Constitutional Reform" in February 1849. The official report of the convention struck a theme that would become very familiar to Kentuckians during the next year. The voters of Kentucky, declared the report, had given their overwhelming support to constitutional revision because they wanted to make their government more responsive to the voters of the state, not because they wanted to abolish slavery. It should be understood, they continued, that the people of Kentucky desired no change in the state constitution's provisions regarding slavery and that the Friends of Constitutional Reform "intend [to mount] a firm and decided resistance to any such change."[8]

Acting on the professed belief that other issues mattered more than slavery, the convention of the Friends of Constitutional Reform approved a platform promising to make the government of Kentucky more responsive to the white citizens of the state through the abolition of life tenure for public officials, a reduction in the number of appointive offices, quick payment of the existing public debt, a restriction in the ability of future legislatures to "contract debts," and the establishment of a sound "system of public instruction." Yet there could be no doubt that members of the convention were most concerned about the issue of slavery: nearly one-half of the platform was devoted to planks supporting the continued existence of slavery in Kentucky.[9]

To promote their cause, the Friends of Constitutional Reform further recommended that supporters should organize conventions in every county to nominate "candidates favorable to their views, and sustain them without regard to former party distinctions." Acting on this advice, proslavery forces in various counties of the state held meetings to nominate candidates for the convention. In many areas, these proslavery slates of candidates were indeed bipartisan "fusion" tickets that appealed to voters from both parties. In some of the larger counties, each of which would send more than one delegate to the convention, proslavery organizers made certain that candidates of both parties were placed on the ticket to emphasize its bipartisan nature. Jefferson, Fayette, Madison, Nelson, and Franklin Counties, among others, had fusion tickets.[10]

The state's antislavery forces began organizing a statewide political network at about the same time as the proslavery groups, although the emancipationists did not establish a formal political organization until three months after the convention of the Friends of Constitutional Reform. The antislavery reformers of Louisville, who had already formed a loose political coalition locally and who controlled the state's only newspaper wholly devoted to antislavery, played a key role in organizing the statewide emancipation movement for the campaign of 1849. In December 1848, a group of eleven prominent Louisvillians headed by Samuel S. Nicholas, the venerable chancellor of the Louisville Chancery Court, issued an antislavery pamphlet, *Slave Emancipation in Kentucky,* which proposed that the emancipationists hold a statewide convention in the spring to organize an antislavery party for the election. At planning meetings in Louisville in January and February of 1849, emancipationists decided to hold the state convention in Frankfort during April. They also appointed a nine-member Corresponding and Executive Committee on Emancipation—all but one of whom had been co-authors of *Slave Emancipation in Kentucky*—to promote antislavery sentiment throughout the state. This committee did its job well: it raised funds for the cause, published several pamphlets, sent speakers from Louisville to address antislavery meetings in other parts of the state, and persistently promoted the upcoming statewide emancipation convention. These efforts were followed in the late winter and early spring of 1849 by antislavery meetings across the state.[11]

In February, the movement received the important endorsement of Henry Clay, who announced in a public letter that it was his "duty" to place his "sentiments" about slavery "permanently upon record." Recalling that he had advocated emancipation in the campaign for delegates to the last state constitutional convention some fifty years earlier, Clay's words rang clear: "how deeply do I lament that a system [of emancipation] . . . had not been then established! If it had been, the State would now be nearly rid of all [its] slaves." Clay proposed as a solution to the problem of slavery the traditional scheme of *post nati* emancipation and colonization. Although Clay's plan of emancipation was hardly new or radical when compared to those offered by abolitionists like Fee or even those offered by Cassius Clay and some of the Louisville emancipationists, it resounded through the state like a thunderbolt. Clay's letter was denounced by

proslavery ideologues—some of whom demanded that he should re-
sign his seat in the United States Senate—and praised by Kentucky's
antislavery advocates, who were greatly encouraged by the support
of the state's most powerful and influential politician.[12]

The specific plan of emancipation that Clay offered, however,
did not much help the state's antislavery forces, who discovered in
the spring of 1849 that they would have to overcome serious internal
divisions before they could come together as a cohesive political group.
Most of Kentucky's antislavery supporters—the handful of the state's
abolitionists excepted—would have agreed with Henry Clay that any
plan of emancipation should be of the gradual, *post nati* variety with
which Kentuckians had long been familiar. There remained, however,
a number of differences among the state's antislavery supporters over
how slavery should be ended and what the antislavery movement
hoped to accomplish under the new constitution. Some antislavery
reformers, including Cassius Clay and a number of emancipationists
in Louisville, asserted that voters of the state considered colonization
impractical and that any proposed scheme of emancipation that included colonization would cause the antislavery movement to be defeated. But such arguments were anathema to most of the state's
antislavery advocates, who vowed that colonization must be part of
any emancipation scheme. Another point of division concerned the
timing of emancipation. If the state were to declare that all slaves born
after a certain date would be freed upon reaching adulthood, which
date should be chosen? Should the process of emancipation begin right
away, or should a more remote date be chosen, a date that might not
arrive for years to come?[13]

A number of the state's antislavery advocates even questioned
whether it would be wise to place any sort of plan of emancipation
in the new constitution. They argued that few voters in the year 1849
would be willing to support a plan of emancipation, even if this plan
were the "prospective" kind that would not begin operating for many
years. Under these circumstances, a more immediate and practical
goal for the antislavery movement would be to establish in the new
constitution procedural mechanisms by which a plan of emancipation could more easily be enacted when the state's voters were ready

for emancipation. Some antislavery supporters hoped to place in the constitution a provision for a referendum on the subject of emancipation, which would be held at some fixed time after the implementation of the new constitution. Other antislavery supporters hoped to place in the new constitution a so-called "open clause," a procedure through which individual amendments could be added to the state's fundamental law without calling a formal constitutional convention to review the entire state constitution. Such a procedure would enable antislavery forces to push for emancipation without having the issue entangled with other, controversial areas of constitutional reform.[14]

Some of the state's antislavery supporters were not willing to go even this far. Although Kentucky's antislavery movement, on the whole, seemed increasingly radical in the late 1840s because people like Cassius Clay and the Louisville emancipationists had become so prominent in the movement, in truth there were many traditional antislavery conservatives whose views about reform had not changed since the 1830s. They argued that slavery was dying of its own cancerous nature and that wise statesmanship consisted mostly of leaving slavery alone to die in peace. Kentuckians should, however, prevent politicians from artificially resuscitating slavery from the throes of death. In this view, antislavery groups should continue to insist that slave importation be prohibited; perhaps they could strengthen this ban by enshrining the principles of nonimportation in the state's new constitution.[15]

For most of the state's antislavery advocates—even those who wanted to place a definite plan of emancipation in the constitution—the cause of nonimportation took on added urgency in February 1849, when the supporters of slavery, after years of unsuccessful efforts, secured the repeal of the Law of 1833 by the General Assembly. Opposition to nonimportation on the part of proslavery ideologues and residents of southwestern Kentucky had been growing steadily during the 1840s, and in recent years several sessions of the General Assembly had come close to repealing the law. The decisive votes for repeal, however, came from those who wanted to discourage the state's antislavery movement by abrogating its principle legislative accomplishment. Instead of being discouraged, however, emancipationists were outraged by the repeal of nonimportation, as were many other Kentuckians who had little connection with the organized antislavery movement. This made the repeal of the Law of 1833 seem like a boon to the state's antislavery movement. Hundreds of Kentuckians who had previously shown little interest in supporting antislavery candidates to the constitutional convention now expressed an interest in voting for emancipationists who would entrench the principle of nonimportation in the new state constitution.[16]

This heightened interest in the antislavery movement, however, was a mixed blessing. The entrance into the antislavery movement of zealous supporters of nonimportation who also opposed a more definite plan of emancipation added even more discord to a movement already rent by internal divisions. These divisions were readily apparent when 157 delegates gathered in Frankfort in April 1849 for the convention to establish a statewide political organization for the emancipationists, a meeting which would eventually become known in Kentucky history as the Frankfort Convention. Among the delegates were such notables as John G. Fee, Cassius M. Clay, William P. Thomasson, John C. Young, John D. Paxton, Robert J. Breckinridge, and Stuart Robinson. By the time the convention gathered, delegates had arrayed themselves into two loose groupings in regard to the convention's platform. One group hoped to place in the new constitution some definite scheme of emancipation; the other sought only to establish in the new constitution the principle of nonimportation and some mechanism through which the people might eventually abolish slavery without having to call another constitutional convention. These two groups became evident during the discussion of the report of the convention's platform committee. The twenty-three–member platform committee consisted of a broad cross section of the state's antislavery movement, including conservative activists like Clay and Thomasson and, in John Fee, at least one outright abolitionist. Nevertheless, the committee was dominated by traditional antislavery conservatives who returned to the convention a report that strongly reflected their views. Although the report proclaimed slavery an evil that should not be "increased or perpetuated," the committee pointedly refrained from urging the immediate enactment of a plan of gradual emancipation. The committee's report recommended only that emancipation candidates support the entrenchment of nonimportation in the new constitution and the incorporation of either the open clause or a provision for a referendum on the subject of slavery at a later date.[17]

After the platform committee presented its report to the convention, seven members of the platform committee—nearly a third of its membership—publicly expressed their dissatisfaction with the report. The most important public dissent came from the two committee members from Louisville and Jefferson County. William L. Breckinridge, the brother of Robert J. Breckinridge and an influential antislavery reformer in his own right, proposed an amendment declaring that slavery "ought to be removed under the new constitution, by some scheme of gradual emancipation and colonization." Breckinridge's amendment, however, was too radical for most members of the convention, and it was soon replaced by a substitute amendment offered by another member of the Louisville and Jefferson County delegation, William P. Thomasson. The substitute amendment, like Breckinridge's original amendment, proposed that the constitutional convention should establish a definite scheme of emancipation, but added that this emancipation scheme should not go into effect immediately.[18]

Debate on the Thomasson amendment occupied most of the convention's time. Supporters of the amendment generally said that the voters of the state would not support the emancipationists if they took "half-way stands" on the most important issue of the day. The committee's report, declared William M.O. Smith of Bourbon County, "will dishearten our friends by its timidity, and throw a gloom over the prospects of the whole party." "The people incline to a bold fight," agreed John F. Holloway of Boyle County, "and they will regard any compromise as a virtual yielding up of the question." On the other hand, critics of the Thomasson amendment maintained that the voters of Kentucky, including many antislavery advocates, would not support a platform as radical as the ones proposed by Breckinridge and Thomasson. "The gentlemen of Louisville or

Jefferson [County], may be far in advance of us," proclaimed Ben Monroe, the president of the Kentucky Colonization Society and the chairman of the platform committee. "The amendment may suit them—[but] it would destroy us. . . . Our work must be done slowly and only after a radical change in public sentiment. If we raise our banner too high, . . . I fear we will do nothing" in the election.[19]

By the second day of the convention, most delegates to the convention obviously agreed with Monroe's assessment, and Thomasson withdrew his amendment to allow Samuel S. Nicholas of Louisville to offer a compromise measure. But the Nicholas amendment proved to be a poorly written, muddled effort that nearly everyone seems to have regarded as inferior to the committee report itself, and the amendment was tabled on the motion of a member of the Louisville delegation. However, compromise was eventually reached. Samuel Shy of Lexington and John F. Holloway, both decided opponents of the committee report, secured slight changes in the wording of the platform, making it so ambiguous that it could be read to support the enactment of either the open clause or a definite scheme of emancipation. Kentucky's emancipationists, the platform declared, upheld "the complete power in the people of Kentucky to enforce and perfect, in or under the new Constitution, a system of gradual prospective emancipation of slaves."[20]

In contrast to the heated discussion of the platform, a resolution establishing a formal, statewide organization to support antislavery candidates for the constitutional convention was passed almost as an afterthought. The convention established a Central Executive Committee, which was to appoint county-level committees to work for the election of antislavery candidates, to coordinate communications between these committees, and to arrange for pro-emancipation speakers throughout the state. Additionally, the committee would be responsible for printing and circulating emancipationist literature in Kentucky. Perhaps as a measure of conciliation to the supporters of the Thomasson amendment and in recognition of the organizational skills of the Louisville emancipationists, Ben Monroe of the Kentucky Colonization Society successfully urged the convention to adopt Louisville's Corresponding and Executive Committee on

Emancipation as the state Central Executive Committee. According to one observer, however, Monroe also "expressed the hope, that no document would be published by the committee, except such as were written by our own citizens. He was decidedly opposed to foreign interference in this matter." Although the Frankfort Convention chose no name for the formal political organization it established, it was known popularly as the Emancipation party.[21]

With the establishment of a state antislavery party to oppose the proslavery fusion tickets already in existence, the stage was set for the most extensive and wide-ranging debate on slavery in Kentucky's history. Emancipationists and proslavery activists alike sent out their best orators and campaign literature across the state. The two groups held rallies to stir up their supporters, and representatives of the two groups occasionally met in public debate. The opponents of slavery spoke of the ruinous effects of slavery on the state's social and economic systems and emphasized that slavery was undermining the well-being of the average white farmer and laborer. Supporters of slavery argued strongly that no acceptable alternative to slavery existed because African colonization was impractical and because no self-respecting white Kentuckian would consent to live among a large population of free blacks. Proslavery activists also told the voters that African-American slavery elevated the status of the average white man by providing the state with black workers to perform the menial tasks that would otherwise have to be done by whites of small means. "It would ill suit . . . our spirited Southern men, without property," argued one proslavery man, "to become shoe-blacks, waiters, and servants of all sorts, who must not sit at the same table with their employers or masters, and must hold themselves in submission to them."[22]

By the beginning of the summer of 1849, the debate on slavery had spread to many parts of the state. In June, Benjamin Coates, a Pennsylvania merchant traveling through the state, reported that "the Emancipation question is being discussed in almost every part of the State that I have been in. . . . It is more exciting than I had supposed and is *the* question of the day overriding all others. . . . It is the principal topic in stage coach and tavern throughout the state."

Coates added, however, that he believed he had "been in some of the strongest Emancipation Counties" and that he could not vouch for the strength of the slavery question in other parts of the state. This was an important qualification, for although there is direct evidence of organized antislavery activity in nearly half the counties of the state and although the debate over slavery undoubtedly extended beyond those counties, in some portions of the state slavery was hardly an issue at all.[23]

In those places where slavery was discussed, the debate took on the same sort of emotional intensity that, by the late 1840s, so often accompanied the discussion of slavery in the United States. This spirit of intensity had been building ever since the voters called for a constitutional convention. During the second, three-day referendum on the convention proposal in 1848, for instance, Kentuckians in the Bluegrass area learned that a group of between fifty-five and seventy-five slaves, armed and led by two white men, had escaped from Fayette, Bourbon, and Mason Counties. That news electrified the state's white residents with the dread of slave insurrection and caused hundreds of volunteer slave hunters to set off in pursuit of the fugitives. After several days, most of these slaves were surrounded in a hemp field north of Cynthiana; after a gun battle in which one slave was killed and a slave hunter was wounded, most of the fugitives were captured. In the following months, there was a minor wave of hysteria in the Bluegrass as whites uncovered other alleged plots of mass slave escapes and insurrection. Public meetings in Lexington and other Bluegrass towns called for "the detection and punishment of abolitionists and others enticing slaves from their owners," and a Lexington newspaper urged that "a more severe example should be made" of those "abolitionists in our midst . . . whose business it is to tamper with and run off our slaves."[24]

Proslavery advocates were not surprised at such events. They firmly believed—as, indeed, did most Kentuckians—that discussion of the issue of slavery was dangerous, for it allegedly encouraged slaves to become restive. Proslavery advocates believed that the events of recent months logically resulted from the discussion of a dangerous issue. What was one to expect, asked one supporter of slavery, when emancipationists like Robert J. Breckinridge were "going about making speeches, the tendency of which is to incite our negroes to cut our throats, and to burn our houses and villages"? The existence of such attitudes among many Kentuckians encouraged acts of condemnation and violence against antislavery supporters, acts which must certainly have suppressed support for emancipation among many voters. For instance, not only did the General Assembly repeal the Law of 1833 in an effort to discourage the state's antislavery movement, but the state House of Representatives also declared, by a vote of ninety-three to zero, that "we, the Representatives of the people of Kentucky, are opposed to abolition or emancipation of slavery in any form or shape whatever, except as now provided for by the Constitution and laws of the State."[25]

As the election of delegates to the constitutional convention approached, the spirit of condemnation and violence against antislavery forces increased. In June, Cassius Clay—although not himself a candidate for the convention—traveled to Foxtown in northern Madison County to participate in a debate with Squire Turner, a local proslavery candidate to the constitutional convention. When Clay made remarks that several of Turner's relatives found insulting, they set upon Clay with pistols, knives, and clubs. Clay was stabbed in the abdomen, but remarkably he wrenched free from his assailants, grabbed a bowie knife, and stabbed Squire Turner's son to death. Clay survived the attack—as he would all others—but was incapacitated for months. Another antislavery man—Benedict Austin of Paducah—was not as lucky as Clay. Austin, an emancipationist candidate for the constitutional convention, was shot and killed by his opponent, Judge James Campbell, during a campaign debate in Paducah during July.[26]

Such incidents of violence and condemnation continued during the election itself. In some places, Kentucky's system of oral voting encouraged acts of retribution against those who voted for emancipationist candidates. Antislavery advocates in Louisville, for instance, charged that several voters were openly "beaten for voting according to their sentiments." Moreover, on the second day of the election in Louisville, a gun battle broke out in the city's first electoral ward between proslavery supporters and a group of antislavery election observers that included Paul Seymour of the Louisville *Examiner*. A proslavery supporter and a small child were shot in the battle. In Georgetown, the vote of Howard Malcom, president of Georgetown College, for an antislavery candidate caused such excitement that the Board of Trustees of the college asked for and received Malcom's resignation.[27]

The atmosphere of desperate anxiety that surrounded the campaign grew worse with the arrival in Kentucky of the epidemic of cholera then spreading throughout the United States. During the summer, Kentuckians watched with justified anxiety as cholera—a disease that killed half of those who caught it—swept across the state. As hundreds of people died in towns like Lexington, Maysville, and Paris, many became understandably preoccupied with the epidemic and, like Judge William B. Kinkead of Frankfort, opened their daily mail or newspapers "with trembling" lest they discover "among the victims of the disease some near relation or friend." Cholera did claim some prominent victims. Governor John J. Crittenden became ill during the epidemic, as did Robert J. Breckinridge, who was running as an antislavery candidate for the constitutional convention from Fayette County. Both men, however, recovered from their illness. Aaron K. Wooley, a proslavery candidate for the convention from Fayette County and the son-in-law of Robert Wickliffe, was not so fortunate. He died of cholera only three days before the election.[28]

Wrongly believing that cholera was caused by a poisonous "miasma" from dying and decaying vegetation, doctors advised Kentuckians to avoid crowded places where there was no circulation of air and to seek shelter from the poisonous gases during the heat of the afternoon. Visitors traveling through Kentucky during that fateful summer reported a strange stillness across the state as hundreds of people took the doctors' advice by abandoning their normal activities or fleeing the cities for the healthful countryside. These circumstances prompted those who participated in the campaign for delegates to approach the contest with even more seriousness and intensity than always accompanied the debate on slavery. Given the prevailing opinions about the causes of cholera, people attending campaign debates held in the heat of the afternoon sun—or meetings in crowded, poorly ventilated rooms—had good reason to believe they were risking their lives for a cause they believed in. Many people were apparently not up to this challenge: during the election in August, voter turnout in cities like Louisville, Lexington, and Frankfort was unusually low, and some observers blamed the fear of cholera for keeping hundreds from the polls.[29]

Because of incomplete election returns, the exact vote tally for this election is difficult to determine today—as it was in 1849. It is, however, possible to say that emancipationist candidates for the convention collectively gathered nearly fifteen thousand votes and that at least two emancipationist candidates were elected to the convention. Emancipationist candidates for the convention did quite well in some areas. They carried the mountain counties of Knox and Harlan with 74.1 percent of the vote and the city of Newport with 59.9 percent. Emancipationists ran well in the city of Louisville and the western counties of Logan and Crittenden, winning 45.2, 45.5, and 42.3 percent of the vote in those places respectively. Overall, emancipationists won 35.1 percent of the vote in those counties for which statistics are known. It is difficult to determine the size of this vote in relation to the statewide vote because election statistics for many counties are unavailable and the party affiliations of some candidates in other counties are unclear. However, if only the 14,801 votes which are known to have been won by emancipationists are considered, it would appear that altogether the emancipationists received at least 9.7 percent of the total statewide vote, a conservative estimate based on the total number of ballots cast in the sixty counties for which electoral statistics are known and the total number of eligible voters in the other forty counties of the state.[30]

The election results are subject to two different interpretations. On one hand, given the time and the place in which the emancipationists were running for election, their showing was quite remarkable. The proportion of the vote won by the Emancipation party, for instance, exceeded the vote won nationally by the Liberty and Free-Soil parties in three of the four presidential elections held from 1840 to 1852, and it was close to the 10.1 percent won for the Free-Soil party by former President Martin Van Buren in 1848. Compared to this national vote won by a former president only one year earlier, the Kentucky emancipationists certainly made a respectable showing by winning the support of 9.7 percent of the voters in a slave state.[31]

On the other hand, Kentucky's emancipationists came nowhere near accomplishing their stated objective—winning control of the constitutional convention—and, thus, their efforts in the election could be considered a failure, even by their own standards. Although the proslavery activists elected as delegates to the constitutional convention remained worried about the supposed strength of antislavery in Kentucky, the popular perception of the election results was dominated by the striking failure of the emancipationists. After all, the movement against slavery in 1849 had been supported by some of Kentucky's leading citizens. It had been endorsed by both of Kentucky's United States senators—including Kentucky's favorite son, Henry Clay—by several current and former members of the state judiciary, by the state's superintendent of public instruction, and by numerous current and former members of the General Assembly. In addition, the movement had been supported by many other leaders of public opinion, including several college presidents, newspaper editors, and prominent ministers. Despite the efforts of these eminent people, the emancipationists had failed abjectly. Most antebellum Kentuckians believed that this failure indicated that it would be politically impossible to implement any scheme of emancipation for many years to come.[32]

This perception was heightened by the supposed impracticality of every known plan of emancipation. Throughout the antebellum era, white Kentuckians had insisted that the state's slaves could not be freed en masse and still remain in Kentucky. Yet by the late 1840s there appeared to be no alternative to abolition "on the soil" except perpetual slavery. Kentuckians had long harbored doubts about the feasibility of African colonization; by the mid-1840s, these doubts were so prevalent in Kentucky that some antislavery reformers like Cassius Clay had urged the emancipationists to abandon colonization as a hopeless cause. Clay and others argued that a more fruitful course would be to educate the voters about the safety of emancipation on the soil. The campaign for delegates to the constitutional convention had undoubtedly reinforced the perception that colonization and, hence, emancipation were impossible, as proslavery ideologues incessantly argued that there was no practical alternative to perpetual slavery. Ironically, the state's antislavery forces, with their inability to agree among themselves about which plan of emancipation was most practical, probably contributed to the popular perception that emancipation was impossible. This belief had become so widespread by the end of the campaign of 1849 that several observers claimed that this perception was the primary cause of the emancipationists' stunning defeat.[33]

After the election of the delegates, the convention itself shored up slavery with important new constitutional buttresses, contributing greatly to the popular belief that it had become impossible to emancipate the state's slaves. At least a third of the delegates elected to the convention had run as proslavery candidates, and most of the others were alarmed at the strength of antislavery sentiment in Kentucky and wanted to design a constitution that would bolster slavery. John L. Ballinger of Lincoln County spoke for many delegates when he proclaimed to the convention that "we have come here to protect, and . . . to perpetuate to posterity" the institution of slavery. Shortly after the convention opened on October 1, 1849, the delegates laid aside the convention's other business to expound upon their views concerning slavery. For the next two and a half weeks of the twelve-week-long convention, the greater portion of the convention's time was taken up with discussions of slavery. Although the delegates eventually went on to discuss other issues, they never really put the slavery question aside. Indeed, throughout the convention, the behavior of most delegates was marked by what one frustrated delegate termed a "morbid sensibility . . . on the slave question." In nearly every question before the convention, delegates scrutinized their actions to determine what effect such actions would have on the preservation of slavery.[34]

Yet if nearly all of the delegates agreed that they should act to strengthen slavery in Kentucky, there existed no firm consensus about how to do this. Two general approaches to the preservation of slavery emerged during the convention. Some delegates believed that the exigency of the times called for radical measures to protect slavery and urged the convention to enact measures ranging from the restriction of the political rights of some whites to an outright prohibition of all forms of emancipation, including the right of individual masters to manumit their slaves and the power of the legislature to enact a statewide plan of compensated emancipation as provided for in the old constitution. Other proslavery delegates, however, believed that with few exceptions, the old constitution had provided adequate guarantees for the preservation of slavery in Kentucky. They argued that radical proposals for the protection of slavery would be counterproductive and that the convention was pursuing a dangerous course in considering such proposals. The voters of the state had placed the control of the convention in the hands of proslavery forces because the supporters of slavery—unlike the emancipationists—had promised not to tinker with the existing slave clause of the old constitution.

Several delegates saw this promise as a double-edged sword: if the voters did not want slavery to be abolished at present, neither did they want to eliminate every possible means of emancipation. They wanted to preserve an escape clause in the constitution, a mechanism whereby the state could rid itself of slaves should the presence of black laborers become intolerable. If the convention were to remove any possibility for emancipation, or if the convention were to place restrictions on the political rights of those potentially favoring antislavery, the delegates' imprudent actions might cause voters to repudiate the new constitution and throw their support to the emancipationists. After reviewing a proposal restricting the political rights of people living in cities like Louisville and Covington, where opposition to slavery was widespread, John W. Stevenson of Kenton County indignantly asked, "How can we, who are pro-slavery men, go home to our people and explain this outrage upon their rights?" The people of Kentucky had proven themselves willing to uphold the rights of slaveholders by electing proslavery delegates to the convention, Stevenson continued, "and shall now a proslavery convention . . . say to those gallant defenders of their rights, that . . . we cannot trust you? . . . Do you not know that the emancipationists . . . would make it a trumpet-note of attack against the result of our labors?"[35]

Throughout the convention many warnings like this were sounded, and some of them were heeded. Several measures adopted by the convention clearly revealed the work of delegates concerned that immoderation might breathe new life into the emancipation movement. Yet the final handiwork of the delegates contained so many important new measures protecting slavery that most Kentuckians came to believe that the convention had removed nearly every possibility for emancipation in Kentucky.

Both approaches to the protection of slavery were evident in the report of the convention's committee on slavery, delivered ten days after the opening of the convention. The committee recommended that the convention adopt most of the language of the existing slave clause of the Constitution of 1799, which had come, in turn, from the Constitution of 1792. Under the committee's proposal, the General Assembly would again be prohibited from emancipating the state's slaves unless it either secured the permission of the slaves' owners or paid the owners a "full equivalent" of the slaves' value. The legislature would again be required to pass special laws allowing slave owners to emancipate their bondsmen, and it would retain the power to pass laws requiring slave owners to "abstain" from injuring their slaves. Once more, the General Assembly would be able to pass laws limiting the importation of slaves for resale, although it would again be prevented from passing laws prohibiting immigrants from bringing their slaves with them.[36]

In addition to retaining these provisions, however, the committee recommended the addition of several new measures, all of which would strengthen the institution of slavery. Most of them were intended to make emancipation more difficult and to restrict the growth of the free black population of Kentucky. One of these provisions was directed squarely at the emancipationists' contention that slaveholders had no property rights over unborn slaves and that the state could therefore free the children of slave mothers at birth without having to compensate the owners of the mothers. The committee's report recommended that the General Assembly should have no "greater power over the after born children of slave mothers than over the slaves then in being." In other words, any plan of *post nati* emancipation enacted by the legislature would have to include a provision for compensating the slave owners. Another proposal would forbid the legislature from authorizing private manumissions without making some provision for removing the freed slaves from the state. Two other proposals would give the General Assembly the power to deport the state's existing population of "free negroes and mulattos" and would require the state to imprison any other free blacks who migrated to Kentucky subsequent to the passage of the constitution.[37]

Even these provisions were not enough to satisfy some supporters of slavery, who immediately challenged the committee's report. Some delegates argued that the proposed slave clause did not do enough to protect slavery from the threat allegedly posed by the free black population. Other delegates feared that slavery would not be safe as long as the General Assembly retained the power to emancipate the state's slaves through compensation. Still other delegates, perhaps the most insistent of them all, wanted to establish a constitutional right for the citizens of Kentucky to import slaves for their own use. Amid the throng of voices calling for even stronger measures to protect the institution of slavery, the committee's frustrated chairman, David Meriwether of Jefferson County—himself no timid supporter of slavery—urged the delegates to act with prudence. If the convention were to adopt strident measures, he asked, "will not this . . . be a powerful argument in the mouth of the abolitionist? Will he not rouse the feelings of the community, and induce them . . . to vote against the constitution?"[38]

After a week of debate on the committee's report, there was no consensus about its disposition and the convention set aside the report to consider other matters. But, of course, there was no end to the slavery question, and through the middle weeks of the convention, as the delegates debated such matters as legislative reapportionment and the constitution's amendatory procedure, proslavery extremists seemed increasingly unwilling to moderate their demands that strong measures be taken to protect slavery. Although many of

the delegates had been elected as reformers pledged to make the government of Kentucky more responsive to the people, some of these
reformers proved all too willing to abandon that cause when the preservation of slavery was at stake, denying, for instance, the use of secret
ballots in elections and making it more difficult for voters to change
the constitution for fear of free expression of the popular will on the
subject of slavery.[39]

The climax of the effort to take radical steps to protect slavery
came in early December, near the end of the convention, as the delegates were drafting the new constitution's bill of rights. On the motion of future United States Senator Garrett Davis of Bourbon
County, the delegates added to the third section of the bill of rights
an amendment proclaiming that "the right of property is before and
higher than any constitutional sanction; and the right of the owner
of a slave to such slave, and its increase, is the same, and as inviolable
as the right of the owner, of any property whatever." In unmistakable
language, the Davis amendment declared that slave owners had an
"inviolable . . . right" to the "increase" of their slave property, thereby
insuring that the new constitution would prohibit any scheme of
post nati emancipation not including a provision for the compensation of slave owners.[40]

The Davis amendment also served as a defining statement of
the extent of the delegates' support for slavery. In the weeks preced-
ing the passage of the Davis amendment, the delegates had periodi-
cally debated the theoretical limits of the convention's power and,
indirectly, the limits of majority rule in Kentucky. Was there a limit
to the authority of the convention and, hence, to that of the citizens? If
a popularly elected constitutional convention spoke with the sovereign
voice of the people of the state, could such a convention abolish slavery or confiscate any other forms of property without providing compensation to the owners or was it legally and morally bound to respect
the property rights of slaveholders? Some delegates insisted that, as a
matter of democratic principle, there could be no limitations placed
on the ultimate authority of the people of Kentucky, as expressed
through a constitutional convention. The citizens of the state, speaking through their representatives meeting in convention, were free to

redesign the framework of government and law in any way they saw fit, even if that meant the abridgment of legally sanctioned property rights. Other delegates adamantly disagreed and wanted to place within the new constitution an unambiguous statement of their views. In the words of one delegate, they wanted there to be "no misunderstanding with regard to this point: . . . the power to destroy property without compensation or the consent of the owner does not exist"—even in the sovereign authority of the people. The delegates found such a statement in the Davis amendment, with its declaration that the right to own slaves was "before and higher than any constitutional sanction."[41]

After the passage of the Davis amendment in early December, the delegates again took up the troublesome issue of the constitution's slave clause, but this time the convention began to pursue a more moderate course. Some delegates who had earlier asked the convention to take strong, affirmative measures to protect slavery now seemed ready to compromise. Those who wanted the convention to take stronger actions to limit the growth of the free black population and to take away the legislature's ability to enact a plan of compensated emancipation were mollified somewhat by the passage of a substitute for the first section of the slave clause. This substitute section, offered by Ninian E. Gray of Christian County, incorporated most of the language of the slave clause of the Constitution of 1799 and added a requirement for the General Assembly to pay for the deportation outside of the state of any slaves the legislature freed through a scheme of compensated emancipation. Gray argued that this measure would not only work against the accumulation of free blacks should the state ever decide to emancipate its slaves, it would also likely make compensated emancipation itself prohibitively expensive.[42]

Comparative moderation also characterized the convention's handling of the slavery committee's proposal that authority to regulate slave importation should be left in the hands of the legislature. Moderation on this issue was not easy to maintain, for there was a large and persistent group of delegates—mostly Democrats—who wanted to guarantee the right of the citizens of Kentucky to import slaves for their own use. They argued that unless the right to import slaves was guaranteed in the constitution, the legislature could again prohibit slave importation, thus limiting the ownership of slaves to Bluegrass "aristocrats," who would grow rich by selling their slaves at inflated prices. A resumption of nonimportation would also limit the ability of the average farmer to advance his social and economic position through the purchase of slaves. In addition, some delegates resented the implicit message that nonimportation sent to the rest of the nation—that the uninhibited growth of slavery in Kentucky was harmful to the state. If slavery was the blessing that most of the delegates took it to be, asked William D. Mitchell of Oldham County, "why should we throw [up] any obstacle to its successful operation?" Elijah Nuttall of Henry County echoed these sentiments: slavery had created "the most enlightened, the richest, and the most cultivated people upon the face of God Almighty's earth," he argued. "Slavery is not an evil, and I want rather more of it."[43]

Other delegates—mostly Whigs—wanted to leave the issue of slave importation in the hands of the state legislature, where it had rested for the past fifty-seven years. These delegates argued that changing the constitutional provision on slave importation would align large segments of voters against the new constitution and possibly drive them to emancipationism. Moreover, re-enacting the old provision on slave importation would pose no immediate threat either to the existence of slavery or to the ability of Kentuckians to import slaves, for the legislature's earlier repeal of the Law of 1833 would likely stand for years to come. These arguments ultimately prevailed, and the convention left the question of slave importation in the hands of the General Assembly.[44]

The convention ended its work on December 20, having made it harder for the people of Kentucky to enact a plan of emancipation and, indeed, having declared that slavery enjoyed an exalted status in Kentucky—a status "before and higher than any constitutional sanction." In one of their last acts, the delegates approved a report that summarized the convention's work and gave a public explanation of their actions. In this report, the delegates announced that they had acted from the assumption that slavery was not an evil, as generations of Kentuckians had insisted it was. Rather, slavery was a positive good, a "great element of wealth, and social and political power, [which] will remain undisturbed and secure, so long as this constitution shall continue the paramount law of the land." Indeed, the delegates had gone so far in trying to protect slavery that, according to one modern legal historian, their handiwork was the most strongly proslavery state constitution yet written in the United States, a document that was the "culmination" of "the process of shoring up slavery's security in the [southern] states . . . which had been going on since the Revolution."[45]

This fact was not lost on the people of Kentucky. The state's Third Constitution convinced many Kentuckians that slavery had become more or less a permanent fixture in their state. This was the opinion of Samuel Freeman Miller, a young attorney from Knox County who was destined to serve a long and distinguished career in the United States Supreme Court. Miller recalled later that "the new constitution of Kentucky . . . fixed slavery more firmly than ever in the people; and left me no reason to suppose that any policy for eradicating slavery, would ever be adopted in Kentucky in my life time." Miller's opinion was echoed by Henry Clay, who noted publicly that the events of 1849 in Kentucky had helped convince him "that no safe mode of gradual emancipation by the operation of law can terminate in any one of the States the existence of slavery much, if any sooner than it will be terminated by the operation of natural causes." One of Clay's most ardent admirers, Abraham Lincoln— who spent two weeks near Frankfort during the constitutional convention—agreed with Clay's assessment, concluding that the results of the debate on slavery in Kentucky in 1849 had national significance: "There is no peaceful extinction of slavery in prospect for us," Lincoln declared in 1855. "The signal failure of Henry Clay, and other good and great men, in 1849, to effect any thing in favor of gradual emancipation in Kentucky, together with a thousand other signs, extinguishes that hope utterly."[46]

For Kentuckians who had always pictured slavery as a necessary evil, the seemingly indisputable evidence that slavery was to be a permanent fixture in Kentucky did not cause them to renounce the belief that slavery was, in the abstract, an evil. However, the idea that slavery was not dying did encourage many Kentuckians to embrace the peculiar institution more tightly. Most white Kentuckians still acknowledged that, according to the abstract principles of justice, all people should be free. They still declared that if the Negro and the Caucasian races had been confined to their own homelands, as God and Nature had intended, it would be best for each race to have the freedom to govern its affairs as it saw fit. But many Kentuckians now believed that blacks and whites were fated to live together in Kentucky. Under these circumstances, slavery—an institution perhaps wrong in the abstract—served the useful function of controlling the Negro race and providing sustenance to blacks and whites alike. And many white Kentuckians argued that such a practical institution should be protected from meddling northerners who did not understand the realities of life among Negroes.[47]

The most immediate effect of this new way of looking at slavery was a marked increase in Kentucky of a mode of political activity that historian William J. Cooper has called the "politics of slavery." In the years before 1850, there had always been room in Kentucky politics for people espousing a cautious, conservative brand of antislavery, like Henry Clay and Joseph R. Underwood. There had always been a degree of acceptance and even success for certain political causes supported by antislavery reformers, such as nonimportation and constitutional reform. After 1850, however, mainstream antislavery politics and public debate on emancipation nearly disappeared in Kentucky as Whig and Democratic politicians alike rushed headlong into the politics of slavery. Further, in the 1850s most political issues were considered at least partly by the criterion of how they affected slavery. The popularity of slavery became so great that competing politicians often tried to win favor among the voters through a game of "one-upmanship," as each candidate tried to portray his opponent as "soft" on the issue of slavery while proclaiming himself to be the true friend of slavery.[48]

Defeat demoralized a large segment of the state's antislavery movement. The movement disintegrated soon after the election of delegates to the constitutional convention in August 1849. Although in the first weeks following the election, some members of the Central Executive Committee of the Emancipation party and the editors of the Louisville *Examiner* talked hopefully of continuing their fight for antislavery and of making the Emancipation party a permanent political organization, it was soon apparent that enthusiasm for organized antislavery activities was on the wane. For instance, subscriptions to the Louisville *Examiner* dropped dramatically after the election of delegates to the constitutional convention. Although several of the state's leading antislavery activists struggled to revive interest in the paper, by the end of 1849—only four months after the election—the editors of the *Examiner* suspended its publication.[49]

Likewise, the state's emancipationists failed miserably in an effort to defeat the final passage of the new constitution. When the constitutional convention adjourned in December 1849, it decided to submit the new constitution to the people in an advisory referendum to be held in May 1850. Although this would be a purely symbolic referendum, with no power to alter the handiwork of the convention, it was believed that a period of debate before the referendum would expose any defects in the new constitution. The constitutional convention would then reconvene in June 1850 to repair these defects and give final approval to the new constitution. Although several of the state's leading emancipationists hoped to rally the voters against the proslavery provisions of the new constitution, most emancipationists showed no interest in this task, and the new constitution was approved by a large margin in a referendum characterized by a low turnout of voters.[50]

The Emancipation party itself limped along for two more years without most of its most prominent supporters. During the gubernatorial campaign of 1851, it nominated Cassius Clay for governor and George D. Blakey of Logan County for lieutenant governor. However, Clay and Blakey were largely ignored in one of the most bitterly partisan statewide elections between Whigs and Democrats in years. Modern voting studies suggest that hundreds of emancipationists either deserted Clay and Blakey to vote for the two major parties or neglected to vote at all. Indeed, the emancipationists received more votes in the city of Louisville alone in 1849 than Clay did throughout the state in 1851.[51]

The demoralization of the antislavery forces manifested itself in several ways. As the low vote for Clay and Blakey suggests, some antislavery supporters like James Speed of Louisville, a former member of the Central Executive Committee of the Emancipation party and a leading emancipationist speaker in 1849, simply dropped out of politics for a time. Other antislavery advocates, like Robert J. Breckinridge, abandoned their antislavery activities and drifted into nativist politics and the new anti-immigrant Know-Nothing party. Some of the state's more radical antislavery activists, like Cassius Clay and John Fee, became increasingly convinced that Kentucky would not voluntarily abolish slavery and changed the focus of their antislavery activities from state politics to national politics.[52]

Although the fortunes of the state's antislavery movement dramatically declined during the 1850s and although Kentuckians embraced slavery with increased ardor, it would be a mistake to assume that Kentuckians had wholeheartedly adopted the same militant attachment to slavery that was rife in the Lower South. While most Kentuckians had apparently decided that slavery was a useful—even beneficial—institution, the preservation of slavery rarely became the all-consuming concern of political life in Kentucky that it did in the Lower South. Despite the growing importance of the "politics of slavery," there remained an important—albeit sharply limited—tolerance for antislavery activity and emancipationists in Kentucky throughout most of the 1850s. While some politicians like Underwood, who lost his bid for re-election in 1852, found that supporting emancipation in the new order of things could be politically fatal, others survived and even prospered. Breckinridge, for instance, found that he could still function effectively as the state's superintendent of public instruction and even work well with the state legislature despite his association with the emancipation movement. "The present Legislature . . . has done all I asked them," wrote Breckinridge just months after the electoral defeat of 1849, "notwithstanding very repeated and very severe attacks on me, as an Emancipationist—an enemy of the New Constitution. . . . [It] ordered over 20,000 copies of [my annual] Report to be printed—as its answer, to all grumbling." Unlike Underwood, Breckinridge ran successfully for re-election as superintendent in 1851. Surviving politically, however, usually required even more restraint and moderation regarding one's antislavery predilections than before. During the campaign of 1851, John C. Young reported to Breckinridge that a group of supporters in Danville—a stronghold of antislavery activism in the 1830s and 1840s—had decided to cancel a campaign rally for Breckinridge. "It was suggested by some that . . . you had enough of the odor of . . . emancipation about you without needing the [addition] to it which . . . might be given by a recommendation from a place like Danville. We were afraid you might exclaim, . . . 'Save me from my friends.'" When Cassius Clay urged Breckinridge to come out more openly in favor of emancipation during the campaign, Breckinridge demurred, citing the state's need for calm and peace on the slavery issue. "Having proved myself faithful to my convictions," Breckinridge said, "I shall now prove myself faithful to the Commonwealth."[53]

This continued tolerance for antislavery activity, combined with the abandonment of such activities by antislavery conservatives like Breckinridge, produced a significant development. Even as support for slavery became stronger within Kentucky, antislavery radicals for the first time became the most influential members of the state's antislavery movement. In Newport, an antislavery workingman named William S. Bailey bought a printing press in 1850; only a few short months after the *Examiner* ceased publication, he gave the state a new antislavery newspaper, the *Newport News*. For more than fifteen years, Bailey kept his paper in operation, using it to espouse the same radical free-labor arguments in evidence in Louisville during the late 1840s.[54]

In Louisville, the antislavery movement became dominated by German immigrants, many of whom were politically radical refugees from the unsuccessful German Revolution of 1848. In 1854, these radicals issued the so-called Louisville Platform, a twelve-point plank of political reform that called for the repeal of the Fugitive Slave Law of 1850, the prohibition of slavery in the western territories, the gradual abolition of slavery in the South, and the establishment of political and social equality between blacks and whites. In the mountains of Kentucky, Cassius Clay—despite his increasing interest in national affairs—worked to convert the traditional ambivalence that many highlanders felt toward slavery into outright antislavery sentiment. And during the mid to late 1850s, Clay worked to incorporate both the antislavery groups of the mountains and the scattered remnants of the statewide Emancipation party into the new Republican party. Along Kentucky's border with the free states, organized slave rescue attempts became more prominent, especially those conducted by the notorious Calvin Fairbank and Delia Webster. The number of slaves rescued by antislavery activists was small—more slaves escaped using their own wits and the assistance of fellow slaves than were rescued by an "underground railroad" of organized outsiders. Nevertheless, organized slave rescues assumed a growing visibility in the 1850s, highlighted by the efforts of Fairbank, Webster, John Parker, Thomas Brown, and others. When combined in the public mind with concerns about organized northern resistance to the recapture of Kentucky's fugitive slaves, efforts to assist and promote slave escapes generated great controversy in Kentucky.[55]

Indeed, so pronounced was the influence of radical antislavery activists in the 1850s that even abolitionists began to play an important role in the state's antislavery movement. Abolitionism in Kentucky grew remarkably in the 1850s, mostly under the aegis of John G. Fee and the American Missionary Association (AMA). Under Fee's leadership, AMA missionaries traversed the eastern part of the state, preaching abolitionism to thousands of Kentuckians. Perhaps more than any single event before the secession crisis of 1860–61, Fee's success in promoting abolitionism in Kentucky demonstrated that, even in the 1850s, the attitudes of most Kentuckians on slavery differed greatly from those of proslavery ideologues in the Deep South. Fee's story is a testament to Kentucky's lingering antislavery potential in the 1850s, for it demonstrated what could still be accomplished through the efforts of a southerner whose moral vision was unclouded by support for racism, concerns about property rights, and fear of social ostracism. Fee's story is one of courage and—ultimately—of failure in the face of adversity, a story that bears closer examination for what it tells us about the struggles of reformers in a slave state and about public opinion in Kentucky on the eve of the Civil War.

7

The Quest for Righteousness

On the night of October 16, 1859, a band of zealous abolitionists, led by veteran antislavery warrior John Brown, stormed into the nation's headlines by seizing the federal arsenal in Harper's Ferry, Virginia. This raid—an attempt to set off a wave of slave insurrections throughout the South—sent shock waves through the teetering edifice of sectional harmony. In the South, John Brown's raid united southerners as perhaps no event had yet done, enlisting southerners of all stripes in the strident defense of their section—and its peculiar institution—and prompting them to call for swift retribution not only against Brown and his followers but also against all manner of antislavery reformers. In the North, John Brown was both praised and damned—at first. Once he was arrested and tried for treason in Virginia, however, Brown's noble demeanor in the face of adversity transformed him, in the eyes of many northerners, into a hero of almost mythic proportions and won him grudging admiration from even his staunchest critics.[1]

One northerner who was drawn to the legendary John Brown was the nation's most famous cleric, Henry Ward Beecher, who found in Brown's trial and impending martyrdom what one modern biographer called "a drama . . . [he] could not resist." Beecher publicly praised Brown's "bold, unflinching, honest" character and kept his congregation fully informed of the events unfolding in Virginia. On November 13, 1859, only two weeks before Brown's death sentence was to be carried out, Beecher welcomed to his pulpit an abolitionist who, like Brown, had chosen to take his antislavery mission to the South, a person Beecher introduced as "a better man than I am" for having the courage to proclaim his convictions precisely where they were least popular. That man was the Rev. John Gregg Fee of Kentucky.[2]

Beecher's guest was an unusual figure in antebellum America. Fee knew slavery with an intimacy few northern abolitionists could match: he had grown up in a slave state among a slaveholding family. Yet unlike most southern opponents of slavery, Fee was a true abolitionist. He believed that slavery and slaveholding were sins from which God expected people to repent, immediately and uncompromisingly. He opposed the colonization of freed slaves and believed that blacks had a God-given right to political and social equality with whites. There were other southerners with similar views, of course. Several famous abolitionists, including James G. Birney, Sarah and Angelina Grimké, James A. Thome, and Moncure D. Conway, had been born and raised in the South. Fee differed from these abolitionists in that he thought it was his duty to remain in the South and carry his antislavery crusade to the slaveholders themselves—and for fifteen years Fee had preached against slavery in Kentucky. These years of hardship and persecution had earned Fee a measure of fame and respect in the North, and now, in November 1859, he had come to Beecher's Plymouth Church in Brooklyn to bring his message to the nation's foremost pulpit. At the age of forty-three, Fee was at the height of his antebellum career.[3]

Fee used his sermon at Plymouth Church to recount his experiences as an abolitionist in a slave state, to chide the North for its own torpor on the slavery issue, and to urge support for the free-labor colony and abolitionist college he was establishing in Kentucky. Fee especially wanted to stir interest in the colony and the school, for he believed that neither enterprise was receiving its due share of support from the free states because northerners were more interested in keeping slavery out of the western territories than they were in destroying slavery where it already existed. Thus, Fee argued before Beecher's congregation, southerners were not the only ones complicit in the sin of slaveholding; northerners shared the guilt because they either defended slavery or refused to use every instrument at their disposal to end human bondage. He urged the congregation to fight slavery with their pocketbooks, and more importantly, with their very lives. Fee exhorted his listeners to move south to the antislavery colony he and his associates were establishing in the foothills of Kentucky, or to go anywhere else in the South where they could battle slavery. Harking back to the events of recent days, Fee's peroration reiterated this plea: "We need more John Browns—," Fee proclaimed, "not in the MANNER OF HIS ACTION, BUT IN HIS SPIRIT OF CON-SECRATION: . . . men who would go, not with carnal weapons, but with the 'sword of the spirit,' the Bible; and who in love would appeal to slaveholders and non-slaveholders—[men who would] . . . be ready, if needs be, to give up property and life" to battle slavery in the South.[4]

The congregation at Plymouth Church responded to Fee's plea—if not with their lives, then at least with their pocketbooks. They contributed to Fee's colony and school a sum of money equivalent to half the preacher's annual salary. For their part, Kentuckians responded less graciously to Fee's sermon. Four days after the speech, the *Louisville Courier* published a garbled account of Fee's speech, writing that "the fanatical abolitionist John G. Fee, while in the East collecting funds for the prosecution of his nefarious work, said that more John Browns were wanted, especially in Kentucky." The *Kentucky Statesman* of Lexington soon commented that "if Fee and his followers try to revolutionize Kentucky with the funds he collected at Beecher's church, they will be resisted with force and blood by the mountaineers." Ominously, in Fee's own county the *Kentucky Messenger* of Richmond pronounced him a "fanatic" and a "bad man," claiming that Fee's brand of abolitionism required that Kentuckians "SHALL BE MURDERED IN COLD BLOOD." Such statements were typical of a growing outrage at what Kentuckians thought Fee had said. By the summer of 1860, this outrage had caused Kentuck-

ians to expel nearly one hundred of Fee's followers from the two antislavery communities they had built.[5]

It is, perhaps, too easy to dismiss the significance of the work of
John G. Fee with the harsh reality of this expulsion. At first glance, it
would appear that this episode was just another example of southern
intransigence on the slavery issue, another chapter in the story of the
hardening of southern opinion on slavery in the 1850s and the resulting suppression of free thought and civil liberties. But, on further
consideration, what is really striking about Fee's life and work is not
that his antebellum career in the South ended so harshly and
abruptly, but rather that for fifteen years he was able to maintain an
abolitionist crusade in the midst of slavery. Fee's story suggests that
even in the 1850s Kentuckians remained ambivalent about the slavery issue, that although they were increasingly willing to defend the
South and slavery against northern opposition, they did not always
see this defense as their highest priority in political and social affairs.

John G. Fee was born on September 9, 1816, to a prosperous,
middle-class family in Bracken County, Kentucky. In 1823, when
Fee was a boy of six, his father owned thirteen slaves, in this county
of small farms and few slaves located just across the river from Ohio.
After a turbulent adolescence and frequent quarrels with his slaveholding father, which would extend into adulthood, Fee packed his
bags for Lane Seminary in Ohio, intending at age twenty-six to enter
the Presbyterian ministry. There, Fee had a religious experience which
set him on the road to his life's work. By now, Fee was an earnest
young Christian who had been troubled for some time by his relationship to slavery. At Lane, long a hotbed of abolitionism and liberal theology, Fee encountered two classmates from the North who
were determined to show their young southern friend the sin of
slaveholding. As Fee remembered in his *Autobiography*, these two students stressed that abolitionism "was fundamental in the religion of
Jesus Christ, and that unless I embraced the principle and lived it in
honest practice, I would lose my soul." Fee struggled over the issue
for some time, knowing "that to embrace the principle and wear the
name [of abolitionist] was to cut myself off from relatives and former
friends," but he finally gave in. "I saw that to have light and peace

from God," Fee remembered later, "I must make the consecration. I said, 'Lord, if needs be, make me an Abolitionist.' The surrender was complete."[6]

This was not the end of Fee's inner struggles over the sin of slaveholding—indeed, it was just the beginning. As he pursued his studies at Lane, Fee pondered the implications that abolitionism would have for his ministry. After considering a career as a missionary in western Africa and a more conventional ministry in the North, Fee decided to return to his native Kentucky, claiming that "because God in his providence had thrown my lot in the land of Slavery, and made me acquainted with its workings, and the feelings of those involved in it, I felt called . . . to the work of preaching the Gospel of love" in the South. Fee eventually accepted a commission from the American Home Missionary Society (AHMS) and the pastorate of a small New School Presbyterian church in Lewis County. Fee's return to his chosen field of labor placed him in an environment where he was constantly forced to re-examine his own involvement with slavery. There was no place in Kentucky—or any other slave state—for someone of Fee's abolitionist sensibilities to avoid confronting thorny questions about his own indirect support of slavery through religious, political, and economic institutions. Neither was it very possible to deceive oneself about the intransigence of most slaveholders on the issue of slavery.[7]

Unlike most other Kentuckians of antislavery sensibilities, Fee did not allow the harsh realities of life in a southern state—or the influence of racism, property, and public opinion—to weaken his stance against slavery. Unlike proponents of the necessary-evil theory, Fee did not temporize. Indeed, throughout Fee's antebellum career, he drifted increasingly toward radical positions on slavery and the methods of reform in an effort to absolve himself from the taint of slavery and to find some effective method of freeing the slaves. In 1846, Fee demonstrated an early version of his abolitionist philosophy in a series of articles on the sin of slaveholding in Cassius Clay's paper, the *True American*; two years later, he expanded these articles into a book called *An Anti-Slavery Manual*. The heart of Fee's abolitionist philosophy was a theologically based radical egalitarianism.

Fee began his theology with a conventional premise, comparing God's authority to the earthly power of a sovereign monarch. God was an active force in the universe who retained "the prerogative of originating laws to regulate human conduct" and demanded that people conform their actions to his laws. To act contrary to the commandments of a sovereign God—that is, to commit sin—was to enter into literal "*rebellion against God*," the punishment for which was eternal damnation.[8]

Fee used traditional doctrines to make an unusual—even controversial—point: that God's sovereign commandments forbade slavery and required people to challenge many of the institutions and laws that existed in nineteenth-century America. Unlike the vast majority of southern churchmen, who believed that the Old Testament's laws on servitude and certain of the Apostle Paul's teachings proved that slavery was a divinely ordained institution, Fee emphatically denied that God's law approved of slavery. Fee claimed that the institution mentioned in such biblical examples was so different from American slavery that they could hardly be seen as the foundation for the South's peculiar institution, and he accused proslavery ideologues of taking "*isolated* passages" from the Bible that "seem to tolerate slavery" and purposefully misreading them to support slavery.[9]

Fee argued that instead of misreading "isolated passages" from the Bible to support slavery, white southerners should look to the "*foundation* principle" of Christianity for advice about their relationship to the black race. Fee's view of these matters was shaped by strong doses of Arminianism. Like many New School Presbyterians, Fee rejected the Calvinist belief that God would save only a few souls from perdition, that each person's fate was settled by God before the creation of the universe, and that humans were utterly incapable of affecting their eternal destiny. Instead, Fee argued that God offered salvation to those who had the faith to follow his laws and damnation to those who did not. If true, then it was imperative that each person have the freedom to obey divine law according to the dictates of his or her own conscience. Hence, Fee believed, the laws God established to govern people's conduct necessarily maximized human liberty.[10]

In Fee's view, this was the heart of the problem of slavery: the peculiar institution of the South inherently prevented slaves from seeking salvation and serving God according to the bidding of their own consciences. Fee claimed that slavery was, at its foundation, "a system of force, and can exist only by force." It was "built . . . upon the principle that one innocent man may be compelled to be the property of another—his powers of body and of mind . . . controlled for the benefit of the master." The slave could not "do any thing, either for himself, his wife, his family, his church, his country, his God, but with the consent of his master." The unnatural—indeed, ungodly—force used to maintain slavery effectively usurped God's sovereign authority to make rules for humanity. Slavery, Fee wrote, "cannot exist without giving to the master this power."[11]

This implicitly egalitarian view of God's moral order echoed Fee's belief that God had not limited salvation to a select group of "visible saints" and instead wanted all people to have the freedom to seek salvation. To Fee, since God did not make niggling distinctions between people, neither should white Americans. Fee argued that the desire of whites to raise such distinctions and the racial prejudices that resulted were ungodly and sinful; as proof, he offered the biblical injunctions that "God hath made of one blood all nations of men," that man should "love his neighbor as himself," and above all, that men should do unto other "men as they would be done by." Fee called the last of these injunctions the "law of impartial love" and proclaimed it "the fundamental law of the Christian religion." The neglect of this principle and the consequential development of racial animosity, Fee argued, were the root causes of slavery. "No man can love his neighbor as himself and hold that neighbor on the scale of a brute—a commodity to be sold," Fee wrote. "No man can do as he would men should do unto him and deprive or continue to deprive another of liberty." If people would only follow the law of love and remove unnatural distinctions among people, slavery would fall away in an instant.[12]

Such appeals played an increasingly prominent role in Fee's rhetoric during the late 1840s, the period during which antislavery became the central focus of Fee's ministry. By April 1846, Fee believed that slaveholders should be excluded from membership in Christian churches, and he had led his own church to follow that principle. If, as Fee thought, "slaveholding is a sin which, . . . if knowingly and deliberately persisted in, must 'exclude the soul from Heaven,'" then slaveholders must be warned of their sin by expulsion from the church. To preach against slavery as sin while allowing people who practiced that sin to remain as members sent the message that the church was not serious about its views on sin; it was, Fee argued, to "bid the slaveholder God speed, and rock him to sleep in his sin." Expulsion of slaveholders from the church would jolt them awake to their sin, thus leading them to a renunciation of sin and a reunion with the church.[13]

The exclusion of slaveholders from Fee's church did not sit well with many of Kentucky's New School Presbyterians. Although nationally the New Schoolers had something of an antislavery reputation, Kentucky's New School Synod was less inclined toward antislavery than its northern counterparts, and, in the fall of 1846, it recommended to the AHMS that Fee no longer receive the Society's financial support. The Synod claimed that since slaveholding was not prohibited by the Presbyterian Confession of Faith, Fee—by urging his congregation to exclude slaveholders—had caused his church to establish a new, divisive standard of church membership. Despite the threat to his income, Fee did not back down, which prompted the Synod to take further action against him. When the Synod met again in September 1847, it censured Fee for his continued resistance to slaveholding church members and instructed the Presbytery to take action against both Fee and his church. The censure was a warning to the heretic to repent from his heresy, but Fee again remained undeterred, proclaiming that "I shall obey God rather than man." He went ahead with his plans to publish the *Anti-Slavery Manual* in February 1848; by the time the Presbytery met in April, Fee's views on the sinfulness of slavery and nonfellowship with slaveholders were readily available in a book widely circulated throughout the state. Not surprisingly, the Presbytery also censured Fee and appointed a committee of ministers "to labor with Bro[ther] Fee and induce him to change his course or withdraw from our connection and also to visit his church . . . and bring them to abandon the new test [of church membership] which they have so unwarrantably set up."[14]

Throughout Fee's conflicts with his denomination, the AHMS continued to support him financially, even though according to the Society's own constitution, it could give aid only to ministers in good standing with their churches. Moral considerations aside, the AHMS was not ready to cut itself off from funds given by antislavery northerners, who, along with rival missionary societies, were watching Fee's case carefully to see if the AHMS was going to "make abolition a test of church standing." At first, Fee was glad to have the Society's support, and he ultimately hoped for a reconciliation with the Presbyterians that would put to rest questions regarding his funding. Fee was reluctant to draw a parallel that a number of abolitionists were drawing: that if it was sinful to associate with slaveholders in a local church body, it was also sinful to associate with them within religious denominations. During his early troubles with the Synod and Presbytery, Fee maintained that as long as he had a fair chance of swaying the minds of Kentucky's New School Presbyterians, duty required him to maintain his connection with them so that he might show them the error of their ways—a principle Fee would soon recant.[15]

By the fall of 1847, Fee had still not renounced this principle, but he had lost hope for Kentucky's New School Presbyterians, and he concluded that he should now break with them. The Synod's willingness to censure him and to accept the argument that Presbyterians in search of doctrinal guidance must look to the Confession of Faith before they looked to the Bible proved to Fee the hopeless corruption of the Presbyterian Church. Fee's new attitude toward the New School Presbyterians was also evident to the committee of ministers appointed by the Presbytery to visit with Fee and his church in the spring of 1848. They urged Fee to withdraw from the Presbyterian Church for everyone's good and offered him an inducement to go: if he and his church withdrew before there were any further troubles, the Presbytery would give him a "letter of dismission" in good standing, by which he could continue to receive the support of the AHMS without further questions about his standing with the Presbyterian Church.[16]

Even as the committee corresponded with Fee, he again revised his opinion of his relationship to the Presbyterian Church and, ironically, with the AHMS. By the summer of 1848, Fee acknowledged that he had been wrong to attempt to reform the Presbyterian Church from within: just as righteous churches should show slaveholders their sin by excommunicating them, so must righteous churches reveal to slaveholding churches their sin by withdrawing from fellowship with them. Further, by the summer of 1848, Fee included the AHMS in his indictment of corrupt religious associations. Fee now argued that by paying the salaries of missionaries in the South whose churches did not exclude slaveholders, the AHMS was supporting slavery, and he wanted no part of it. In August 1848, Fee returned his commission from the AHMS, saying that "though our influence[,] name[,] and means may be very small yet we ought to give neither of these to build up an association which builds up . . . a great curse to the land[,] the enemy of religion, as well as the happiness of man." At about the same time, both Fee and his church asked for a severance of their relationship with the Presbytery, which was granted at its next meeting in the spring of 1849.[17]

Fee's emerging policy of nonfellowship with slaveholding churches was a version of "come-outerism," a religious movement that enjoyed a great vogue among abolitionists in the 1840s and 1850s. The term came from the biblical injunction that Christians should "come out" of corrupt churches: "Be ye not unequally yoked together with unbelievers: for what fellowship hath righteousness with un-righteousness? . . . Wherefore come out from among them, and be ye separate, saith the Lord, and touch not the unclean *thing*; and I will receive you." Antislavery come-outerism took two different forms. In one, antislavery churches seceded from proslavery ecclesiastical organizations. The withdrawal of Fee's church from the New School Presbyterian Church came in a period that saw many similar secessions in the North and the corresponding formation of several antislavery come-outer sects. The other variety of antislavery come-outerism was more anarchical, involving a rejection of not only proslavery churches but also church forms and hierarchies. Its adherents rejected not only proslavery denominations, but also denominationalism in general; in extreme cases, they rejected the use of pastors, church buildings, and structured church meetings.[18]

Fee initially embraced the more moderate "nonfellowship" version of come-outerism, but after his exodus from the New School Synod in 1848, he embraced portions of the anarchistic version of come-outerism by rejecting the very idea of religious denominations. When he now looked at his treatment by the Presbyterians and the AHMS, Fee detected in their actions the same sort of motivation that had caused slavery. People had created denominational labels and "sectarian peculiarities" to distinguish themselves from and, hence, raise themselves above other Christians, just as whites created unnatural racial barriers to elevate their status above other people. The resulting assortment of sectarian creeds and doctrines only encouraged humanity's desire to create unnatural distinctions among people and fostered in members of religious denominations a sinful desire to enforce doctrinal orthodoxy rather than to uphold the word of God. Fee thought that this tendency had clearly been demonstrated in his various trials before the Synod. When Fee would not conform to the Presbyterians' doctrine, they tried to force him to conform by withholding his salary and censuring him, and to Fee, this represented an inherent problem with denominations. The power of denominations to coerce individual believers through creeds, licenses, pastoral salaries, and church trials represented—as slaveholding did—the ability to use unnatural force to enforce the will of one group of people upon another. Thus, denominations created an intermediary between the individual believer and God, which—like slavery—affected an individual's ability to seek salvation according to the calling of his own conscience.[19]

After 1848, Fee increasingly referred to unnatural distinctions between people as "caste," asserting that it was "harder to get men to act against [caste], than against slaveholding," because the love of distinctions was the underlying sin, and slavery only its symptom. The goal of Fee's ministry, then, became not just the abolition of slavery but also the elimination of caste. For instance, in the late 1840s Fee attacked secret societies like the Masons and Odd Fellows, claiming that the restricted membership of these fraternal organizations gave "one class of men an unknown and an undue advantage over the other members of society."[20]

Likewise, Fee openly criticized Kentucky's antislavery colonizationists, arguing that the only motive for colonizing blacks in Africa came from prejudice and a refusal to accept blacks as members of American society. Fee came to believe that the prejudice of colonizationists and other white Kentuckians had less to do with race or skin color than it did with the universal desire among people to elevate themselves by magnifying small differences between groups of people into insurmountable social barriers. "[I]t is not instinctive aversion to color" that creates racial prejudice against blacks, Fee argued, but rather a learned "association" between the African American's color and the "degraded . . . condition his color has been made to assume." As proof, Fee pointed to caste distinctions that were clearly not produced by racial animosity. Caste, Fee wrote, "exists in India among people of the same color. It exists in Europe among people of the same color. It exists in our own country toward those of a different color or complexion; and toward those of the same [white] complexion. . . . [I]t is caste that excludes the free white laborers from the first table, and from the family of many slaveholders and aristocrats."[21]

Fee's attacks on the prejudice of the colonizationists and the general broadening of his ministry into anticaste activities continued after his commissioning by the American Missionary Association in October 1848. Formed in 1846 specifically to rival the AHMS and "to discountenance slavery," the founders of the AMA hoped it would force the older missionary society to withdraw support from slaveholding missionaries and churches, or failing this, to take away the older society's northern sources of financial support. Further, under the leadership of such antislavery stalwarts as Lewis Tappan, Amos A. Phelps, George Whipple, and Simeon S. Jocelyn, the Association took a strongly anticaste and mildly antisectarian position. While the AMA did not disparage denominations per se, it pointedly renounced any "ecclesiastical jurisdiction over the missionaries" and announced that its funds were available to "any person of evangelical sentiments . . . who is not a slaveholder," regardless of their sectarian affiliation.[22]

Under the aegis of the AMA, Fee's churches—the church in Lewis County and a newer congregation in Bracken County—merged the themes of antislavery, antisectarianism, and anticaste and embraced the free church movement. Begun as a reaction against the pervasive practice of charging pew rents, the free church movement held that people should not be closed off from hearing God's word because of poverty. The church, they argued, should not be segregated by wealth, with those who could afford rented pews sitting apart from those required to use free, pauper pews. Fee's churches agreed, and as Fee noted in 1851, his congregations were "equally free to *all persons*" so that all "have equal rights, equal chances and encouragements to hear the gospel." Some, including Fee and his churches, asserted that this egalitarian doctrine also meant that free churches should not shut people out because they refused to submit to an "authoritarian creed"; individuals should be free to find salvation according to their own consciences. Requirements for church membership would be kept to a bare minimum in Fee's churches; candidates for membership were required to make "a profession only of those doctrines *essential* to salvation" so that, in Fee's words, "we would not trammel a brother's conscience in non-essentials" such as the "mode of baptism" or the "doctrine of election and reprobation, or the opposite doctrines." One doctrine, however, that the churches considered essential to salvation was the repudiation of slaveholding: owners of slaves could not become members of the churches.[23]

Before 1850, Fee's evolving free churches apparently thought of themselves as free, *white* churches. In barring both slaveholders and slaves from full membership, Fee's churches conformed to the racial standards of that day. Only ten years earlier, the American Anti-Slavery Society still prohibited blacks from addressing its meetings; in 1850, many northern churches still had a "negro pew." Fee, of course, had already told the world that the law of love required the removal of all unnatural distinctions among people. It is unclear why Fee tolerated his churches' racial policies before 1850, but when his churches were formally deciding to accept free-churchism in 1850, Fee challenged them to consider the implications of their actions. If both caste and slaveholding were sinful, should they not include blacks in the church as well as exclude slaveholders? Were they going to eliminate the pauper's pew only to protect the "negro pew"? The churches voted for consistency: they would admit blacks to church membership on a full and equal basis. Blacks would be able to vote on all matters before the church, sit wherever they wanted within the building, and receive communion with the white members of the church. Fee thought the adoption of such practices made the churches fully worthy of the name each had chosen for itself: "A Free Church of Christ."[24]

By the early 1850s, Fee's anticaste beliefs caused him to challenge many conventional tenets of American racial thought. Fee discounted the seemingly conclusive evidence offered by physicians like Josiah Nott and Samuel Cartwright that Caucasians and Negroes were not separate races of humanity, but entirely different species. Fee believed this to be nonsense; in his view, not only did the Bible clearly state that "God hath made of ONE *blood all nations of men*," but the best scientific evidence available bore this out. To explain the differences between the races, Fee relied on Lamarckism, the theory that acquired characteristics are passed from parents to their children. He believed that any human's skin turned dark in warm climates, and that when people were exposed to a hot climate for a long period of time, their natural skin color became slightly darker, a characteristic that they passed on to their children. Over the course of many generations, the accumulated changes left the descendants with "*constitution[s]*" that were "*radically changed*" from their ancestors. Further, if ever-shifting environmental factors brought about racial characteristics, as Fee thought, then blacks and whites who lived in the same American climate would eventually become alike: whites would become darker and blacks, lighter. How then would southerners justify slavery?[25]

Although by the standards of Fee's day this was an enlightened view of racial differences, by today's standards Fee does not appear quite so free from prejudice: he clearly shared some of the racial stereotypes of his day and sometimes spoke disparagingly of blacks as a race. Environmental factors might determine racial characteristics, but it was clear to Fee that humanity controlled many of these factors and that many racial characteristics of blacks had been caused by poor or uncivilized standards of living. "Poverty of diet," "filthiness of living," "the miasma of decaying vegetation," and the lack of "the arts and comforts of *civilization* in giving . . . appropriate food, clothing, and shelter from extreme heat, or cold," all ensured that "savages, because of constant exposure to these causes, are always *darker than civilized men in the same climate.*"[26]

What is striking about Fee, though, is not that he failed to free himself completely from the mores of the society in which he had been raised, but that he came as close to achieving this as nearly anyone did in his day. Historians have known for years that few northern abolitionists were completely free of prejudice, and even among these comparatively tolerant men and women, Fee's record stands out; indeed, it is remarkable how little prejudice Fee seemed to feel. Fee rarely used racial stereotypes; he never considered allegedly inferior characteristics of African Americans as unchangeable; and he always emphasized that whites who shared the same environment shared many of the same characteristics. In fact, Fee argued that the tables had once been turned: during ancient times the ancestors of America's slaves had been known the world over as a highly advanced race, at the same time that the ancestors of the "enlightened and refined nations of Europe" were "ignorant, and rude barbarians." Remove "the incubus of slavery, and the withering blight of unholy prejudice," Fee wrote, and blacks would "shoot into intellectual and moral greatness."[27]

Fee's movement away from personal racial antipathy and toward anticaste beliefs is perhaps best illustrated by the development of what may have been his most controversial position: that interracial marriage was preferable to the continuation of sin and prejudice. Miscegenation in the South had been going on for centuries, but it was a delicate subject for southerners, to say the least. A violation of racial taboos, miscegenation was something that everyone knew about but few acknowledged. About the only type of "amalgamation" that anyone mentioned was the prospective version: that is, the kind that supposedly would result from abolition. Fee was aware of these arguments, and in the late 1840s he presented himself as an opponent of amalgamation, like many northern abolitionists. He claimed that, by removing black women from the predatory power of their masters, abolition would restrict, not foster, miscegenation. But even as he presented himself as an opponent of miscegenation, Fee worried more about the fact that slavery caused the coercion of black women and sexual relations outside of marriage than about miscegenation per se.[28]

By the mid-1850s, Fee was openly endorsing interracial marriage. He called the argument that abolition would lead to amalgamation an "appeal to prejudices" in order "to defend our sins." Would it not be better if the black and white races were merged through interracial marriage and the birth of mulatto children than for "unholy prejudice" between the races to continue? "Better that we have black faces than bad hearts, and reap eventually the torments of hell," he wrote. "We may have pure hearts if our faces should, after the lapse of a century or two, be a little tawny." Fee's ideas on this subject eventually saw their fruition at Berea College, the school he founded and guided for nearly forty years, where during Reconstruction interracial dating between students was officially sanctioned by the college's board of trustees.[29]

Such ideas did not win Fee many friends in Kentucky during the early 1850s, a fact driven home to Fee by several violent, physical assaults he endured during the period. Indeed, the obvious resistance of Kentuckians to Fee's antislavery and anticaste ideas in the early to mid-1850s increasingly drew his attention away from questions concerning the abolitionist's relationship to ecclesiastical organizations to broader ones concerning his own relationship to the political society in which he lived. When confronting these questions, Fee was forced to deal with troubling questions about the manner in which his political relationship with people corrupted by slavery paralleled his former ecclesiastical relationship with slaveholding churchmen. Had a sovereign God commanded his followers to separate themselves from earthly political arrangements and the laws of unregenerate people?

This was, of course, the question of higher law that nearly all abolitionists faced. Abolitionists arrived at vastly different solutions to this problem. Some, like William Lloyd Garrison, advocated a variety of political come-outerism. Garrison saw in human government the same sort of coercive power over the individual's conscience that Fee saw in religious denominations, and he saw in the North's political union with southern slaveholders the same sort of corrupting association with sinners that Fee saw in his former ties with the Presbyterian Church and the AHMS. Therefore, Garrison advised abolitionists to avoid association with sinful people and coercive institutions by refusing to vote, and he urged the North to demonstrate the immorality of slavery by seceding from political union with the South. Most abolitionists consciously rejected the application of come-outerism to human society. Believing it to be either their religious or civic duty to reform slavery through the political system, abolitionists participated in the formation of several antislavery political parties from the late 1830s to the 1850s, including the Liberty party in 1839, the Free-Soil party in 1848, and the Republican party in 1856.[30]

For a number of abolitionists from the evangelical tradition, the decision to participate in electoral politics forced them to face harder and more enduring moral dilemmas than Garrison experienced. Like Garrison, they feared the seemingly inevitable tendency of politics to corrupt its participants; unlike him, they could not conscientiously avoid politics. Finding even the regular antislavery parties too willing to sacrifice principle for electoral gain, abolitionists like Lewis Tappan, William Goodell, and Gerrit Smith created tiny antislavery splinter parties in the late 1840s and 1850s, often referred to generically as the Radical Political Abolitionists.[31]

Like the circle of abolitionists dominated by Tappan, Goodell, and Smith into which he was increasingly being drawn during the 1850s, Fee also felt the conflict between politics and morals. Throughout his life, Fee showed an unusual interest in political action, but until the end of the Civil War he never found a party that satisfied him. From the beginning of his career, Fee stressed that antislavery political action was incumbent on the Christian abolitionist. The Bible enjoined people to use any resources at their disposal to free the slave, and if these included political action, then abolitionists must use that too. A Christian must vote, organize political parties, or serve in office, if called. "How shall we pray for God's kingdom to come," asked Fee, "when we stay at home, and let wicked men put forward wicked rulers, who will perpetuate the devil's kingdom?" Yet Fee worried often that people became so involved in antislavery politics that they forgot the reason why "'we enter our protest against slavery, . . . for the grand reason that it is sin against God. When we lose sight of that fact, we lose our hold upon conscience.'" By itself, Fee wrote, "mere political action will not, cannot" destroy slavery. "Public sentiment must be changed first. The mere politician will not do this. The work must be done by those imbued with the spirit of Christ." Fee himself affirmed the primacy of his ministerial duties and eschewed political office for fear that it would take him away from a more useful service: awakening the conscience of his fellow Kentuckians.[32]

Ironically, in the late 1840s and early 1850s Fee's need to be above politics—to avoid public office while preaching moral principles with a political application—helped ease him into political alliances with people of less advanced views. Fee seemed to realize that a person like Cassius Clay, the politician, complemented Fee, the moralist, perfectly. Fee would set down general principles of morality and leave it to practical politicians like Clay to translate them into policies and to make the necessary political compromises. As long as Fee could view a compromise as a forward step toward the complete accomplishment of a broader political goal and as long as the compromise required him to do no "positive wrong," Fee could support it. But Fee stood ready to "come out" from any party if it stopped progressing toward his larger goal or if it required him to sin.[33]

This position eased Fee's conscience about making political alliances with people of less advanced views, and before the mid-1850s he eagerly sought political allies among Kentucky's more conservative antislavery forces. By far Fee's most important and enduring political ally among Kentucky's emancipationists was Cassius M. Clay. Although Clay's abolitionism was far from perfect, the two men shared many assumptions about slavery, and in many ways their positions were closer to each other than to the mass of Kentucky's anti-slavery reformers. By the late 1840s, both men opposed coloniza-tion, both believed that northerners had a rightful voice in the issue of slavery, and both refused to compromise their belief that slavery should be absolutely abolished. Although Fee himself recognized many of Clay's faults and doubted him to be a Christian—an impor-tant consideration for someone of Fee's religious perspective—he believed that Clay was "noble in many respects" and, as he told Clay, "that God has raised you up to do a good work." For his part, Clay believed Fee was "as pure and noble a man as ever breathed." There was a deep and abiding affection between the men, a friendship that far outlasted their political alliance. Both the friendship and the alli-ance began in the late 1840s, when Fee and Clay had several oppor-tunities to cooperate in antislavery work. As previously noted, in 1846 Fee sent Clay a series of articles for publication in the *True American*; two years later, after Fee had enlarged and compiled the articles into his *Anti-Slavery Manual*, Clay distributed the book in central Kentucky. The next year, Fee returned the favor by circulat-ing Clay's newly published *Writings* in northeastern Kentucky. Also during the late 1840s, Clay spoke in Fee's churches several times, and Fee tolerated—but did not approve of—his friend's enlistment in the army during the Mexican War.[34]

Upon Clay's return from Mexico, the two men again worked together, this time in the effort to elect emancipationists to the state's constitutional convention. In the spring of 1849, Clay helped Fee campaign against proslavery candidates in northern Kentucky; in April, Fee journeyed to the state capital to attend the Frankfort Emancipation Convention, where he was chosen to be a member of the platform committee. Although he was disturbed by the conserva-tive approach to antislavery he heard espoused by most delegates—especially by their denials that slavery was sinful and their declarations of support for colonization—Fee refrained from speaking out strongly against the delegates' conservatism, for fear of disrupting the fragile accord of the meeting. Perhaps at no other time in Fee's career did his desire to secure a successful political alliance so completely win out over his desire to make certain that his actions were morally unimpeachable. In this he mirrored Clay's views on the subject: Clay told the convention that although he disagreed with the conservative tone of its platform, he supported it for the sake of unity. "If we gain not all we want," Clay argued, "we at least gain all the circumstances around us authorize us to hope for."[35]

After the antislavery candidates' devastating loss in the fall elections, with the movement dispirited and disorganized, Fee wrote to Clay that "so far from 'giving up the ship,' . . . I feel that . . . we have achieved a great victory—[by seeing a] party organized and the way opened to the *Polls*." Fee suggested to Clay a number of strategies for building up the Emancipation party, and he remained active in the party through the state's gubernatorial election of 1851, in which Clay, running as the party's candidate, was soundly defeated. The next year, however, Fee and Clay—along with several other luminaries of the Emancipation party—joined the national Free-Soil party. Fee campaigned within the state for the Free-Soilers' presidential candidate and served as a Free-Soil candidate for presidential elector. The climax of Fee's and Clay's cooperation with the Free-Soil party came in September 1852, when they hosted George W. Julian, the party's vice presidential candidate, in a series of speaking engagements in and around Fee's churches.[36]

At the same time, events drew the careers of Fee and Clay closer together, an occurrence that eventually led to Fee's most significant contribution to Kentucky antislavery. During the early fifties, Fee decided to expand the scope of his ministry by building schools, employing colporteurs, and bringing other antislavery missionaries to Kentucky. In the late 1840s, the northern leadership of the AMA had doubted that antislavery missions could survive in the South, but Fee's success in Kentucky caused them to rethink their position, and they backed Fee's plans for expanding his ministry. Under Fee's leadership, the AMA's work grew during the 1850s to include operations throughout eastern Kentucky. The colporteurs—itinerant purveyors of religious literature—were probably the most important members of this operation, in terms of the sheer number of people reached. Every year, the AMA's colporteurs distributed thousands of copies of Fee's antislavery pamphlets and other religious documents.

Wherever they went, the colporteurs prepared the way for the coming of AMA schools and churches by talking to people about religion and slavery. Colporteurs and missionaries alike found their eastern Kentucky audiences remarkably receptive. Their reports indicated that, although they often found small groups of people who were hostile to the AMA's mission, the large mass of common men and women were willing to read their tracts, listen to their sermons, and at least tolerate the presence of active abolitionists in the community; it is clear that the colporteurs, missionaries, and schools introduced literally thousands of Kentuckians to the AMA's brand of antislavery before the Civil War.[37]

Heartened by his friend's success, Cassius Clay saw in Fee's expanding missionary field a chance to build an antislavery political constituency in the mountains and foothills of southeastern Kentucky, a base from which he might launch a successful antislavery candidacy for Congress. Clay hoped that the establishment of come-outer churches would nurture the region's undercurrent of antislavery sentiment and attract other antislavery activists to move to the area. During the early 1850s, Clay strongly urged the AMA to establish a church in Madison County—his own home county—as the foundation for an antislavery community, a goal he achieved by 1853. To make this proposed community in Madison County even more attractive to potential antislavery settlers, Clay—who owned hundreds of acres of land near the new church—let it be known that he intended to give away much of his land and to sell the rest at low prices to people of right principles.[38]

Fee also saw the antislavery potential of Clay's proposed community, and when the pastor of the Madison County church had to be replaced in September 1854, Fee decided to take charge of the church personally. Upon his arrival in Madison County, Fee named the still-unsettled community Berea, from the biblical town whose residents had "received the word with all readiness of mind and searched the scriptures daily." Fee believed that the new community would provide him with a base of operations in the heart of Kentucky from which he could further expand his ministry. Berea was situated between the mountains of southeastern Kentucky and the heart of the state's slaveholding region. It would be an "outpost" on the frontier of enemy country. Churches established by the AMA, Fee wrote, "however small, . . . would be nucleuses around which others would gather—centers from which light would radiate"—and, together with antislavery schools, would make "public sentiment so aroused that the death knell of slavery would soon be heard."[39]

Fee's conception of the antislavery potential of the Berea community was not narrowly religious, though. Fee and his co-workers hoped that Berea would become a center for immigration from the free states—an antislavery "colony," as they often called it—and from the outset they made it clear that they wanted all types of settlers, not just professional missionaries, to come to Berea and, as one of Fee's associates put it, "help this people build up [a] good society, good schools, and a pure Christianity." These settlers, Fee hoped, would build a prosperous community founded on the principles of Christian egalitarianism, abolitionism, and free labor, a model in both religion and economics for the South to emulate. To secure this end, the Bereans—as all of Fee's co-workers were called, regardless of their place of residence—began promoting northern settlement of the Berea colony in national publications during the fall of 1855, which attracted a trickle of northern settlers to Berea over the next four years. Berea also quickly became a settling point for some antislavery Kentuckians and the center of AMA activities in Kentucky.[40]

The establishment of a community of Christian abolitionists in the midst of slavery raised for Fee a number of questions about Berea's relationship to the outside world, especially about the extent to which the Bereans were to be governed by God's law rather than man's. This issue troubled Fee because he recognized, to some degree, the authority of both types of law, and it pained him that human and divine law seemed to be so often at odds. For Fee, of course, the claims of divine law always remained paramount. Living in an imperfect, slaveholding world in which human law seemed routinely to contravene divine law, Fee idealized the concept of a network of Christians living among other people but functioning as a separate community under the sole governance of God's sovereignty. These

Christians would have their own code of living that had little to do with the prevailing laws of human society.[41]

Fee demonstrated his commitment to the doctrine of higher law in regard to the issue of fugitive slaves. Fee's record on fugitive slaves is difficult to assess, because he never left a record that he ever helped a fugitive find freedom. But his pronouncements on the subject were daring—even dangerous—for a southerner living among people for whom the issue of fugitive slaves was a matter of urgent concern. In publications intended for distribution in the South, Fee praised the fugitives, suggesting that since God did not recognize the existence of slavery, neither should the slave or the Christian. Nothing in God's law prevented a slave from "assum[ing] to himself . . . personal ownership, and walk[ing] off." Likewise, God's law required the Christian to help a black man who came to him for assistance on the same terms that he would help a white man, even though the Christian knew that by humanity's law the black man was a slave. Fee praised those whites who helped fugitives and announced publicly that he could never return a fugitive who came to him for help because "God forbade that the servant should be delivered up, 'that was escaped from his master.'"[42]

Fee's belief in higher law influenced another activity of the Bereans, the distribution of Bibles to slaves. The AMA had shown an early interest in giving Bibles to slaves, and it regularly provided Bibles for Fee and his co-workers to distribute among Kentucky's bondsmen. Unlike most southern states, it was not illegal in Kentucky to teach slaves to read and write or to give them literature to read—provided, of course, that the slaves' masters consented. Fee ignored this last element of the law: although Fee would not enter a farm without the owner's permission to give Bibles to slaves, when a slave came to Fee and asked him for a Bible, Fee obliged without regard for the consent of the master. Further, when slaves did not come to him, he went to them: Fee and the colporteurs he supervised sought out slaves along roadsides, in churches, or at the houses of other slaves to give them Bibles. Before handing them the scriptures, Fee and his associates inquired only whether the bondsmen wanted the Bible and sometimes whether they could read, but not whether their masters approved of the transaction. Fee showed so little regard for the consent of masters that he sometimes gave Bibles to slaves for them to distribute to other slaves.[43]

Fee was firmly committed to such practices, continuing them even over the vehement objections of his friend Clay. In fact, Fee's Bible distribution policy and its underlying rationale that Christians were governed first by God's law, not man's, sparked the first recorded argument between Clay and Fee. Clay pleaded with his friend to seek the permission of masters before giving Bibles to their slaves. "If you offer the bible [and] the masters deny [it], . . . then you have done your duty—the responsibility rests upon *them* not you," Clay argued. "Any other communication with the slave except through the master is not to be thought of by us," for this is the only "*safe* ground of opposition to slavery. . . . It is the *creature of law*—and we propose not to violate the law—but to *unmake it by law.*"[44]

For all of Clay's admonitions, Fee himself was not immune to the claims of human government. Although Fee idealized the community of Christians who lived as though humanity's law did not exist, he also believed that human government had been given to people by God to implement certain elements of divine law: to provide order on Earth, to punish sin, and to promote salvation. The fact that "*government* is of Divine appointment," Fee thought, meant that Christians should obey earthly governors to some degree. Ideally, no great conflict between human law and God's law should exist because the very process of conducting an earthly government required people to reconcile human and divine law. If God had instituted human governments to accomplish some divine purpose, Fee argued, then the proper function of human legislators was to search the scriptures to find and enact the true moral law, the divinely ordained principles of right that should guide relationships between people.[45]

This notion was rooted, like Fee's whole antislavery philosophy, in his belief that God was the active sovereign of the universe, with the ultimate power to make laws for human conduct. In Fee's eyes, jurists and legislators could not create law themselves; they could only implement pre-existing principles of natural law. "Men are only

. . . law bringers," Fee wrote. "God is the source of all true law." In Fee's conception of law lay the source of much of his difference with Clay over the distribution of Bibles to slaves. When Clay insisted that slavery was a "creature of law," his premise was that humanity was the source of law and could make or unmake slavery at its discretion. Fee's natural-law formulation, on the other hand, assumed that God was the ultimate source of law and that human governments could make no laws exceeding the grant of authority given to them by God. Thus, slave codes and all other laws "contrary to natural right" lacked "the elements of true law," for they had come into being only through the "usurpation" of God's authority by humans. In God's eyes, slavery was null and void, literally "incapable of legalization" by human legislators.[46]

There still remained the question of whether a Christian was obliged to obey a human government when it had exceeded what seemed to be its God-given authority. Fee's answer was a qualified no. If the conflict between human law and higher law operated merely as an inconvenience or injury to the Christian, he was commanded by God to obey human government because disobedience to an inconvenient or even personally oppressive law promoted general disobedience to government and fostered within the Christian's character such unrighteous traits as anger, impatience, and infidelity. But if human law went beyond mere harm to the Christian—if it *required* him to sin—he was bound by his religion to disobey human law. "I may suffer wrong, but not *do* wrong," Fee wrote. "I would endure a grievous tax—an unjust one, until by persevering efforts we could secure a repeal of the oppressive law. But when [legislative] enactments or political parties require me to *do* a positive wrong— an immorality to man, and an act of impiety to God—. . . then I must in obedience to God's higher law, refuse obedience to the mere human law." In such a case, however, Christians must submit nonviolently to whatever punishment the earthly government chose to inflict on the person who preferred God's law to man's.[47]

Fee was generally quite conservative in determining when a human law ceased being merely an inconvenient or oppressive requirement on the individual and became instead a requirement for him to sin, and he usually advised Christians to pay their taxes, sit on juries, and serve in the military if required to do so. Fee even advised slaves not to be insubordinate, lest by resisting the exercise of the master's unjust and unwarranted authority, they destroy in themselves those "*Christian virtues*" which were "*essential to the perfection of Christian character.*" Yet if Fee advised slaves not to be insubordinate, he certainly did not tell them to remain in bondage. Indeed, Fee's advice to slaves about higher law practically called on them to escape. He argued that the biblical requirement for all Christians, including slaves, to follow God before man might make it a slave's religious duty to escape, much as it had been the ancient Hebrews' duty to escape from Egyptian slavery when the Pharaoh commanded "that they should not go out to sacrifice, without his consent." If American slavery had been merely an injustice to the slave, he should not disobey the master. But in Fee's view, by definition slavery took from the slave "the privilege of worshipping his God as he chooses." The Bible's strictures against insubordination, Fee wrote, "are never to be so construed as to prevent a man from PEACEFULLY withdrawing to a place . . . where he can serve God better. No claims of man, or society, may contravene those of God, or of conscience."[48]

This and other highly individualistic appeals to the higher-law doctrine constituted a major theme of Fee's early career, informing as they did his belief in the sinfulness of slavery, his critique of denominationalism, and his thoughts about his relationship to the government and the world around him. It was a theme that fit well with the circumstances of Fee's own early career as a reformer. As an abolitionist in a slave state and as a Christian minister in a seemingly unregenerate world, Fee's conception of himself as a reformer was that of a solitary individual seeking to change the world through the power of persuasion, the force of logic, and the appeal of truth. One of Fee's prime concerns, then, was to uphold those God-given liberties that sustained righteous people in a hostile world: the freedom to follow one's conscience in the face of overwhelming opposition and to proclaim one's personal beliefs openly and without fear of retribution.

Fee's quest for righteousness had given him a transforming moral vision that most Kentuckians—as proponents of the necessary-evil theory—lacked. Fee would not compromise or temporize, unlike the majority of Kentuckians who ultimately accommodated themselves to the pressures exerted by racism, property rights, and social stigma. And unlike most conservative emancipationists after their defeat in the constitutional struggle of 1849, Fee would not give up. However, during the mid-1850s, the events of Fee's life and of national politics caused Fee to wonder if reform could in fact be achieved by the upholding the right of individuals to follow their consciences or to proclaim their beliefs. Facing determined and sometimes violent opposition, Fee now asked a question that Kentucky's more conservative antislavery reformers dared not ask: Did the persistence of coercive opposition make it imperative for reformers to resort to coercion themselves?

8

The Relevance and
Irrelevance of John G. Fee

Fee's re-examination of the tactics of reform coincided with a similar re-examination by American abolitionists in general, in response to the rise of popular antislavery in the North and the increased intransigence of slaveholders in the South. These developments affected Fee as well, in some ways even more than it did his northern counterparts, for southern intransigence had a far more direct effect on his life than it did on an abolitionist in Boston or New York. In Fee's case—and for many northern abolitionists as well—the events of the mid-1850s caused him to abandon much of his hope that abolition would come about through the tactics of moral suasion: the efforts of reformers like himself to convince slaveholders of the error of their ways. By the mid-1850s, Fee stood ready to adopt more coercive tactics in the fight against slavery. If slaveholders refused to free their slaves, they must be forced to do so by the legal and political system; should they respond with violence, then their efforts must be met in kind.

Fee's embrace of coercive tactics in the mid-1850s was ironic, for much of his career until then had been dedicated to ameliorating coercive human relationships, whether between master and slave, re-

ligious denomination and communicant, or government and citizen. Yet like Fee's earlier concern for protecting individual rights from
majoritarian coercion, his growing interest in democratic political
power reflected his desire to free people from all restraints that prevented them from following God's higher law. What if citizens started
voting like Christians and electing leaders concerned with implementing higher law? Would not democracy become a forum in which
God's will could be made known through the collective voice of his
followers? Could constitutional restraints prevent a righteous host
from using the ballot to effect "self-evident truths" in law? If human
governments were designed by some higher authority to secure
humanity's "inalienable rights," could any earthly restraints on this
government prevent it from accomplishing its mission?[1]

At the same time, Fee looked to the North and to the federal
government to find his righteous majority. This change of perspective represented a modification of Fee's early conception of effective
methods of reform and of his own role as a reformer. Fee initially
assumed that effective political action against slavery would have to
occur at the state level, and he directed most of his political activities
to state politics. Ultimately, of course, Fee believed that all types of
political action, whether by state or national government, offered
defective solutions to the problem of slavery as long as prejudice—
the real foundation of slavery—remained in people's hearts. Abolition would be effected only by reformers like Fee who showed the
nation its sin and pointed the way to salvation.[2]

However, in the mid-1850s Fee's views on the efficacy of a national political solution to slavery began to change. Events at home
caused Fee to experience a crisis of faith regarding his own antislavery ministry, as Fee and his co-workers experienced serious incidents
of mob violence, which threatened to overwhelm them. The first
such incident occurred in March 1855 when Fee arrived at Dripping
Springs in Garrard County to debate the subject of colonization with
William Davis, a local lawyer. A mob of forty men refused to allow
Fee to speak and demanded that he pledge never to preach again in
that neighborhood. When Fee insisted that he had the right of free
speech, the men placed him on his horse, and they "forced [the]

horse along" the road "with boards and sticks" for two hours while taunting Fee with "vile abuse, and constant threats." The mob eventually released Fee, shaken but unharmed. In the following days, however, a flurry of public meetings near Dripping Springs denounced Fee and his co-workers, demanding that they cease their antislavery activities in the area. Such open displays of mob violence and opposition to abolitionism, the continuing refusal of slaveholders to see the error of their ways, and the unwillingness of even nonslaveholders to act against slavery made Fee doubtful of the effectiveness of his ministry and increasingly receptive to new modes of antislavery action. As he saw it, "The people are slow to receive the truth, or at least, to act on it," and meanwhile, "the poor slave toils on—his chains are being multiplied. It will certainly be a *mercy* to him to adopt the *speediest* means [of abolition] possible."[3]

At the same time, Fee witnessed the phenomenal rise of the new Republican party in the North. The sudden appearance of an avowedly antislavery political party that might attract a plurality of the North's voters made Fee hopeful that northerners were finally becoming enlightened on the slavery issue, and it made him believe that political action might now be a more effective and humane solution to the issue of slavery than moral suasion alone. Yet Fee had mixed emotions about the Republican party. As with many abolitionists, Fee's excitement about the rise of the new party was tempered by nagging doubts about the party's watered-down principles; he feared that "the prevailing type of Republicanism is a disposition to let the slave pass by." At first, Fee actively participated in the new party and, along with his longtime political ally Cassius Clay, organized the first Kentucky branch of the Republican party in the spring of 1856. Fee also served on the committee that called and organized the first Republican National Convention in Philadelphia, which was scheduled for June 1856. But although Clay remained ecstatic over the new party, Fee could not shake his concern that the Republicans' moderate program of opposing the extension of slavery into the territories was "tedious, uncertain, and, at best, still leaves one half of the nation under the blighting curse of slavery." At the same time, Fee moved closer to William Goodell, Gerrit Smith, and the Radical

Political Abolitionists, reformers who, like Fee, looked to principles of higher-law doctrine and constitutional theory to reconcile the conflict between individual rights and majority rule—between their own need for freedom of conscience and their desire to muster coercive political power against others—and to justify an unprecedented assumption of power by a national government in order to abolish slavery. In January 1856—while still working with the Republicans—Fee joined the Radicals' newly formed American Abolition Society, and in June of that year he told Gerrit Smith, the Radicals' presidential candidate, that "my present conviction is that the radical position is nearest right [and] I do not expect to attend the Republican [National] Convention."[4]

Fee's growing involvement with the Radicals worried his friend Clay. As early as July 1855, Clay had warned Fee away from the Radicals' political and constitutional doctrines, arguing that "we cannot stand on them in the South." In fact, Fee's association with the Radicals and their majoritarian, higher-law doctrines caused a growing estrangement between Fee and Clay, a conflict that by the summer of 1856 would end their antislavery partnership. The two men quarreled privately about higher law between the summers of 1855 and 1856; their conflict became public at a Fourth of July picnic they hosted at Slate Lick Springs in Madison County. Fee opened the day's festivities with a long speech that outlined his version of Radical constitutionalism, without explicitly endorsing the Radical party; Clay followed with a stinging refutation of Fee's constitutional theories. When the speeches were finished, so was the decade-long alliance between the men. Although both men tried at various times to renew their cooperation, and although they remained friendly for several years, they could never again work together as they once had.[5]

What Fee and Clay debated at Slate Lick Springs and what they continued to argue about in subsequent days was the Radicals' notion that a national majority could exercise direct, coercive power against slavery, and that, in fact, God authorized the United States government to abolish slavery. Fee realized that this position was problematic. A fundamental principle of American constitutional law before the Civil War was that the federal government lacked the direct power to abolish slavery within the states themselves. Few people, even among abolitionists, challenged this principle. Fee himself believed that while God may have given the federal government the power to abolish slavery, the Founding Fathers might not have been so generous. In Fee's view, the Founders, like all human lawmakers, were imperfect people trying to find and enact God's law; hence their understanding of that higher law was imperfect and they sometimes acted out of expediency rather than principle. While Fee believed that the Founders had not wanted slavery to be a permanent institution or intended to make the Constitution a proslavery document, he still thought "the framers and people intended to tolerate slavery at least until 1808 [and] possibly longer."[6]

Yet unlike many other antislavery reformers who recognized the Founders' expediency—Republicans like Clay, who believed that the Constitution was neutral on the subject of slavery, and Garrisonian abolitionists, who believed the Constitution was a thoroughly proslavery document—Fee now accepted the Radicals' doctrine that the Founders' intentions did not significantly limit the federal government's ability to abolish slavery. Indeed, Fee wanted to go beyond the Founders' intentions: he proposed to remake the Constitution into an antislavery document by discovering what "the *words* of the constitution—not [the] intentions of [the] framers or adopters—allow *us to do.*" If the Founders had not intentionally granted the federal government all of the powers necessary to implement its God-given authority to abolish slavery, people of Fee's day could adapt the Constitution to fulfill God's calling.[7]

Even as he called for Americans of his time to change the meaning of the Constitution, Fee knew that jurists of the mid-nineteenth century did not look kindly upon either the intentional reinterpretation of the Constitution or the discarding of the Founders' intentions, and he tried to ground his argument in legal theories that connected his antislavery rendering of the Constitution with the original design of the Constitution. This concern, and his own interest in finding mechanisms by which the Constitution could be made to resemble God's law, attracted him to the system of English common law and Blackstonian concepts of natural law. Like Fee, Sir

William Blackstone, the great eighteenth-century commentator on English law, had argued that in many respects the primary function of human legislators was to discover and implement principles of natural law. Their efforts, however, were often flawed. Thus, when faced with specific cases in which human law was not clear, judges should assume a legislative intent to enact natural law and rule according to their own understanding of that law. Fee claimed that American courts had long accepted the maxim that when a judge interpreted a law that seemed to abridge natural rights—unless the legislative intention to do so was clear and unmistakable—he should apply the law in a way that upheld natural rights. Fee argued, therefore, that judges served constantly to refine human law into an increasingly close approximation of natural law.[8]

Given the Blackstonian strain in American legal thought, Fee believed that if he could demonstrate historically that the Founders had intended to enact higher law—that the Constitution "was designed for Freedom," as Fee put it—and that the Founders had placed mechanisms in the Constitution allowing subsequent generations to refine the Constitution into a closer approximation of higher law should experience prove the Founders' creation to be imperfect, then his appeal for a deliberate reinterpretation of the nation's fundamental law would be constitutionally valid. Guarantees of civil rights, while not originally intended to apply to slaves, could rightly be applied to them by modern Americans.[9]

Consequently, Fee set out to prove that the Constitution was indeed "designed for freedom": that while the Founding Fathers compromised the truth by refusing to abolish slavery through the Constitution, they had created a general framework of liberty in the Constitution that, they believed, would work against the system of slavery. They never intended for the Constitution to be used to protect slavery and "did not expect slavery to live long under the then prevailing sentiment of liberty and equal rights." Thus, while the Founders wrote a Constitution which sometimes recognized the fact that slavery existed and, as a practical matter, regulated certain aspects of it—such as the recovery of fugitive slaves—they refused to establish slavery positively in the Constitution and, in Fee's words, "were careful not to . . . do any thing that would seem to imply the legality of Slavery." Fee pointed to the very language of the Constitution as proof that the Founders had recognized the fact—but not the legality—of slavery. They had scrupulously avoided using the word *slave* in the Constitution, lest that hated word stain their work and imply the constitutionality or morality of the peculiar institution.[10]

A question remained, however—one so provocative and so counter to the prevailing legal and cultural norms that few people even dared ask it. Did the state governments have the legal authority to establish slavery within their borders? Most Americans of Fee's day, even those holding grandiose conceptions of federal power, believed that the greater portion of governmental powers was meant to be exercised by state governments. They viewed the Constitution as an agreement among the peoples of the various states, one granting to the federal government and prohibiting to the state governments a limited number of powers, while reserving to the people in each state the ability to determine how much of the great residual power to govern would be granted to their state governments. Fee departed radically from this consensus, challenging the doctrine of state sovereignty and asserting that state authority to establish slavery had been taken away by the ratification of the United States Constitution. Fee worried that the doctrine of state sovereignty granted to the people of the states almost unlimited powers, including the power to destroy what Fee thought was the very purpose of the Constitution, the provision of a framework of liberty for the nation. If "the majority of the people of each State, in convention assembled, may decree that . . . [any] unoffending member . . . of this commonwealth may be made a Slave, . . ." Fee wrote, "then our State governments become the vilest despotisms under the sun—yea their power is so great that they may destroy the whole national government."[11]

Drawing arguments from Radical constitutionalism, Fee claimed that the antidote to state sovereignty lay in what has been called "one of the most confused and unprecedented areas of American constitutional development" before the Civil War, the concept of citizenship. Few Americans agreed about what made a person a citizen of either his state or his nation; about what rights, privileges, and immunities belonged to a person as a result of his citizenship in either a state or the nation; or about what restrictions and obligations a person's citizenship in one polity placed on the government of another. If there was even a rough preponderance of opinion on these questions, it was that, in terms of rights and privileges, an individual's primary citizenship was to his state; that an individual had few federal rights; that these rights posed few restrictions on his state; and that even federal rights were to be primarily enforced by the states.[12]

Fee's notion of citizenship differed sharply from this consensus, and his concept of national citizenship anticipated doctrines later established in the Fourteenth Amendment. Fee believed that there was such an entity as national citizenship, separate from and above state citizenship; that it belonged to every person born in the United States; and that it invested a person with certain rights that neither states nor private individuals could abridge. The cornerstone of these national citizenship rights, Fee believed, was the guarantee of the Fifth Amendment that "no person shall be deprived of life, liberty, or property, without due process of law." Fee took this not in the narrow, procedural sense—that every person accused of crime has a right to a fair trial—but in the broader, more modern substantive sense—that unless convicted of a crime in a fair trial, every person has a right to liberty. Fee believed that the language of this amendment and the principles set forth in the Declaration of Independence—a document that helped define the sort of government the Founders were seeking to create—applied the guarantee of liberty to all "resident[s] of the United States" without regard for "color, or race," a formulation that included the nation's slave population. If slaves were citizens, and if states were limited in their actions against such citizens by the Fifth Amendment, then state laws that sustained such an obvious abridgment of liberty as slavery were unconstitutional. In Fee's view, the Fifth Amendment had freed all slaves, and if judges were fair and honest in their interpretation of the Constitution, they would declare state laws establishing slavery to be unconstitutional.[13]

With his enunciation of black citizenship and judicial power, Fee believed he had embraced constitutional doctrines that held great promise for ending slavery through a court challenge, and he urged other abolitionists to press the Fifth Amendment argument upon judges. In truth, Fee's strategy raised so many historical and legal problems as to require a judicial revolution of some magnitude to solve. Fee himself realized that no state judge in Kentucky—or any other slave state—was likely to declare slavery unconstitutional, and his strategy depended explicitly upon getting a case to federal court. But there was little reason to hope that a federal court would even accept jurisdiction in Fee's proposed test case. When Fee first embraced the Radicals' judicial solution to slavery in 1856, the United States Supreme Court had *never* declared a provision of a state constitution to be in violation of the United States Constitution, and it had only once accepted jurisdiction in a case in which the constitutionality of a state constitution was at issue, a case which was still pending. Given that it had recently reaffirmed that the first eight amendments to the Constitution did not restrict the actions of states, the Supreme Court would likely dismiss such a case based on the Fifth Amendment.[14]

The merit of Fee's argument was that courts sometimes change their minds. What is radical doctrine and strained argument one day can become established constitutional law the next. Fee did not have much hope that state judges in Kentucky or other slave states would change their minds, and his strategy of trying to get a case before a federal judge looked beyond the slave states for the source of antislavery action. Neither did he have much hope that existing federal judges would be very sympathetic to the slave. Fee's strategy depended explicitly on the appointing of federal judges with antislavery sentiments, which in turn, of course, required the election of a president who would appoint such judges and a Senate that would confirm them. Such a notion underlay Fee's argument that the Constitution should be intentionally reinterpreted for antislavery purposes: he frequently characterized judges as people who consciously interpreted law to carry out specific policies and the federal judiciary as "the instrument of a *national* party."[15]

The image is striking. At the same time that he was calling for a politicized judiciary, he was repeating his traditional plea for courts "to enforce . . . the revealed will of God." If, as in Fee's view, judges were to be both the arm of a party and seekers after truth, then they must be the arm of a righteous party, a moral majority. It is in this context that the importance of Blackstonian concepts on Fee's thought becomes apparent. If judges serve to refine general human laws, then as political judges they serve to bring the acts of the majority more closely in line with natural law—to allow a Christian democracy to continually remake its government.[16]

If, as Fee believed, a radical judiciary offered the best hope for ending slavery throughout the United States, his judicial strategy did nothing to relieve the personal dilemma over his own role as a reformer in an unjust world, a dilemma which the events of the mid to late 1850s were heightening. Before the Constitution could be reinterpreted to free the slaves, judges would have to be appointed by officials elected by an antislavery majority; but there was no assurance that the existing antislavery majority in the North, as represented by the Republican party, would appoint the right kind of people to the courts. For Fee this raised a continuing question about his own political involvement: "Should I support the Republican Party," he asked, or "stand off with a few and keep away from the movement . . . until I could get men to take abolitionist ground?" This was a question Fee would not be able to answer in the election year of 1856, when, despite his accession to Radical constitutionalism, he could not decide between the Republican presidential candidate, John C. Frémont, and the Radical candidate, Gerrit Smith. When on election day the voters of Madison County announced their oral votes for president, the voice of John Fee—who thought it was a Christian's religious duty to vote—remained silent. Indeed, Fee would waver between the Republicans and some more radical alternative throughout the late 1850s and into the Civil War years, alternately attracted by the Republicans' prospects for success and repulsed by their conservatism.[17]

Fee's dilemma over the tactics of reform, however, went far beyond questions of political action. In the late 1850s, the slaveholders' challenge to Fee and his mission in Kentucky intensified and became increasingly violent, so much so that it seemed to Fee that it might crush out his work in the mountains of Kentucky. This challenge and the slaveholders' general recalcitrance raised other questions in

Fee's mind. Were Christians confined to the use of political force? Had God authorized people to use righteous violence to free the slave? Fee's views on the use of violence have, in many ways, proved to be the most problematic aspect of his thought. Fee's mild manner and his own professions that he was a man of peace misled many of his contemporaries and subsequent historians alike into thinking that he abjured the use of violence. Cassius Clay saw the truth of the matter more clearly: he remarked without elaboration in his memoirs that Fee "was at first a non-resistant; but, further along, allowed his friends to use force." Clay's observation was astute, a quality arising out of his intimate and sometimes painful acquaintance with Fee's views on the use of violence. In the early part of his career, Fee did embrace a form of nonresistance—albeit one that did not completely disavow violence—and in the mid to late 1850s, the same factors that caused Fee to lose some faith in moral suasion and to embrace majoritarianism increasingly convinced him that, in some cases, abolitionists could righteously use violence to further their cause.[18]

Nonviolent abolitionists of the antebellum years often called themselves nonresistants. The name came from Jesus' injunction to "resist not evil": "Ye have heard that it hath been said, An eye for an eye, and a tooth for a tooth: But I say unto you, That ye resist not evil: but whosoever shall smite thee on thy right cheek, turn to him the other also." However, the term nonresistant could justly be applied to people holding widely divergent opinions about the use of violence. At the very least, nonresistance implied a simple restraint on the nonresistant's ability to defend himself against minor abuses. In the minds of abolitionists like William Lloyd Garrison or Nathaniel P. Rogers, however, nonresistance called for the abolition of all forms of violence and coercive force. They decried not only violent self-defense but also subtler forms of coercive force, such as governments. Beyond Clay's observation that Fee, for a time, had embraced nonresistance, there is no evidence that Fee ever called himself a nonresistant, perhaps because of the term's association with the Garrisonians and their theory of "no-governmentism"; in addition, his peace views never matched those of the Garrisonians. Nevertheless, Fee's early views on the issue generally accorded with those of other friends and associates of Lewis Tappan who sometimes called themselves nonresistants. That is, although Fee deplored violence, he did believe in a narrowly conceived right of self-defense.[19]

Before the mid-1850s, Fee advised people to use violence "only as a last resort . . . to save body or life." This standard prohibited violent self-defense, even when facing violent opposition, so long as loss of life or serious injury at the hands of another party was not certain. Likewise, during his early career Fee excluded from his standard of rightful self-defense even the defense of civil rights against the violent suppression of those rights, an important concession for a reformer asserting free speech in an unpopular cause. "Where we cannot maintain our rights," Fee argued, "an attempt to do so by resistance becomes wrong from inexpediency, and perhaps blasphemy." This belief matched Fee's views on civil disobedience and his advice to slaves. As long as violence was aimed only at the abridgment of rights and not at life or religious duty, the Christian was obliged to bear the abridgment but could apply to the courts for relief. To do otherwise was to risk committing "blasphemy" by engendering in one's self feelings of sinful hatred. Further, Fee insisted, if a Christian was not permitted to resist violent opposition to the exercise of rights, then logically he should not carry arms to defend those rights. Fee even argued that people should not carry arms for self-defense, claiming that such habits made it more likely that opponents would initiate violence—or that, in the heat of an argument, weapons intended for self-defense would be used in other ways.[20]

These views contributed to the emerging friction between Fee and Clay after the summer of 1855. As his numerous brawls involving free speech suggest, Clay was hardly timid about defending his rights. Since the late 1840s, Fee had worried about Clay's proclivity for violence, and after Fee moved to Berea in 1854, their increasingly close association prompted Fee to worry that his own mission would be tainted by Clay's violence. The episode that brought Fee's concern to the fore occurred soon after the incident with the mob at Dripping Springs. Following the attack on Fee, Clay had rushed to his friend's defense, speaking throughout the area in favor of Fee's freedom of speech, rallying local supporters to express their support for

Fee, and even meeting with representatives of the mob to try and allay their hostility to Fee.[21]

Public outcry against Fee continued for several months after Dripping Springs and spread to nearby Rockcastle County where, in July 1855, a public meeting in the county seat passed resolutions threatening Fee and Clay with death, should they ever speak there again. This was an especially pernicious threat to Fee because he saw Rockcastle County as the center of his antislavery mission, and the two men viewed this challenge as a special opportunity to uphold symbolically Fee's freedom of speech by refusing to back down before the threat. On July 21, the day of Fee's next regularly scheduled speaking engagement in Rockcastle County, the two men—accompanied by a group of their friends—went to the Scaffold Cane meetinghouse, where Fee spoke "without interruption." Clay immediately followed Fee's remarks with a theatrical demonstration of support for the preacher that, in the hands of northern storytellers, became the source of legend—and myth. With a Bible, a copy of the United States Constitution, and a pistol arrayed before him on the lectern, Clay allegedly thundered: "For those who obey the law of God I appeal to this Book; for those who obey the law of the land I appeal to this document," and—with his hand now clutching the pistol—"for those who recognize the law of force, here is my defense. . . . Free speech shall be maintained; Fee shall be heard." Whether or not this story is true in all its details, there can be no doubt that Clay was armed that day and that both men addressed the congregation while "surrounded by armed followers."[22]

The story of the Scaffold Cane affair received wide coverage in the northern antislavery press, much of it favorable. However, the incident embarrassed Fee and he told Clay how he felt. Before Scaffold Cane, Fee's opposition to violence had wavered as he weighed the morality of allowing others to defend his right of free speech when the government refused to do so. In the end, Fee apparently turned down Clay's offer of armed protection and was surprised when Clay and his supporters made a show of force. Fee privately scolded Clay for carrying concealed weapons at Scaffold Cane and openly criticized Clay's tactics, writing to the northern press to correct "the impression that the way for the gospel has to be opened by an armed force." He cited several examples of places in Kentucky, even in Rockcastle County, where, "without weapons or armed friends, we had free speech on the subject of slavery." Such criticism only increased the differences driving Fee and Clay apart in the mid-1850s. Ironically, though, the break between the men caused Fee to move closer to Clay's position on the use of violence. After 1856, when Fee confronted mob violence he did so without the assurance of Clay's support, and this fact made Fee more fearful that his life and work would be snuffed out unless he and his followers defended themselves.[23]

Fee's thoughts began to evolve during a seven-month period of extraordinary violence, which touched the very heart of his southeastern Kentucky operations. After the Scaffold Cane affair, Rockcastle County seemed so secure and promising a field of labor that Fee and his followers debated moving the base of their operations there from Berea. They had hit upon the idea of building an antislavery school and college to help attract settlement from the North, and a group of Fee's friends in Rockcastle County had donated land for the college at Cummins. The Bereans began an integrated primary school on that spot in January 1857, at the same time redoubling their efforts to promote their antislavery colonies and proposed college in the northern press.[24]

But in the summer of 1857 things began to go awry in and around Rockcastle County. While Fee was preaching at the Cummins schoolhouse on June 21, a group of men gathered around the school, apparently intending to stop the meeting. Nothing came of the incident, but five days later arsonists burned down the schoolhouse. Fee immediately began to raise money for a new building and moved his preaching services into the house of A.G.W. Parker, an AMA colporteur under his supervision. About two weeks after the Cummins school had been burned, Fee got word that another of his co-workers, J. Clark Richardson, had been "mobbed and beaten" at Williamsburg in nearby Whitley County; one month after the school burning, Fee himself experienced another taste of mob violence in Rockcastle County. On July 19, thirty to forty armed men stopped Fee's preaching service at the Parker house in Cummins and forcibly carried Fee away, apparently intending to do him harm. Fee was saved from injury by inclement weather, which made the mob lose interest in their task, and they released Fee after warning him not to return to Rockcastle County.[25]

This incident did not end Fee's troubles, however. Less than a week later, Fee's congregation at Cummins voted to ask him back to the area. Soon thereafter, during the first week of August, someone set fire to the house occupied by A.G.W. Parker, whose family barely escaped from their burning home. Fee's congregation in Rockcastle County, which had not backed down when their school building was burned and their preacher was mobbed, shuddered now that a private residence had been attacked. Members of the congregation refused to allow their houses to be used for Fee's preaching. Moreover, Fee's efforts to prosecute the Cummins mob in the Rockcastle County Court failed. According to Fee, not only did the grand jury fail to indict the men, but the judge also "threw his influence on the side of the mob, gave up his court-house to them . . . to pass resolutions against us. . . . Quite a number of men last week at Court swore publickly that they would take my life." Two weeks later, Fee and Richardson confronted another mob in neighboring Laurel County. When Fee and Richardson arrived for an engagement on August 22, they "found a mob with guns in their hands" who would not let the men speak.[26]

During this summer of trials, Fee took self-defense much more seriously than he had in the past. The same man who had once thought that people should not even prepare to defend themselves could now be heard praising his followers for being "ready [to] 'take aim and fire' if need be—they intend to show a determination not to surrender the life of their friend." The man who had once been reticent to defend himself now publicly announced his intention to defend himself and his family. The man who in 1855 had criticized Clay for maintaining that armed resistance was necessary for the spread of antislavery was writing in 1857 that he believed that "the people . . . will have to defend themselves against the lawless with their rifles if needs be or we shall have to give up the field . . . in some places."[27]

Fee also turned his attention toward getting Clay once again to take on precisely the role for which Fee had once criticized him for assuming, that of Fee's armed protector. When Fee was mobbed at Parker's house in Cummins, a member of the congregation immediately left for Berea to warn Fee's family and friends. Twenty-four people, including Fee's wife Matilda, rushed from Berea to find Fee and—if necessary—rescue him from the mob. Another person left Berea for White Hall to rouse Clay and bring him to Fee's rescue. The party from Berea searched for twelve hours before they discovered that Fee had been released unharmed. Clay, for his part, refused to come to Fee's aid, citing the two men's political differences. Clay's inaction deeply hurt Fee, who wrote Clay that, however much they disagreed about politics, Clay should have come to Fee's defense. "Protection is the duty of man to his fellow [man]," argued Fee. "When the officer cannot or will not [protect someone] then the people exorcise [sic] the right belonging to them [to do it]. This the friends here are determined to do. . . . You ought to [also]."[28]

Fee's disappointment at Clay's new aloofness turned to despair when, after several months of quiet in the fall of 1857, Fee and his co-workers again faced violence. In January 1858, at Lewis Chapel—some twenty-three miles north of Berea, near the border of Madison County—Fee faced the most dangerous mob incident of his life. On January 16, thirty men dragged Fee and colporteur Robert Jones from the church where Fee had been preaching and took them to the nearby Kentucky River, where the mob threatened to dunk both men in the icy water "till there was no breath" in them, unless the abolitionists promised to leave the area and never return. When Fee and Jones refused, the colporteur was ordered to strip naked in the winter chill and given a beating that left him bedridden for days. The mob then put Fee and Jones on a horse, escorted them five miles toward Berea, and left them with a warning never to return.[29]

Less than a week later, another of Fee's schools was burned to the ground; this time, the target was the school directed by George Candee in Pulaski County. Hostility against Candee soon became so strong that he had to leave the county. According to Fee, threats of violence against himself reached such a fevered pitch that "the male members of the church" at Berea "with others who were friends, held three formal councils" to warn him that they could defend him no longer and to ask Fee to leave the area for his own safety. During this period, Fee wrote to Simeon S. Jocelyn, the corresponding secretary of the AMA, that "there is still some threatening by the mob. Some Republican friends are ready to give me up—the mob know[s] it. Most of the church members stand firm. Clay stands entirely aloof. We may be crushed out." Desperate, Fee again begged Clay for the same sort of support that Clay had provided in the weeks following the Dripping Springs incident. "I feel the need of *protection*, . . ." Fee informed Clay. "*Immediate* action on your part will inspire courage on the one hand and intimidate on the other. The cause of God and humanity are at stake—To strike is life[;] inaction is death to us."[30]

Fee wanted Clay's support both to "intimidate" and to "inspire courage." The latter was important to Fee, for under the weight of his persecutions and thoughts of failure, his spirits were flagging. Although during these trying months of persecution he frequently proclaimed the glory and effectiveness of martyrdom, in truth he found martyrdom a heavy cross to bear. Especially in the months after the Lewis Chapel incident, Fee grew depressed about his suffering and the continuing threat mobs posed to his ministry, concluding that "I shall probably live secluded, struggle with adversity, and die a premature death, worn out with care and toil." James S. Davis, Fee's associate in northern Kentucky, visited Berea in April 1858, and Fee's physical and mental condition so disturbed him that he noted publicly that "should the constant strain of a year past continue," Fee "will break down under its overwhelming weight." Privately, Davis told Jocelyn that "I found Bro[ther] Fee in a state of great depression. . . . The vacillation and weakness of some of the brethren was to Bro[ther] Fee a source of anxiety. . . . From these causes, his bodily strength was giving away."[31]

Thus, by the spring of 1858, mob violence had only heightened Fee's crisis of faith over his ability to touch the slaveholder's conscience. Not only did Fee's mission appear increasingly ineffective, but also it looked as though his mission might be suppressed. But, at the same time, Fee reached a new understanding of the methods he would have to use to free the slave, a realization that he could not rely on men like Clay to fight his battles for him and that he might have to take rifle in hand to defend himself and maintain his ministry. This change of heart is, perhaps, best seen in Fee's new conception of the antislavery martyr. Fee had long idealized the Christian martyr as the person who bore physical persecution or even death without resistance. But after the Lewis Chapel affair, for the first time Fee praised Elijah P. Lovejoy, the man who had died with a gun in his hand while defending his antislavery press, as a martyr. "The death of Lovejoy was no loss to the cause of Human Freedom in this nation," Fee wrote. "He perhaps has accomplished far more by his death than by his life. . . . His violent death gave immortality to his name, embodiment and perpetuity to his words, and sent every sentiment to the hearts and consciences of men, with an electric power which death in a righteous cause alone can inspire."[32]

After the spring of 1858, Fee was cheered by the undeniable fact that he had persevered and by the recognition that his ministry seemed to be flourishing again. The focus of this newfound hope was the effort of Fee and his associates to establish their long-dreamed-of antislavery college in Kentucky. By April 1858, the persecution of the Bereans had quieted sufficiently for Fee and his associates to continue with their plans to start the college, which they now prudently decided should be built in Berea. In that month, Fee asked a recent graduate of Oberlin College, John A.R. Rogers, to come to Berea and put the primary school there on a sound footing, in preparation for the establishment of the college. Rogers succeeded in this task, and shortly after his arrival Fee reported happily to Clay that "we have a first rate school with encouraging prospects . . . [and] more than formerly attend our [church] meetings."[33]

Indeed, the entire area surrounding Berea seemed happy that someone was finally bringing education to the mountains of Kentucky. At the end of the first school term, Fee and his associates combined their annual Fourth of July celebration with an "exhibition" for the Berea School to mark the end of the school year, and they were heartily surprised when nearly six hundred people showed up for the event. The entire exhibition provided a surprising and cheering day for the Bereans. They heard William Davis, the lawyer who had been scheduled to debate Fee at Dripping Springs some three years earlier, denounce the mob. Several slaveholders publicly praised the quality of the abolitionists' school and the day's exhibition. Even two members of the Cummins mob rather sheepishly joined in the festivities. Soon thereafter, Fee began soliciting funds to purchase 120 acres of land at Berea, and he and several supporters met to hammer out the constitution and bylaws of the college. In September 1858, Fee began a triumphant tour of the North to raise funds for the planned college and to attend the annual meeting of the AMA.[34]

When Fee returned from the North in November, however, he found trouble brewing at the school. The centerpiece of Fee's anticaste crusade, the proposed college, was to be open to people of all races, as was consistent with both the Bereans' philosophy and the established practice of their primary schools. However, unlike some of the AMA schools in Kentucky, the primary school at Berea had never had any blacks apply for admission, and so "the question of having colored children come into the school room, with white children, had not come practically before the people" of the area. The talk of opening an integrated college as an adjunct to the primary school brought the issue out in the open, and during Fee's absence some locals voiced opposition to integration. When Fee returned from his fund-raising tour, he found that several of the trustees of the proposed college "thought it best not to purchase" land "until the people of this district should decide whether an Anti Cast[e] school should be taught here."[35]

Had this controversy involved only the proposed college and the purchase of land, it would not have become as serious as it did. But the issue naturally extended into the question of what Fee and Rogers would do if blacks tried to attend the existing primary school. This meant that the people who lived around Berea would have something to say about the school's policy on integration. Since Fee and his associates received partial support for the school from the state's public school fund, the school was subject to the general supervision of the district school trustees. Elections for the trustees were to be held in the spring of 1859, and some residents of the area realized that if enemies of integration were elected as school trustees that they could prevent the admission of blacks to the primary school. Rogers announced before the election that if trustees prohibited blacks from attending the school, he would quit teaching there. The question before the voters, then, was, Which goal was more important to the white community: preventing black children from going to school with white ones or maintaining a quality elementary school? The voters answered resoundingly by electing trustees favorable to the integrated school by a margin of three to one, a remarkable occurrence in a slave state. Soon thereafter, the college's trustees approved the constitution and bylaws for Berea College, which proclaimed: "The object of this College shall be to furnish the facilities for a thorough education to *all* persons of good moral character. . . . This college shall be . . . opposed to sectarianism, slaveholding, caste, and every other wrong institution or practice."[36]

But classes did not begin at Berea College in 1859, nor at any time before the end of the Civil War. The peace that had existed since the spring of 1858 was abruptly shattered in May 1859. For the next year, a "reign of terror" descended on the Bereans, culminating in their expulsion from the state. The way Fee and his associates met this challenge showed how much they now accepted the necessity of defending themselves. The "reign of terror" began on May 1, when twenty armed men prevented James S. Davis from speaking in Mason County, charging that he had assisted a slave in killing his master. Davis left for Berea to allow the situation to cool down, but upon returning home in early June, he found threats still against him. On Davis's first Sunday back in Mason County, most of the men in the congregation stayed outside and guarded the church building. John Rogers, Davis's brother-in-law, wrote that during this period, Davis's "principles were so obnoxious and threats against him so abundant that one of his deacons often when he was preaching, sat in front of the pulpit with a loaded gun in his hand."[37]

Shortly after Davis returned to northern Kentucky, Fee himself faced another mob. At the conclusion of Fee's regular preaching appointment in Estill County on July 25, a group of men entered the building where he had been speaking and warned Fee not to return.

The members of the congregation, however, stood up for Fee, who wrote triumphantly, "The friends present told them in unmistakable terms that I should have the privilege of speaking." Fee viewed this episode as a ringing victory because, as he saw it, the congregation had prevented another incident like Lewis Chapel by standing up to the mob and threatening to resist them. The mob had withdrawn "not from regard to right," Fee wrote, "but because the majority of the good citizens were determined to resist them and maintain freedom of speech." Fee thought the result was that "manifest good was done. I do not think I have seen a more promising field in interior Kentucky. I trust God is opening an effectual door in our State."[38]

Three months later, Fee left for another fund-raising tour of the North and his ill-fated appointment at Henry Ward Beecher's Plymouth Church. The reaction in Kentucky to Fee's sermon followed hard upon the first newspaper accounts of the speech. Within two weeks of the speech, there were so many threats of violence that Rogers issued a public appeal for calm. Rogers and Matilda Fee soon wrote to Fee, who was still in the North, "asking him to clarify his remarks so that they could counter the attacks" against him. By the second week in December, several public meetings in Richmond discussed the proper way to handle the "Fee party." On December 11, three of Fee's associates—George Candee, William Kendrick, and the unlucky Robert Jones—were confronted in Laurel County by a mob, which shaved off the men's hair and beards and covered their heads with tar. Kendrick wrote to the Association that "the excitement is so great here, . . . the probability is that all the brethren at Berea will be killed or driven out. They intend to kill Mr. Fee, if he should come to K[entuck]y." Given such threats, friends and family persuaded Fee not to return to Berea but to wait a few days to see what would happen. He did not have long to wait: two days before Christmas, a party of sixty men, representing the earlier public meetings in Richmond, ordered twelve families from Berea to leave the state within ten days, on pain of death. After some debate about the proper course of action and after appealing to the governor of Kentucky for protection—an appeal that was refused—on December 29 more than thirty Bereans left their homes.[39]

Most of the exiled Bereans went to Cincinnati, but several went to Bracken County to join the other significant grouping of Fee's followers. After meeting his wife in Cincinnati, Fee joined them in Bracken County during the second week of January. But the situation there was nearly as unsettled as in Berea, and on January 25, 1860, a committee of fifty men delivered an order for eight families to leave the state by February 4. Fee at first wanted to resist the expulsion order, but his supporters in Bracken County balked at the suggestion. According to Fee, they told him that "'Our first impulse was to take our rifles and stand with you: but . . . we find that we will be utterly overwhelmed by the opposing power, and if you stay we shall all be driven away.'" Fee noted sadly that "the friends[,] even my father[-]in[-]law[,] thought I ought to go away[.] There was but one man there who said he would stand [by me]." Fee decided to leave the state rather than see all of his supporters driven out, but he hoped to return when "passion[s] subside and reaction begin[s]" to build on the base of support they provided. Although he acted for the sake of expediency, Fee did not derive much satisfaction from abandoning the field without a fight, and he noted ruefully to Clay that "a few resolute men could make the mobs quail."[40]

Fee did eventually return to his native state. During the Civil War, he toured the state several times to gauge the situation, and in April 1864, Fee did come home again. Upon his return, he threw himself into the work of educating black soldiers stationed at Camp Nelson in Jessamine County and into the task of opening Berea College. Indeed, after the war the "co-education of the races" became Fee's major work. He believed that blacks and whites should be educated together so that it would be clear to the world that blacks could compete equally with whites. In this respect, Fee succeeded in making Berea College the most remarkable experiment in interracial education in post–Civil War America: at no other institution of higher learning, not even at Oberlin College, were nearly equal numbers of blacks and whites educated together in integrated facilities.[41]

Fee's practice after the war was consistent with his antebellum teachings. As an antislavery southerner, Fee knew better than anyone that beyond the issue of slavery lay the issue of prejudice; for slavery and its fruits to come to an end, ultimately prejudice had to be defeated. Even when he came to believe that political solutions to slavery would have to precede moral ones, he never forgot his basic belief that political solutions alone were not sufficient to end the fruits of slavery. Fee's battle against prejudice became the main thrust of his antislavery warfare. It occupied most of his time with the building of antislavery and anticaste schools, churches, and communities, with which Fee tried to show people truth through example. He hoped that the example of racial equality in these institutions would break down people's prejudices and that, as still-receptive children, the young people taught in his schools would learn egalitarianism. Finally—and to him most importantly—Fee believed that the Christianity preached in these institutions could serve as a mighty counterweight to the entrenched power of prejudice, greed, and peer pressure, and literally transform men's lives and attitudes, as it had his own.

Fee's belief that prejudice was the central problem of race relations in America did not differ greatly from that of Kentucky's conservative antislavery supporters. The difference between Fee and these conservatives was that Fee was not just a southern antislavery reformer, he was a southern abolitionist. Lacking Fee's transforming vision of the sin of slaveholding and prejudice, the antislavery conservatives were never able to break free from their racism, their class interests, and their natural caution. Fee believed that prejudice could and should be eliminated; the conservatives had doubts on both counts. If Fee's position as an abolitionist distinguished him from other southern antislavery supporters, so did his position as a southerner distinguish him from other abolitionists. His southern perspective kept him concerned about convincing slaveholders of their sin long after many northern abolitionists had abandoned the slaveholder to concentrate on mobilizing an already aroused North into antislavery warfare. Even after Fee lost much of his original optimism about the possibility of the slaveholder's salvation in the mid-1850s, he never lost sight of the need to save them or abandoned his mission to them.

Fee's southern perspective was clearest on this point: his whole ministry was based on his belief that something should be done in the South. In this context, Fee's importance stands out. He was one of the few southern abolitionists in American history who abandoned neither abolitionism nor the South. His accession to majoritarianism and violence in the mid-1850s, thus, represented an attempt to reconcile these two seemingly irreconcilable goals. The symbol of Lovejoy became a shield against flagging zeal and hostile mobs; the national Christian majority became a weapon against intractable states and unregenerate people. In the process of seeking a workable political solution that was both charitable to the slave and faithful to God, Fee embraced nationalistic ideas that anticipated Reconstruction and placed him on the cutting edge of American political thought. It is remarkable to find such a far-advanced position, embraced by only a handful of prewar northerners, being fervently proclaimed by a minister in a slave state.

Indeed, Fee's advanced position made him essentially irrelevant in his home state. His ideas departed so far from mainstream thought and interests in Kentucky that they cut him off from the very audience he was trying to win. Isolated from Kentucky, he had little chance before the war of affecting the broad currents of public opinion throughout the state. Fee's appeal for national majorities to free the slave flew in the face of one of the South's most cherished shibboleths, that only southerners acting through their state governments could deal with the peculiar institution. Fee's demand for immediate abolition, his advice that slaves should escape if they could, his call for social equality and political rights for blacks, and his public approval of interracial marriage guaranteed that Fee would not win many friends in a slave state.

What is surprising, though, is that given Fee's extreme positions, Kentucky paid as little attention to him as it did. A parallel development, occurring many years earlier and in the North, is instructive here. In 1831, the mayor of Boston received a letter from Robert Y. Hayne, United States senator from South Carolina, asking him "what measures might be taken to suppress the *Liberator* immediately." The mayor had never heard of the *Liberator* and was surprised that anyone in South Carolina could be so alarmed by such a paper published in his city. He promptly dispatched someone to investigate the matter, to see if indeed such a paper was being published in Boston. Although as the later mobs against Garrison in Boston would indicate, the city was no great friend of Garrison, abolitionism, or racial equality, neither was it so alarmed by these things that it was constantly on its guard against them. Kentucky's reaction to Fee was surprisingly similar to Boston's original reaction to Garrison. Berea was only forty miles from Lexington, the heart of Kentucky's slaveholding region. Within one day's journey of Berea lived literally thousands of slaves—yet for years the great mass of Kentuckians seemed almost unconcerned about Fee.[42]

Further, Fee received a remarkably warm reception in some places. While Fee admitted that he chose his ground carefully and that his message would not be received everywhere in Kentucky, Fee's "open ground" included nearly one-third of the state. While his churches remained small and Fee always lived under the threat of violence, he often attracted large audiences and experienced relatively few actual instances of violence. Within Fee's "open ground," he and his associates never went anywhere where they could not find an audience and a sympathetic hearing; in many places, people were willing to hear even the northerners Fee brought in to speak against slavery. Wherever Fee and his associates went, they converted people to their abolitionist faith, and throughout the area Fee found pockets of already eager antislavery supporters. Perhaps most important, wherever Fee and his associates went they found people who cared more about the fact that Fee and company brought with them a school and a church than they did about the fact that the missionaries bringing them were abolitionists. These people might not have been strong opponents of slavery, but neither was slavery the central focus of their lives. Securing an education for their children and a place to worship concerned them more than absolutely guaranteeing the security of slavery.

In the end, this was the real relevance of John G. Fee: he tested the limits of his state's toleration. His fifteen-year ministry in a slave state was not just a testimony that southern public opinion was sometimes sensitive on the issue of slavery. Fee's ministry was also a testimony to the fact that most white Kentuckians—compared with most white southerners—were sufficiently moderate in their defense of slavery to tolerate a person like Fee for many years. Kentuckians were not yet ready to abandon slavery, but neither had they given themselves over wholly to it.

When the Civil War came sixteen months after Fee's expulsion from Kentucky, the state remained committed to its uneasy status quo of straddling the fence on the issues of slavery and sectionalism, until the war made fence-straddling impossible. Kentucky maintained a policy of neutrality during the first months of the fighting, refusing to join the Confederates in a struggle to save slavery from all possible northern threats, but also refusing to join northerners in a struggle to save the Union from secessionists. When neutrality finally proved impossible after September 1861, Kentucky supported the Union war effort, arguing that loyalty to the Union was the surest guarantee of the preservation of slavery, even as it became abundantly clear that the Union war effort was destroying slavery in the South. After the war, Kentuckians remained proud of the moderate character of the state's people, which had produced statesmen, sectional compromisers, and Unionists in the era of Henry Clay, while they also embraced a Neo-Confederate revival, which largely erased popular memory of Kentucky's support for the Union in the era of the Civil War. Imagining an idyllic community of benevolent masters who created the mildest form of slavery in America before the war, Kentuckians embraced the hard racism which produced segregation, discrimination, and lynching after the war.

In the end, Kentucky's moderation—its theory that slavery was a necessary evil—had the effect of preserving slavery and white domination of the state. Kentuckians demonstrated that their moderation on the issue of slavery was little different, in its effects, from immoderation. Expected to be the first to give up slavery because of its moderation, Kentucky actually became one of the last two states to give up slavery—because of that same moderation. Kentucky's highest ideals became not the antebellum period's vision of the African American's innate humanity and abstract right to freedom, but the postbellum period's support for the Lost Cause and white supremacy.

Through years of controversy, Kentucky tried to serve two masters: God and Mammon—their highest ideals and their love of the things and ways of this world. Caught between their potential for antislavery idealism and their loyalty to racism, property, and reputation, Kentuckians found they could not successfully serve two masters. For in loving one, they came to hate the other.

Notes

List of Abbreviations

ACS	American Colonization Society
ACSR	American Colonization Society Records, Library of Congress
AFIC	American Freedmen's Inquiry Commission
AM	*American Missionary*
AMA	American Missionary Association
AMAA	American Missionary Association Archives, Amistad Research Center, Tulane University
AR	*African Repository*
BFP	Breckinridge Family Papers, Library of Congress
Birney	James G. Birney
Breckinridge	Robert J. Breckinridge
CG	*Cincinnati Gazette*
CHGR	*Colonization Herald and General Register* (Philadelphia)
CJ	*Cincinnati Journal*
Cowan	Alexander M. Cowan
CMC	Cassius Marcellus Clay
CRBO	*Christian Register and Boston Observer*
CWSP	Charles W. Short Papers, Filson Historical Society
DAB	*Dictionary of American Biography*
Davis	James S. Davis
Ex	*Examiner* (Louisville)
Fee	John Gregg Fee
FHS	Filson Historical Society
Finley	Robert S. Finley
FWP	Federal Writers' Project
GB	Gamaliel Bailey
Goodell	William Goodell
GSP	Gerrit Smith Papers, Syracuse University Library
Gurley	Ralph R. Gurley

HJ	Kentucky, General Assembly, House, *Journal*
HC	Henry Clay
Jacobs	John A. Jacobs
JGFP	John G. Fee Papers, Berea College
Jocelyn	Simeon S. Jocelyn
JRUP	Joseph R. Underwood Papers, Western Kentucky University
KCS	Kentucky Colonization Society
KN	*Kentucky News* (Newport)
LB	Dwight L. Dumond, ed., *Letters of James Gillespie Birney, 1831–1857*, 2 vols. (New York: Appleton-Century, 1938)
LC	*Louisville Courier*
Li	*Liberator* (Boston)
LJ	*Louisville Journal*
McLain	William McLain
Morehead	James T. Morehead
NASS	*National Anti-Slavery Standard* (New York)
NE	*National Era* (Washington, D.C.)
NI	*National Intelligencer* (Washington, D.C.)
NR	*Niles' Register* (Baltimore, Washington, D.C., Philadelphia)
NYT	*New York Times*
NYTr	*New York Tribune*
OBP	Orlando Brown Papers, Filson Historical Society
OG	*Old Guard* (Frankfort)
Peers	Benjamin O. Peers
PF	*Pennsylvania Freeman* (Philadelphia)
PrH	*Presbyterian Herald* (Louisville)
RA	*Radical Abolitionist*
Re	*Republic* (Washington, D.C.)
Rogers	John A.R. Rogers
SJ	Kentucky, General Assembly, Senate, *Journal*
Smith	Gerrit Smith
SPCP	Salmon P. Chase Papers, Historical Society of Pennsylvania
Tappan	Lewis Tappan
UK	University of Kentucky
Underwood	Joseph R. Underwood
WCMC	Horace Greeley, ed., *The Writings of Cassius Marcellus Clay, Including Speeches and Addresses* (New York: Harper & Brothers, 1848; reprint ed., New York: Negro Universities Press, 1969)
Whipple	George Whipple
WK	*West Kentuckian* (Paducah)
WPA	Works Progress Administration/Work Projects Administration
WSB	William S. Bailey
Young	John C. Young

1. The Necessary Evil

1. HC [Scaevola] to the Electors of Fayette County, April 16, 1798, HC [Scaevola] to the Citizens of Fayette, February 1799, in Hopkins et al., eds., *Papers of Clay,* 1:6, 14; Van Deusen, *Life of Henry Clay,* 19–21; Coward, *Kentucky in the New Republic,* 107, 118, 161; Aron, *How the West Was Lost,* 89–95.

2. HC to Richard Pindell, February 17, 1849, in *NR,* March 21, 1849.

3. For discussions of Clay's views on slavery, see Remini, *Henry Clay,* 7–8, 26–28, 179–82, 439–40, 483–89, 507–11, 525–26, 617–20, 627, 693–94, 740; Maness, "Henry Clay and Slavery"; Eaton, *Henry Clay,* 117–36; Aron, *How the West Was Lost,* 89–101, 143–49; Howe, *Political Culture,* 132–37; Van Deburg, "Henry Clay," 132–46; Coleman, "Clay, Kentucky and Liberia," 309–22; Jones, "Clay and Expansion," 241–62; Troutman, "Emancipation," 179–81; Troutman, "Clay and 'Ashland,'" 159–74.

4. Matt. 6:24. For a sampling of the use of this analogy, see L. Clarke, *Narrative,* 97–98; Abraham Lincoln, "Speech at Peoria, Illinois, October 16, 1854," in Nicolay and Hay, eds., *Works of Lincoln,* 2: 244–47; Cheever, *God against Slavery,* 12.

5. John C. Calhoun, "Speech on the Reception of Abolition Petitions, Delivered in the Senate, February 6th, 1837," in Crallé, ed., *Works of Calhoun,* 2:631.

6. John Irwin to John Irwin, Sr., February 26, 1839, Irwin Papers; Birney to Theodore D. Weld, July 17, 1834, in Barnes and Dumond, eds., *Letters of Weld, Weld and Grimké,* 1:158; Young to Charles Hodge, June 15, [1836], Thurman Collection; Almeron Dowd to Emily Curtis, August 23, 1845, Dowd Papers; Fee to Milton Badger and Charles Hall, January 18, 1848, typescript in JGFP; Fee to the Members and Friends of the AMA, May 1854, AMAA 43243–44; Fee to Whipple, January 16, 1854, AMAA 43212; George Candee to Jocelyn, March 13, 1860, AMAA 43857–58; Otis B. Waters to AMA, n.d., in AMA, *Annual Report* (1857), 65; "The Young Men's Colonization Society of Pennsylvania" (Speech of Benjamin B. Smith), *AR* 11 (March 1835):93; *New York Spectator,* January 16, 1835, in "Colonization Meeting" (Speech of Benjamin B. Smith), *AR* 11 (January 1835):16–17; Paxton, *Letters on Slavery,* 155; William M.O. Smith to Breckinridge, April 7, 1849, BFP 134:24755–56; Breckinridge to Samuel Steel, April 17, 1849, BFP 134:24773–74; George W. Williams to Messrs. Lyle and Walker, n.d., clipping in William M.O. Smith to Breckinridge, April 28, 1849, BFP 134:24785–86; Garrett Davis to Messrs. Lyle and Walker, n.d., clipping in William M.O. Smith to Breckinridge, April 28, 1849, BFP 134:24785–86; Peers to Gurley, December 11, 1826, February 5, 1827, ACSR 2:185–86, 3:352–53; Finley to Gurley, April 12, 1831, ACSR 30:4884–85; Breckinridge to Gurley, May 5, 1832, ACSR 39:6508; Cowan to McLain, November 24, 1847, ACSR 108(2):29718–19; GB to John Scoble, January 19, 1845, in Abel and Klingberg, eds., *Side-Light,* 202–3; Spalding, "'Dissertation on the Civil War,'" 76–79; Appleton, "Englishman's Perception," 62.

7. Among works demonstrating the distinctiveness and importance of the Upper South within southern history are W. Freehling, *Road to Disunion;* W. Freehling, *The South vs. The South;* B. Fields, *Slavery and Freedom;* Crofts, *Reluctant Confederates;* Inscoe, *Mountain Masters;* Ash, *Middle Tennessee;* Cimprich, *Slavery's End;* Knupfer, *The Union as It Is;* Holt, *Political Crisis;* Remini, *Henry Clay;* Ayers and Willis, eds., *The Edge of the South;* Dunn, *Abolitionist in the Appalachian South.* Tise, *Proslavery,* 97–123, is a convenient listing of some of the shared propositions among theories of slavery.

8. In 1850, there were 7,497 slaves in the mountain counties, compared to 10,889 slaves in Fayette County. At the same time, however, 134,763 whites lived in the mountain counties, compared to 11,178 whites in Fayette County. The statistics in this paragraph have been derived from U.S., Office of the Census, *Seventh Census: 1850*, 611–12; U.S., Office of the Census, *Statistical View*, 94; "Appendix to Mr. Helm's Speech," *OG* 1 (February 21, 1850):47–48; Berlin, *Slaves without Masters*, 136, 396–99; Barton, "'Good Cooks and Washers,'" 436–37. The proportion of blacks in the population of the mountain region of Kentucky was lower than it was in any other state of the southern Appalachians. See Murphy, "Slavery and Freedom," 151–69. The most authoritative source on slavery in Kentucky is Lucas and Wright, *History of Blacks in Kentucky*, vol. 1: *From Slavery to Segregation*. Other works on slavery based on black sources include: Sprague, "Kentucky Pocket Plantation," 69–86; Harrison, "Slavery Days," 242–57; Harrison, ed., "Folklore," 25–30, 53–60. Two older, but still helpful, books are Coleman, *Slavery Times in Kentucky* and McDougle, *Slavery in Kentucky*.

9. U.S., Office of the Census, *Seventh Census: Report*, 86–97, 155–60; U.S., Office of the Census, *Statistical View*, 238–47; Aron, *How the West Was Lost*, 124–69; Sears, "Working Like a Slave," 4–7; Barton, "'Good Cooks and Washers,'" 436–60. Hemp was an important cash crop in the Bluegrass region and it was cultivated almost exclusively with slave labor because the crop was so "very dirty, and so laborious that scarcely any white man will work at it" (*The Farmers' Register* 3 [1836]:612, quoted in Hopkins, *Hemp Industry in Kentucky*, 24–25). Nevertheless, staple crops like hemp played a far less important role in the economy of Kentucky than crops like cotton, rice, and sugar did in the economy of the Lower South. Ironically, Kentuckians may have been wrong in believing that an economic base of labor-intensive staple crops was necessary to support slavery. In Kentucky, for instance, slaves were successfully employed in relatively large mining and manufacturing operations. Slaves were used in the processing of salt; in the mining of coal, iron, and saltpeter; and in the manufacture of paper, iron products, cotton textiles, and hemp products, such as rope and bagging. See Starobin, *Industrial Slavery*, 17–19, 22–23, 81, 296; B. Faust, "Saltpetre Mining," 330; Hill and DePaepe, "Saltpeter Mining," 251; Talley, "Salt Works," 108; Hopkins, *Hemp Industry in Kentucky*, 135–39.

10. U.S., Office of the Census, *Statistical View*, 94.

11. See, for instance, Martin, "Anti-Slavery in Kentucky," 11–12, 63–78, 139–47; Adams, "Neglected Period of Anti-Slavery," 17–56, 249–52; W. Smith, *Political History*, 1:2–40; S. Weeks, "Anti-Slavery in the South," 88–130.

12. W. Freehling, *Prelude to Civil War*, 76–79, 82, 327–28; W. Freehling, "Founding Fathers and Slavery," 81–93; W. Freehling, *Reintegration of American History*, especially 12–33, 138–75; W. Freehling, *Road to Disunion*, especially 118–210, 462–74; Degler, *Other South*, 13–123; Berlin, *Slaves without Masters*, 86–87, 184–92; J.C. Miller, *Wolf by the Ears*; A. Freehling, *Drift toward Dissolution*, 96–109; Ashworth, *Slavery, Capitalism, and Politics*, vol. 1: *Commerce and Compromise*, 192–285; Goodman, *Of One Blood*; Snay, *Gospel of Disunion*, 20–28. For a discussion of the historiography of southern antislavery, see Harrold, *Abolitionists and the South*, 9–25.

13. Drew Gilpin Faust, "Introduction: The Proslavery Argument in History," in D.G. Faust, ed., *Ideology of Slavery*, 5–6; Jenkins, *Pro-Slavery Thought*, especially 39–49; McColley, *Slavery and Jeffersonian Virginia*; Tise, *Proslavery*. Genovese, *The World the Slaveholders Made*, 130–36, acknowledges that some southerners had misgivings about slavery but emphasizes the similarity in southern thought on slavery between the Revo-

lutionary and antebellum periods. See Allen, "Proslavery Thought," 75–90, for evidence of continuity in the proslavery argument from Kentucky.

14. For southern efforts to resolve the conflict between slavery and republican liberty, see Ford, *Southern Radicalism*; Sinha, *Counterrevolution of Slavery.*

15. Genovese, *The World the Slaveholders Made*, 143–50; Foster, "Guilt over Slavery," 665–94; Charles G. Sellers, Jr., "The Travail of Slavery," in Sellers, ed., *Southerner as American*, 40–71; Morrow, "Proslavery Argument," 79–94; Kenneth M. Stampp, "The Southern Road to Appomattox," in Stampp, *Imperiled Union*, 246–69; Beringer et al., *Why the South Lost the Civil War*, 336–67; Thomas Jefferson to John Holmes, April 22, 1820, in Peterson, ed., *Writings*, 1434. Genovese has argued that some southerners experienced guilt regarding abuses of the masters' powers. While still defending slavery in the abstract, they feared that the defeat of the Confederacy was divine retribution for their failure to live up to the biblical standard for masters. See Genovese, *Consuming Fire*. Among historians who argue that southern society faced various dilemmas associated with slavery are Greenberg, *Masters and Statesmen*; Oakes, *Slavery and Freedom*; Genovese, *Slaveholders' Dilemma.*

16. This duality has introduced considerable terminological confusion among historians, who have disagreed over whether to describe the necessary-evil theory as antislavery or proslavery. Finding that "faulty semantics" had contributed to "faulty analysis," William W. Freehling proposed that such terms be abandoned in regard to the necessary-evil theory and suggested a new one: "conditional termination." See W. Freehling, *Road to Disunion*, 122–23. I prefer to treat the necessary-evil theory more as a common set of assumptions shared by most antebellum Kentuckians. Certain issues and approaches running counter to these assumptions were instantly removed from consideration. Beyond these areas of consensus, there remained many areas of disagreement about slavery; hence there were both proslavery and antislavery Kentuckians operating within the parameters of the necessary-evil theory.

17. A.H. Triplett to McLain, May 30, July 29, 1844, March 7, July 1, 1845, April 4, 1848, ACSR 94:24107–8, 95:24332, 97(1):25179, 99(1):25530–31, 110(1):30679.

18. A.H. Triplett to McLain, May 30, July 29, 1844, March 7, July 1, 1845, January 16, February 13, 1846, April 4, 1848, April 7, 1849, ACSR 94:24107–8, 95:24332, 97(1):25179, 99(1):25530–31, 101(1):26476, 101(2):26573–74, 110(1):30679, 114(1):33146.

19. On Clay's changing positions, see Remini, *Henry Clay*, 26–28; Aron, *How the West Was Lost*, 95–97.

20. Breckinridge to Samuel Steel, April 17, 1849, BFP 134:24773–74; Garrett Davis to Messrs. Lyle and Walker, n.d., clipping in William M.O. Smith to Breckinridge, April 28, 1849, BFP 134:24785–86; Paxton, *Letters on Slavery*, 155; Peers to Gurley, December 11, 1826, February 5, 6, 1827, September 5, 1828, February 7, 1829, ACSR 2:185–86, 3:352–55, 11:1864–65, 13:2309–10; Finley to Gurley, April 12, 1831, ACSR 30:4884–85; Breckinridge to Gurley, October 4, 1831, May 5, 1832, ACSR 34:5600, 39:6508; Franklin Knight to Samuel Wilkeson, November 30, 1839, ACSR 76(2):16303–4; Jacobs to McLain, September 13, 1845, ACSR 99(2):25852–53; GB to John Scoble, January 19, 1845, in Abel and Klingberg, eds., *Side-Light*, 202–3; Harrold, *Abolitionists and the South*, especially 31–32, 37; *Day of Small Things*, 34.

21. For examples of proslavery arguments derived from the necessary-evil doctrine, see Buck, *Slavery Question*; W.S. Brown, "Strictures on Abolitionism," 485–91; Kentucky, *Report of the Debates*, 71–76.

22. Fladeland, *Birney,* 1–30; Lamb, "Birney," 83–101.

23. Henkle, *Life of Bascom,* 1–155; Collins and Collins, *Kentucky,* 1:453–55; *DAB* 2:30–32, s.v. "Bascom, Henry Bidleman."

24. Henry B. Bascom, "Claims of Africa; or, An Address in Behalf of the American Colonization Society," in Ralston, ed., *Works of Bascom,* 2:251–52, 285; Mathews, *Slavery and Methodism,* 94–96, 104–5; Birney to Gurley, July 12, 1832, January 24, 1833, in *LB,* 1:9, 51; Fladeland, *Birney,* 37–74.

25. Fladeland, *Birney,* 23–24, 37–38, 52–53, 75–124; Plantation Record Book of Birney, 1824, cited in *LB,* 1:52; Lamb, "Birney," 93–134.

26. Bascom, *Methodism and Slavery,* 6; Bailey, *Shadow on the Church,* 214–15, 222, 239–40; Henkle, *Life of Bascom,* 384–98; Mathews, *Slavery and Methodism,* 246–90; Purifoy, "Methodist Episcopal Church, South, and Slavery," 67–84, 198–200; Bascom, Greene, and Parsons, *Brief Appeal;* Sutton, *Methodist Church Property Case.*

27. Bascom, *Methodism and Slavery,* 7, 10, 30, 41, 46–47, 66, 78, 84–85, 122; Purifoy, "Methodist Episcopal Church, South, and Slavery," 180–81, 185–86.

28. John C. Calhoun to Thomas G. Clemson, June 23, 1845, John C. Calhoun to James H. Hammond, July 7, August 2, 1845, in Jameson, ed., "Correspondence of Calhoun," 2:665–68.

29. James H. Hammond to John C. Calhoun, August 18, 1845, John C. Calhoun to James H. Hammond, August 30, September 28, 1845, in Jameson, ed., "Correspondence of Calhoun," 2:1045–47, 2:669–70, 672–73.

2. The Colonizationist Imperative

1. Thornton A. Mills to Birney, July 1, 1833, in *LB,* 1:80; James Freeman Clarke to *CRBO,* August 15, 1836, in "Colonization," *AR* 12 (October 1836):321; J. Robertson et al. to HC, August 22, 1836, in *AR* 12 (October 1836):316–17; "Colonization Movements," *AR* 12 (September 1836):265–66, 268–69; James Freeman Clarke to Margaret Fuller, July 29, 1836, in J.W. Thomas, ed., *Letters of Clarke,* 122; Howard, "Pendleton," 195; Martin, "Anti-Slavery in Kentucky," 3; Allen, "Debate," 136; Staudenraus, *African Colonization,* 136, 141–43, 170, 184; "Life Members of the American Colonization Society," *AR* 22 (February 1846):70; *WCMC,* 331; HC to Gurley, December 22, 1836, in "Letter from Mr. Clay," *AR* 13 (January 1837):38; Kentucky, *Acts* (1832–33), ch. 223, sec. 4; Peers to Gurley, December 11, 1826, February 7, 1829, ACSR 2:185–86, 13:2309–10; Jacobs to Gurley, December 4, 1829, ACSR 19:3338–39; Finley to Gurley, April 12, 1831, ACSR 30:4884–85; Breckinridge to Gurley, October 4, 1831, ACSR 34:5600; W.C. Matthews to McLain, September 18, 1844, August 16, 1847, ACSR 95:24482–83, 107(2):27276–77; Finley to McLain, September 11, 1845, ACSR 99(2):25824–25.

2. Breckinridge, *Question of Negro Slavery,* 14; Peers to Gurley, February 5, 1827, ACSR 3:352–53.

3. Allen, "Debate," 144–47; Bennett, "All Things," 165–66; Friedman, *Inventors of the Promised Land,* 213; Finley to Joseph Gales, May 7, 1834, ACSR 58(3):10259–60; Finley to McLain, August 29, 1846, ACSR 103(2):27288–89; J. Robertson et al. to HC, August 22, 1836, in *AR* 12 (October 1836):316; James Freeman Clarke to *CRBO,* August 15, 1836, in "Colonization," 321; "Prospects in Kentucky," *AR* 5 (March 1829):27; "Rev. Mr. Bascom's Agency," *AR* 6 (December 1830):310–11; "Contribu-

tions to the American Colonization Society, from 23d July, to 13th August, 1829," *AR* 5 (August 1829):190.

4. James Freeman Clarke to *CRBO,* August 15, 1836, in "Colonization," 321; "Colonization Movements," 265–70; *Lexington Intelligencer,* September 10, 1836, in "Auxiliary Societies," *AR* 12 (October 1836):303; "Colonization Meetings," *AR* 12 (October 1836):306; Charles W. Short to William Short, April 14, May 10, 1839, CWSP; "The Colonization Cause in Louisville, Ky.," *AR* 15 (May 1839):154; Staudenraus, *African Colonization,* 236–37, 251; J.C. Talbot to Samuel Wilkeson, September 20, 1839, ACSR 75(2):16015; W.L. Tannehill to Samuel Wilkeson, October 31, 1839, ACSR 76(1):16147. Apathy regarding colonizationism continued in Louisville well into the 1840s. See George W. Fagg to McLain, April 22, 1844, ACSR 94:24007; Cowan to McLain, October 10, 1845, ACSR 100(1):26013–14.

5. Peers to Gurley, February 7, 1829, ACSR 13:2309–10; Bennett, "All Things," 33, 66–68, 172; Cowan to McLain, December 23, 1844, February 20, 1845, ACSR 96(2):24793–94, 97(2):25095–96.

6. For writings on colonizationism in Kentucky, see Allen, "Debate"; Allen, "Southern Colonizationists," 92–111; Allen, "'All of Us Are Highly Pleased,'" 97–109; Allen, "Southern Critics of Slavery," 169–90; Bennett, "All Things"; Coleman, "Clay, Kentucky and Liberia," 309–22; Coleman, "Kentucky Colonization Society," 1–9; Finnie, "Antislavery in the Upper South," 319–42; Keith, "Joseph Rogers Underwood," 117–32; Martin, "Anti-Slavery in Kentucky," 49–62. On colonizationism in general, see Staudenraus, *African Colonization;* W. Freehling, *Reintegration of American History,* 138–57; Goodman, *Of One Blood,* 1–64; Stevenson, *Life in Black and White,* 277–85; Melish, *Disowning Slavery,* 192–99, 212–18.

7. HC, "Remarks on the 26th of August, 1836," 297–301; Bennett, "All Things," 39; Finley to Gurley, April 12, 1831, ACSR 30:4884–85; Breckinridge to Gurley, August 16, 1831, ACSR 32:5372–73; Allen, "Southern Colonizationists," 98; Finnie, "Antislavery in the Upper South."

8. Danville Colonization Society, *Constitution,* art. 2, in Danville Colonization Society, "Constitution and Proceedings"; "Colonization Movements," 268; HC, *Colonization Society of Kentucky,* 15; "Twenty-First Annual Meeting of the American Colonization Society" (Speech of HC), *AR* 14 (January 1838):17–19; "Addresses Delivered at the Annual Meeting" (Speech of HC), *AR* 26 (February 1850):44–45; Bennett, "All Things," 33, 47; Underwood, *Colonization Society of Bowlinggreen,* 8.

9. Breckinridge, "Speech," 138; Breckinridge, "Black Race," 139; Robinson, "Address," 140; Adam Beatty to John Payne, April 21, 1829, in Greene, ed., "Antislavery in Kentucky," 85; Peers to Gurley, February 7, 1829, ACSR 13:2309–10; Paxton, *Letters on Slavery,* 13–14; Bennett, "All Things," 48–49; Staudenraus, *African Colonization,* 144–46.

10. "Early History of the American Colonization Society" (Speech of HC), *AR* 12 (February 1836):51–55; Kentucky, *Report of the Debates,* 928–29; Bullock, "Address," 99–110; Philip Lindsey to McLain, December 27, 1844, ACSR 97(2):24846–47; Cowan to McLain, January 28, February 20, 1845, ACSR 97(1):24984–85, 97(2):25095–96; "Proceedings of the American Colonization Society at the Nineteenth Annual Meeting" (Speech of HC), *AR* 12 (January 1836):9–10; HC, *Colonization Society of Kentucky,* 17; "Twenty-First Annual Meeting" (Speech of HC), 17–18; Young, "Address," in KCS, *Annual Report* (1833), 10; Underwood, *Colonization Society of Kentucky,* 7–8.

11. Fee, *Anti-Slavery Manual,* 171; Fee, *Colonization;* Birney, *Letter on Coloniza-*

tion, 11–12, 29; Birney to John Winslow et al., May 29, 1835, in Huch, ed., "Birney," 358–59; Allen, "Debate," x; Allen, "Southern Critics of Slavery," 189–90; Breckinridge, "Hints on Colonization," 285; Underwood, *Colonization Society of Kentucky,* 9; Underwood, *Speech upon the Resolution to Censure,* 11.

12. Charles W. Short to William Short, November 15, 1837, CWSP; Breckinridge to Gurley, October 4, 1831, ACSR 34:5600; George W. Fagg to Samuel Wilkeson, September 19, 1839, ACSR 75(2):16013–14; Henry Wingate to Gurley, October 31, 1839, ACSR 76(1):16148; Franklin Knight to Samuel Wilkeson, November 30, 1839, ACSR 76(2):16303–4; Cowan to McLain, May 2, October 10, November 27, 29, 1845, February 13, July 2, 1846, August 10, October 9, 1847, April 21, 1848, ACSR 98:25378–79, 100(1):26013–14, 100(2):26230–31, 26241–42, 101(2):26573–74, 103(1):27051–53, 107(2):29256–57, 108(1):29440–41, 110(1):30778–79; W.C. Matthews to McLain, November 29, 1845, August 16, 1847, ACSR 100(2):26238, 107(2):27276–77; Bullock, "Address," 106, 108; "Resolutions of the Kentucky Synod on Colonization," *AR* 22 (January 1846):30; Underwood to Birney, April 11, 1840, in *LB,* 1:552; Breckinridge, "Hints on Colonization," 290–91; Breckinridge, "Speech," 142–43; Breckinridge, "Black Race," 140–41; HC to N.W. Pollard, September 6, 1851, in M.E. Thomas, ed., "Henry Clay Replies," 263–65; Bennett, "All Things," 49, 96–97; HC, *Colonization Society of Kentucky,* 19; Thomas Dolan to McLain, March 25, 1846, ACSR 101(2):26715–16; Joseph Bryan to McLain, March 28, 1846, ACSR 101(2):26725–26.

13. McClung, "Address," 133–49; Bullock, "Address," 108; Breckinridge, "Hints on Colonization," 288. For a discussion of the ways in which the migratory experience of white Americans shaped colonizationist thinking, see W. Freehling, *Reintegration of American History,* 150–51.

14. Charles W. Short to William Short, May 28, 1830, January 10, May 3, June 3, August 27, 1838, January 12, 1839, January 30, 1848, CWSP; Skaggs, "Short," 55–56, 61–62, 117–18, 143, 149–51, 172; Staudenraus, *African Colonization,* 127, 243; Charles W. Short to ACS, July 2, 1838, in *AR* 14 (September 1838):229. For other biographical information on Short and his family, see *DAB* 17:127–28, s.v. "Short, Charles Wilkins"; Davies, "Short," 208–49; Titley, "Short," 29–31; T. Speed, "Political Club," 77–79.

15. Charles W. Short to William Short, November 15, 1837, October 28, 30, 1838, April 14, 1839, John P. Campbell to Charles W. Short, October 25, 1838, CWSP.

16. Charles W. Short to William Short, January 12, February 24, March 10, April 14, July 3, August 18, October 6, 1839, CWSP.

17. Charles W. Short to William Short, November 17, 24, 1839, March 8, 1840, January 5, February 9, March 7, July 28, 1841, CWSP.

18. Charles W. Short to William Short, November 17, 24, December 19, 1839, January 12, November 14, 1840, February 9, March 7, 24, July 28, 1841, September 28, 1842, CWSP. According to Short, Gist was the name of "a family to which his [Charles's] father belonged" (Charles W. Short to William Short, July 4, 1840, CWSP). Over 40 percent of all colonists died within six years of their migration to Liberia. See Shick, "Liberian Colonization," 56.

19. Charles W. Short to William Short, July 24, 1840, February 9, March 24, 30, April 1, 1841, December 8, 1847, CWSP; Charles Gist to Charles W. Short, December 21, 1847, in *Ex,* May 26, 1849. According to Deborah Skaggs, in 1849 Charles Gist

was convicted in a Liberian court for killing his "wife's lover" and was executed for the murder (Skaggs, "Short," 151).

20. Cowan, *Liberia, as I Found It*, 179; John B. Pinney to ACS, n.d., in "Twenty-Seven Slaves Offered to the Society," *AR* 20 (August 1844):251; Underwood to Elizabeth C. Underwood, December 15, 1851, JRUP; Finley to Joseph Gales, May 7, 1834, ACSR 58(3):10259–60; Franklin Knight to Samuel Wilkeson, November 30, 1839, ACSR 76(2):16303–4; W. Hodge and John Triplett to McLain, February 19, 1844, ACSR 93(2):23762; A.H. Triplett to McLain, May 30, 1844, July 1, 1845, January 16, 1846, April 4, 1848, ACSR 94:24107–8, 99(1):25530–31, 101(1):26476, 110(1):30679; Jacobs to McLain, December 4, 1844, September 13, 1845, ACSR 96(2):24772, 99(2):25852–53; Cowan to McLain, October 21, 1845, September 27, November 1, 1847, ACSR 100(1):26058–59, 108(1):29404–5, 108(2):29589–90; Thomas Dolan to McLain, January 28, February 11, March 7, 1846, ACSR 101(1):26523–24, 101(2): 26557, 26657–58; Underwood to McLain, June 20, 1848, ACSR 110(2):31080; N.M. Goodson to McLain, October 29, 1849, ACSR 116(1):34; B.B. Crump to McLain, October 30, 1849, ACSR 116(1):34; McPheeters, "Reminiscences," 224–25; Stone, "Address on Colonization," 198.

21. Without question, the racial egalitarianism of the abolitionists was more significant than the vestiges of racism that remained in their thinking. This argument has been made most forcefully by Goodman, *Of One Blood*. On racism among abolitionists, see Litwack, *North of Slavery*, 216–30; Pease and Pease, "Antislavery Ambivalence," 686–95; Walters, *Antislavery Appeal*, 56–60; Friedman, *Gregarious Saints*, 160–95.

22. For discussions of skepticism about the antislavery credentials of colonizationists, see Finnie, "Antislavery in the Upper South," and Allen, "Southern Colonizationists," 92–95.

23. Petition of James B. Townsend, n.d., OBP; Peers to Gurley, September 5, 1828, February 7, 1829, ACSR 11:1864–65, 13:2309–10; Finley to Gurley, April 12, 1831, ACSR 30:4884–85; Breckinridge to Gurley, October 4, 1831, ACSR 34:5600; George W. Fagg to Gurley, March 27, 1844, ACSR 93(2):23919; A.H. Triplett to McLain, July 29, 1844, ACSR 95:24332; Cowan to McLain, August 1, 1845, ACSR 99(1):25659–60; Underwood, *Colonization Society of Bowlinggreen*, 6, 20–21; KCS, *Proceedings* (1831), 4; Augusta *Reflector*, April 8, 1829, in Greene, ed., "Antislavery in Kentucky," 79; HC, *Colonization Society of Kentucky*, 22; Breckinridge, "Hints on Colonization," 293–96; Mayes, "Address," 21; Paxton, *Letters on Slavery*, 3, 13–14; Morehead, "Address," in KCS, *Annual Report* (1834), 25; Fee, *Colonization*, 28; Birney, *Letter on Colonization*, 7; Young to Charles Hodge, June 15, [1836], Thurman Collection; Breckinridge, "Black Race," 136–37.

24. James Freeman Clarke to *CRBO*, August 15, 1836, in "Colonization," 321; Robinson, "Address," 144–45; "Convention of the Friends of African Colonization Held in the Capitol, Washington City, May 4th, 1842" (Speech of Morehead), *AR* 18 (June 1842):176; Breckinridge, "Black Race," 139, 142; HC, "Remarks on the 26th of August, 1836," 298–300; HC, *Colonization Society of Kentucky*, 7, 14–15, 21, 23; "Twenty-First Annual Meeting" (Speech of HC), 17–19; Paxton, *Letters on Slavery*, 157–58; "Addresses at Annual Meeting" (Speech of HC), 44; Breckinridge, "Speech," 144–45; "Colonization Movements," 269; Mayes, "Address," 20; Morehead, "Address," 21; KCS, *Proceedings* (1831), 4; Underwood, *Colonization Society of Kentucky*, 7; Louisville *Protestant and Herald*, n.d., in "A Plan for Raising $2,000 for the Colonization Cause," *AR* 20 (October 1844):309; Jacobs to McLain, September 13, 1845, ACSR 99(2):25852–53.

25. Underwood, *Colonization Society of Kentucky,* 7–8, 10; Underwood, *Coloniza-tion Society of Bowlinggreen,* 8–9; Underwood to McLain, October 17, 1844, ACSR 96(1):24612–13; Collins and Collins, *Kentucky,* 2:739–41; Priest, "Underwood," 286–303; Keith, "Joseph Rogers Underwood"; Baber, "Underwood," 47–54; "Hon. Joseph R. Underwood," 609–14; Underwood, *Speech upon the Resolution to Censure;* U.S., Congress, House, *Congressional Globe,* 30th Cong., 1st sess., 1847–48, *Appendix,* 306–13; Eaton, ed., "Minutes and Resolutions," 541–45; Underwood to Elizabeth C. Underwood, December 17, 1849, January 13, 16, 1850, March 14, December 30, 1852, January 21, 26, 1853, Elizabeth C. Underwood to Underwood, January 2, 25, 31, February 1, 15, 1850, JRUP; *PrH,* n.d., in "Sailing of the Rothschild for Liberia," *AR* 22 (March 1846):92; Bennett, "All Things," 79.

26. Underwood, *Colonization Society of Kentucky,* 14–15.

27. Birney to Smith, January 31, 1835, Birney to Tappan, February 3, 1835, in *LB,* 1:175, 178; Underwood, *Colonization Society of Kentucky,* 14–15; Fee, *Coloniza-tion,* 14–15; Fee to CMC, September 18, 1849, JGFP. The impact of Underwood's plan was calculated from statistics in Kentucky, General Assembly, *Second Auditor's Report,* no. 13 (1844–45), *Legislative Documents,* 74–75; Kentucky, General Assembly, *Second Auditor's Report,* no. 10 (1848–49), *Legislative Documents,* 264–65; Kentucky, General Assembly, *Second Auditor's Report,* no. 10 (1850–51), *Legislative Documents,* 306–7.

28. Birney, *Letter on Colonization,* 7; William Martin to Lundsford Yandell, September 6, 1845, Yandell Family Papers; Peers to Gurley, December 11, 1826, February 5, 6, March 26, 1827, September 5, 1828, ACSR 2:185–86, 3:352–53, 354–55, 4:517–18, 11:1864–65; Jacobs to Gurley, December 4, 1829, ACSR 19:3338–39; Breckinridge to Gurley, August 16, 1831, May 5, 1832, ACSR 32:5372–73, 39:6508; B. Mills to McLain, February 5, 1844, ACSR 93(1):23690–91; A.H. Triplett to McLain, May 30, July 29, 1844, July 1, 1845, January 16, 1846, ACSR 94:24107–8, 95:24332, 99(1):25530–31, 101(1):26476; Jacobs to McLain, September 13, 1845, March 11, 1849, ACSR 99(2):25852–53, 113(3):32969–70; W.C. Matthews to McLain, August 16, 1847, ACSR 107(2):27276–77; Cowan to McLain, November 24, 1847, May 10, June 10, 1848, May 9, 1849, ACSR 108(2):29718–19, 110(1):30866–67, 110(2):31029–30, 114(2):33328–29; Samuel Hatch to McLain, June 22, 1849, ACSR 114(2):33530–31; E.P. Pratt to McLain, September 12, 1849, ACSR 115(2):34. See also Stone, "Address on Colonization," 198–200; Ramage, "Bluegrass Patriarch," 63–64, 67.

29. Klotter, *The Breckinridges,* 37–91; Klotter, "Slavery and Race," 375–97; Mayse, "Breckinridge"; Vaughan, *Breckinridge;* Sandlund, "Breckinridge," 145–54; Gilliam, "Breckinridge, 1800–1871," 207–23, 319–36; Gilliam, "Breckinridge: Kentucky Unionist," 362–85; Howard, "Breckinridge Family," 37–56; Howard, "Breckinridge in 1849," 328–43; E. Moore, "Breckinridge," 285–94; Tapp, "Breckinridge during the Civil War," 120–44; Tapp, "Breckinridge and the Year 1849," 125–50; Breckinridge, "Hints on Colonization," 296–97; Breckinridge to Gurley, August 16, 1831, ACSR 32:5372–73; Breckinridge, *Hints on Slavery,* 11; Breckinridge, "Address before the Colonization Society of Kentucky," 171.

30. HC, *Colonization Society of Kentucky,* 8, 24; Breckinridge, "Address before the Colonization Society of Kentucky," 171, 176; Mayes, "Address," 11, 21–22; Young, "Address," 10–17, 20–21, 30; Morehead, "Address," 19–21, 25–26; Underwood, *Colo-nization Society of Kentucky,* 7, 10–11, 19; Bullock, "Address," 109–10; McClung, "Address," 134–35, 137–40; Robinson, "Address," 141–42, 151–53; Breckinridge, "Black

Race," 137, 145; KCS, *Proceedings* (1831), 4; KCS, *Annual Report* (1834), 5. Every such annual address delivered between 1829 and 1851 that has survived to this day expressed the hope that slavery would be ended by colonization.

31. Finley to Gurley, April 12, 16, 1831, ACSR 30:4884–85, 4904–5; Breckinridge to Gurley, August 16, 1831, ACSR 32:5372–73; Peers to Gurley, February 7, 1829, ACSR 13:2309–10.

32. Breckinridge to Gurley, August 16, 1831, ACSR 32:5372–73.

33. For biographical information on Wickliffe, see Ramage, "Bluegrass Patriarch," 51–71; Ramage, "Love and Honor," 115–33; Collins and Collins, *Kentucky,* 2:199–200; Ranck, *History of Lexington, Kentucky,* 382; Townsend, *Lincoln,* 53, 80, 108–9, 177–83 passim; Coleman, *Slavery Times in Kentucky,* 32–33, 133–34, 150–51, 302–4, 312–13.

34. Wickliffe, *Speech on Monday, the 9th of November, 1840,* 44; Tapp, "Wickliffe and Breckinridge," 156–70; Wickliffe, *Speech on the Second Day of September, 1843,* 14–15. On the Wickliffe-Breckinridge controversy in general, see Klotter, *The Breckinridges,* 70–73.

35. Wickliffe, *Further Reply,* 55; Wickliffe, *Speech on Monday, the 9th of November, 1840,* 44; *Louisville Public Advertiser,* April 19, 1830, quoted in Martin, "Anti-Slavery in Kentucky," 57; Cowan to McLain, January 28, February 20, July 15, October 21, 1845, September 29, 1846, ACSR 97(1):24984–85, 97(2):25095–96, 99(1):25596–97, 100(1):26058–59, 103(2):27425–26; Kentucky, *Report of the Debates,* 94–95, 99, 115, 488, 574–75, 918; Breckinridge, "Black Race," 138.

36. "Colonization Movements," 266.

37. HC, "Speech of January 21, 1851," 106, 108; Young, "Address," 10; Danville Colonization Society, "Constitution and Proceedings"; Breckinridge, "Address before the Colonization Society of Kentucky," 176; Bullock, "Address," 109; Robinson, "Address," 140, 144; "Colonization Movements," 266–67; KCS, *Proceedings* (1848), 4; Cowan to McLain, October 1, 1844, ACSR 96(1):24558–59; "Twenty-First Annual Meeting" (Speech of HC), 17–18; HC, *Colonization Society of Kentucky,* 14–15; HC, "Remarks on the 26th of August, 1836," 299–300; HC, "Speech on Abolition Petitions," 61; Breckinridge, "Hints on Colonization," 292; "Convention, May 4th, 1842" (Speech of Morehead), 176. Breckinridge said that Clay tried to reassure the slaveholders that colonization posed no threat to slavery with "reasonings [that] do not . . . do justice to his own sentiments or this subject" (Breckinridge to Gurley, August 16, 1831, ACSR 32:5372–73).

38. Morehead, "Address," 15; HC, "Speech on Abolition Petitions," 61; "Twenty-First Annual Meeting" (Speech of HC), 17; Underwood, *Colonization Society of Bowlinggreen,* 9, 17–20.

39. Finnie, "Antislavery in the Upper South."

40. Kentucky, *Report of the Debates,* 71, 83, 94, 488, 918, 928; Underwood, "Colonization and Gradual Emancipation," 321–23; Robinson, "Address," 152–54; Breckinridge, "Speech," 137; Breckinridge, "Black Race," 140, 146; Finley to Gurley, October 20, 1832, ACSR 45:7577–78; John T. Edgar to Gurley, February 28, 1833, ACSR 47:7993–94; Finley to Philip R. Fendall, September 27, 1834, ACSR 58(3):10263–64; Cowan to McLain, December 23, 1844, May 2, August 1, October 10, 21, 27, November 29, 1845, February 13, May 14, July 2, September 29, 1846, December 25, 1849, ACSR 96(2):24793–94, 98:25378–79, 99(1):25659–60, 100(1):26013–14, 26058–59, 26103–4, 100(2):26241–42, 101(2):26573–74, 102(2):26887–88, 103(1):27051–53, 103(2):27425–26,

116(2):34; W.C. Matthews to McLain, November 29, 1845, August 16, 1847, ACSR 100(2):26238, 107(2):27276–77; Finley to McLain, August 29, 1846, ACSR 103(2): 27288–89; Petition of James B. Townsend, n.d., OBP; McClung, "Address," 144; "Twenty-First Annual Meeting" (Speech of HC), 18–19; Bennett, "All Things," 110–11, 113–16.

41. Paxton, *Letters on Slavery,* 157, see generally, 156–63, 177; Finley to Philip R. Fendall, June 23, September 27, 1834, ACSR 58(3):10261–64; George W. Fagg to Samuel Wilkeson, September 19, 1839, ACSR 75(2):16013–14; Cowan to McLain, November 1, 1847, ACSR 108(2):29589–90; W. Freehling, *Reintegration of American History,* 148–49; Melish, *Disowning Slavery,* 193–94.

42. HC, *Colonization Society of Kentucky,* 20–21; "Early History" (Speech of HC), 51; HC to J. Robertson et al., September 3, 1836, in *AR* 12 (October 1836):316–17; HC to N.W. Pollard, September 6, 1851, in M.E. Thomas, ed., "Henry Clay Replies," 264–65; Remini, *Henry Clay,* 670; Mayes, "Address," 9–10; "Convention, May 4th, 1842" (Speech of Morehead), 168–69, 171; Bullock, "Address," 105–6; Robinson, "Address," 152–53; Daniel Mayes to Gurley, August 9, 1832, ACSR 43:7110–11; L.W. Dunlap to Corresponding Secretary, ACS, September 13, 1834, ACSR 58(2):10230–31; Franklin Knight to Samuel Wilkeson, November 30, 1839, ACSR 76(2):16303–4; Jacobs to McLain, November 22, 1844, ACSR 96(1):24678–79; Cowan to McLain, November 29, 1845, August 10, October 9, November 1, 9, 1847, April 6, 1848, February 14, October 19, 1849, ACSR 100(2):26241–42, 107(2):29256–57, 108(1):29440–41, 108(2):29589–90, 29629–30, 110(1):30690–91, 113(2):32776–78, 116(1):34; Finley to Philip R. Fendall, September 27, 1834, ACSR 58(3):10263–64; Peers to Gurley, February 7, 1829, ACSR 13:2309–10. On the national level, the ACS tried to scotch support for non-African colonization. See Staudenraus, *African Colonization,* 85–87.

43. Kentucky, *Report of the Debates,* 24, 72–73, 78, 94–95, 102–3, 573, 853, 859, 919, 923–25, 930–33; Cowan to McLain, November 24, 1847, April 21, 1848, April 24, December 25, 1849, ACSR 108(2):29718–19, 110(1):30778–79, 114(1):33243–44, 116(2):34; William P. Thomasson to McLain, June 5, 1849, ACSR 114(2):33445.

44. Kentucky, *Report of the Debates,* 24, 71, 573, 575; Squire Turner to John C. Breckinridge, January 14, 1850, BFP 136:25242a–42b; Kentucky, *Acts* (1850–51), ch. 15, art. 9, sec. 1, art 11.

45. HC, *Colonization Society of Kentucky,* 22; HC, "On the Public Lands," in Colton, ed., *Works of Henry Clay,* 7:487–515; HC, "Remarks on the 26th of August, 1836," 300. See also Peers to Gurley, March 26, 1827, September 5, 1828, ACSR 4:517–18, 11:1864–65; Remini, *Henry Clay,* 394–95; Underwood, *Colonization Society of Kentucky,* 14–15; Mayes, "Address," 9–11; Underwood, "Colonization and Gradual Emancipation," 321; U.S., Congress, House, *Congressional Globe,* 30th Cong., 1st sess., 1847–48, *Appendix,* 306–13; Cowan to McLain, December 23, 1844, ACSR 96(2):24793–94; W. Freehling, *Reintegration of American History,* 149.

46. Underwood, *Colonization Society of Kentucky,* 15; HC, *Colonization Society of Kentucky,* 17; Young, "Address," 9, 31; Robinson, "Address," 151; Morehead, "Address," 123; HC, "Speech of January 21, 1851," 107; Underwood, *Colonization Society of Bowlinggreen,* 22; Bullock, "Address," 104, 107–8, 110; Peers to Gurley, February 6, 1827, ACSR 3:354–55; Jacobs to Gurley, December 6, 1828, ACSR 12:2078–79; George W. Fagg to Samuel Wilkeson, September 19, 1839, ACSR 75(2):16013–14; B. Mills to McLain, February 5, 1844, ACSR 93(1):23690–91; W.C. Matthews to McLain, September 18, 1844, ACSR 95:24482–83; Underwood to McLain, October

17, 1844, ACSR 96(1):24612–13; Cowan to McLain, February 20, July 15, 1845, November 1, 1847, ACSR 97(2):25095–96, 99(1):25596–97, 108(2):29589–90; Jacobs to McLain, March 11, 1849, ACSR 113(3):32969–70; E.P. Pratt to McLain, September 12, 1849, ACSR 115(2):34; Stone, "Address on Colonization," 198–200; Mills, "Expedition to Liberia," 167–68.

47. Young, "Address," 9; "Convention, May 4th, 1842" (Speech of Morehead), 176; Kentucky, *Report of the Debates,* 918; George W. Williams to Messrs. Lyle and Walker, n.d., clipping in William M.O. Smith to Breckinridge, April 28, 1849, BFP 134:24785–86. See Wyatt-Brown, *Southern Honor,* 27–32, 368–69, on southern fatalism.

48. "Convention, May 4th, 1842" (Speech of Morehead), 168–69, 175–76; Bullock, "Address," 104–5, 107; Breckinridge, "Speech," 140–41, 143–45; Young, "Address," 9–10, 30–31; Cowan to McLain, October 1, 1844, November 27, 1845, ACSR 96(1):24558–59, 100(2):26230–31; Underwood to McLain, October 17, 1844, ACSR 96(1):24612–13; Jacobs to McLain, September 13, 1845, ACSR 99(2):25852–53; HC, *Colonization Society of Kentucky,* 25; PrH, n.d., in "The Republic of Liberia," AR 28 (October 1852):296–99.

49. Morehead, "Address," 18, 25; McClung, "Address," 149; "Early History" (Speech of HC), 51; HC, "Speech of January 21, 1851," 107; Young, "Address," 31–32; "Proceedings of the Annual Meeting" (Resolutions of John J. Crittenden), AR 13 (January 1837):34; "Convention, May 4th, 1842" (Speech of Morehead), 122–23; A.H. Triplett to McLain, July 29, 1844, ACSR 95:24332.

50. Jacobs to McLain, September 13, 1845, ACSR 99(2):25852–53; N.M. Goodson to McLain, October 29, 1849, ACSR 116(1):34; Fee to McLain, December 17, 1856, quoted in Bennett, "All Things," 198; Fee, *Anti-Slavery Manual,* 171; Birney to Smith, January 31, 1835, in *LB,* 1:175; Birney, *Letter on Colonization,* 35–43. During the seven-year period from 1831 to 1837, the American Board of Commissioners for Foreign Missions (ABCFM), the largest of the American foreign missionary societies, spent well over one million dollars on foreign missions. This statement is based on statistics in the annual *Report* of the ABCFM: (1831) 103–10, (1832) 127–35, (1833) 143–49, (1834) 132–38, (1835) 118–24, (1836) 118–24, (1837) 129–34. See Friedman, *Inventors of the Promised Land,* 237–41, for a different interpretation of Birney's views on colonization. It should be obvious that I disagree with Friedman's contention that the colonization societies' "argument for Christian uplift was shabby and contrived," at least as it applies to the KCS (195).

51. Friedman, *Inventors of the Promised Land,* 189–90, see generally 180–219; Morehead, "Address," 25, 30; Underwood, *Colonization Society of Kentucky,* 20; Cowan to McLain, October 1, 1844, ACSR 96(1):24558–59; Underwood, *Slavery Question,* 14; McClung, "Address," 147; Breckinridge, "Hints on Colonization," 289; PrH, n.d., in "Republic of Liberia," 298–99; Breckinridge, "Speech," 141; Young, "Address," 31; Jacobs to McLain, September 13, 1845, ACSR 99(2):25852–53; Breckinridge, "Black Race," 143.

52. "Operations in Kentucky," AR 22 (October 1846):304; PrH, n.d., in "Alexander High School," AR 27 (May 1851):148; N.M. Goodson to McLain, October 29, 1849, ACSR 116(1):34; Cowan to McLain, October 9, 1847, ACSR 108(1):29440–41; HC, *Colonization Society of Kentucky,* 16; "Twenty-First Annual Meeting" (Speech of HC), 17; "Addresses at Annual Meeting" (Speech of HC), 44; "Convention, May 4th, 1842"

(Speech of Morehead), 172, 175; Breckinridge, "Black Race," 142–43; Bullock, "Address," 106–7; Mayes, "Address," 20; *PrH,* n.d., in "Republic of Liberia," 296–97.
53. Paxton, *Letters on Slavery,* 159.
54. *PrH,* n.d., in "Republic of Liberia," 296–97; Finley to Gurley, April 12, 1831, ACSR 30:4884–85; Shannon, *Philosophy of Slavery,* 17–18; Kentucky, *Report of the Debates,* 94, 99, 575, 928; *LJ,* n.d., in "Free Negroes and Colonization," *AR* 27 (July 1851):204–5; Paxton, *Letters on Slavery,* 157; Robinson, "Address," 154; "Addresses at Annual Meeting" (Speech of HC), 44.
55. Morehead, "Address," 18; Kentucky, *Report of the Debates,* 100–101, 925; Breckinridge, "Hints on Colonization," 284, 297–98; [Young], *Address to the Presbyterians,* 23–24; "Convention, May 4th, 1842" (Speech of Morehead), 173.

3. The Dilemma of Conservative Reform

1. Young, "President Young on Slavery," 120; [Young], *Address to the Presbyterians,* 20, 24; Young to Birney, May 29, 1847, in *LB,* 2:1075–76; Jacobs, "Young," 157–58; Young, *Duties of Masters,* 4–6; Shannon, *Philosophy of Slavery,* 22; Col. 4:1. For biographical information on Young, see *DAB* 20:629, s.v. "Young, John Clarke"; Jacobs, "Young," 151–66; Ormond Beatty, "Danville Social and Literary Club, History," in Danville Literary and Social Club, *History,* 10–14; Groves, "Centre College," 312–17.
2. Samuel Crothers to Young, February 14, 1835, in *CJ,* February 27, March 16, 1835; Ritchie, ed., *Life & Writings of Crothers,* 183–93; Young, "President Young on Slavery," 120–23; Theodore D. Weld to Birney, January 23, 1835, in *LB,* 1:172.
3. Young, "The Doctrine of Immediate Emancipation Unsound," in [Young], *Address to the Presbyterians,* 33, 64; Beatty, "Danville Social and Literary Club," 7; Birney to Tappan, March 19, 1835, March 17, 1836, August 8, 1837, Birney to Smith, March 21, 1835, Birney, manuscript enclosures in Thomas Ayers to Birney, n.d., Young to Birney, March 22, August 4, 1837, October 21, 1838, May 29, 1847, in *LB,* 1:188–89, 222, 312, 377–79, 402, 412, 472, 2:1074–77; Young to *CJ,* March 7, 1835, in *CJ,* March 27, 1835; Young, "President Young on Slavery," 120–21, 123; Young to Charles Hodge, June 15, [1836], Thurman Collection; Young to Charles Hodge, July 6, 1836, Young Papers; Tappan to William Lloyd Garrison, February 25, 1836, cited in Merrill and Ruchames, eds., *Letters of Garrison,* 2:54.
4. On the affinities between Kentucky's Whig party and the antislavery movement, see Peers to Gurley, March 26, 1827, September 5, 1828, ACSR 4:517–18, 11:1864–65; Jacobs to McLain, March 11, 1849, ACSR 113(3):32969–70; William L. Breckinridge to Breckinridge, February 14, 1849, BFP 133:24658; Breckinridge to Samuel Steel, April 17, 1849, BFP 134:24773–74; R.C. Grundy to Breckinridge, June 19, 1849, BFP 134:24879; Frank Ballenger to Breckinridge, July 13, 1849, BFP 135:24945; Robert O. Morris to Breckinridge, November 28, 1849, BFP 135:25138–41. On the concept of southern slaves as an antislavery group, see Dillon, *Slavery Attacked.* My discussion of Kentucky's antislavery conservatives has been influenced especially by Howe, *Political Culture;* Degler, *Other South,* 13–123; Barkan, "Whig Persuasion," 367–95; M. Wilson, *Space, Time, and Freedom;* T. Brown, *Politics and Statesmanship;* Kohl, *Politics of Individualism.*
5. Phillips, *American Negro Slavery,* 261–308, 327–30; Elkins, *Slavery,* 81–139; Coleman, *Slavery Times in Kentucky,* vii; Appleton, "Englishman's Perception," 60; Hopkins, *Hemp Industry in Kentucky,* 62–63; A. Young, "Task and Gang Labor," 41–

66; A. Young, "Cellars and African-American Slave Sites," 107–15; A. Young, "Risk Management," 26–27; Sprague, "Kentucky Pocket Plantation," 77–78; W. Johnson, *Soul by Soul,* 190–94. On the task system, see Morgan, "Work and Culture," 563–99. From a study of Civil War pension files, Richard Steckel calculated that in 1860, 69 percent of marriages among American slaves living on farms with fewer than 24 slaves were interfarm marriages. See Steckel, *Economics,* 226–31. Compare the discussion below to Lucas and Wright, *History of Blacks in Kentucky,* vol. 1: *From Slavery to Segregation,* 42–43.

    6. Blassingame, *Slave Community,* 251; Dunaway, "Diaspora, Death, and Sexual Exploitation," 128–49; Genovese, *Roll, Jordan, Roll,* 414; R.M. Miller and J.D. Smith, eds., *Dictionary of Afro-American Slavery,* s.v. "Miscegenation," by Laurence Glasco; Bancroft, *Slave Trading,* 89–90; Hopkins, *Hemp Industry in Kentucky,* 17, 47; Tadman, *Speculators and Slaves,* 12; Sutch, "Breeding of Slaves for Sale," 210; Dunaway, "Put in Master's Pocket," 116–32. Although Bluegrass planters relied on slave labor to cultivate hemp, this crop was not labor-intensive. A small number of slaves could raise a large hemp crop. This fact prompted additional complaints from planters who raised hemp, like Henry Clay and Robert J. Breckinridge, about the oversupply of slaves in the Bluegrass region. For an overview of labor practices, see Hopkins, *Hemp Industry in Kentucky,* 4–5, 24–30. The excess of slaves in the Bluegrass region also promoted the widespread practice of slave-hiring, in which slaves were rented out to others. See Barton, "'Good Cooks and Washers,'" 436–60.

    7. Charles W. Short to William Short, November 15, 1837, CWSP; Anderson, *From Slavery to Affluence,* 40–41; Marrs, *Life and History,* 21–25; Nelson Sanders to Susan Fishback, January 5, 1848, Shelby Family Papers; Robert Johnson to Thomas Dolan, August 20, 1846, Coleman Papers; FWP interviews with America Morgan, Bert Mayfield, Will Oats, Wes Woods, George Scruggs, Harriet Mason, Susan Dale Sanders, Mary Woodridge, and Hannah Davidson, n.d., in U.S., WPA, *Slave Narratives,* 5:142, 7:16, 19, 26, 29–32, 45, 106–10, 12:32; Henry Bibb to William Gatewood, March 23, 1844, Henry Bibb to Albert G. Sibley, October 7, 1852, Lewis Richardson, "Speech of Lewis Richardson," AFIC interviews with A.T. Jones and George Dunn, 1863, "Stories of Runaway Slaves," Lewis Hayden Autobiography in Blassingame, ed., *Slave Testimony,* 48–49, 53, 164, 430–32, 438–39, 516–17, 697; Jackson, *Narrative,* iii-iv, 7, 9; L. Clarke, *Narrative,* 14–15, 65–66, 76–77, 81–82; H. Smith, *Fifty Years,* 88; Lucas and Wright, *History of Blacks in Kentucky,* vol. 1: *From Slavery to Segregation,* 51–52; J.C. Meadors interview with Addie Murphy, August 13, 1938, in J. Winston Coleman, Jr., ed., "Slave Interviews, Notes and Data on Kentucky Slavery," 123, Coleman Papers; Bennett, "All Things," 96–97; Howard, "Black Testimony," 142–43, 154, 156–57; Coulter, *Civil War in Kentucky,* 350–51. Compare this interpretation of the harshness of slavery in Kentucky to that presented in Klotter, *The Breckinridges,* 64–65.

    8. L. Clarke, *Narrative,* 31, see also 34, 81; Bibb, *Narrative,* 46–47. Slave escapes from Kentucky are highlighted in J. Parker, *His Promised Land,* 71–151; Franklin and Schweninger, *Runaway Slaves,* 70–71, 97–98, 113–17, 120–21, 263–64. For slave resistance in Kentucky generally, see Lucas and Wright, *History of Blacks in Kentucky,* vol. 1: *From Slavery to Segregation,* 57–83. Michael Tadman estimates that in the states of the Upper South, 22–35 slaves successfully escaped annually for every 100,000 slaves during the 1850s. If Tadman's estimated rate of escape is correct for Kentucky, 46–79 slaves successfully escaped each year from the state. This calculation is based on statistics in Tadman, *Speculators and Slaves,* 239; Berlin, *Slaves without Masters,* 396–97.

9. Stedman, *Bluegrass Craftsman,* 112, 136; McPheeters, "Reminiscences," 224; A. Young, "Cellars and African-American Slave Sites," 110–11; Lucas and Wright, *History of Blacks in Kentucky,* vol. 1: *From Slavery to Segregation,* 55; Coleman, *Slavery Times in Kentucky,* 79–80. On the concept and evolution of the slaves' economy, see Morgan, "Work and Culture"; Berlin, *Many Thousands Gone,* 33–38, 57, 68–70, 134–38, 157–58, 164–66, 202–6, 269–71, 276, 301–2, 312–13, 346–48, 387–88.

10. FWP interview with Joana Owens, n.d., in U.S., WPA, *Slave Narratives,* 7:46–47; "$3,125 Reward," Broadside Collection; Jackson, *Narrative,* 8–9; *Columbus Dispatch,* February 9, 1932, in Coleman, ed., "Slave Interviews," 128–30, Coleman Papers; H. Smith, *Fifty Years,* 72, 95; Lewis Clarke, "Leaves from a Slave's Journal of Life," AFIC interview with A.T. Jones, 1863, "Stories of Runaway Slaves," in Blassingame, ed., *Slave Testimony,* 160, 430, 520–21; L. Clarke, *Narrative,* 72; Anderson, *From Slavery to Affluence,* 11, 31. For biographical information on Anderson, see Wax, "Anderson: A Kentucky Slave," 255–73; Wax, "Anderson, Ex-Slave," 163–92.

11. Anderson, *From Slavery to Affluence,* 11; Henry Bibb interview with John Moore, 1851, "Stories of Runaway Slaves," in Blassingame, ed., *Slave Testimony,* 275, 518; L. Clarke, *Narrative,* 26, 77–78, 81; Jackson, *Narrative,* 17; H. Smith, *Fifty Years,* 16.

12. Anderson, *From Slavery to Affluence,* 8–10; Marrs, *Life and History,* 10; L. Clarke, *Narrative,* 24–30; H. Smith, *Fifty Years,* 27–28, 37–38, 94–95, 106, 155–56; Jackson, *Narrative,* 27–28; FWP interview with Sophia Word, n.d., in U.S., WPA, *Slave Narratives,* 7:66–68; Fee, *Anti-Slavery Manual,* 144, 176–77; Birney to John Winslow et al., May 29, 1835, in Huch, ed., "Birney," 357; Breckinridge to Mary Hopkins Cabell Breckinridge, February 12, 1850, BFP 137:25296; McPheeters, "Reminiscences," 224; L. Clarke and M. Clarke, *Narrative,* 119–20.

13. H. Smith, *Fifty Years,* 51–53, 63–65, 68–71, 72–73, 83–85, 89, 92–93, 114–15, 135–38, 140; L. Clarke and M. Clarke, *Narrative,* 71–74, 180; FWP interviews with Harriet Mason and Sophia Word, n.d., in U.S., WPA, *Slave Narratives,* 7:31–32, 66–68; Jefferson T. Craig Diary, entry for April 18, 1855, 66, Local History Reports, Box 4; Ramage, "Bluegrass Patriarch," 55–58; L. Clarke, *Narrative,* 66–68, 72, 220; L. Clarke, "Leaves from a Slave's Journal of Life," 160.

14. Bibb, *Narrative,* 42–44; L. Clarke and M. Clarke, *Narrative,* 73, 125; Weisenburger, *Modern Medea;* FWP interview with Sophia Word, n.d., in U.S., WPA, *Slave Narratives,* 7:66–68; H. Smith, *Fifty Years,* 17–19, 20, 61, 113–14, 128–30, 133–35; Mary Breckinridge Maltby, "Recollections of War Times in Kentucky When I Was a Little Girl," 2–5, 8, typescript in Local History Reports, Box 4; Coleman, *Slavery Times in Kentucky,* 88. The Garner case has been made famous in modern times by Toni Morrison's Pulitzer Prize-winning novel *Beloved* and the movie version based on it.

15. Oakes, *Ruling Race,* 183, see generally 179–84.

16. Underwood, *Colonization Society of Bowlinggreen,* 24; Young, *Duties of Masters,* 25; William L. Breckinridge to Breckinridge, August 19, 1848, BFP 131:24324; William P. Hart to Breckinridge, March 17, 1849, BFP 133:24716; Breckinridge to William L. Breckinridge, January 11, 1850, BFP 136:25303; Breckinridge to Mary Hopkins Cabell Breckinridge, February 12, 1850, BFP 137:25296; Cowan to McLain, October 9, 1847, ACSR 108(1):29440–41; McPheeters, "Reminiscences," 224–25; John Thomas Croxton to Henry Croxton, March 29, 1855, in R. Miller, "Croxton," 284; Craig Diary, entries for October 13, 1854, April 23, July 23, September 17, 1855, 45, 67, 77, 82, Local History Reports, Box 4; Nicholas et al., *Slave Emancipation,* 3.

17. Underwood, *Slavery Question,* 18; Peers to Gurley, March 26, 1827, ACSR 4:517–18; Breckinridge, *Question of Negro Slavery,* 12.

18. Underwood, *National Politics,* 10; Breckinridge, "Black Race," 135–36; HC to John Greenleaf Whittier, July 22, 1837, in Hepler, ed., "Whittier Hears from Clay," 172; HC to Thomas M. Peters and John M. Jackson, July 27, 1844, in *NR,* August 31, 1844; HC to Stephen F. Miller, July 1, 1844, in *NR,* August 3, 1844; HC to *NI,* September 23, 1844, in *NR,* October 5, 1844; HC to *NI,* April 17, 1844, in *NR,* May 4, 1844.

19. Underwood, *Colonization Society of Bowlinggreen,* 24; HC, *Colonization Society of Kentucky,* 12; HC, "Speech of January 21, 1851," 110.

20. Underwood, *National Politics,* 30; William Campbell Preston, quoted in [J. Speed et al.], *Address,* 8–9. This address exists in two significantly different forms, and I have chosen to cite each separately. Hereinafter, [J. Speed et al.], "Address," in *Ex,* February 24, 1849, will refer to the original version of the address as published in *Ex.* [J. Speed et al.], *Address,* will refer to the later, revised version of the address. The members of the committee that wrote this address were identified in *Ex,* February 3, 1849.

21. Underwood, *Speech upon the Resolution to Censure,* 12; "Convention, May 4th, 1842" (Speech of Morehead), 176; Breckinridge, *Question of Negro Slavery,* 12. My discussion of the conservatives' thoughts on race owes much to Fredrickson, *Black Image,* chaps. 1–5.

22. Breckinridge, "Speech," 142; Breckinridge, "Hints on Colonization," 285; Robinson, "Address," 144; Morehead, "Address," 26; Underwood, *Colonization Society of Kentucky,* 9; Underwood, *Colonization Society of Bowlinggreen,* 7.

23. Underwood, *Colonization Society of Kentucky,* 9, 17; Underwood, *Speech upon the Resolution to Censure,* 13; Nicholas et al., *Slave Emancipation,* 4; HC, "Reply to Mr. Mendenhall," in Colton, ed., *Works of Henry Clay,* 9:388; Remini, *Henry Clay,* 526, 618, 693; Breckinridge, "Speech," 142–43; Breckinridge, *Question of Negro Slavery,* 14; Underwood, *Colonization Society of Bowlinggreen,* 4.

24. Breckinridge, "Hints on Colonization," 285; George W. Johnson, quoted in *Ex,* October 28, 1848; Fredrickson, *Black Image,* 43–96; McClung, "Address," 148; Breckinridge, *Question of Negro Slavery,* 13; Cleros [pseud.], "Shall Kentucky Continue a Slave State" in [Garrett et al.], *Address to the Non-Slaveholders,* 9. The members of the committee that wrote the *Address to the Non-Slaveholders* were identified in *Ex,* April 14, 21, 1849.

25. HC, "Remarks on the 26th of August, 1836," 297; Young, "President Young on Slavery," 120–21; [Young], *Address to the Presbyterians,* 27; Young, "Address," 8–9, 15, 28–29; Breckinridge, "Black Race," 141.

26. HC to Richard Pindell, February 17, 1849, in *NR,* March 21, 1849. For the argument that lower-class whites might benefit from enslavement, see Buck, *Slavery Question,* 13–14.

27. [Young], *Address to the Presbyterians,* 24; Cowan to McLain, October 9, 1847, ACSR 108(1):29440–41; HC, *Colonization Society of Kentucky,* 13; HC, "Speech of January 21, 1851," 109.

28. McClung, "Address," 148–49; Underwood, *Colonization Society of Kentucky,* 4; *LJ,* n.d., in "Free Negroes and Colonization," 205.

29. Mayes, "Address," 16; Bullock, "Address," 102; Young, "Address," 28–29; "Convention, May 4th, 1842" (Speech of Morehead), 173.

30. *LJ*, n.d., in "Free Negroes and Colonization," 204–5; KCS, *Annual Report* (1834), 5; Bullock, "Address," 102–3.

31. Mayes, "Address," 20; Fee, *Anti-Slavery Manual,* 171; Friedman, *Inventors of the Promised Land,* 195.

32. Mayes, "Address," 16; [Young], *Address to the Presbyterians,* 7–8; Nicholas et al., *Slave Emancipation,* 4; Paxton, *Letters on Slavery,* 156; Underwood, *Colonization Society of Bowlinggreen,* 16, 21; HC, *Colonization Society of Kentucky,* 12–13; Underwood, *Colonization Society of Kentucky,* 9, 21, 23–24. In speaking of antiliteracy laws, Mayes was referring to the South as a whole, not about Kentucky, where there were no such laws. Compare this paragraph to Howe, *Political Culture,* 134. On the conservatives' belief in the inevitability of a slave revolt, see additionally Paxton, *Letters on Slavery,* 155–56; Nicholas et al., *Slave Emancipation,* 4; Breckinridge, "Speech," 143; Mayes, "Address," 21.

33. *WK*, n.d., in *Ex,* February 3, 1849.

34. Underwood, *Slavery Question,* 10–11; *WCMC,* 282; Breckinridge, "Hints on Colonization," 298–300; Young, "Immediate Emancipation," 44, 48.

35. Nicholas et al., *Slave Emancipation,* 6; Breckinridge, *Question of Negro Slavery,* 5, 7–8, 12–14; Underwood, *Slavery Question,* 10; *WCMC,* 281–82.

36. Underwood, *Colonization Society of Bowlinggreen,* 4–5; McClung, "Address," 142.

37. HC, *Colonization Society of Kentucky,* 18–19; Mayes, "Address," 18–19; Underwood, *Colonization Society of Bowlinggreen,* 4–5; Bullock, "Address," 99–101; Young, "President Young on Slavery," 121; [Young], *Address to the Presbyterians,* 11; [J. Speed et al.], *Address,* 11.

38. [Young], *Address to the Presbyterians,* 6, 16; Breckinridge, *Question of Negro Slavery,* 12; [J. Speed et al.], *Address,* 4–5, 10, 12; Underwood, *Colonization Society of Bowlinggreen,* 9, 13–14; John Irwin to John Irwin, Sr., and Mary Irwin, January 31, 1840, Irwin Papers; Breckinridge to Samuel Steel, April 17, 1849, BFP 134:24773–74; *WCMC,* 68–69, 74–75, 226, 269, 378; Wickliffe, *Speech on Monday, the 10th Day of August, 1840,* 14; Nicholas et al., *Slave Emancipation,* 3, 7; [J. Speed et al.], "Address," in *Ex,* February 24, 1849.

39. Underwood, *Colonization Society of Bowlinggreen,* 9–10; [Young], *Address to the Presbyterians,* 14–15.

40. [J. Speed et al.], *Address,* 9; Underwood, *National Politics,* 9–10; Meyers, *Jacksonian Persuasion,* especially 1–23.

41. Breckinridge, *Question of Negro Slavery,* 7–10; *WK,* n.d., in *Ex,* February 3, 1849; Underwood, *Colonization Society of Kentucky,* 3, 6, 21; Bullock, "Address," 109; Underwood, *Slavery Question,* 14.

42. Underwood to Elizabeth C. Underwood, December 19, 1852, January 26, 1853, JRUP; "HMU," typescript enclosure in Underwood to Elizabeth C. Underwood, December 19, 1852, JRUP. On Espy, see *DAB* 6:185–86, s.v. "Espy, James Pollard."

43. [J. Speed et al.], *Address,* 5, 10; Nicholas et al., *Slave Emancipation,* 3; *WCMC,* 225–26; *WK,* n.d., in *Ex,* February 3, 1849; see generally [J. Speed et al.], *Address,* 3–11; Nicholas et al., *Slave Emancipation,* 1–3.

44. Nicholas et al., *Slave Emancipation,* 3; McClung, "Address," 134–36; Bullock, "Address," 109.

45. [J. Speed et al.], *Address,* 10; Nicholas et al., *Slave Emancipation,* 2; Bullock, "Address," 109–110. See Robinson, "Address," 146–49, for a fascinating discussion of how progress was removing slavery in the South.

46. Nicholas et al., *Slave Emancipation,* 1–2; Underwood, "Colonization and Gradual Emancipation," 323–24; McClung, "Address," 137; HC, *Colonization Society of Kentucky,* 10–12; Young, "Address," 24–25; Petition of James B. Townsend, n.d., OBP; HC, *Colonization Society of Kentucky,* 10.

47. HC, *Colonization Society of Kentucky,* 10; Young, "Address," 24–25; Bullock, "Address," 109; Underwood, *Slavery Question,* 14; Underwood, *Colonization Society of Kentucky,* 19–21; WCMC, 224; Underwood, *Colonization Society of Bowlinggreen,* 13; Nicholas et al., *Slave Emancipation,* 7; John Irwin to John Irwin, Sr., and Mary Irwin, August 16, 1832, John Irwin to Ellis Irwin, August 23, 1832, Irwin Papers.

48. Underwood, *Colonization Society of Bowlinggreen,* 13–15; Underwood, *Colonization Society of Kentucky,* 19; [J. Speed et al.], "Address," in *Ex,* February 24, 1849; [J. Speed et al.], *Address,* 6; Nicholas et al., *Slave Emancipation,* 6–7; WCMC, 224–25.

49. Underwood, *Colonization Society of Bowlinggreen,* 15; Nicholas et al., *Slave Emancipation,* 7; Breckinridge, *Question of Negro Slavery,* 4–5; WCMC, 227.

50. Breckinridge, *Question of Negro Slavery,* 11–12; [J. Speed et al.], *Address,* 1, 3–5, 7, 9; [J. Speed et al.], "Address," in *Ex,* February 24, 1849; Young, "Address," 21; Underwood, *Colonization Society of Kentucky,* 20; "Young Men's Society" (Speech of Benjamin B. Smith), 93; John Thomas Croxton to Henry Croxton, March 29, 1855, in R. Miller, "Croxton," 284–86; Bennett, "All Things," 49; Nicholas et al., *Slave Emancipation,* 2–3; For evidence that slavery did, in fact, prompt a sizable migration from the Upper South to the free states, see Finnie, "Antislavery Movement in the South"; Schwarz, *Migrants against Slavery,* especially 1–17.

51. [J. Speed et al.], *Address,* 4–5; [J. Speed et al.], "Address," in *Ex,* February 24, 1849; Nicholas et al., *Slave Emancipation,* 2; Underwood, *Colonization Society of Bowlinggreen,* 10.

52. [J. Speed et al.], *Address,* 4–5.

4. The Limits of Political Action

1. Breckinridge, "Speech," 140.

2. Breckinridge, *Question of Negro Slavery,* 13–14; Young, "President Young on Slavery," 123; "Twenty-First Annual Meeting" (Speech of HC), 18; Nicholas et al., *Slave Emancipation,* 7.

3. Stampp, *Peculiar Institution,* 253; Breckinridge, *Question of Negro Slavery,* 5; Breckinridge, *Speech in the Court-House Yard,* 8–9; WCMC, 118, 120. See nonimportation bills in *HJ* (1839–40), 303–4; *HJ* (1840–41), 93–95; *SJ* (1840–41), 252–53; *HJ* (1842–43), 206; *SJ* (1843–44), 205–7; *HJ* (1844–45), 112–13; *SJ* (1844–45), 153–54.

4. WCMC, 69, 118–19; D.B. Davis, *Problem of Slavery in Western Culture,* 135–44; Breckinridge, *Question of Negro Slavery,* 4–5; Coward, *Kentucky in the New Republic,* 138.

5. WCMC, 69; Breckinridge, *Question of Negro Slavery,* 4; GB to John Scoble, January 19, 1845, in Abel and Klingberg, eds., *Side-Light,* 202–3.

6. Breckinridge, *Hints on Slavery,* 13; Martin, "Anti-Slavery in Kentucky," 90–96; Mathias, "Slavery," 4–5; Kentucky, *Report of the Debates,* 554–55. The vote in favor of the Nonimportation Act of 1833 was 56–32 in the House and 23–12 in the Senate.

7. Kentucky, *Acts* (1814–15), ch. 268, secs. 2, 4; Kentucky, *Acts* (1832–33), ch. 223, secs. 1, 2, 4, 8; Breckinridge, *Hints on Slavery,* 13.

8. Bancroft, *Slave Trading,* 272; C. Fields, "Kentucky's Third Constitution," 133,

142–46; Mathias, "Slavery," 5–6, 8–10, 13–15; Martin, "Anti-Slavery in Kentucky," 64–69, 95–97; John McLarning, quoted in *Li,* April 20, 1849; Kentucky, *Report of the Debates,* 82–83, 490, 554–55; Wickliffe, *Speech on Monday, the 10th Day of August, 1840;* Wickliffe, *Circular;* GB to John Scoble, January 19, 1845, in Abel and Klingberg, eds., *Side-Light,* 202–3.

9. *HJ* (1837–38), 385–86; *HJ* (1840–41), 95–96, 206–7; *HJ* (1841–42), 364–65; *HJ* (1842–43), 207–11; *HJ* (1844–45), 113–14; *HJ* (1847–48), 269–71; CMC, *Review of the Late Canvass;* WCMC, 58–76, 118–36; Smiley, *Lion of White Hall,* 43–54; Underwood, "Colonization and Gradual Emancipation," 324.

10. Breckinridge, *Speech in the Court-House Yard,* 17.

11. Underwood, *Slavery Question,* 10, see generally, 9–11; Underwood, *Colonization Society of Kentucky,* 8; Young, "President Young on Slavery," 121; Young, "Immediate Emancipation," 48; Breckinridge, "Hints on Colonization," 298–99; Young, *Duties of Masters,* 13–15; Cowan to McLain, November 24, 1847, ACSR 108(2):29718–19. On the use of familial imagery by the defenders of slavery, see McCurry, *Masters of Small Worlds,* especially 208–38.

12. Young, "President Young on Slavery," 120–21; Young, "Immediate Emancipation," 36–42; Cowan to McLain, November 24, 1847, ACSR 108(2):29718–19; Underwood to Birney, May 6, 1840, in *LB,* 1:562; [Young], *Address to the Presbyterians,* 16, 26–28; Underwood, *Slavery Question,* 13; William T. McElroy Journal, entry for mid-February 1852; Breckinridge, "Hints on Colonization," 299–300.

13. [Young], *Address to the Presbyterians,* 10–16; Young, *Duties of Masters,* 4–7, 10–15; Underwood, *Colonization Society of Bowlinggreen,* 9–10, 13, 16; George W. Fagg to Samuel Wilkeson, September 19, 1839, ACSR 75(2):16013–14; A.H. Triplett to McLain, July 1, 1845, January 16, 1846, ACSR 99(1):25530–31, 101(1):26476; Martin, "Anti-Slavery in Kentucky," 130; Jacobs to McLain, March 11, 1849, ACSR 113(3):32969–70; Breckinridge, *Question of Negro Slavery,* 7; Nicholas et al., *Slave Emancipation,* 1.

14. See, for instance, McColley, *Slavery and Jeffersonian Virginia;* Cohen, "Jefferson and Slavery," 503–26; Cooper, *Liberty and Slavery,* 33–35. For a discussion of antislavery colonizationists in Kentucky who freed their own slaves, see Allen, "'All of Us Are Highly Pleased,'" 97–109.

15. Breckinridge, *Question of Negro Slavery,* 8; Nicholas et al., *Slave Emancipation,* 5; [J. Speed et al.], "Address," 11; John Thomas Croxton to Henry Croxton, March 29, 1855, in R. Miller, "Croxton," 284; Kentucky, *Report of the Debates,* 928; Underwood, *Colonization Society of Bowlinggreen,* 23; Barton, "'Good Cooks and Washers,'" 436–60.

16. Elkins, *Slavery,* 140–206; Stewart, "Politics and Belief," 74–97; *LJ,* August 15, 1836, in "Colonization Movements," 267; HC, "Speech on Abolition Petitions," 51–52; Underwood, *Slavery Question,* 11–12; Birney to Theodore D. Weld, July 17, 21, 1834, in Barnes and Dumond, eds., *Letters of Weld, Weld and Grimké,* 1:158, 161; James M. Buchanan to Birney, December 2, 1835, Birney to Tappan, March 17, 1836, in *LB,* 1:277–78, 312. For a sophisticated interpretation of how the abolitionists' individualism and anarchism undermined their ability to fight slavery, see Perry, *Radical Abolitionism.*

17. Genovese, *Political Economy of Slavery,* 206–8.

18. Harriet L. Smith to Harriet Richards Campfield Boswell, May 8, 1838, Smith

Papers, UK; William Lloyd Garrison to Isaac Knapp, May 8, 1838, in Merrill and Ruchames, eds., *Letters of Garrison*, 2:357.

19. Breckinridge to William H. Seward, November 6, 1855, in *NYT,* November 15, 1855; Breckinridge to Charles Sumner, July 11, 1855, in *NYT,* July 25, 1855; Breckinridge, "Past Course," 426–42; Republican Party, *Proceedings*, 177–81; Klotter, *The Breckinridges*, 76, 84–88; Gilliam, "Breckinridge: Kentucky Unionist," 362–85; Tapp, "Breckinridge during the Civil War," 120–44; Mayse, "Breckinridge," 535–630. Breckinridge's letters were responses to Seward's speech of October 19, 1855 (*NYT,* October 22, 1855), and Sumner's speech of May 1855 (*NYTr,* May 16, 1855).

20. "Nineteenth Annual Meeting" (Speech of HC), 10–11; HC, "Speech on Abolition Petitions," 60–61; HC to John Greenleaf Whittier, July 22, 1837, in Hepler, ed., "Whittier Hears from Clay," 171–72; HC to Birney, November 3, 1838, in Boromé, ed., "Clay and Birney," 123–24; Bullock, "Address," 100, 106; "A Check Given to Abolition in Kentucky," *AR* 11 (September 1835):285; Underwood to Birney, April 11, 1840, in *LB,* 1:552; John Irwin to John Irwin, Sr., February 26, 1839, Irwin Papers; Bennett, "All Things," 74; Danville Colonization Society, "Constitution and Proceedings"; Nicholas et al., *Slave Emancipation,* 1; Breckinridge, "Hints on Colonization," 303; Jacobs to McLain, March 11, 1849, ACSR 113(3):32969–70; "Colonization Movements," 266; Klotter, *The Breckinridges,* 68–70.

21. Kentucky, *Second Constitution* (1799), art. 7, sec. 1; Zilversmit, *First Emancipation,* 180–84, 193–99; *WCMC,* 209.

22. Kentucky, *Second Constitution* (1799), art. 9.

23. C. Fields, "Kentucky's Third Constitution," 10–13; Martin, "Anti-Slavery in Kentucky," 33.

24. Ireland, *County Courts*; Ireland, "Aristocrats All," 365–83. On the general defects of the Second Constitution, see C. Fields, "Kentucky's Third Constitution."

25. Coward, *Kentucky in the New Republic*; Van Deusen, *Life of Henry Clay,* 19–21; James Freeman Clarke to CRBO, August 15, 1836, in "Colonization," 321; John Irwin to John Irwin, Sr., February 26, 1839, Irwin Papers; Peers to Gurley, December 11, 1826, February 5, 1827, ACSR 2:185–86, 3:352–53; GB to John Scoble, January 19, 1845, in Abel and Klingberg, eds., *Side-Light,* 202–3; C. Fields, "Kentucky's Third Constitution," 25–26; Martin, "Anti-Slavery in Kentucky," 98–103.

26. *HJ* (1834–35), 85–86, 137–38; *SJ* (1834–35), 30, 95–97; *HJ* (1835–36), 85–86; *SJ* (1835–36), 124–25, 134–35; *SJ* (1836–37), 60, 129–31; *HJ* (1837–38), 35–36, 102–4, 121–23; Martin, "Anti-Slavery in Kentucky," 99–103; C. Fields, "Kentucky's Third Constitution," 25–27; James Freeman Clarke to CRBO, August 15, 1836, in "Colonization," 321; "Young Men's Society" (Speech of Benjamin B. Smith), 93–94; *CJ,* n.d., in "Gradual Emancipation in Kentucky," *AR* 11 (August 1835):256; Webb, "Bristow," 142–58; *Ex,* May 26, June 2, 1849; Collins and Collins, *Kentucky,* 2:481, 651.

27. Wood, *Creation of the American Republic,* 306–89, 532–36; Breckinridge, *Question of Negro Slavery,* 2, 5–6, 12; *WCMC,* 45.

28. Republican Party, *Proceedings,* 179; Breckinridge, *Question of Negro Slavery,* 12. It should be noted that Breckinridge, in this speech before the Republican National Convention of 1864, was praising the right of Americans to change their constitution.

29. HC, "Speech on Abolition Petitions," 61; HC to Birney, November 3, 1838, in Boromé, ed., "Clay and Birney," 123–24; Eaton, *Henry Clay,* 79, 81; *WCMC,* 46–47. For general Whig opposition to the convention, see C. Fields, "Kentucky's Third Constitution," 20–29.

30. *WCMC,* 47–48; Underwood, *Colonization Society of Bowlinggreen,* 24; Breckinridge, *Hints on Slavery,* 3.

31. Stanton, Thome, and Cox, *Debate at the Lane Seminary;* Jacobs to Gurley, December 4, 1829, ACSR 19:3338–39; Harrison, *Antislavery Movement,* 43; English, "Fee," 11–12; Fladeland, *Birney,* 75–124; Martin, "Anti-Slavery in Kentucky," 75, 106. On the abolitionists' postal campaign, see Wyatt-Brown, *Lewis Tappan,* 142–66; Wyatt-Brown, "Postal Campaign," 227–38.

32. Morehead, quoted in Martin, "Anti-Slavery in Kentucky," 107, see also 103; HC to Birney, November 3, 1838, in Boromé, ed., "Clay and Birney," 123–24; *WCMC,* 45–46; *HJ* (1837–38), 121–23.

33. The results of the referendum are given in *SJ* (1838–39), 278–79. Out of 104,622 eligible voters, only 28,170 voted for the convention. See also Martin, "Anti-Slavery in Kentucky," 103–10.

5. The Crisis at the Door

1. Smiley, *Lion of White Hall,* 11–13, 21–25, 33–37, 43–53; Siegel, *White Hall,* 9–11; *HJ* (1835–36), 85–86; *HJ* (1837–38), 35–36, 102–4, 121–23; *HJ* (1840–41), 93–96, 204–7; CMC to Brutus J. Clay, December 4, 1831, in C. Clay, ed., "Unpublished Letters," 9 (the editor of this article was a relative of Clay and will be hereinafter referred to as C. Clay); CMC to Elihu Burritt, January 30, 1844, in *Li,* March 1, 1844; *WCMC,* 45–49, 174–75. Cassius Clay believed his father had been the largest slaveholder in Kentucky. See CMC, *Life,* 25.

2. *WCMC,* 53–57; CMC, *Review of the Late Canvass,* 5–7; Smiley, "Cassius M. Clay and Southern Industrialism," 317–21; Smiley, *Lion of White Hall,* 26–30, 34–42. Henry and Cassius Clay were second cousins, though their personal relationship was not close. On Clay's kinship to Henry Clay, see Smiley, *Lion of White Hall,* 3–25, 252.

3. Collins and Collins, *Kentucky,* 1:325–27; Mathias, "Common Schools," 222–27; Mallalieu and Akural, "Kentucky Banks," 297–303; Gilliam, "Letcher," 9–27; C. Fields, "Kentucky's Third Constitution," 85–92; Burckin, "Urban Middle Class," 99–100; Smiley, *Lion of White Hall,* 41; CMC to Brutus J. Clay, November 11, 1841, quoted in Siegel, *White Hall,* 15. For a dissenting view of the depression in Kentucky, see Paine, "Union," 89.

4. CMC to C.D. Cleveland, October 25, 1845, in *NASS,* November 6, 1845; CMC to Salmon P. Chase, April 15, 1842, SPCP; *WCMC,* 51, 54, 58–76, 117–36, 163–66; Genovese, *Political Economy of Slavery,* 172; Woodman, "Profitability," 305–6.

5. Compare this interpretation to Smiley, *Lion of White Hall,* 36–42.

6. *WCMC,* 142–44, 232–33, 235, 248–49, 331, 339–40.

7. Ibid., 143–44, 233, 235, 337–40; "Life Members," 70.

8. Smiley, "Clay and Fee," 204; Pease and Pease, *Bound with Them in Chains,* 76; Degler, *Other South,* 55–60; *WCMC,* 187; CMC to William C. Bloss, January 16, 1846, in *PF,* January 22, 1846; CMC to *New York World,* February 19, 1861, quoted in Smiley, "Clay and Fee," 204.

9. *WCMC,* 170, 174, 180–81, 187, 198–99, 206–7, 231, 234–35, 247–49, 253–55, 292–93, 337–40, 378, 381–82, 470–71; CMC to Gentlemen, July 11, 1844, in *Li,* September 13, 1844. Compare this interpretation to Harrold, *Abolitionists and the South,* 23, 132–35; Harrold, "Clay on Slavery and Race," 42–56.

10. *WCMC,* 267–68, 339–40.

11. CMC to Salmon P. Chase, December 21, 1842, January 19, 1844, January 28, July 3, 1845, March 20, May 2, 1846, July 14, 1848, SPCP; CMC to Edmund Quincy, May 14, 1844, in *Li*, June 7, 1844; CMC to Gentlemen, July 11, 1844, in *Li*, September 13, 1844; CMC to Pliny Warren, April 1, 1846, Clay Papers, UK; CMC to Christian Donaldson, March 25, 1853, in *Li*, May 6, 1853; *WCMC*, 157–59, 278, 450–51; CMC to W.J. McKinney, March 20, 1844, in *Li*, April 5, 1844.

12. *WCMC*, 267–68, 292–93, 339–40.

13. The most notable of these confrontations was Clay's long-running feud with the powerful Wickliffe family, involving not only a war of words and electoral battles, but also a duel between Clay and Robert Wickliffe, Jr., and a nearly fatal brawl between Clay and a man Clay believed to be a paid assassin hired by the Wickliffes. See Smiley, *Lion of White Hall*, 38–39, 43–53, 60–63, 83, 86.

14. *WCMC*, 211–18, 284–85, 313; Harrison, "*True American,*" 30–49; Smiley, *Lion of White Hall*, 90–91, 211–12; CMC to Smith, February 14, 1845, Clay Papers, UK; CMC to Salmon P. Chase, July 3, 1845, SPCP; J. Speed Smith to Brutus J. Clay, July 12, 1845, in C. Clay, ed., "Unpublished Letters," 15–16; CMC to *NI*, December 1845, in *PF*, January 8, 1846; CMC to Horace Greeley, January 18, 1846, in *PF*, January 29, 1846.

15. J. Speed Smith to Brutus J. Clay, July 12, 1845, in C. Clay, ed., "Unpublished Letters," 15–16; Almeron Dowd to Emily Curtis, August 23, 1845, Dowd Papers; D.M. Craig to E.F. Berkley, August 19, 1845, in "Old Letter," 197–98; Smiley, *Lion of White Hall*, 91–99; Harrison, "*True American,*" 36–41; Harrison, "Anti-Slavery Career," 304–6; *WCMC*, 287, 294–95, 317–18; Eaton, *Freedom-of-Thought Struggle*, 187–89, 193–94; Pease and Pease, *Bound with Them in Chains*, 69–70. For Clay's version of the suppression of the True American, see *WCMC*, 287–326. Other documents associated with the suppression of the *True American* may be found in *Li*, August 29, 1845; *NASS*, September 4, 1845. Historians disagree about the motives for the attack on Clay's paper. David Smiley argued strongly that slaveholders worried that the *True American* undermined the support of white nonslaveholders for slavery (Smiley, *Lion of White Hall*, 87–88, 97–98, 101–2; Smiley, ed., "View of the Suppression," 320). While such concerns clearly played a role in stirring up anger against Clay, he assumed that Lexingtonians feared their slaves more than they feared nonslaveholding whites. Clay sought to relieve public concerns about the influence of his inflammatory editorial on blacks by claiming that it was meant for "the white millions" of the South (*WCMC*, 288). For examples of Clay's argument that he was not trying to start a slave insurrection, see, CMC to Lyman Clary, September 18, 1845, in *Li*, October 24, 1845; CMC to *NI*, December 1845, in *PF*, January 8, 1846; *WCMC*, 288–89, 291, 297, 314–19.

16. Smiley, *Lion of White Hall*, 104; *WCMC*, 478; CMC to Salmon P. Chase, June 30, 1846, December 27, 1847, SPCP; CMC to Maria Weston Chapman, June 30, 1846, in *Li*, July 17, 1846.

17. There is no modern, published study of Vaughan's career. For biographical information, see Tallant, "Slavery Controversy in Kentucky," 226–27.

18. CMC to Salmon P. Chase, September 27, 1843, January 19, February 20, 1844, SPCP; Harrold, "Southern Strategy," 21–36.

19. Tappan to George W. Alexander, February 23, 1847, Tappan to John Scoble, June 30, 1847, in Abel and Klingberg, eds., *Side-Light*, 219, 224; Salmon P. Chase to Smith, September 1, 1846, GSP; C. Clay, ed., "Unpublished Letters," 122–23; Smiley, *Lion of White Hall*, 115.

20. Mary Jane Clay to Brutus J. Clay, June 17, 29, July 9, September 5, October 11, November 8, 1846, Paul Seymour to Brutus J. Clay, October 6, 22, 1846, in C. Clay, ed., "Unpublished Letters," 123–30; Mary Jane Clay to Fee, October 28, 1846, JGFP. For the abolitionist reaction to Clay's enlistment in the army, see Tappan to George W. Alexander, February 23, 1847, in Abel and Klingberg, eds., *Side-Light,* 221–22; William Lloyd Garrison to Elizabeth Pease, June 20, 1849, in Merrill and Ruchames, eds., *Letters of Garrison,* 2:622–23. See Harrold, "Clay and the Abolitionists," 101–19, for evidence that abolitionists had not entirely given up on Clay.

21. Salmon P. Chase to Smith, September 1, 1846, GSP; Mary Jane Clay to Brutus J. Clay, July 9, September 28, 1846, Paul Seymour to Mary Jane Clay, October 22, 1846, in C. Clay, ed., "Unpublished Letters," 125–27, 129–30; Mary Jane Clay to Fee, October 28, 1846, JGFP. Salmon P. Chase viewed Brutus Clay as "an open and avowed enemy of the [antislavery] movement" who used the paper's financial troubles as a pretext to close the paper (Salmon P. Chase to Charles Sumner, November 26, 1846, in Bourne, ed., "Diary and Correspondence of Chase," 2:111). Mary Jane Clay's letters, however, show clear distress about the financial burden that the *True American* was placing on her husband's finances. See Mary Jane Clay to Brutus J. Clay, October 11, 1846, in C. Clay, ed., "Unpublished Letters," 128; Siegel, *White Hall,* 16.

22. Salmon P. Chase to Charles Sumner, November 26, 1846, in Bourne, ed., "Diary and Correspondence of Chase," 2:112; Edgar Needham to Fee, January 9, 1847, Joseph Glazebrook to Fee, October 29, 1847, JGFP.

23. Edgar Needham to Fee, February 7, 1847, JGFP; John C. Vaughan to Smith, April 9, 1847, GSP. See also Cowan to McLain, November 24, 1847, ACSR 108(2): 29718–19; Samuel Hatch to McLain, June 22, 1849, ACSR 114(2):33530–31.

24. Edgar Needham to Fee, January 9, February 7, 1847, Tappan to Fee, November 2, 1847, Paul Seymour to Fee, March 7, 1848, Hugh S. Fullerton to Fee, December 9, 1846, JGFP; Fee to Tappan, November 17, 1846, in *AM,* o.s., 1 (January 1847):23–24; Tappan to George W. Alexander, February 23, 1847, Tappan to John Scoble, June 30, 1847, in Abel and Klingberg, eds., *Side-Light,* 219–22, 224.

25. CMC to Salmon P. Chase, June 30, 1846, SPCP; Salmon P. Chase to Charles Sumner, November 26, 1846, in Bourne, ed., "Diary and Correspondence of Chase," 2:111–12; Salmon P. Chase to Smith, September 1, 1846, John C. Vaughan to Smith, April 9, 1847, GSP; Charles Sumner to Salmon P. Chase, December 12, 1846, in Palmer, ed., "Small Minority," 165–66. On the importance which northern abolitionists placed on the publication of Vaughan's paper, see Harrold, *Abolitionists and the South,* 34.

26. John C. Vaughan to Smith, April 9, 1847, GSP; Edgar Needham to Fee, January 9, February 7, April 9, 1847, JGFP; *Ex,* June 19, 1847.

27. On the abandonment of colonization by some conservatives, see Samuel S. Nicholas, "Emancipation," in *Ex,* March 17, 1849; William L. Breckinridge to *Louisville Democrat,* February 22, 1849, in *Ex,* March 3, 1849; William L. Breckinridge to Breckinridge, February 6, 1849, BFP 133:24645–46; William P. Thomasson to McLain, June 5, 1849, ACSR 114(2):33445; Samuel Hatch to McLain, June 22, 1849, ACSR 114(2):33530–31; Harrold, *Abolitionists and the South,* 131.

28. The profile of Louisville emancipationists presented in the remainder of this chapter was developed by compiling, from the published proceedings of antislavery meetings in 1849, a list of 136 people who were prominent in the emancipation movement. These lists were printed in *Ex,* February 3, 17, March 24, 31, April 7, 14, May 5,

12, June 9, 16, July 28, 1849. Information on 113 of these people was found in: *Biographical Encyclopaedia of Kentucky,* 24–25, 69–70, 102, 125, 174, 215–16, 252, 257–59, 268–69, 312, 384, 401–2, 423–24, 461–62, 496, 520, 533, 564, 639–40, 670, 680–82, 741, 748; Johnston, ed., *Memorial History of Louisville,* 1:83, 85, 87–88, 130, 377, 380–82, 386, 413–15, 639–41, 2:484–86, 493–97, 559–60, 621–23, 650–51; *Biographical Cyclopedia of Kentucky,* 67, 145, 173, 181, 564–66; Collins and Collins, *Kentucky,* 1:87–88, 95–96, 108, 128, 170–71, 189, 222, 224, 235, 243, 2:357; G. Collins, *Louisville Directory for 1848,* 5–231 passim; Jegli, *Jegli's Directory for 1848–1849,* 6–8, 10, 12–16, 23, 25, 27–35, 37, 41, 63–254 passim; Jegli, *Directory for 1851–1852,* 49–286 passim; Kirwan, *Crittenden,* 98, 158; Burckin, "Urban Middle Class," 51–53, 178–79, 187. For the almost single-minded concern for the economic effects of slavery, see Nicholas et al., *Slave Emancipation;* [J. Speed et al.], *Address;* James Speed Diary, entry for April 19, 1844, quoted in J. Speed, *Speed,* 17 (the author of this book was the grandson of the book's subject). On boosterism, see Boorstin, *Americans,* 113–65; Burckin, "Urban Middle Class," 8–9, 54. For an example of boosterism in Louisville, see Casseday, *History of Louisville,* 247–55. Louisville's antebellum economic competition with Cincinnati is surveyed in Curry, *Rail Routes South,* 8–21.

29. [Garrett et al.], *Address to the Non-Slaveholders,* 3–4; Stafford, "Slavery in a Border City," 29–30, 120–42. It is impossible to determine from the published census report the exact proportion of males employed in manufacturing in southern cities in 1850 because the census shows only county level data for this statistic. Nevertheless, it is possible to establish a numerical range within which the actual proportion of adult males employed in manufacturing in a given city will fall. To determine this range for the ten largest cities in the South in 1850, I have divided the number of people employed in manufacturing in each city by the number of males above the age of 15 who lived in the city and also by the number of adult males who lived in the corresponding county. This calculation shows that in 1850, between 44.0 and 59.4 percent of Louisville's male population was employed in manufacturing establishments. Louisville's nearest competitors on this count were Baltimore, where between 36.5 and 45.1 percent of the adult males were employed in manufacturing; and Richmond, Virginia, where between 30.6 and 45.6 percent of the adult males were employed in manufacturing. These figures were calculated from statistics in U.S., Office of the Census, *Seventh Census: 1850,* 218–20, 232–34, 242–55, 334–38, 354–64, 414–21, 466–73, 600–610, 644–54; U.S., Office of the Census, *Statistical View,* 199, 205, 211, 247, 253, 271, 307, 325, 331, 397–98. See Goldin, *Urban Slavery,* 17–18, 25–27, for a discussion of the methodological problems in determining the proportion of workers in antebellum southern cities.

30. [Garrett et al.], *Address to the Non-Slaveholders,* 2–7. The minutes of the workingmen's meeting, held on April 10, 1849, are in *Ex,* April 14, 1849. On the relationship between urban workingmen in the South and slavery, see Berlin and Gutman, "Natives and Immigrants," 1175–1200; Goldin, *Urban Slavery,* 28–33; Starobin, *Industrial Slavery,* 211–14; Johnson and Roark, *Black Masters,* 173–94, 198–200, 256–61, 266–70, 275–82.

31. *LC,* August 6, 1849; Kentucky, *Report of the Debates,* 568. The antislavery politicians from Louisville who served in the state House of Representatives in the 1840s and the years they served were: William F. Bullock (1840–41, 1841–42); William E. Glover (1842–43, 1845–46); James S. Speed (1843–44, 1844–45); Charles M. Thruston (1844–45); James Speed (1847–48); Robert F. Baird (1849–50). See Collins

and Collins, *Kentucky,* 2:357. On Thomasson, see Johnston, ed., *Memorial History of Louisville,* 2:621–23; *Biographical Directory of the American Congress,* 1808, s.v. "Thomasson, William Poindexter." Though Thomasson twice voted for the Wilmot Proviso in 1846, during the next session of Congress, he twice voted against it. See U.S., Congress, House, *Congressional Globe,* 29th Cong., 1st sess., 1845–46, 1217–18; U.S., Congress, House, *Congressional Globe,* 29th Cong., 2d sess., 1846–47, 573. For Thomasson's explanation of his actions concerning the Wilmot Proviso, see U.S., Congress, House, *Congressional Globe,* 29th Cong., 2d sess., 1846–47, *Appendix,* 166–69; Paine, "Union," 61–62.

32. Jegli, *Jegli's Directory for 1848–1849,* 6–8, 10, 12–13, 25; Kentucky, *Report of the Debates,* 103–6, 468–69, 476–78, 491–94, 510–14, 535–39, 571–78, 609–10; Cox, *Remarks,* 9–10. There was significant criticism of city dwellers' efforts to take away the farmers' slaves. See Ann Mary Crittenden (Mrs. Chapman) Coleman to Breckinridge, July 24, 1849, BFP 135:24969; John H. Heywood to Breckinridge, September 18, 1849, BFP 135:25063.

33. Young to Birney, May 29, 1847, in *LB,* 2:1076; *LJ,* January 23, 1849, in *Ex,* February 3, 1849.

34. Richard French to Howell Cobb, September 10, 1848, in Phillips, ed., "Correspondence of Toombs, Stephens, and Cobb," 2:126.

6. The Crossroads

1. *HJ* (1843–44), 108–9; *HJ* (1844–45), 50, 99–101; *HJ* (1845–46), 97–100; *SJ* (1845–46), 91–92; *HJ* (1846–47), 70–73; *SJ* (1846–47), 50–53; C. Fields, "Kentucky's Third Constitution," 156–61; GB to John Scoble, January 19, 1845, in Abel and Klingberg, eds., *Side-Light,* 202–3.

2. In the first referendum, out of 136,945 eligible voters, 92,639 supported the calling of a constitutional convention. In the second referendum, out of 139,922 eligible voters, 101,828 supported the calling of a constitutional convention. The results of the two referenda are in Kentucky, *Report of the Debates,* 3–4.

3. Coleman, *Slavery Times in Kentucky,* 313–14; Harrison, *Antislavery Movement,* 56; Eaton, ed., "Minutes and Resolutions," 542; C. Fields, "Kentucky's Third Constitution," 161–66; *LC,* February 6, 1849, in *Ex,* February 10, 1849; *Indianapolis State Journal,* n.d., in *NR,* October 4, 1848; CMC to Salmon P. Chase, January 28, 1845, SPCP; Charles W. Short to William Short, December 8, 1847, January 30, 1848, CWSP; Underwood, "Colonization and Gradual Emancipation," 324; GB to John Scoble, January 19, 1845, in Abel and Klingberg, eds., *Side-Light,* 202–3; James G. Blaine to Thomas B. Searight, January 14, 1848, April 8, 1849, quoted in Dodge, *Blaine,* 90–91, 95; *Ex,* August 4, 1847, October 28, 1848; Martin, "Anti-Slavery in Kentucky," 120–21; Cox, *Remarks*; Kentucky, *Report of the Debates,* 101.

4. CMC to Salmon P. Chase, January 28, 1845, SPCP; Joseph Glazebrook to Fee, October 29, 1847, JGFP; William L. Breckinridge to Breckinridge, February 6, 1849, BFP 133:24645–46; William M.O. Smith to Breckinridge, April 7, 1849, BFP 134:24755–56; Young to Birney, May 29, 1847, in *LB,* 2:1076–77; *HJ* (1845–46), 44, 97–100; Underwood, *Colonization Society of Bowlinggreen,* 24; Underwood, "Colonization and Gradual Emancipation," 324; Breckinridge to S.R. Williams, November 17, 1848, BFP 132:24462–63; Cowan to McLain, July 2, 1846, ACSR 103(1):27051–53;

Turner, "Kentucky State Politics," 124; CMC, *Life,* 176–77; H. Wilson, *Slave Power,* 2:175; Dorris, "Turner," 37. Note, however, that Underwood came to support the calling of a constitutional convention before the second referendum was held.

5. Volz, "Party, State, and Nation," 69–70; Turner, "Kentucky State Politics," 123–24; C. Fields, "Kentucky's Third Constitution," 84–85, 110–26, 162–65, 169–83, 188–89; Collins and Collins, *Kentucky,* 1:332–33; Little, *Ben Hardin,* 509–18; Shaler, *Kentucky,* 213–16; Ireland, *County Courts,* 156–70; Gilliam, "Letcher," 9–27; Mathias, "Common Schools," 214–34; Vaughan, *Breckinridge,* 35–109.

6. Volz, "Party, State, and Nation," 69–72; Paine, "Union," 25–26; Robert O. Morris to Breckinridge, November 28, 1849, BFP 135:25138–41; I.H. Holeman to Orlando Brown, February 17, 1850, OBP; Little, *Ben Hardin,* 512–13. As of 1849, no Democratic candidate had won the governor's chair since 1832. No Democratic presidential nominee had carried the state since 1828. Since 1835, Democrats had never held more than 43 percent of the seats in either house of the state legislature, and for half of the years between 1835 and 1849, Democrats numbered fewer than 36 percent of the House and 32 percent of the Senate. Finally, Democrats won only 25 of the 92 congressional elections held in Kentucky between 1835 and 1849. For Kentucky's electoral statistics, I have relied on: Greeley, ed., *Tribune Almanac,* vol. 1: 1838 ed., 28–29, 1840 ed., 25–26, 1841 ed., 23–24, 1844 ed., 56, 1845 ed., 51, 1846 ed., 48, 1847 ed., 48, 1848 ed., 46–47, 1849 ed., 54–55, 1850 ed., 48; J. Moore, ed., *Guide to U.S. Elections,* 720, 724, 731, 734, 738, 741, 745; Collins and Collins, *Kentucky,* 1:39, 41–43, 47, 49, 51, 53, 55, 57, 59; Ireland, *County Courts,* 112–13.

7. Cowan to McLain, June 10, 1848, April 24, 1849, ACSR 110(2):31029–30, 114(1):33243–44; Jacobs to McLain, March 11, 1849, ACSR 113(3):32969–70; Harrison, *Antislavery Movement,* 56; Eaton, ed., "Minutes and Resolutions," 542; Turner, "Kentucky State Politics," 123–24; Martin, "Anti-Slavery in Kentucky," 120–25; Coleman, *Slavery Times in Kentucky,* 314; Howard, "Kentucky Presbyterians," 231–32; Breckinridge to Samuel Steel, April 17, 1849, BFP 134:24773–74; C.W. Anderson et al. to Breckinridge, June 8, 1849, BFP 134:24868–69; Robert O. Morris to Breckinridge, November 28, 1849, BFP 135:25138–41.

8. *Ex,* February 17, 1849.

9. Ibid.; Volz, "Party, State, and Nation," 72; C. Fields, "Kentucky's Third Constitution," 163–65. According to the minutes of the convention, all provisions of the platform concerning slavery passed unanimously. Although before the opening of the convention the meeting's organizers had billed it only as a constitutional reform convention, contemporaries recognized that the convention was to be a meeting of proslavery forces. See *Ex,* February 3, 10, 1849.

10. *Ex,* February 17, 1849; Robertson, *Scrapbook,* 318; Breckinridge to Samuel Steel, April 17, 1849, BFP 134:24773–74; C.W. Anderson et al. to Breckinridge, June 8, 1849, BFP 134:24868–69; Robert O. Morris to Breckinridge, November 28, 1849, BFP 135:25138–41; Martin, "Anti-Slavery in Kentucky," 132, 134–35; Tapp, "Breckinridge and the Year 1849," 136–38; Volz, "Party, State, and Nation," 74–75.

11. Nicholas et al., *Slave Emancipation*; William L. Breckinridge to Breckinridge, February 6, 14, March 17, 1849, BFP 133:24645–46, 24658, 24714; *Ex,* February 3, 17, 24, March 3, 17, 24, 31, April 7, 14, 21, 28, 1849; *NASS,* February 15, 22, 1849; Martin, "Anti-Slavery in Kentucky," 124–26, 129–30; Tallant, "Slavery Controversy in Kentucky," 261; Robert Wallace et al. to Breckinridge, March 8, 1849, BFP 133:24705; *Li,* April 27, 1849; *CHGR,* May 1849; CMC, *Life,* 488–91; Howard, "Kentucky Pres-

byterians," 221–23; Coleman, *Slavery Times in Kentucky,* 274–75; Townsend, *Lincoln,* 161.

12. HC to Richard Pindell, February 17, 1849, in *NR,* March 21, 1849; De Lolme [pseud.] to Thomas F. Marshall and I.H. Holeman, n.d., in *OG* 1 (April 4, 1850):155. Clay's plan of emancipation was nearly identical to the one he established in his will for the emancipation of his own slaves. See Eaton, ed., "Clay's Will," 1–9; Troutman, "Emancipation," 179–81; Eaton, *Henry Clay,* 135–36; Van Deusen, *Life of Henry Clay,* 419–20. Although Clay's letter surprised most observers, some emancipationists knew of Clay's intention to support emancipation months in advance. See Breckinridge to S.R. Williams, November 17, 1848, BFP 132:24462–63. On the reaction of Kentuckians to Clay's letter, see Jacobs to McLain, March 11, 1849, ACSR 113(3):32969–70; *Li,* June 15, 1849; *NR,* June 13, 1849; Mathias, "Slavery," 12. On the reaction of southerners outside Kentucky to Clay's letter, see Brookes, *Defense of Southern Slavery,* 160–61. On northern reaction to Clay's letter, see Samuel Steel to Breckinridge, March 20, 1849, BFP 134:24725; *Li,* March 16, 23, 30, April 6, 27, 1849; William Lloyd Garrison to HC, March 16, 1849, in Merrill and Ruchames, eds., *Letters of Garrison,* 3:608–13; Norton, "Religious Press," 149.

13. *Ex,* February 17, 24, March 24, 31, April 7, 14, 21, 28, 1849; *Ex,* n.d., in *CHGR,* July 1849; William L. Breckinridge to Breckinridge, February 6, 1849, BFP 133:24645–46; Howard, "Pendleton," 203.

14. Eaton, ed., "Minutes and Resolutions," 544; Howard, "Pendleton," 198–99; James Madison Pendleton to Fortunatus Cosby, Jr., John H. Heywood, and Noble Butler, April 7, 1849, in *Ex,* April 14, 1849; Breckinridge to Samuel Steel, April 17, 1849, BFP 134:24773–74; John B. Bibb to Breckinridge, May 1, 1849, BFP 134:24794; William Garnett to Breckinridge, May 22, 1849, BFP 134:24830; James Matthews to Breckinridge, May 30, 1849, BFP 134:24844–45; C.W. Anderson et al. to Breckinridge, June 8, 1849, BFP 134:24868–69; Frank Ballenger to Breckinridge, July 2, 1849, BFP 134:24888; George D. Blakey to Breckinridge, July 10, 1849, BFP 135:24936; Jacobs to McLain, March 11, 1849, ACSR 113(3):32969–70; Howard, "Breckinridge in 1849," 334–35.

15. James Madison Pendleton to Fortunatus Cosby, Jr., John H. Heywood, and Noble Butler, April 7, 1849, in *Ex,* April 14, 1849; *Ex,* March 24, April 7, 28, 1849.

16. *SJ* (1848–49), 274–78, 284–85, 316–17, 363; *HJ* (1848–49), 263–69, 272–74, 282–84, 449–50; *Li,* April 20, 1849; Martin, "Anti-Slavery in Kentucky," 95–97; Harrison, *Antislavery Movement,* 55–56; Mathias, "Slavery," 13–15; *Ex,* March 24, 31, April 7, 1849; Jacobs to McLain, March 11, 1849, ACSR 113(3):32969–70; Townsend, *Lincoln,* 158–59. The vote in the House to repeal the Law of 1833 was 56–42. The vote in the Senate was 22–16. On the legislative history of nonimportation in the 1840s, see *HJ* (1839–40), 40, 303–4; *SJ* (1839–40), 34, 47–48, 142–44, 147; *HJ* (1840–41), 68, 74, 93–96, 204–7; *SJ* (1840–41), 73–74, 138, 251–54, 369, 422–25; *HJ* (1841–42), 93–94, 257, 364; *SJ* (1841–42), 149, 165, 264, 281; *HJ* (1842–43), 136, 205–11; *SJ* (1842–43), 22, 108, 194–95, 221–22; *HJ* (1843–44), 38, 45; *SJ* (1843–44), 22, 205–7; *HJ* (1844–45), 50, 112–14; *SJ* (1844–45), 24, 75–76, 152–55; *HJ* (1845–46), 31, 84, 127; *SJ* (1845–46), 11, 51, 85, 150; *HJ* (1846–47), 20, 55, 109–12, 115–16, 246–47, 311–13, 325–26; *SJ* (1846–47), 126, 144; *HJ* (1847–48), 33, 268–71, 276–84, 300–305; *SJ* (1847–48), 25, 34, 54, 106–9, 234–35. See Mathias, "Slavery," 14, for a different interpretation of the effect of the repeal of the Law of 1833.

17. The minutes of the Frankfort Convention were published in *Ex,* May 5, 1849;

NASS, June 21, 1849. For historians' discussion of the convention, see Martin, "Anti-Slavery in Kentucky," 130–32; Howard, "Pendleton," 199–200; Howard, "Kentucky Presbyterians," 224–26; Tapp, "Breckinridge and the Year 1849," 133–34; Gregory, "Question of Slavery," 92; Harrison, "Anti-Slavery Career," 309–10; Harrison, *Antislavery Movement*, 57; Allen, "Southern Colonizationists," 107–9.

18. *NASS*, June 21, 1849.

19. Ibid. After the Frankfort Convention, Holloway became the emancipationist candidate from Boyle County for the constitutional convention. For details of his involvement with the emancipation movement in 1849, see *Ex*, March 31, June 23, 1849. On Monroe, see KCS, *Proceedings* (1849), 3–4; *Ex*, April 28, 1849.

20. CMC, *Life*, 176; *NASS*, June 21, 1849.

21. *NASS*, June 21, 1849. On the concern of many traditional conservatives about the involvement of some Kentucky emancipationists with northern abolitionists, see George D. Blakey to Breckinridge, July 10, 1849, BFP 135:24936; *NASS*, February 15, 1849; Norton, "Religious Press," 146; *Ex*, February 3, April 14, 28, 1849.

22. Haskin, *To the Voters*, 9; Tapp, "Breckinridge and the Year 1849," 135–46; Martin, "Anti-Slavery in Kentucky," 131–34; Howard, "Pendleton," 200–201; Howard, "Kentucky Presbyterians," 227–32, 235–36; Howard, "Breckinridge in 1849," 336–41.

23. Benjamin Coates to Walter, June 20, 1849, Coates Papers. Coates was an avid antislavery colonizationist. See Benjamin Coates to J. Miller McKim, June 29, 1849, in *CHGR*, September 1849; Coates, *Cotton Cultivation*. I have found evidence of organized antislavery activities in 47 of Kentucky's 100 counties, as indicated by the occurrence of one or more of the following: a public antislavery meeting, the nomination of an antislavery candidate to the constitutional convention, a public debate or speech on emancipation, an invitation issued by a group of people to a speaker to deliver an antislavery speech, or the presence at the Frankfort Convention of a delegation from that county. These counties were: Ballard, Barren, Bath, Boone, Bourbon, Boyle, Bracken, Caldwell, Campbell, Clark, Clay, Crittenden, Estill, Fayette, Franklin, Garrard, Harlan, Henry, Jefferson, Kenton, Knox, Laurel, Letcher, Lewis, Lincoln, Livingston, Logan, McCracken, Madison, Mason, Mercer, Monroe, Muhlenberg, Nelson, Nicholas, Oldham, Owen, Owsley, Perry, Pulaski, Scott, Shelby, Spencer, Trimble, Warren, Wayne, Woodford. See *Ex*, February 3, 17, 24, March 17, 24, 31, April 7, 14, 21, 28, May 5, 12, 19, 26, June 2, 9, 16, 23, July 7, 14, 28, August 4, 11, 18, 1849; Clay Harlan to Orlando Brown, August 14, 1849, OBP; Frank Ballenger to Breckinridge, July 2, 1849, BFP 134:24888.

24. *Lexington Observer and Reporter*, August 9, September 27, October 11, November 6, 1848; Pratt Diary, entry for August 24, 1848, 1:283; E.H. Goulding to My Dear Friend, August 11, 1848, Manuscript Vertical File, UK; Collins and Collins, *Kentucky*, 1:57; Coleman, *Slavery Times in Kentucky*, 88–92, 106; Townsend, *Lincoln*, 154–55; Stampp, *Peculiar Institution*, 138–39; Aptheker, *Slave Revolts*, 338–39; Harrison, "Anti-Slavery Career," 311; William L. Breckinridge to Breckinridge, August 15, 17, 19, 29, 1848, BFP 131:24314–15, 24320–21, 24324, 24341–42; Mary Hopkins Cabell Breckinridge to Breckinridge, August 19, 1848, BFP 131:24322–23. It should be noted that slaves bore the brunt of the persecution caused by the mass slave escape, which, as one white Kentuckian observed, "called forth severe rules and regulations for the poor blacks" (Pratt Diary, entry for August 24, 1848, 1:283).

25. Kentucky, *Report of the Debates*, 72, 97, 884; Tapp, "Breckinridge and the Year

1849," 131–32; *HJ* (1848–49), 233–35; *Ex,* February 10, 1849; *NR,* February 14, 1849; Martin, "Anti-Slavery in Kentucky," 124. The resolution was not as strongly proslavery as it would appear. The original draft of the resolution unconditionally condemned emancipation. The House softened it by adding the statement that it opposed emancipation "except as now provided for by the Constitution and laws of the State." This change of wording was approved 63–30. See Williams, "Lincoln's Closest Friend," 30.

26. CMC, *Life,* 184–87; CMC to T.I. Goddin, July 2, 1849, in *Li,* July 13, 1849; Smiley, *Lion of White Hall,* 138–42; Harrison, "Anti-Slavery Career," 310–11; Coleman, *Slavery Times in Kentucky,* 315–16; *Li,* August 10, 1849; Townsend, *Lincoln,* 163–64; Channing, *Kentucky,* 106. Clay never stood trial for the killing of Cyrus Turner, perhaps because Clay's actions were clearly taken in self-defense. Austin was identified as an antislavery candidate in *Ex,* July 14, 1849.

27. *Ex,* August 11, 18, 25, September 1, 1849; *NASS,* August 16, 1849; Pratt Diary, entry for August 15, 1849, 1:308–9; Pendleton, *Reminiscences,* 94–95; *Baptist Banner,* August 22, 29, September 12, 26, 1849, August 14, 1850; *Tennessee Baptist,* September 13, 20, 1849; [Hutchinson], "Malcom," 321; Meyer, *Georgetown College,* 61–73; Eaton, *Freedom-of-Thought Struggle,* 222; Howard, "Pendleton," 202–3; *DAB* 12:220, s.v. "Malcom, Howard."

28. Rosenberg, *Cholera Years,* 101–72; Baird, "Cholera's First Visit," 228–40; Baird, "Asiatic Cholera," 327–41; William B. Kinkead to Isaac Shelby, August 1, 1849, Shelby Family Papers; Breckinridge to Mary Hopkins Cabell Breckinridge, July 6, 1849, BFP 135:24935; William L. Breckinridge to Breckinridge, July 10, 1849, BFP 135:24938; Virginia Breckinridge to Breckinridge, July 12, ca. 14, 30, 1849, BFP 135:24942, 24949, 24983; Breckinridge to Richard Martin, July 14, 1849, BFP 135:24947; Breckinridge to Virginia Breckinridge, July 26, 1849, Grigsby Papers; Clay Harlan to Orlando Brown, August 14, 1849, OBP; Pratt Diary, entry for August 3, 1849, 1:305–6; Samuel Shy to Breckinridge, July 5, 1849, BFP 135:24933–34; Howard, "Breckinridge in 1849," 339–41; Townsend, *Lincoln,* 165–68, 172–74; Tapp, "Breckinridge and the Year 1849," 144. Collins and Collins, *Kentucky,* 1:59, claims that during the epidemic there were 164 deaths from cholera in Paris, 191 deaths in Maysville, and 394 deaths in Lexington.

29. Rosenberg, *Cholera Years,* 75–78; Baird, "Cholera's First Visit," 228–29, 236; Baird, "Asiatic Cholera," 327–36; Benjamin Coates to Walter, June 20, 1849, Coates Papers; Thomas N. Lindsey to Orlando Brown, August 31, 1849, OBP; Breckinridge to Mary Hopkins Cabell Breckinridge, July 6, 1849, BFP 135:24935; William L. Breckinridge to Breckinridge, July 10, 1849, BFP 135:24938; Breckinridge to Richard Martin, July 14, 1849, BFP 135:24947; J.N. Garrard to Breckinridge, July 14, 1849, BFP 135:24951; Cowan to McLain, September 11, 1849, ACSR 115(2):34; E.P. Pratt to McLain, September 12, 1849, ACSR 115(2):34; Cowan to McLain, December 25, 1849, ACSR 116(2):34; Bennett, "All Things," 136; Townsend, *Lincoln,* 171; Howard, "Breckinridge in 1849," 340–41; Virginia Breckinridge to Breckinridge, July 12, ca. 14, 18, 27, 29, 30, 1849, BFP 135:24942, 24949, 24954, 24979, 24981, 24983; Tapp, "Breckinridge and the Year 1849," 144–45. One history of Madison County claims that 60 percent of the population of Richmond left that town during the epidemic. See Ellis, Everman, and Sears, *Madison County,* 100. A comparison of the voter turnout rate in the congressional elections of 1847 and 1849 demonstrates the impact of the cholera epidemic. For instance, in Jefferson and Fayette Counties, the voter turnout rate de-

clined by 20.3 and 13.4 percent respectively between 1847 and 1849. These figures have been calculated from statistics in Kentucky, General Assembly, *Second Auditor's Report,* no. 10 (1848–49), *Legislative Documents,* 79, 125, 127, 169, 195, 213; Kentucky, General Assembly, *Second Auditor's Report,* no. 10 (1849–50), *Legislative Documents,* 85, 132, 135, 177, 203, 221; Greeley, ed., *Tribune Almanac,* vol. 1: 1848 ed., 46, 1850 ed., 48.

30. These statistics have been computed from election returns and population statistics in Crittenden Executive Papers, 1848–49, Section 2, Box 111, Jackets 766–73; *Ex,* August 11, 18, 1849; *LJ,* August 9, 10, 11, 1849; "Helm's Speech," 47–48. Antislavery candidates were identified from the election returns above and from the following sources: *Ex,* March 24, May 5, 19, 26, June 16, 23, 1849; Clay Harlan to Orlando Brown, August 14, 1849, OBP; Samuel F. Miller to Sir, April 16, 1867, Lanman Papers. Note that the 14,801 votes I have counted for antislavery candidates is 42 percent higher than the traditional figure of 10,394 votes. See Norton, "Religious Press," 151. However, there exist estimates of the total emancipationist vote that are closer to my vote count than to the traditionally cited figure. See Kentucky, *Report of the Debates,* 114, 336–37. The two emancipationist candidates who are known to have been elected were Silas Woodson, representing Knox and Harlan Counties, and Ira Root, representing Kenton County.

31. This summary of the Free-Soil vote in 1848 is based on statistics in Blue, *Free Soilers,* 142.

32. Mathias, "Slavery," 14–15; C. Fields, "Kentucky's Third Constitution," 168–69, 188–89; Ann Mary Crittenden (Mrs. Chapman) Coleman to Breckinridge, July 10, 1849, BFP 135:24940; Jacobs to Breckinridge, August 24, 1849, BFP 135:25040–41. Some proslavery delegates to the constitutional convention, however, were influenced by a fear that unless they took preemptive action, the influence of people like Henry Clay would lead Kentucky to adopt a scheme of emancipation. See Kentucky, *Report of the Debates,* 101–3, 865, 951–52; De Lolme (pseud.) to Thomas F. Marshall and I.H. Holeman, n.d., in *OG* 1 (April 4, 1850):155.

33. *Ex,* October 28, 1848; Haskin, *To the Voters,* 5, 14; Kentucky, *Report of the Debates,* 71, 83, 94–95, 99–101, 115, 488, 514–15, 918, 924–25, 928–29; De Bow, "Kentucky," 205; *Ex,* n.d., in *CHGR,* July 1849; Cowan to McLain, May 9, December 25, 1849, ACSR 114(2):33328–29, 116(2):34; Chamberlain, "Evolution of State Constitutions," 208–10; Bennett, "All Things," 123, 136–37; *Li,* June 22, 1849; Helm, "Remarks," 59; Robinson, "Address," 150–51; Martin, "Anti-Slavery in Kentucky," 122–23, 131–32, 134; Harrison, *Antislavery Movement,* 58; Harrison, "Anti-Slavery Career," 309; Mayse, "Breckinridge," 271; Robertson, *Scrapbook,* 326; Gregory, "Question of Slavery," 93–94.

34. Kentucky, *Report of the Debates,* 138, 464, 485, 508–10, 843; Channing, *Kentucky,* 107; Gregory, "Question of Slavery," 94–101, 107; Cowan to McLain, December 25, 1849, ACSR 116(2):34; Martin, "Anti-Slavery in Kentucky," 135–36; Mathias, "Kentucky's Third Constitution," 7–9. For general histories of the convention, see C. Fields, "Kentucky's Third Constitution," 190–318; Paine, "Union," 98–135; Chamberlain, "Evolution of State Constitutions," 182–252; Burckin, "Urban Middle Class," 298–403; Bruce, "Constitutional Convention," 131–62; Willis, "History," 28:305–29, 29:52–81; B. Young, *History,* 48–60; Dietzman, "Constitutions," 122–25. The election returns identified twenty-four delegates as proslavery candidates. Another ten delegates were elected over persons identified as antislavery candidates. Twenty-two other delegates

had perfect proslavery voting records on the four key slavery-related issues considered by the convention. Between October 17 and December 5, when delegates were supposedly discussing other issues, delegates gave at least sixty-three speeches on slavery. By the end of the convention, at least fifty-one of the one hundred delegates had publicly addressed the issue of slavery.

35. Kentucky, *Report of the Debates*, 76–77, 116–17, 450–53, 481, 508–10, 518–19, 564, 842–43, 846–47, 858–59, 869–70; Breckinridge to Samuel Steel, April 17, 1849, BFP 134:24773–74.

36. Kentucky, *Report of the Debates*, 69–70.

37. Ibid.

38. Ibid., 77, see generally 77–143 passim.

39. Ibid., 312–16, 336–37, 448–580 passim, 596–97, 743–44, 841–43, 947–52, 987–94 passim; Helm, "Remarks," 58–61; Robinson and Brush, *Memorial*; James Matthews to Breckinridge, May 30, 1849, BFP 134:24844–45; C.W. Anderson et al. to Breckinridge, June 8, 1849, BFP 134:24868–69; Clark, *History of Kentucky*, 302–3. For a different interpretation, see Paine, "Union," 99; Chamberlain, "Evolution of State Constitutions," 212–52; Burckin, "Urban Middle Class," 298–403.

40. Kentucky, *Third Constitution* (1850), art. 13, sec. 3; Kentucky, *Report of the Debates*, 815, 856–61. Before voting on this clause, the convention divided it into two sections. The first section, which declared that the right of property was "higher than any constitutional sanction," was approved 65–23. The second section, which declared that the property rights of slaveholders were the same as any other property rights, was approved 77–10. See Tallant, "Slavery Controversy in Kentucky," 293–94, for a discussion of the passage of the Davis amendment.

41. Kentucky, *Report of the Debates*, 377–78, 794, 804–15, 856–61, 862–79; Wiecek, *Sources of Antislavery Constitutionalism*, 279. As a part of their effort to add a definitive statement of the right of white Kentuckians to own slaves, the delegates added to the bill of rights another section which proclaimed: "Absolute, arbitrary power over the lives, liberty, and property of freemen, exists no where in a republic—not even in the largest majority" (Kentucky, *Third Constitution* [1850], art. 13, sec. 2). This section was approved by a final vote of 57–30.

42. Kentucky, *Report of the Debates*, 914–21. Gray's amendment was substituted for section one of the proposed slave clause by a vote of 74–14 and subsequently adopted by a vote of 55–36. As another sign of the delegates' increasing willingness to compromise, the convention defeated the proposal to give the legislature power to deport the existing free black population. No vote was recorded on this measure. The convention, however, did require the legislature to bar the future immigration of free blacks by a vote of 72–8. See Ibid., 923–35.

43. Ibid., 78, 82–83, 105, 138–39, 143, 486–90, 535, 573.

44. Ibid., 76–77, 936–37. On December 12, thirty-two delegates voted to place in the constitution a provision guaranteeing the right of citizens to import slaves for their own use. Nine delegates voted to place a nonimportation clause in the constitution. Forty-seven delegates voted against both proposals, thereby leaving the issue of slave importation in the hands of the General Assembly.

45. Ibid., 1088; Wiecek, *Sources of Antislavery Constitutionalism*, 279. Historians have traditionally commented that the majority of delegates speaking on slavery called it a necessary evil. See, for instance, Martin, "Anti-Slavery in Kentucky," 136–37; Harrison, *Antislavery Movement*, 59–60. My reading of the debates, however, indicates

that of the twenty-three delegates who spoke directly to the question of whether slavery was a necessary evil or positive good, eighteen called it a positive good and only five said that it was a necessary evil.

46. Smiley, *Lion of White Hall*, 142–43; Harrison, *Antislavery Movement*, 61; Gregory, "Question of Slavery," 108; Mayse, "Breckinridge," 272; Mathias, "Slavery," 14–15; Samuel F. Miller to Sir, April 16, 1867, Lanman Papers; Ross, "Hill-Country Doctor," 430–62; Swinford, "Miller," 37–38; Fairman, *Miller*, 3–17; Underwood, *Slavery Question*, 12; Breckinridge, "Black Race," 136–37; Pendleton, *Reminiscences*, 94; HC, "Speech of January 21, 1851," 108; U.S., Congress, Senate, *Congressional Globe*, 31st Cong., 1st sess., 1849–50, pt. 1, 404; Remini, *Henry Clay*, 770; Abraham Lincoln to George Robertson, August 15, 1855, in Basler, ed., *Works of Lincoln*, 3:317–19; Miers, gen. ed., *Lincoln Day by Day*, vol. 2: *1849–1860*, 23–24. Compare Henry Clay's assessment with Cassius Clay's, given in CMC, *Speech Delivered August 1, 1851*, 1–2.

47. Shackleford, ed., *Life of Pinkerton*, 71–72; W.S. Brown, "Strictures on Abolitionism," 485–91; Underwood, *Slavery Question*, 13; Breckinridge, "Black Race," 138; George Candee to Jocelyn, March 13, 1860, AMAA 43857–58; Otis B. Waters to AMA, n.d., in AMA, *Annual Report* (1857), 65; Fee to the Members and Friends of the AMA, May 1854, AMAA 43243–44.

48. Cooper, *Politics of Slavery*; Volz, "Party, State, and Nation," 40, 60–64, 79–80, 95, 107, 118–24, 134, 137, 140–44, 164, 173, 213–14, 223–24, 257–59, 268–69, 314–15, 324–43; Gilliam, "Lexington Press," 48–54; Gilliam, "Kansas and Slavery," 225–30; Farrelly, "Harlan's Formative Period," 400–401; Cowan to McLain, December 25, 1849, ACSR 116(2):34; Paine, "Union," especially 159, 164–65, 185–88, 191, 198, 215, 225, 228–29. For a different interpretation, which argues that the politics of slavery "have severe limitations for understanding Kentucky," see Paine, "Union," especially 11, 241.

49. *Ex*, August 11, September 8, 15, 1849; Fee to CMC, September 18, 1849, JGFP; Jacobs to Breckinridge, August 24, 1849, BFP 135:25040–41; John H. Heywood to Breckinridge, September 18, 1849, BFP 135:25063; Samuel Steel to Breckinridge, September 28, 1849, BFP 135:25072; Howard, "Breckinridge in 1849," 342–43; Fee to Tappan, October 30, 1849, quoted in Reynolds, "Antislavery Campaign in Kentucky," 48. There was also an unsuccessful effort to begin a new antislavery newspaper in Lexington and to merge the *Examiner* with it. See Jacobs to Breckinridge, August 24, 1849, BFP 135:25040–41; John H. Heywood to Breckinridge, September 18, 1849, BFP 135:25063.

50. Kentucky, *Report of the Debates*, 1061–83, 1103, 1110–11; Robert O. Morris to Breckinridge, November 28, 1849, BFP 135:25138–41; Joseph Cabell Harrison to Breckinridge, February 14, 1850, BFP 137:25308d-8e; Paine, "Union," 135; Volz, "Party, State, and Nation," 77–82. The new constitution was approved by 77.9 percent of the vote, with 71,653 voters approving the new constitution and 20,302 opposing it.

51. CMC, *Speech Delivered August 1, 1851*; Smiley, *Lion of White Hall*, 142–48; Steely, "Antislavery Movement in Kentucky," 149–53; Turner, "Kentucky State Politics," 130–33; Volz, "Party, State, and Nation," 82–104. George D. Blakey became one of Kentucky's most important antislavery politicians in the 1850s and was active in both the state Free-Soil party and the state and national Republican parties. See Tallant, "Slavery Controversy in Kentucky," 304–5. Although Clay did not win many votes, he may have been responsible for electing a Democrat as governor for the first time since the election of 1832. A modern statistical study of the election claims that in a contest

decided by 850 votes, nearly all of Clay's votes—more than enough to swing the election to the Democrats—came from Whigs. See Volz, "Party, State, and Nation," 98–100; CMC to Salmon P. Chase, August 12, 1851, SPCP; CMC to Joshua R. Giddings, September 3, 1851, quoted in Long, "Giddings," 33; CMC, *Life,* 212–13.

52. Williams, "James and Joshua Speed," 61–62, 64–68; CMC to Salmon P. Chase, August 12, 1851, SPCP; Mayse, "Breckinridge," 272–355; Volz, "Party, State, and Nation," 152, 156–57; Smiley, *Lion of White Hall,* 147–49; and chap. 8 below.

53. Breckinridge to S.R. Williams, February 27, 1850, BFP 137:25339; S.R. Williams to Breckinridge, April 10, 1850, BFP 137:25401–02; Breckinridge to Samuel Steel, April 17, 1849, BFP 134:24773–74; Klotter, *The Breckinridges,* 58–60; Young to Breckinridge, April 21, 1851, BFP 140:25916–17; Breckinridge quoted in Smiley, *Lion of White Hall,* 142. There were occasional indications that some persons who had been antislavery conservatives in the 1830s and 1840s were less than enthusiastic supporters of the new proslavery consensus of the 1850s. See, for instance, Volz, "Party, State, and Nation," 52–56, 88–90, 111–15, 243–44, 295–301, 305–12, 315, 348–53.

54. Wigham, *Anti-Slavery Cause,* 46–51; Steely, "Bailey," 274–81; Steely, "Antislavery Movement in Kentucky," 179–92; Harrold, *Abolitionists and the South,* 29–30, 39–40, 43, 147–48.

55. *Ex,* May 5, 1849; McGann, *Nativism in Kentucky,* 60–66; Wittke, *German-Language Press,* 86–89, 98–99, 111–12, 171; Wittke, *Against the Current,* 91–95; Wittke, *Refugees of Revolution,* 163–65; Eitel W. Dobert, "The Radicals," A.E. Zucker, "Biographical Dictionary of the Forty-Eighters," in Zucker, ed., *Forty-Eighters,* 178–79, 287, 290, 303; Weisert, "Dembitz," 7–8; Barney, "Turnverein," 134–37; Baldwin, "Germans in Louisville," 84–88; Barney, "German Turners," 344–57; Malberg, "Republican Party," 8–13, 17–33; Smiley, *Lion of White Hall,* 149–67; and chaps. 7–8 below; Fairbank, *During Slavery Times*; Webster, *Kentucky Jurisprudence*; *Miss Delia A. Webster,* Webster Kentucky Farm Association, *By-Laws*; Runyon, *Delia Webster*; Coleman, "Webster and Fairbank," 129–42; J. Parker, *His Promised Land,* 71–151; T. Brown, *Three Years in the Kentucky Prisons*; Harrold, *Abolitionists and the South,* 64–83; Weisenburger, *Modern Medea*; Middleton, "Law and Ideology," 347–72; Yzenbaard, "Crosswhite Case," 131–43; Sherwood, "One Flame in the Inferno," 40–47; B. Wilson, "Kentucky Kidnappers," 339–58; Gara, "Fugitive Slave Law," 116–28; Strassweg, "Horace Bell," 105–8. For the underground railroad generally, see Gara, *Liberty Line.*

7. The Quest for Righteousness

1. Oates, *To Purge This Land with Blood.*

2. Rugoff, *The Beechers,* 383; *Independent,* November 3, 10, 1859; Wendell Phillips, "John Brown and Harpers Ferry," in Filler, ed., *Wendell Phillips,* 96; Stewart, *Holy Warriors,* 173–74; Bartlett, *Wendell Phillips,* 212; "Rev. John G. Fee," *AM,* n.s., 3 (December 1859):276.

3. See Wyatt-Brown, *Lewis Tappan,* 317–18, for an appraisal of Henry Ward Beecher and Plymouth Church. For appraisals of Fee's influence and importance within the abolitionist movement, see Harrold, *Abolitionists and the South,* 88–89, 92, 95; Howard, *Evangelical War against Slavery and Caste,* 94, 146; Sears, *Day of Small Things*; Sears, *Kentucky Abolitionists.*

4. "Rev. John G. Fee," 276–77; *NYTr,* November 14, 1859; Fee, "To the Citizens of Madison County," 13; see also C.H. Johnson, "Fee," 93.

5. *LC,* November 17, 1859, Lexington *Kentucky Statesman,* November 30, 1859, quoted in English, "Fee," 155–56; Richmond *Kentucky Messenger,* n.d., in *NASS,* January 21, 1860; AMA, *Annual Report* (1859), 40; "Rev. John G. Fee," 277; E. Peck and E. Smith, *Berea's First 125 Years,* 19–20.

6. Fee, *Autobiography,* 12–14, 17; English, "Fee," 1–32; "Rev. John G. Fee," 276; *NASS,* January 21, 1860. See Gamaliel Bailey's statements about Fee's early opposition to slavery in *NE,* August 19, 1847, August 16, 1855; and evidence in English, "Fee," 11–12:

7. Fee, *Anti-Slavery Manual,* vii; Fee, *Autobiography,* 15–16; English, "Fee," 15–16; Sears, *Day of Small Things,* 4, 34, 92, 94, 96; Fee to Milton Badger and Charles Hall, July 3, October 28, 1845, January 3, 1846, Fee to Charles Hall, May 15, 1846, Fee to Milton Badger and Charles Allen, April 1, 1846, typescripts in JGFP.

8. Fee, *Anti-Slavery Manual,* vii; Fee, *Non-Fellowship,* 7, 39. Aside from these two works, Fee's other significant antislavery publications are: Fee, *Sinfulness;* Fee, *Non-Fellowship;* Fee, *Colonization;* Fee, *Slavery Question.* For a general discussion of God's sovereignty in abolitionist thought, see Perry, *Radical Abolitionism,* especially 32–54.

9. Fee, *Anti-Slavery Manual,* 18–25, 33–38, 87; Fee, *Sinfulness,* 15–17, 19; Fee to *LC,* n.d., in *NASS,* April 21, 1855.

10. Fee, *Anti-Slavery Manual,* 19, 71, 85, 87, 216; Fee, *Autobiography,* 13–14; Fee, *Non-Fellowship,* 11; Fee to Milton Badger and Charles Allen, April 1, 1846, typescript in JGFP; Warford, "Radical Tradition," 152; Warford, "Piety, Politics, and Pedagogy," 74–82. For a discussion of the theology of New School Presbyterians, see Marsden, *New School Presbyterian Experience,* 1–58. The influence of Arminianism on Fee's theology may have been a remnant of his early attraction to Methodism. See Fee, *Autobiography,* 12–13.

11. Fee, *Anti-Slavery Manual,* 13, 86, 90, 128–29, 137; Fee to *LC,* n.d., in *NASS,* April 21, 1855.

12. Fee to American Tract Society, n.d., in *AM,* n.s., 3 (September 1859):200; Fee to *LC,* n.d., in *NASS,* April 21, 1855; Fee, *Non-Fellowship,* 4, 6; Fee, *Anti-Slavery Manual,* 140, 175; Fee, *Autobiography,* 49, 56–59; Fee to Goodell, January 10, 1856, in *RA,* March 1856; Fee to the Members and Friends of the AMA, May 1854, AMAA 43243–44; Fee, *Slavery Question,* 4.

13. Fee, *Colonization,* 11; Fee to *LC,* n.d., in *NASS,* April 21, 1855; Fee to WSB, n.d., in *KN,* September 8, 1856, clipping in JGFP; Fee, *Anti-Slavery Manual,* 216; Fee to Milton Badger and Charles Allen, April 1, 1846, typescript in JGFP; Green, "Northern Missionary Activities," 156; Fee to Whipple and Tappan, May 8, 1850, AMAA 43050–53; Fee, *Non-Fellowship,* 15, 21.

14. Fee to Milton Badger and Charles Hall, April 1, September 30, 1846, September 28, 1847, June 27, 1848, Fee to Charles Hall, May 15, 1846, typescripts in JGFP; Davis to Whipple, December 18, 1857, AMAA 43532–34; Fee, *Non-Fellowship,* 19; Fee, *Autobiography,* 35–36; H. Parker, "New School Synod," 72–73, 79–80. On the relationship of New School Presbyterians to slavery, see Marsden, *New School Presbyterian Experience,* 88–103, 119, 250–51; Staiger, "Presbyterian Schism," 391–414; H. Parker, "New School Synod," 79–89.

15. Amos A. Phelps to Fee, June 17, 1846, Goodell to Father, September 14, 1850, JGFP; Kuykendall, "'Southern Enterprize,'" 178–83; Griffin, "Benevolent Societies,"

195–216; Fee to Milton Badger and Charles Hall, June 27, 1848, typescript in JGFP; Fee, *Non-Fellowship,* 19–20; Fee, *Autobiography,* 21.

16. Fee to Milton Badger and Charles Hall, September 28, 1847, typescript in JGFP; Eliphaz P. Pratt, Benjamin Mills, and E.M. Wright to Fee, June 16, 1848, JGFP.

17. Fee, *Non-Fellowship,* 18–21; Fee, *Autobiography,* 21; Fee to Milton Badger and Charles Hall, July 29, August 29, September 13, 1848, typescript in JGFP; Benjamin Mills to Fee, March 12, 1849, JGFP.

18. 2 Cor. 6:14, 17; Rev. 18:4; J.L. Thomas, *Liberator,* 318–23; Perry, *Radical Abolitionism,* 92–128; McKivigan, "Antislavery 'Comeouter' Sects," 142–60.

19. See Fee to John C. Vaughan, n.d., different portions of which are quoted in *PF,* June 20, 1850, and *True Democrat,* June 1, 1850, cited in U.S., WPA, *Annals of Cleveland,* part 1, 33:36; Fee to Goodell, May 29, 1850, September 10, 1851, JGFP; Fee, *Autobiography,* 36–37, 39–40, 191, 194–95, 200–201; Fee to Whipple, November 7, 1851, AMAA 43119–21; Fee, *Non-Fellowship,* 65; Fee to Charles Hall, May 15, 1846, Fee to Milton Badger and Charles Hall, September 28, 1847, typescripts in JGFP; Fee, *Anti-Slavery Manual,* 153.

20. Fee to Whipple, August 11, 1851, AMAA 43105; Fee, *Autobiography,* 52, see also, 51–55; Fee to Goodell, May 29, 1850, September 10, 1851, JGFP; Fee to Milton Badger and Charles Hall, January 18, 1848, typescript in JGFP. Opposition to secret societies was as a major theme in Fee's reformist career, prompting his opposition to the Sons of Temperance and the Know-Nothing party before the Civil War and his support for the National Christian Association and the American party after the war. See Fee to GB, February 16, 1855, in *NE,* March 15, 1855; Roberts, "Crusade against Secret Societies," 382–400; Taylor, "Beyond Immediate Emancipation," 260–74; Kilby, *Minority of One,* 190, 198–99.

21. Fee, *Anti-Slavery Manual,* 171; Fee to Whipple and Tappan, May 8, 1850, AMAA 43050–53; Fee, *Colonization,* 16–23, 31–32.

22. AMA, *Constitution,* arts. 3, 7–8, in *AM,* n.s., 2 (November 1858):289; Green, "Northern Missionary Activities," 147–56; Wyatt-Brown, *Lewis Tappan,* 287–95; De Boer, "Role of Afro-Americans," 22–44, 73–86; Harrold, *Abolitionists and the South,* 36; Steely, "Antislavery Movement in Kentucky," 27.

23. P. Johnson, *Shopkeeper's Millennium,* 116; Cole, "Free Church Movement," 284–97; Wyatt-Brown, *Lewis Tappan,* 65, 176–79, 340–41; Fee to Whipple, August 9, September 7, 1850, August 11, 1851, AMAA 43075, 43085, 43105; Fee to Goodell, May 29, 1850, September 10, 1851, JGFP; Fee, *Non-Fellowship,* 29, 57, 63; Fee to Whipple, July 19, 1853, in *AM,* o.s., 7 (September 1853):91; Fee to the Members and Friends of the AMA, May 1854, AMAA 43243–44; Fee to Jocelyn, July 9, 1858, AMAA 43637–39.

24. Friedman, *Gregarious Saints,* 163; Litwack, *North of Slavery,* 196–98, 206–13, 217, 219–20; Fee to Whipple, August 11, 1851, AMAA 43105; Fee to GB, August 19, 1851, in *NE,* September 11, 1851; Fee, *Autobiography,* 57–59; Reynolds, "Antislavery Campaign in Kentucky," 90; Steely, "Antislavery Movement in Kentucky," 51; Harrold, *Abolitionists and the South,* 97–98; Fee to Goodell, May 29, July 23, 1850, Goodell to Father, September 14, 1850, JGFP.

25. Fredrickson, *Black Image,* 43–96; Fee, *Anti-Slavery Manual,* 183–216, especially 183, 188–90; Fee, *Sinfulness,* 5. Fee was citing Acts 17:26.

26. Fee, *Autobiography,* 63; Fee, *Anti-Slavery Manual,* 19, 143–44, 147, 149, 186, 189, 198–99; Fee to J.S. Batchelder, n.d., in *AM,* o.s., 10 (May 1856):51; Fee to Charles

Hall, May 15, 1846, typescript in JGFP; Fee to Children, January 19, 1858, AMAA 43544–48; Fee to American Tract Society, n.d., in *AM*, 3 (September 1859):200.

27. Fee, *Anti-Slavery Manual*, 143–44, 155–56, 167, 198–99, 203–15. My views of the abolitionists' racial prejudice have been influenced by Litwack, *North of Slavery*, 216–30; Friedman, *Gregarious Saints*, 160–95; Walters, *Antislavery Appeal*, 56–69; Pease and Pease, "Antislavery Ambivalence," 686–95.

28. Walters, *Antislavery Appeal*, 75–76; Fee, *Anti-Slavery Manual*, 175–76, 192.

29. Fee, *Colonization*, 27; P. Nelson, "Interracial Education," 17–18; Drake, *One Apostle*, 52–53.

30. Dillon, *Abolitionists*, 150, 156–58. For Fee's critique of disunionism, see Fee to Goodell, January 10, 1856, in *RA*, March 1856.

31. Wiecek, *Sources of Antislavery Constitutionalism*, 250–51.

32. Fee, *Non-Fellowship*, 60–61; Fee to Daniel R. Goodloe, September 15, 1859, in *AM*, n.s., 3 (November 1859), 257; Fee to the Annual Meeting, n.d., in *AM*, n.s., 4 (November 1860):256; Fee to Tappan, June 10, 1847, AMAA 43012; Fee to Whipple and Tappan, May 8, 1850, AMAA 43050–53; Fee to Whipple, April 29, 1853, AMAA 43162; Fee to Jocelyn, April 8, 1858, AMAA 43608; Fee to *Re*, November 5, 1857, clipping in JGFP; Fee to CMC, September 17, 1857, JGFP; Steely, "Antislavery Movement in Kentucky," 182.

33. Fee to Daniel R. Goodloe, September 15, 1859, in *AM*, n.s., 3 (November 1859):257; Fee to CMC, December 12, 1859, in CMC, *Life*, 575–76; Fee to CMC, August 3 (postscript dated August 8), 1857, JGFP; Reynolds, "Antislavery Campaign in Kentucky," 152.

34. Fee to Smith, April 12, 1858, GSP; Fee to CMC, August 17, September 18, 1849, August 3, September 17, 1857, 1858, April 24, 1859, JGFP; Fee to *CG*, April 9, 1860, clipping in JGFP; Lexington *True American*, July 22, 1846, quoted in Steely, "Antislavery Movement in Kentucky," 46; CMC, *Speech from the Capitol Steps*, 3; CMC, *Life*, 494–96, 570–73; Fee, *Anti-Slavery Manual*, vii; Fee to the Members and Friends of the AMA, May 1854, AMAA 43243–44; Fee, *Autobiography*, 88, 126–28; CMC to *Ex*, June 9, 20, 1849, in *Ex*, June 23, 30, 1849; Fee to Tappan, November 17, 1846, in *AM*, o.s., 1 (January 1847):23–24; Embree, "Kentucky Crusader," 101.

35. Fee to *Ex*, June 20, 1849, in *Ex*, June 30, 1849; CMC, *Life*, 494–96; CMC to *Ex*, June 9, 1849, in *Ex*, June 23, 1849; Fee to AMA, n.d., in *AM*, o.s., 3 (March 1849):45; *NASS*, June 21, 1849; Fee to CMC, September 18, 1849, JGFP; Fee, *Sinfulness*, 8, 10.

36. Fee to CMC, August 17, September 18, 1849, Benjamin Mills to Fee, November 8, 1849, JGFP; Reynolds, "Antislavery Campaign in Kentucky," 48–49; Fee, *Non-Fellowship*, 2; Steely, "Antislavery Movement in Kentucky," 93; Fee to *NE*, October 5, 1852, in *NE*, October 14, 1852; Julian, *Political Recollections*, 125–27; CMC, *Life*, 479, 500; Riddleberger, *Julian*, 86–87; G. Clarke, *Julian*, 132–33; Collins and Collins, *Kentucky*, 1:66; Harrold, *Abolitionists and the South*, 127.

37. Green, "Northern Missionary Activities," 157; Harrold, *Abolitionists and the South*, 88–89, 95; Reynolds, "Antislavery Campaign in Kentucky," 83–84, 88; Steely, "Antislavery Movement in Kentucky," 25–133.

38. CMC to Salmon P. Chase, March 12, 1854, SPCP; Fee to the Members and Friends of the AMA, May 1854, AMAA 43243–44; Fee to GB, September 25, 1854, in *NE*, October 5, 1854; Fee to Goodell, July 23, 1850, JGFP; CMC, *Life*, 570–71; Warford, "Radical Tradition," 151–52; E. Peck and E. Smith, *Berea's First 125 Years*, 1–

2; Smiley, "Clay and Fee," 207–8; Reynolds, "Antislavery Campaign in Kentucky," 73–78.

39. Fee to the Members and Friends of the AMA, May 1854, AMAA 43243–44; Reynolds, "Antislavery Campaign in Kentucky," 28–29, 92–93, 99, 121; Steely, "Antislavery Movement in Kentucky," 53–54; Ellis, Everman, and Sears, *Madison County,* 105–12; Acts 17:11; Fee to CMC, June 22, October 17, 1854, JGFP; Fee to Whipple, May 23, 1854, AMAA 43241; Fee to American Tract Society, n.d., in *AM,* n.s., 3 (September 1859):201; Fee to Jocelyn, January 8, 1858, February 28, 1859, AMAA 43553–57, 43723–24.

40. J. Clark Richardson to AMA, September 16, 1859, AMAA 43796–97; Peter West to Jocelyn, December 22, 1857, AMAA 43540; Fee to Jocelyn, March 24, 1855, February 28, 1859, AMAA 43308–10, 43723–24; Fee, "Emigration to Kentucky," December 13, 1856, AMAA 43123–26; Warford, "Radical Tradition," 154–57; Warford, "Piety, Politics, and Pedagogy," 72; Harrold, *Abolitionists and the South,* 121–25; Fee to Jocelyn, July 7, 1855, in *AM,* o.s., 9 (August 1855):78; Davis, "Shall Kentucky Be Free?—Emigration Thither," February 13, 1857, AMAA 43439–40; Davis to Jocelyn, February 28, 1857, AMAA 43445–46; Davis to AMA, June 29, 1857, in *AM,* n.s., 1 (August 1857):189; Otis B. Waters, "A Christian Colony in Kentucky," February 16, 1857, AMAA 43443; William E. Lincoln to AMA, n.d., AMAA 43519A; William E. Lincoln, "For the Missionary," March 1858, AMAA 43602; George Candee to Jocelyn, August 12, 1858, March 13, 1860, AMAA 43654–55, 43857–58; Rogers, "Kentucky," 257–58; Reynolds, "Antislavery Campaign in Kentucky," 110–16.

41. Fee, *Anti-Slavery Manual,* 107, 110, 114.

42. Fee to *Re,* November 5, 1857, clipping in JGFP; Fee to WSB, March 8, 1855, in *NASS,* April 21, 1855; Fee to CMC, April 18, 1856, October 26, 1857, JGFP; Fee, "To the Citizens of Madison County," 13; Harrold, *Abolitionists and the South,* 98–99, 102–3; Fee, *Anti-Slavery Manual,* 36, 53, 55–56, 94–95; Fee, *Sinfulness,* 30–31; Fee to *CG,* April 9, 1860, Fee to WSB, n.d., in *KN,* September 8, 1856, clippings in JGFP. Fee claimed he did not "tamper" with slaves, by which I believe he meant he did not seek out slaves to convince them to escape. Fee argued that such activities would help individual slaves, but it would do little to help the large majority of slaves. Fee acknowledged, however, that "our preaching indirectly excites the slaves" because "a wronged and outraged people will be aroused by every ray of light . . . which shows their wrongs" (Fee to J. Joplin, John Adams, R.G. Williams, and M.J. Miller, July 18, 1855, AMAA 43328).

43. McKivigan, "Bibles for Slaves Campaign," 62–64, 77; Harrold, *Abolitionists and the South,* 98–99; Howard, *Evangelical War against Slavery and Caste,* 40–42; James M. West to AMA, n.d., in AMA, *Annual Report* (1852), 45; James Gillespie to AMA, May 19, 1849, in *AM,* o.s., 3 (July 1849):77; Fee to AMA, October 5, 1859, in *AM,* n.s., 3 (November 1859):256–57; Matilda Hamilton Fee to Jocelyn, October 17, 1856, AMAA 43406.

44. CMC to Fee, July 8, 1855, JGFP. It is obvious from the letter that Fee and Clay had argued the point before this date.

45. Fee to WSB, n.d., in *KN,* September 8, 1856, clipping in JGFP; Fee, *Non-Fellowship,* 58–59; Fee, *Anti-Slavery Manual,* 134–36.

46. Fee, *Autobiography,* 130, 137; W. Nelson, "Judicial Reasoning," 525–26; Cover, *Justice Accused,* 8–30; Fee to Smith, October 6, 1856, January 28, 1857, GSP; Fee to

Goodell, January 10, 1856, in *RA*, March 1856; Fee to WSB, n.d., in *KN*, August 25, 1856, clipping in JGFP.

47. Fee, *Anti-Slavery Manual*, 92–93; Fee, *Sinfulness*, 4; Fee, "To the Citizens of Madison County," 13; Fee to WSB, n.d., in *KN*, September 8, 1856, Fee to *CG*, April 9, 1860, clippings in JGFP. Compare these letters with Fee to CMC, August 17, 1849, JGFP.

48. Fee, *Anti-Slavery Manual*, 21–22, 92, 94–95, 178–79; Fee to WSB, n.d., in *KN*, September 8, 1856, Fee to *CG*, April 9, 1860, clippings in JGFP; Fee, *Non-Fellowship*, 5; Fee, *Sinfulness*, 25–31.

8. The Relevance and Irrelevance of John G. Fee

I have adapted the title of this chapter from Gordon Wood's "The Relevance and Irrelevance of John Adams." See Wood, *Creation of the American Republic*, chap. 14.

1. Fee to Jocelyn, June 14, 1859, AMAA 43768–70; Fee, "To the Citizens of Madison County," 14; Fee, *Slavery Question*, 1–2; Fee to *CG*, April 9, 1860, clipping in JGFP; Fee to CMC, May 10, 1856, JGFP; Fee to Goodell, January 10, 1856, in *RA*, March 1856; Steely, "Antislavery Movement in Kentucky," 82.

2. Fee to Whipple and Tappan, May 8, 1850, AMAA 43050–53.

3. Fee to Smith, March 8, 1855, January 28, 1857, GSP; Fee to Jocelyn, March 24, 1855, AMAA 43308–10; Fee to CMC, July 12, 1858, JGFP; Fee, *Autobiography*, 96–101; Fee to GB, July 25, 1855, in *NE*, August 16, 1855; CMC, *Life*, 75–77; *NE*, August 2, 9, 1855; CMC to Samuel Evans, August 5, 1855, clipping in Clay Papers, FHS; Howard, "Clay and the Republican Party," 59–61; Fee to Goodell, January 10, 1856, in *RA*, March 1856; Fee to Smith, June 11, 1856, copy in JGFP.

4. Fee to Goodell, January 10, 1856, in *RA*, March 1856; Fee to GB, February 16, 1855, in *NE*, March 15, 1855; Fee to CMC, May 10, 1856, JGFP; Fee to WSB, n.d., in *KN*, September 8, 1856, clipping in JGFP; Friedman, *Gregarious Saints*, 225–52; Malberg, "Republican Party," 8–12; Julian, "Republican Convention," 320; Reynolds, "Antislavery Campaign in Kentucky," 82, 146–48; Smiley, *Lion of White Hall*, 154–56; Howard, "Clay and the Republican Party," 62–68; Fee to Smith, June 11, 1856, copy in JGFP; Harrold, *Abolitionists and the South*, 146–47; Perkal, "American Abolition Society," 57–71.

5. CMC to Fee, July 8, December 18, 1855, Fee to CMC, April 18, May 10, 1856, JGFP; English, "Fee," 145–46. For accounts of Fee's and Clay's speeches at Slate Lick Springs, see CMC to *Richmond Messenger*, December 28, 1859, in CMC, *Life*, 236–37; Fee to WSB, n.d., in *KN*, August 25, September 1, 8, 1856, CMC to Davis, October 8, 1857, clippings in JGFP. Clay had long-standing objections to the Radicals' constitutional theories. See *WCMC*, 369–70; CMC to Smith, November 20, 1857, GSP; CMC, *Speech from the Capitol Steps*, 6. On Radical constitutionalism, see Wiecek, *Sources of Antislavery Constitutionalism*, 249–75; Wiecek, "*Somerset*," 119–25; Barnett, "Slavery Unconstitutional," 977–1014; Cover, *Justice Accused*, 154–58.

6. Fee to *CG*, April 9, 1860, clipping in JGFP; Fee to CMC, May 10, 1856, March 9, September 17, 1857, JGFP; Steely, "Antislavery Movement in Kentucky," 82; Wiecek, *Sources of Antislavery Constitutionalism*, 15–16; Hyman and Wiecek, *Equal Justice under Law*, 88–89, 92; Fee to Smith, June 11, 1856, copy in JGFP; "Mr. Fee in

Boston," *AM*, n.s., 5 (July 1861):157. For a fuller discussion of Fee's constitutional argument, see Tallant, "Slavery Controversy in Kentucky," 371–84.

7. Wiecek, *Sources of Antislavery Constitutionalism,* 202–48; Foner, *Free Soil,* 73–102; Fee to Smith, June 11, 1856, copy in JGFP. This appeal to the words over the intentions of the Founders was typical of Radical constitutionalists. See Cover, *Justice Accused,* 157; Wiecek, *Sources of Antislavery Constitutionalism,* 263–64; Kraditor, *Means and Ends,* 195–96. For a modern analysis which finds merit in the Radicals' method of constitutional interpretation, see Barnett, "Slavery Unconstitutional," 977–1014. Compare Fee's position to the so-called adequacy constitutionalism of the Civil War era. See Hyman and Wiecek, *Equal Justice under Law,* 234–35, 266, 389–97, 401–4.

8. Blackstone, *Commentaries,* 1:3–92, 3:426–55, 4:400–436; Hart, "Law of Nature," 169–74; P. Lucas, "Blackstone," 142–58; Willman, "Blackstone," 39–70; Posner, "Blackstone and Bentham," 569–606; Cover, *Justice Accused,* 15–17, 22–26; Wiecek, "*Somerset,*" 119–22; Fee to WSB, n.d., in *KN,* September 1, 1856, Fee to *Re,* November 5, 1857, clippings in JGFP; Fee to CMC, 1856, JGFP.

9. Fee to *CG,* April 9, 1860, clipping in JGFP; Fee, *Anti-Slavery Manual,* 73–75; Wiecek, *Sources of Antislavery Constitutionalism,* 264.

10. "Mr. Fee in Boston," 157; Fee to *CG,* April 9, 1860, Fee to WSB, n.d., in *KN,* September 1, 1856, clippings in JGFP; Fee to Goodell, January 10, 1856, in *RA,* March 1856.

11. Fee to WSB, n.d., in *KN,* August 25, 1856, clipping in JGFP; Fee to CMC, May 10, 1856, JGFP; Hyman and Wiecek, *Equal Justice under Law,* 211–12.

12. Hyman and Wiecek, *Equal Justice under Law,* 94–95, 181, 299–302; Kettner, *American Citizenship,* 248–333; Wiecek, *Sources of Antislavery Constitutionalism,* 165–66.

13. Fee to WSB, n.d., in *KN,* August 25, September 1, 1856, Fee to *CG,* April 9, 1860, Fee to *Re,* November 5, 1857, clippings in JGFP; Fee, *Anti-Slavery Manual,* 98; Fee to Goodell, Tappan, and Smith, January 12, 1857, Fee to Smith, November 13, 1857, GSP; Fee to CMC, March 9, August 3, 27, September 17, 1857, JGFP; Fee to Smith, June 11, 1856, copy in JGFP; Fee, *Colonization,* 44; Cover, *Justice Accused,* 156.

14. Fee to Smith, June 11, 1856, copy in JGFP; Fee to Goodell, Tappan, and Smith, January 12, 1857, GSP; Hyman and Wiecek, *Equal Justice under Law,* 24, 373; Wiecek, *Sources of Antislavery Constitutionalism,* 266–67. Between 1855 and 1857, Fee himself tried to instigate a test case on the issue of whether the actions of private individuals were limited by the Fifth Amendment's guarantee of due process. The case that was pending when Fee adopted the Radicals' judicial solution to slavery was *Dodge v. Woolsey,* 18 How. (59 U.S.) 331 (1856). The Supreme Court issued its ruling in the case on April 8, 1856, nearly three months after Fee had clearly expressed support for a judicial solution to slavery. See 15 *Lawyers' Edition* 401; Fee to Goodell, January 10, 1856, in *RA,* March 1856. The Court ruled on the first eight amendments in the cases of *Barron v. Mayor of Baltimore,* 7 Pet. (32 U.S.) 243 (1833); *Permoli v. Municipality No. 1 of New Orleans,* 3 How. (44 U.S.) 589 (1845).

15. Fee to *Re,* November 5, 1857, Fee to WSB, n.d., in *KN,* September 8, 1856, clippings in JGFP; Fee to Smith, June 11, 1856, copy in JGFP; Fee to CMC, August 3 (postscript dated August 8), 1857, JGFP.

16. Fee to *Re,* November 5, 1857, clipping in JGFP.

17. Fee to Jocelyn, Whipple, Tappan, and Goodell, April 4, 1857, AMAA 43458; Fee to Pennsylvania Anti-Slavery Society, October 3, 1859, in *NASS,* October 15, 1859;

Goodell to Fee, August 6, 1857, Fee to CMC, August 3 (postscript dated August 8), September 17, 1857, April 24, 1859, JGFP; Fee to *Re*, November 5, 1857, clipping in JGFP; Fee to CMC, December 12, 1859, in CMC, *Life*, 575–76; Fee to Smith, April 12, 1858, GSP; Fee to Daniel R. Goodloe, September 15, 1859, in *AM*, n.s., 3 (November 1859):257; *RA*, October 1858; Reynolds, "Antislavery Campaign in Kentucky," 153.

18. W.I. Fee, *Bringing in Sheaves*, 10; *NYTr*, n.d., in *AM*, n.s., 4 (February 1860):38; *Cincinnati Commercial*, December 27, 1859, in *AM*, n.s., 4 (February 1860):37; Smiley, "Clay and Fee," 203–4; C.H. Johnson, "Fee," 92–93; CMC, *Life*, 77; CMC to Samuel Evans, August 5, 1855, clipping in Clay Papers, FHS. Fee's changing views on the use of violence mirrored those of northern abolitionists. See Perry, *Radical Abolitionism*, 231–67; Friedman, *Gregarious Saints*, 196–222. Compare my discussion of Fee's views on the use of violence to Harrold, "Violence and Nonviolence," 15–38.

19. Matt. 5:38–39; Perry, *Radical Abolitionism*, 56–58. For the beliefs of Tappanite nonresistants and Fee's general agreement with those beliefs, see Mabee, *Black Freedom*, 4, 15–20, 147, 236–38, 259, 374–78.

20. Fee to CMC, June 31, 1849, in CMC, *Life*, 574; Fee, *Sinfulness*, 28; Fee, "Free Speech and Free Churches in Kentucky," September 1855, AMAA 43338–40; CMC to Fee, December 18, 1855, Goodell to Fee, August 6, 1857, JGFP; Fee, *Autobiography*, 101; Fee to Whipple, September 7, 1850, AMAA 43085; Fee to Jocelyn, July 21, 29, 1857, AMAA 43488–90, 43492–93; Fee et al., "Appeal to the People," 33; "Non-Resistance—The Missionary's Best Defense," *AM*, o.s., 9 (September 1855):87.

21. CMC to Samuel Evans, August 5, 1855, clipping in Clay Papers, FHS; CMC to *CG*, July 19, 1855, in *NASS*, August 4, 1855; CMC, *Life*, 75–77; Fee to Jocelyn, July 7, 1855, in *AM*, o.s., 9 (August 1855):78; Fee to GB, July 25, 1855, in *NE*, August 16, 1855; Fee, "Free Speech and Free Churches in Kentucky," September 1855, AMAA 43338–40; W.H. Kirtley to Col. Johnson, July 2, 1855, in *NASS*, July 28, 1855; John Adams, Sr. et al. to CMC, July 12, 1853, in *NE*, August 9, 1855; *NE*, May 10, June 14, August 2, 16, 1855; *Li*, August 3, 1855; Howard, "Clay and the Republican Party," 59–61.

22. *NE*, August 2, 1855; Fee to CMC, August 3, 1857, CMC to Fee, July 8, December 18, 1855, JGFP; Fee to GB, July 25, 1855, in *NE*, August 16, 1855; CMC to *CG*, July 19, 1855, in *NASS*, August 4, 1855; Howard, *Evangelical War against Slavery and Caste*, 72–76. CMC quoted in English, "Fee," 145. Clay later claimed that this story was apocryphal because such actions would have been uncharacteristic of him: "Had I laid my pistol on the bookboard, some enemy was most likely to seize it" (CMC, *Life*, 76).

23. Reynolds, "Antislavery Campaign in Kentucky," 107; Fee to Jocelyn, June 7, 1855, AMAA 43325; Fee to J. Joplin, John Adams, R.G. Williams, and M.J. Miller, July 18, 1855, AMAA 43328; Fee, "Free Speech and Free Churches in Kentucky," September 1855, AMAA 43338–40; CMC to Fee, December 18, 1855, JGFP; Embree, "Kentucky Crusader," 101; Sears, *Day of Small Things*, 40. See "Non-Resistance," 87; Wyatt-Brown, *Lewis Tappan*, 333; for critical assessments of the Scaffold Cane incident.

24. Fee to Jocelyn, November 9, 1855, December 3, 1856, January 14, 1857, AMAA 43343–45, 43415–17, 43433–34; Fee to Jocelyn, June 2, 1858, in *AM*, n.s., 2 (August 1858):211; Fee to AMA, November 22, 1856, in *AM*, n.s., 1 (January 1857):7; Fee, *Autobiography*, 95–96, 111; Rogers, *Birth of Berea College*, 37–40; Reynolds, "Antislavery Campaign in Kentucky," 168; E. Peck and E. Smith, *Berea's First 125 Years*, 9;

Hall and Heckman, "Berea's First Decade," 323–39; Steely, "Antislavery Movement in Kentucky," 64; Drake, *One Apostle,* 16.

25. Fee to Jocelyn, June 14, 26, July 15, 21, 1857, AMAA 43478–79, 43481, 43484–85, 43488–90; *AM,* n.s., 1 (November 1857):248–49; AMA, *Annual Report* (1858), 50; J.M McLain to *Free Presbyterian,* n.d., in *Li,* August 14, 1857; Fee to CMC, July 28, 1857, JGFP; Fee, *Autobiography,* 105–110; Otis B. Waters to AMA, n.d., in AMA, *Annual Report* (1858), 66–67.

26. Fee to Jocelyn, July 21, August 14, September 4, 1857, AMAA 43488–90, 43498, 43508–9; Fee to CMC, August 3 (postscript dated August 8), August 27, September 17, 1857, JGFP; Fee, *Autobiography,* 96.

27. Fee to CMC, August 27, 1857, JGFP; Fee to Jocelyn, August 20, 1857, AMAA 43503–4; English, "Fee," 150.

28. Fee to Jocelyn, July 29, 1857, AMAA 43492–93; Fee, *Autobiography,* 109–11; CMC, *Speech from the Capitol Steps,* 2–3; Fee to CMC, August 3, 27, 1857, JGFP; Fee to *Re,* November 5, 1857, Fee to *CG,* April 9, 1860, clippings in JGFP.

29. Otis B. Waters to Jocelyn, January 19, 1858, AMAA 43564–65; Fee to GB, February 12, 1858, in *NE,* March 4, 1858; Fee, *Autobiography,* 112–22; Fee to CMC, January 19, 1858, JGFP.

30. Fee, *Autobiography,* 122–23; George Candee to Jocelyn, January 23, 1858, AMAA 43569–70; George Candee to *NYTr,* n.d., in AMA, *Annual Report* (1858), 65–66; Fee to Jocelyn, February 5, 9, 1858, AMAA 43572–74, 43579–81; Fee to CMC, January 20, 1858, JGFP.

31. Fee to Jocelyn, n.d., in *AM,* n.s., 1 (August 1857):189; Fee to Jocelyn, July 21, August 14, September 4, 1857, January 8, February 9, 1858, AMAA 43488–90, 43498, 43508–9, 43553–57, 43579–81; Fee to CMC, August 27, 1857, JGFP; Fee to GB, February 12, 1858, in *NE,* March 4, 1858; Fee to Children, January 19, 1858, AMAA 43544–48; Fee et al. to the Friends and Patrons of the AMA, April 8, 1858, AMAA 43609; Fee, *Autobiography,* 121; Davis to the Readers of the *AM,* April 15, 1858, AMAA 43611; Davis to Jocelyn, May 4, 1858, AMAA 43618–19; Fee to Smith, March 29, 1862, GSP; Howard, *Evangelical War against Slavery and Caste,* 112–13.

32. Fee to GB, February 12, 1858, in *NE,* March 4, 1858; Fee to Jocelyn, April 12, 1859, AMAA 43750–53; Friedman, *Gregarious Saints,* 214–18.

33. Fee, *Autobiography,* 111–12, 125–26; Rogers, *Birth of Berea College,* 51; E. Peck and E. Smith, *Berea's First 125 Years,* 6, 9; Reynolds, "Antislavery Campaign in Kentucky," 144–45, 168; Fee to CMC, April 14, 1858, JGFP; Fee to Jocelyn, June 2, 1858, in *AM,* n.s., 2 (August 1858):211; Fee to Smith, July 15, 1858, GSP; English, "Fee," 153, 162; Ellis, Everman, and Sears, *Madison County,* 137–44.

34. Fee to CMC, July 12, 1858, JGFP; Fee to Smith, July 15, 1858, GSP; Fee to Jocelyn, July 9, 1858, AMAA 43637–39; Fee, *Autobiography,* 132–37; Ellis, Everman, and Sears, *Madison County,* 142–44; Rogers, *Birth of Berea College,* 60–65.

35. Fee to Jocelyn, December 3, 1856, April 12, 1859, AMAA 43415–17, 43750–53; Fee to AMA, November 22, 1856, in *AM,* n.s., 1 (January 1857):7; Fee to Smith, March 10, 1859, GSP; Rogers, *Birth of Berea College,* 68.

36. Berea College Bylaws, quoted in Fairchild, *Berea College,* 21–22; Fee to Smith, March 10, 1859, GSP; Fee to Jocelyn, April 12, 1859, AMAA 43750–53; Rogers, *Birth of Berea College,* 68; Reynolds, "Antislavery Campaign in Kentucky," 174; Steely, "Antislavery Movement in Kentucky," 66; Ellis, Everman, and Sears, *Madison County,* 135–36, 140–41.

37. Rogers, *Birth of Berea College,* 37; Davis to Jocelyn, June 6, 1859, AMAA 43763–64; J.B. Mullett to Fee, July 26, 1859, JGFP; Steely, "Antislavery Movement in Kentucky," 116.

38. Fee to Jocelyn, July 7, 1859, AMAA 43782–83; Many Citizens to Fee, June 25, 1859, JGFP.

39. Reynolds, "Antislavery Campaign in Kentucky," 179–81; "Citizens of Kentucky Expelled for Entertaining Free Sentiments," *AM,* n.s., 4 (February 1860):38–40; *CG,* December 31, 1859, in *NASS,* January 14, 1860; AMA, *Annual Report* (1859), 49–50; William Kendrick to Jocelyn, December 13, 1859, AMAA 43823; Fee, *Autobiography,* 149; Fee to CMC, December 12, 1859, in CMC, *Life,* 576; Fee, "To the Citizens of Madison County," 13–14; Rogers, *Birth of Berea College,* 74–81; Hall and Heckman, "Berea's First Decade," 335–36; Rogers to Jocelyn, December 3, 28, 1859, AMAA 43819, 43828; "Expulsion," *AM,* n.s., 4 (March 1860):65; Sears, *Day of Small Things,* 293–306.

40. Collins and Collins, *Kentucky,* 1:82; "Expulsion," 64–65; Fee to Jocelyn, January 25, 1860, AMAA 43841–42; Fee, *Autobiography,* 149–53; E. Peck and E. Smith, *Berea's First 125 Years,* 19–20; Fairchild, *Berea College,* 31–37; Sears, *Day of Small Things,* 306–73; Fee to CMC, February 28, 1860, JGFP; Moncure D. Conway to *NASS,* January 12, 1860, in *NASS,* January 21, 1860; "Citizens of Kentucky Expelled," 40; Fee to *CG,* April 9, 1860, clipping in JGFP. Throughout the early weeks of 1860, Fee's followers continued to be expelled from their homes. Cassius Clay later listed ninety-four people from the Berea area who left the state as a result of the various expulsions of Fee's followers. See additionally Ellis, Everman, and Sears, *Madison County,* 158; *NASS,* April 14, 1860; John G. Hanson to Jocelyn, March 13, 1860, AMAA 43855–56; Drake, *One Apostle,* 30–37; "Exiled Missionaries," *AM,* n.s., 4 (May 1860):111.

41. McPherson, *Abolitionist Legacy,* 244. On Berea College after the Civil War, see generally, 244–61; P. Nelson, "Interracial Education," 13–27; Warford, "Piety, Politics, and Pedagogy," 133–39; Burnside, "Suspicion versus Faith," 237–66. On Camp Nelson and Fee's efforts on behalf of the freedmen, see Sears, *"Practical Recognition";* Sears, "Camp Nelson," 29–45; M. Lucas, "Camp Nelson," 439–52; Gutman, *Black Family,* 370–75, 379; Howard, *Black Liberation,* 112–21; McPherson, *Struggle for Equality,* 413; Warford, "Piety, Politics, and Pedagogy," 108–11. On Fee's general postwar work on behalf of freedmen and racial equality, see Sears, *Utopian Experiment.*

42. J.L. Thomas, *Liberator,* 136–37; Merrill, *Against Wind and Tide,* 54.

Bibliography

Primary Sources

Manuscript Collections

Berea, Ky. Berea College Library. Special Collections Department. John G. Fee Papers.

Bowling Green, Ky. Western Kentucky University. Kentucky Library. Joseph R. Underwood Papers.

Frankfort, Ky. Kentucky Department for Libraries and Archives. Governor John J. Crittenden Executive Papers.

Georgetown, Ky. Scott County Public Library. Local History Reports.

Lexington, Ky. University of Kentucky Library. Special Collections Department. Broadside Collection.

Lexington, Ky. University of Kentucky Library. Special Collections Department. Cassius M. Clay Papers.

Lexington, Ky. University of Kentucky Library. Special Collections Department. J. Winston Coleman, Jr., Papers on Slavery.

Lexington, Ky. University of Kentucky Library. Special Collections Department. E.H. Goulding to My Dear Friend, August 11, 1848. Manuscript Vertical File.

Lexington, Ky. University of Kentucky Library. Special Collections Department. William M. Pratt Diary, Vol. 1: 1838–52.

Lexington, Ky. University of Kentucky Library. Special Collections Department. Shelby Family Papers.

Lexington, Ky. University of Kentucky Library. Special Collections Department. Benjamin B. Smith Papers.

Louisville, Ky. Filson Historical Society. Orlando Brown Papers.

Louisville, Ky. Filson Historical Society. Cassius M. Clay Papers.

Louisville, Ky. Filson Historical Society. Benjamin Coates Papers.

Louisville, Ky. Filson Historical Society. Almeron Dowd Papers.

Louisville, Ky. Filson Historical Society. John W. Grigsby Papers.

Louisville, Ky. Filson Historical Society. John Irwin Papers.

Louisville, Ky. Filson Historical Society. Charles Lanman Papers.

Louisville, Ky. Filson Historical Society. William T. McElroy Journal.

Louisville, Ky. Filson Historical Society. Charles W. Short Papers.
Louisville, Ky. Filson Historical Society. Edward C. Thurman Collection of Stampless
Covers Representing Towns and Cities of Kentucky.
Louisville, Ky. Filson Historical Society. Yandell Family Papers.
Louisville, Ky. Filson Historical Society. John C. Young Papers.
New Orleans, La. Tulane University. Amistad Research Center. American Missionary
Association Archives.
Philadelphia, Pa. Historical Society of Pennsylvania. Salmon P. Chase Papers.
Syracuse, N.Y. Syracuse University Library. Gerrit Smith Papers.
Washington, D.C. Library of Congress. American Colonization Society Records.
Washington, D.C. Library of Congress. Breckinridge Family Papers.

Collected Letters and Writings

Abel, Annie Heloise, and Frank J. Klingberg, eds. *A Side-Light on Anglo-American Rela-
tions, 1839–1858: Furnished by the Correspondence of Lewis Tappan and Others
with the British and Foreign Anti-Slavery Society.* Lancaster, Pa.: Assoc. for the Study
of Negro Life and History, 1927.
Barnes, Gilbert H., and Dwight L. Dumond, eds. *Letters of Theodore Dwight Weld,
Angelina Grimké Weld and Sarah Grimké, 1822–1844.* 2 vols. New York: Appleton-
Century, 1934.
Basler, Roy P., ed. *The Collected Works of Abraham Lincoln.* 9 vols. New Brunswick, N.J.:
Rutgers Univ. Press, 1953–55.
Blassingame, John W., ed. *Slave Testimony: Two Centuries of Letters, Speeches, Interviews,
and Autobiographies.* Baton Rouge: Louisiana State Univ. Press, 1977.
Boromé, Joseph A., ed. "Henry Clay and James G. Birney: An Exchange of Views."
Filson Club History Quarterly 35 (April 1961):122–24.
Bourne, Edward G., ed. "Diary and Correspondence of Salmon P. Chase." *Annual Re-
port of the American Historical Association for the Year 1902.* 2 vols. Washington,
D.C.: GPO, 1903.
Clay, Cassius M., ed. "Cassius M. Clay, 'Lion' of White Hall: Some Unpublished Let-
ters Of and About." *Filson Club History Quarterly* 31 (January 1957):3–22; (April
1957):122–46.
Colton, Calvin, ed. *The Works of Henry Clay: Comprising His Life, Correspondence and
Speeches.* 10 vols. New York: Putnam's, 1904.
Crallé, Richard K., ed. *The Works of John C. Calhoun.* 6 vols. New York: Appleton,
1851–55.
Dumond, Dwight L., ed. *Letters of James Gillespie Birney, 1831–1857.* 2 vols. New
York: Appleton-Century, 1938.
Eaton, Clement, ed. "Henry Clay's Last Will." *University of Kentucky Libraries Bulletin,*
no. 1 (1949), 1–9.
———. "Minutes and Resolutions of an Emancipation Meeting in Kentucky in 1849."
Journal of Southern History 14 (November 1948):541–45.
Filler, Louis, ed. *Wendell Phillips on Civil Rights and Freedom.* New York: Hill & Wang,
1965.
Gifford, James M., ed. "Some New Light on Henry Clay and the American Coloniza-
tion Society." *Filson Club History Quarterly* 50 (October 1976):372–74.
Greeley, Horace, ed. *The Writings of Cassius Marcellus Clay, Including Speeches and Ad-

dresses. New York: Harper & Brothers, 1848; reprint ed., New York: Negro Univs. Press, 1969.

Greene, Lorenzo J., ed. "Antislavery in Kentucky." *Midwest Journal* 2, no. 2 (Summer 1950), 76–87.

Harrison, Lowell H., ed. "The Folklore of Some Kentucky Slaves." *Kentucky Folklore Record* 17 (April/June 1971):25–30; (July/September 1971):53–60.

Hepler, John C., ed. "John G. Whittier Hears from Henry Clay." *Register of the Kentucky Historical Society* 51 (April 1953):171–72.

Hopkins, James F., et al., eds. *The Papers of Henry Clay.* 11 vols. Lexington: Univ. of Kentucky Press (vols. 1–5); Lexington: Univ. Press of Kentucky (vols. 6–11), 1959–92.

Huch, Ronald K., ed. "James Gillespie Birney and the New England Friends." *Register of the Kentucky Historical Society* 67 (October 1969):350–59.

Jameson, J. Franklin, ed. "Correspondence of John C. Calhoun." *Annual Report of the American Historical Association for the Year 1899.* 2 vols. Washington, D.C.: GPO, 1900.

Merrill, Walter M., and Louis Ruchames, eds. *The Letters of William Lloyd Garrison.* 6 vols. Cambridge: Belknap Press of the Harvard Univ. Press, 1971–81.

Nicolay, John G., and John Hay, eds. *Complete Works of Abraham Lincoln.* Rev. ed. 12 vols. New York: Francis D. Tandy, 1905.

"An Old Letter Concerning Cassius M. Clay and the *True American.*" *Filson Club History Quarterly* 22 (July 1948):197–98.

Palmer, Beverly Wilson, ed. "From Small Minority to Great Cause: Letters of Charles Sumner to Salmon P. Chase." *Ohio History* 93 (Summer/Autumn 1984):164–83.

Peterson, Merrill D., ed. *Thomas Jefferson: Writings.* New York: Library of America, 1984.

Phillips, Ulrich Bonnell, ed. "The Correspondence of Robert Toombs, Alexander H. Stephens, and Howell Cobb." *Annual Report of the American Historical Association for the Year 1911.* 2 vols. Washington, D.C.: GPO, 1913.

Ralston, Thomas N., ed. *Posthumous Works of the Rev. Henry B. Bascom. . . .* 4 vols. Nashville: Stevenson & Owen, 1855.

Ritchie, Andrew, ed. *The Life & Writings of Rev. Samuel Crothers. . . .* Cincinnati: Moore, Wilstach, Keys, 1857.

Shackleford, John, Jr., ed. *Life, Letters and Addresses of Dr. L.L. Pinkerton.* Cincinnati: Chase & Hall, 1876.

Smiley, David L., ed. "A View of the Suppression of *The True American.*" *Filson Club History Quarterly* 29 (October 1955):320–23.

Thomas, John Wesley, ed. *The Letters of James Freeman Clarke to Margaret Fuller.* Hamburg, West Germany: Cram, de Gruyler, 1957.

Thomas, Mary Elizabeth, ed. "Henry Clay Replies to a Labor Recruiter from Trinidad." *Register of the Kentucky Historical Society* 77 (Autumn 1979):263–65.

Autobiographies and Memoirs

Anderson, Robert Ball. *From Slavery to Affluence: Memoirs of Robert Anderson, Ex-Slave.* Hemingford, Neb.: Hemingford Ledger, 1927.

Bibb, Henry. *Narrative of the Life and Adventures of Henry Bibb, An American Slave.* New York: Macdonald & Lee, 1849.

Clarke, Lewis. *Narrative of the Sufferings of Lewis Clarke*. . . . Boston: David H. Ela, 1845.

Clarke, Lewis and Milton Clarke. *Narrative of the Sufferings of Lewis and Milton Clarke*. . . . Boston: Bela Marsh, 1846.

Clay, Cassius M. *The Life of Cassius Marcellus Clay: Memoirs, Writings, and Speeches*. . . . Cincinnati: J. Fletcher Brennan, 1886.

Fairbank, Calvin. *During Slavery Times: How We "Fought the Good Fight" to Prepare "The Way."* Chicago: Patriotic Publishing, 1890.

Fee, John G. *Autobiography of John G. Fee, Berea, Kentucky.* Chicago: National Christian Assoc., 1891.

Fee, William I. *Bringing in Sheaves: Gleanings from Harvest Fields in Ohio, Kentucky and West Virginia.* Cincinnati: Cranston & Curts, 1896.

Jackson, Andrew. *Narrative and Writings of Andrew Jackson, of Kentucky.* . . . Syracuse, N.Y.: Daily and Weekly Star, 1847.

Julian, George W. *Political Recollections, 1840 to 1872*. Chicago: Jansen, McClurg, 1884.

Marrs, Elijah P. *Life and History of the Rev. Elijah P. Marrs, First Pastor of Beargrass Baptist Church.* Louisville: Bradley & Gilbert, 1885; reprint ed., Miami, Fla.: Mnemosyne, 1969.

McPheeters, Addison. "Illinois Commentary: The Reminiscences of Addison McPheeters." *Journal of the Illinois State Historical Society* 67 (April 1974):212–26.

Parker, John P. *His Promised Land: The Autobiography of John P. Parker, Former Slave and Conductor on the Underground Railroad.* Edited by Stuart Seely Sprague. New York: Norton, 1996.

Pendleton, James Madison. *Reminiscences of a Long Life.* Louisville: Baptist Book Concern, 1891.

Rogers, John A.R. *Birth of Berea College: A Story of Providence.* Philadelphia: Coates, 1904; reprint ed., Berea, Ky.: Berea Clg. Press, 1933.

Smith, Harry. *Fifty Years of Slavery in the United States of America.* Grand Rapids: West Michigan Printing, 1891; reprint ed., Mount Pleasant, Mich.: Clarke Hist. Library, Central Michigan Univ., n.d.

Stedman, Ebenezer H. *Bluegrass Craftsman: Being the Reminiscences of Ebenezer Hiram Stedman, Papermaker, 1808–1885.* Edited by Frances L.S. Dugan and Jacqueline P. Bull. Lexington: Univ. of Kentucky Press, 1959.

Newspapers and Periodicals

African Repository and Colonization Journal 4 (January 1829)-28 (December 1852).

American Missionary, o.s., 1 (January 1847)-n.s., 5 (July 1861).

Cincinnati Journal, February 27, March 16, 27, 1835.

Colonization Herald and General Register, May, July, September 1849.

Frankfort *Old Guard,* February 21, April 4, 1850.

Independent, November 3, 10, 1859.

Lexington Observer and Reporter, August 9, September 27, October 11, November 6, 1848.

Liberator, March 1, April 5, June 7, July 19, September 13, 1844; August 22, 29, September 4, October 24, 1845; July 17, 1846; March 16, 23, 30, April 6, 20, 27, June 15, 22, July 13, August 10, 1849; May 6, 1853; August 3, 1855; August 14, 1857.

Louisville *Baptist Banner,* August 22, 29, September 12, 19, 26, 1849; August 14, 1850.

Louisville Courier, August 6, 1849.
Louisville *Examiner,* June 19, August 4, 1847; October 28, November 4, 1848; January 27, February 3, 10, 17, 24, March 3, 17, 24, 31, April 7, 14, 21, 28, May 5, 12, 19, 26, June 2, 9, 16, 23, 30, July 7, 14, 28, August 4, 11, 18, 25, September 1, 8, 15, 1849.
Louisville Journal, August 9, 10, 11, 1849.
Nashville *Tennessee Baptist,* September 13, 20, 1849.
National Anti-Slavery Standard, September 4, November 6, 1845; February 15, 22, June 21, August 16, 1849; April 21, July 28, August 4, September 8, 1855; October 15, 1859; January 14, 21, April 14, 1860.
National Era, August 19, 1847; September 11, 1851; October 5, 1854; March 15, May 10, June 14, August 2, 9, 16, 1855; March 4, 1858.
New York Times, July 25, October 22, November 15, 1855; August 21, 1881.
New York Tribune, May 16, 1855; November 14, 1859.
Niles' Register, May 4, August 3, 31, October 5, 1844; October 4, 1848; February 14, 21, March 21, June 13, 1849.
Pennsylvania Freeman, January 8, 22, 29, 1846; October 23, 1852.
Radical Abolitionist, March 1856; October 1858.

Public Documents

Barron v. Mayor of Baltimore. 7 Pet. (32 U.S.) 243 (1833).
Dodge v. Woolsey. 18 How. (59 U.S.) 331 (1856).
————. 15 *Lawyers' Edition* 401.
Kentucky. *Acts of the General Assembly.* 1814–15, 1832–33, 1850–51.
————. *Report of the Debates and Proceedings of the Convention for the Revision of the Constitution of the State of Kentucky, 1849.* Frankfort, Ky.: A.G. Hodges, 1849.
————. *Second Constitution* (1799).
————. *Third Constitution* (1850).
Kentucky. General Assembly. *Second Auditor's Report,* no. 13. 53d Gen. Assemb., 1844–45. *Legislative Documents.*
————. *Second Auditor's Report,* no. 10. 57th-59th Gen. Assembs. 1848–51. *Legislative Documents.*
Kentucky. General Assembly. House. *Journal.* 43d-57th Gen. Assembs. 1834–49.
Kentucky. General Assembly. Senate. *Journal.* 43d-57th Gen. Assembs. 1834–49.
Permoli v. Municipality No. 1 of New Orleans. 3 How. (44 U.S.) 589 (1845).
U.S. *Constitution.*
U.S. Congress. House. *Congressional Globe.* 29th Cong., 1st sess.-30th Cong., 1st sess. 1845–48.
U.S. Congress. Senate. *Congressional Globe.* 31st Cong., 1st sess. 1849–50.
U.S. Office of the Census. *The Seventh Census of the United States: 1850.* Washington, D.C.: Robert Armstrong, 1853.
————. *The Seventh Census: Report of the Superintendent of the Census for December 1, 1852; to Which is Appended the Report for December 1, 1851.* Washington, D.C.: Robert Armstrong, 1853.
————. *Statistical View of the United States.* Washington, D.C.: Beverley Tucker, 1854.
U.S. Work Projects Administration. Federal Writers Project. *Slave Narratives: A Folk History of Slavery in the United States from Interviews with Former Slaves.* 17 vols.

Vol. 5: *Indiana Narratives*; Vol. 7: *Kentucky Narratives*; Vol. 12: *Ohio Narratives*. Washington, D.C.: Library of Congress Microfiche, 1941.

U.S. Works Progress Administration. *Annals of Cleveland, 1818–1935: A Digest and Index of the Newspaper Record of Events and Opinions*. 59 vols. Cleveland: Works Progress Administration, 1937.

Other Primary Sources

American Board of Commissioners for Foreign Missions. *Report*. Boston: Crocker & Brewster, 1831–37.

American Missionary Association. *Annual Report*. New York: American Missionary Assoc., 1850–61.

Bascom, Henry B. *Methodism and Slavery: With Other Matters in Controversy between the North and the South . . . in the Case of Bishop Andrew*. Frankfort, Ky.: Hodges, Todd & Pruett, 1845.

Bascom, Henry B., A.L.P. Greene, and C.B. Parsons. *Brief Appeal to Public Opinion in a Series of Exceptions to the Course and Actions of the Methodist Episcopal Church. . . .* Louisville: Morton & Griswold, 1848.

Birney, James G. *Letter on Colonization, Addressed to the Rev. Thornton J. Mills, Corresponding Secretary of the Kentucky Colonization Society*. New York: Anti-Slavery Reporter, 1834.

Blackstone, William. *Commentaries on the Laws of England*. 1st ed. 4 vols. Oxford: Clarendon, 1765–69; reprint ed., Chicago: Univ. of Chicago Press, 1979.

Breckinridge, Robert J. "An Address Delivered before the Colonization Society of Kentucky, at Frankfort, on the 6th Day of January, 1831." *African Repository* 7 (August 1831):161–80.

———. "The Black Race: Some Reflections on its Position and Destiny, as Connected with Our American Dispensation; a Discourse Delivered before the Kentucky Colonization Society, at Frankfort, on the 6th of February, 1851." *African Repository* 27 (May 1851):129–46.

———. "Hints on Colonization and Abolition; with Reference to the Black Race." *Biblical Repertory and Theological Review* 5 (July 1833):281–305.

———. *Hints on Slavery: Founded on the State of the Constitution, Laws and Politics of Kentucky, Thirteen Years Ago*. N.p., 1843.

———. "Mr. Breckinridge's Speech." *African Repository* 14 (May 1838):136–45.

———. "The Past Course and Present Duty of Kentucky." *Danville Quarterly Review* 4 (September 1864):426–42.

———. *The Question of Negro Slavery and the New Constitution of Kentucky*. Lexington: n.p., 1849.

———. *The Second Defense of Robert J. Breckinridge against the Calumnies of Robert Wickliffe. . . .* Louisville: Prentice and Weissinger, 1841.

———. *Speech of Robert J. Breckinridge, Delivered in the Court-House Yard at Lexington, Ky. on the 12th Day of October, 1840, in Reply to the "Speech of Robert Wickliffe." . . .* Lexington: N.L. & J.W. Finnell, 1840.

———. *The Third Defense of Robert J. Breckinridge against the Calumnies of Robert Wickliffe. . . .* Baltimore: R.J. Hatchett, 1843.

Brookes, Iveson L. *A Defense of Southern Slavery against the Attacks of Henry Clay and Alexander Campbell*. Hamburg, S.C.: Robinson and Carlisle, 1851.

Brown, Thomas. *Brown's Three Years in the Kentucky Prisons, from May 30, 1854, to May 18, 1857.* Indianapolis: Indianapolis Journal, 1858.

Brown, W.S. "Strictures on Abolitionism: National Colonization of the Free Black Population of the United States Advocated." In Josiah Priest. *Bible Defence of Slavery; or, The Origin, History, and Fortunes of the Negro Race. . . .* 6th ed. Louisville: J.F. Brennan, 1851.

Buck, William C. *The Slavery Question.* Louisville: Harney, Hughes & Hughes, 1849.

Bullock, William F. "Address of Judge Bullock." *African Repository* 23 (April 1847):99–110.

Casseday, Ben. *The History of Louisville, from Its Earliest Settlement till the Year 1852.* Louisville: Hull, 1852.

Cheever, George B. *God against Slavery and the Freedom and Duty of the Pulpit to Rebuke It, as a Sin against God.* Cincinnati: American Reform Tract and Book Soc., 1857.

Clay, Cassius M. *A Review of the Late Canvass, and R. Wickliffe's Speech on the "Negro Law," by C.M. Clay, September 25, 1840.* Lexington: N.L. Finnell, 1840.

———. *Speech of C.M. Clay, at Lexington, Ky., Delivered August 1, 1851.* N.p., [1851].

———. *Speech of Cassius M. Clay, at Frankfort, Ky., from the Capitol Steps, January 10, 1860.* Cincinnati: n.p., 1860.

Clay, Henry. *An Address Delivered to the Colonization Society of Kentucky, at Frankfort, December 17, 1829.* Lexington: Thomas Smith, 1829.

———. "Mr. Clay's Remarks at the Colonization Meeting Held in Lexington, Ky. on the 26th of August, 1836." *African Repository* 12 (October 1836):297–301.

———. "Speech of Mr. Clay, on the Subject of Abolition Petitions." *African Repository* 15 (February 1839):50–64.

———. "Speech of the Hon. H. Clay, Delivered at the Annual Meeting of the Am. Col. Society, January 21, 1851." *African Repository* 27 (April 1851):105–14.

Coates, Benjamin. *Cotton Cultivation in Africa. . . .* Philadelphia: C. Sherman, 1858.

Collins, Gabriel. *Gabriel Collins' Louisville and New Albany Directory, and Annual Advertiser for 1848.* Louisville: G.H. Monsarrat, [1848].

Collins, Lewis, and Richard H. Collins. *History of Kentucky.* 2 vols. Covington, Ky.: Collins, 1882.

Cowan, Alexander M. *Liberia, as I Found It, in 1858.* Frankfort, Ky.: A.G. Hodges, 1858.

Cox, Leander M. *Remarks of Leander M. Cox of Fleming, . . . as to the Expediency of Calling a Convention. . . .* Frankfort, Ky.: Hodges, Todd & Pruett, 1846.

Danville Colonization Society. "Constitution of the Danville Colonization Society and Proceedings of Meetings, May 16, 1829 to May 15, 1835; Followed by a List of Members." Typescript in the Filson Historical Society, Louisville, Kentucky.

Danville Literary and Social Club. *Danville Literary and Social Club, "Anaconda," History and Semi-Centennial Celebration, December 27, 1889, 1839–1889.* Danville, Ky.: Advocate, [1889].

DeBow, James D.B. "Kentucky." *De Bow's Review,* o.s., 7 (September 1849):191–205.

Fairchild, E.H. *Berea College, Ky.: An Interesting History.* Cincinnati: Elm Street, 1875.

Fee, John G. *An Anti-Slavery Manual, Being an Examination in the Light of the Bible, and of Facts, into the Moral and Social Wrongs of American Slavery, with a Remedy for the Evil.* Maysville, Ky.: Herald, 1848; reprint ed., New York: Arno, 1969.

———. *Colonization: The Present Scheme of Colonization Wrong, Delusive, and Retards Emancipation.* Cincinnati: American Reform Tract and Book Soc., [1854].

————. *Non-Fellowship with Slaveholders the Duty of Christians.* New York: John A. Gray, 1851.

————. *The Sinfulness of Slaveholding Shown by Appeals to Reason and Scriptures.* New York: John A. Gray, 1851.

————. "To the Citizens of Madison County, Kentucky." *American Missionary,* n.s., 4 (January 1860):13–14.

————. *Why Agitate the Slavery Question?* Cincinnati: n.p., [1862].

Fee, John G., et al. "Appeal to the People of the United States." *American Missionary,* n.s., 4 (February 1860):32–33.

[Garrett, Squire O.W., et al.] *Address to the Non-Slaveholders of Kentucky.* Louisville: Corresponding and Executive Committee on Emancipation, 1849.

Greeley, Horace, ed. *The Tribune Almanac for the Years 1838 to 1868. . . .* 2 vols. New York: New York Tribune, 1868.

Haskin, Joseph. *To the Voters of Mercer and Anderson Counties.* Frankfort, Ky.: Kentucky Yeoman, 1849.

Helm, John L. "Remarks of Hon. John L. Helm, in Committee of the Whole Senate, . . . in Relation to the Submission of the New Constitution." Frankfort *Old Guard* 1 (February 21, 1850):53–61.

Henkle, Moses Montgomery. *The Life of Henry Bidleman Bascom, D.D., LL.D., Late Bishop of the Methodist Episcopal Church, South.* Louisville: Morton & Griswold, 1854.

"Hon. Joseph R. Underwood." *American Review* 7 (June 1848):609–14.

[Hutchinson, Enoch.] "Biographical Sketch of Rev. Howard Malcom, D.D." *Baptist Memorial, and Monthly Record* 10 (1851):318–24.

Jacobs, John A. "The Men of Danville, No. 1: A Biographical Sketch of the Rev. John C. Young, D.D., Late President of Centre College." *Danville Quarterly Review* 4 (March 1864):151–66.

Jegli, John B. *A Directory for 1851–1852. . . .* Louisville: J.F. Brennan, 1851.

————. *John B. Jegli's Louisville Directory for 1848–1849.* Louisville: John C. Noble, 1848.

Johnston, J. Stoddard, ed. *Memorial History of Louisville from Its First Settlement to the Year 1896.* 2 vols. Chicago: American Biographical, n.d.

Kentucky Colonization Society. *Proceedings.* Frankfort, Ky., 1831, 1848–49.

————. *Annual Report.* Frankfort, Ky., 1833–34.

Little, Lucius P. *Ben Hardin: His Times and Contemporaries, with Selections from His Speeches.* Louisville: Courier-Journal, 1887.

McClung, John A. "Address of John A. McClung, Esq." *African Repository* 24 (May 1848):133–49.

Mills, Thornton A. "Second Western Expedition to Liberia." *Christian Messenger* 7 (June 1833):167–68.

Miss Delia A. Webster, of Vermont: Her Treatment by the Slaveholders of Kentucky. N.p., [1857].

Nicholas, Samuel S., et al. *Slave Emancipation in Kentucky.* Louisville: n.p., 1849.

Paxton, John D. *Letters on Slavery, Addressed to the Cumberland Congregation, Virginia.* Lexington: Abraham T. Skillman, 1833.

Ranck, George W. *History of Lexington, Kentucky: Its Early Annals and Recent Progress. . . .* Cincinnati: Robert Clarke, 1872.

Republican Party. National Convention. *Proceedings of the First Three Republican Na-*

tional Conventions of 1856, 1860, and 1864, . . . as Reported by Horace Greeley. Minneapolis: Charles W. Johnson, 1893.

Robertson, George. *Scrapbook on Law and Politics, Men and Times.* Lexington: A.W. Elder, 1855.

Robinson, Stuart. "Rev. Mr. Robinson's Address." *African Repository* 25 (May 1849):141–45.

Robinson, Stuart, and George W. Brush. *Memorial of Messrs. Robinson and Brush, Referred to in the Foregoing Proceedings.* N.p., 1849.

Rogers, John A.R. "Kentucky—Come and See." *American Missionary,* n.s., 2 (October 1858):257–58.

Shaler, Nathaniel S. *Kentucky: A Pioneer Commonwealth.* Boston: Houghton, Mifflin, 1885.

Shannon, James. *Philosophy of Slavery, as Identified with the Philosophy of Human Happiness: An Essay.* Frankfort, Ky.: A.G. Hodges, 1849.

Spalding, David. "Martin John Spalding's 'Dissertation on the American Civil War.'" *Catholic Historical Review* 52 (April 1966):66–85.

Speed, James. *James Speed: A Personality.* Louisville: John P. Morton, 1914.

[Speed, James, et al.] *Address to the People of Kentucky on the Subject of Emancipation.* Louisville: Corresponding and Executive Committee on Emancipation, 1849.

Stanton, Henry B., James A. Thome, and Samuel H. Cox. *Debate at the Lane Seminary, Cincinnati; Speech of James A. Thome of Kentucky, Delivered at the Annual Meeting of the American Anti-Slavery Society, May 6, 1834. . . .* Boston: Garrison & Knapp, 1834.

Stone, Barton W. "An Humble Address to the Christians, on the Colonization of Free People of Color." *Christian Messenger* 3 (June 1829):198–200.

Sutton, R. *The Methodist Church Property Case: Report of the Suit of Henry B. Bascom, and Others, "vs.," George Lane, and Others. . . .* Richmond, Va.: John Early, 1851.

Underwood, Joseph R. *Address Delivered before the Colonization Society of Bowlinggreen, on the 4th July, 1832.* N.p., 1832.

———. *An Address Delivered to the Colonization Society of Kentucky, at Frankfort, Jan. 15, 1835.* Frankfort, Ky.: A.G. Hodges, 1835.

———. "Colonization and Gradual Emancipation." *African Repository* 24 (November 1848):321–24.

———. *Speech on Hon. J.R. Underwood, of Kentucky on the Slavery Question Delivered in Senate of the United States, Tuesday, April 3, 1850.* Washington, D.C.: Congressional Globe Office, 1850.

———. *Speech of Hon. J.R. Underwood on the Subject of National Politics Delivered at Elkton, Ky., July 17, 1851.* Bowling Green, Ky.: R.J. Smith, 1851.

———. *Speech of Mr. J.R. Underwood, upon the Resolution Proposing to Censure John Quincy Adams for Presenting to the House of Representatives a Petition Praying for the Dissolution of the Union. . . .* Washington, D.C.: National Intelligencer, 1842.

Waters, Otis B. "A Christian Colony in Kentucky." *American Missionary,* n.s., 1 (May 1857):104–5.

Webster, Delia A. *Kentucky Jurisprudence: A History of the Trial of Miss Delia A. Webster at Lexington, Kentucky, Dec'r 17–21, 1844. . . .* Vergennes, Vt.: E.W. Blaisdell, 1845.

Webster Kentucky Farm Association. *By-Laws of the Webster Kentucky Farm Association, with a Brief Description of the Origin and Object.* Boston: Rand & Avery, 1858.

Wickliffe, Robert. *Circular of Robert Wickliffe to His Constituents.* N.p., [1841].

————. *A Further Reply of Robert Wickliffe, to the Billingsgate Abuse of Robert Judas Breckenridge, Otherwise Called Robert Jefferson Breckenridge.* Lexington: Kentucky Gazette, 1843.

————. *Reply of Robert Wickliffe, to Robert J. Breckenridge.* Lexington: Observer & Reporter, 1841.

————. *Speech of Robert Wickliffe, Delivered before a Mass Meeting of the Democracy of Kentucky, at the White Sulphur Spring, in the County of Scott, on the Second Day of September, 1843.* Frankfort, Ky.: Wm. Tanner, [1843].

————. *Speech of Robert Wickliffe, Delivered in the Court House, in Lexington, on Monday, the 10th Day of August, 1840, upon Resigning His Seat as Senator from the County of Fayette, More Especially in Reference to the "Negro Law."* Lexington: Observer & Reporter, 1840.

————. *Speech of Robert Wickliffe in Reply to Rev. R.J. Breckenridge, Delivered in the Court House in Lexington, on Monday, the 9th of November, 1840.* Lexington: Observer & Reporter, 1840.

Wigham, Eliza. *The Anti-Slavery Cause in America and Its Martyrs.* London: A.W. Bennett, 1863.

Wilson, Henry. *History of the Rise and Fall of the Slave Power of America.* 8th ed. 3 vols. Boston: Houghton, Mifflin, 1874.

[Young, John C.] *An Address to the Presbyterians of Kentucky, Proposing a Plan for the Instruction and Emancipation of Their Slaves.* Cincinnati: Taylor & Tracy, 1835.

Young, John C. "President Young on Slavery." *African Repository* 11 (April 1835):119–23.

[————]. *Scriptural Duties of Masters: A Sermon Preached in Danville, Kentucky, in 1846.* New York: American Tract Soc., [1846].

Secondary Sources

Adams, Alice Dana. "The Neglected Period of Anti-Slavery in America (1808–1831)." *Radcliffe College Monographs,* no. 14 (1908).

Allen, Jeffrey Brooke. "'All of Us Are Highly Pleased with the Country': Black and White Kentuckians on Liberian Colonization." *Phylon* 43 (Summer 1982):97–109.

————. "The Debate over Slavery and Race in Antebellum Kentucky: 1792–1850." Ph.D. diss., Northwestern Univ., 1973.

————. "Did Southern Colonizationists Oppose Slavery? Kentucky, 1816–1850 as a Test Case." *Register of the Kentucky Historical Society* 75 (April 1977):92–111.

————. "The Origins of Proslavery Thought in Kentucky, 1792–1799." *Register of the Kentucky Historical Society* 77 (Spring 1979):75–90.

————. "Were Southern White Critics of Slavery Racists? Kentucky and the Upper South, 1791–1824." *Journal of Southern History* 44 (May 1978):169–90.

Appleton, Thomas H., Jr. "An Englishman's Perception of Antebellum Kentucky: The Journal of Thomas Smith, Jr., of Lincolnshire." *Register of the Kentucky Historical Society* 79 (Winter 1981):57–62.

Aptheker, Herbert. *American Negro Slave Revolts.* New York: Columbia Univ. Press, 1943.

Aron, Stephen. *How the West Was Lost: The Transformation of Kentucky from Daniel Boone to Henry Clay.* Baltimore: Johns Hopkins Univ. Press, 1996.

Ash, Stephen V. *Middle Tennessee Society Transformed, 1860–1870: War and Peace in the Upper South.* Baton Rouge: Louisiana State Univ. Press, 1988.

Ashworth, John. *Slavery, Capitalism, and Politics in the Antebellum Republic,* Vol. 1: *Commerce and Compromise, 1820–1860.* Cambridge: Cambridge Univ. Press, 1995.

Ayers, Edward L., and John C. Willis, eds. *The Edge of the South: Life in Nineteenth-Century Virginia.* Charlottesville: Univ. Press of Virginia, 1991.

Baber, George. "Joseph Rogers Underwood, Jurist, Orator and Statesman of Kentucky." *Register of the Kentucky Historical Society* 10 (May 1912):47–54.

Bailey, David T. *Shadow on the Church: Southwestern Evangelical Religion and the Issue of Slavery, 1783–1860.* Ithaca: Cornell Univ. Press, 1985.

Baird, Nancy D. "Asiatic Cholera: Kentucky's First Public Health Instructor." *Filson Club History Quarterly* 48 (October 1974):327–41.

———. "Asiatic Cholera's First Visit to Kentucky: A Study in Panic and Fear." *Filson Club History Quarterly* 48 (July 1974):228–40.

Bancroft, Frederic. *Slave Trading in the Old South.* Baltimore: J.H. Furst, 1931.

Barkan, Elliott R. "The Emergence of a Whig Persuasion: Conservatism, Democratism, and the New York State Whigs." *New York History* 52 (October 1971):367–95.

Barnett, Randy E. "Was Slavery Unconstitutional before the Thirteenth Amendment? Lysander Spooner's Theory of Interpretation." *Pacific Law Journal* 28 (Summer 1997):977–1014.

Barney, Robert Knight. "America's First Turnverein: Commentary in Favor of Louisville, Kentucky." *Journal of Sport History* 11, no. 1 (Spring 1984), 134–37.

———. "German Turners in American Domestic Crisis: Jahnistic Ideals in Clash with Southern Sentiment during the Antebellum and Civil War Periods." *Stadion* 4 (1978):344–57.

Bartlett, Irving H. *Wendell Phillips: Brahmin Radical.* Boston: Beacon, 1961.

Barton, Keith C. "'Good Cooks and Washers': Slave Hiring, Domestic Labor, and the Market in Bourbon County, Kentucky." *Journal of American History* 84 (September 1997):436–60.

Bennett, Charles R. "All Things to All People: The American Colonization Society in Kentucky, 1829–1860." Ph.D. diss., Univ. of Kentucky, 1980.

Beringer, Richard E., et al. *Why the South Lost the Civil War.* Athens: Univ. of Georgia Press, 1986.

Berlin, Ira. *Many Thousands Gone: The First Two Centuries of Slavery in North America.* Cambridge: Harvard Univ. Press, 1998.

———. *Slaves without Masters: The Free Negro in the Antebellum South.* New York: Pantheon, 1974.

Berlin, Ira, and Herbert G. Gutman. "Natives and Immigrants, Free Men and Slaves: Urban Workingmen in the American South." *American Historical Review* 88 (December 1983):1175–1200.

Biographical Cyclopedia of the Commonwealth of Kentucky. Chicago: John M. Gresham, 1896; reprint ed., Easley, S.C.: Southern Hist. Press, 1980.

Biographical Directory of the American Congress, 1774–1971. Washington, D.C.: GPO, 1971.

Biographical Encyclopaedia of Kentucky of the Dead and Living Men of the Nineteenth Century. Cincinnati: J.M. Armstrong, 1878; reprint ed., Easley, S.C.: Southern Hist. Press, 1980.

Blassingame, John W. *The Slave Community: Plantation Life in the Antebellum South.* Rev. ed. New York: Oxford Univ. Press, 1979.

Blue, Frederick J. *The Free Soilers: Third Party Politics, 1848–54.* Urbana: Univ. of Illinois Press, 1973.

Boorstin, Daniel J. *The Americans: The National Experience.* New York: Random House, 1965.

Brown, Thomas. *Politics and Statesmanship: Essays on the Whig Party.* New York: Columbia Univ. Press, 1985.

Bruce, Helm. "The Constitution and Constitutional Convention of 1849." *Proceedings of the Kentucky State Bar Association* (1918), 131–62.

Burckin, Alexander Irwin. "The Formation and Growth of an Urban Middle Class: Power and Conflict in Louisville, Kentucky, 1828–1861." Ph.D. diss., Univ. of California, Irvine, 1993.

Burnside, Jacqueline G. "Suspicion versus Faith: Negro Criticisms of Berea College in the Nineteenth Century." *Register of the Kentucky Historical Society* 83 (Summer 1985):237–66.

Ceplair, Larry. "Mattie Griffith Browne: A Kentucky Abolitionist." *Filson Club History Quarterly* 68 (April 1994):219–31.

Chamberlain, Oscar B. "The Evolution of State Constitutions in the Antebellum United States: Michigan, Kentucky, and Mississippi." Ph.D. diss., Univ. of South Carolina, 1996.

Channing, Steven A. *Kentucky: A Bicentennial History.* New York: Norton, 1977.

Cimprich, John. *Slavery's End in Tennessee, 1861–1865.* University, Ala.: Univ. of Alabama Press, 1985.

Clark, Thomas D. *A History of Kentucky.* Lexington: John Bradford, 1960.

———. "The Slave Trade between Kentucky and the Cotton Kingdom." *Mississippi Valley Historical Review* 21 (December 1934):331–42.

Clarke, Grace Julian. *George W. Julian.* Indiana Historical Collections, vol. 11. Indianapolis: Indiana Hist. Commission, 1923.

Cohen, William. "Thomas Jefferson and the Problem of Slavery." *Journal of American History* 56 (December 1969):503–26.

Cole, Charles C., Jr. "The Free Church Movement in New York City." *New York History* 34 (July 1953):284–97.

Coleman, J. Winston, Jr. "Delia Webster and Calvin Fairbank—Underground Railroad Agents." *Filson Club History Quarterly* 17 (July 1943):129–42.

———. "Henry Clay, Kentucky and Liberia." *Register of the Kentucky Historical Society* 45 (October 1947):309–22.

———. "The Kentucky Colonization Society." *Register of the Kentucky Historical Society* 39 (January 1941):1–9.

———. "Lexington's Slave Dealers and Their Southern Trade." *Filson Club History Quarterly* 12 (January 1938):1–23.

———. *Slavery Times in Kentucky.* Chapel Hill: Univ. of North Carolina Press, 1940.

Cooper, William J., Jr. *Liberty and Slavery: Southern Politics to 1860.* New York: Knopf, 1983.

———. *The South and the Politics of Slavery, 1828–1856.* Baton Rouge: Louisiana State Univ. Press, 1978.

Coulter, E. Merton. *The Civil War and Readjustment in Kentucky.* Chapel Hill: Univ. of North Carolina Press, 1926.

Cover, Robert M. *Justice Accused: Antislavery and the Judicial Process.* New Haven: Yale Univ. Press, 1975.

Coward, Joan Wells. *Kentucky in the New Republic: The Process of Constitution Making.* Lexington: Univ. Press of Kentucky, 1979.

Crofts, Daniel W. *Reluctant Confederates: Upper South Unionists in the Secession Crisis.* Chapel Hill: Univ. of North Carolina Press, 1989.

Curry, Leonard P. *Rail Routes South: Louisville's Fight for the Southern Market, 1865–1872.* Lexington: Univ. of Kentucky Press, 1969.

Davies, P. Albert. "Charles Wilkins Short, 1794–1863: Botanist and Physician." *Filson Club History Quarterly* 19 (July 1945):131–55; (October 1945):208–49.

Davis, David B. *The Problem of Slavery in Western Culture.* Ithaca: Cornell Univ. Press, 1966.

————. *Slavery and Human Progress.* New York: Oxford Univ. Press, 1984.

De Boer, Clara Merritt. "The Role of Afro-Americans in the Origin and Work of the American Missionary Association: 1839–1877." Ph.D. diss., Rutgers Univ., 1973.

Degler, Carl N. *The Other South: Southern Dissenters in the Nineteenth Century.* New York: Harper & Row, 1974.

————. "The Peculiar Dissent of the Nineteenth Century South." In Alfred F. Young, ed. *Dissent: Explorations in the History of American Radicalism,* 109–35. De Kalb: Northern Illinois Univ. Press, 1968.

————. "Racism in the United States." *Journal of Southern History* 38 (February 1972):101–8.

Dictionary of American Biography. 25 vols. New York: Scribner's, 1932.

Dietzman, Richard P. "The Four Constitutions of Kentucky." *Kentucky Law Journal* 15 (January 1927):116–27.

Dillon, Merton L. *The Abolitionists: The Growth of a Dissenting Minority.* De Kalb: Northern Illinois Univ. Press, 1974.

————. *Slavery Attacked: Southern Slaves and Their Allies, 1619–1865.* Baton Rouge: Louisiana State Univ. Press, 1990.

————. "Three Southern Antislavery Editors: The Myth of the Southern Antislavery Movement." *Publications of the East Tennessee Historical Society,* no. 42 (1970), 47–56.

Dodge, Mary A. [Gail Hamilton]. *Biography of James G. Blaine.* Norwich, Conn.: Henry Bill, 1895.

Donald, David. "The Proslavery Argument Reconsidered." *Journal of Southern History* 37 (February 1971):3–16.

Dorris, Jonathan T. "Major Squire Turner: Lawyer, Statesman, and Economist." *Filson Club History Quarterly* 25 (January 1951):33–50.

Drake, Richard B. *One Apostle Was a Lumberman: John G. Hanson and Berea's Founding Generation.* Berea, Ky.: Berea Clg. Press, 1975.

Dubofsky, Melvin. "Daniel Webster and the Whig Theory of Economic Growth: 1828–1848." *New England Quarterly* 42 (December 1969):551–72.

Dunaway, Wilma A. "Diaspora, Death, and Sexual Exploitation: Slave Families at Risk in the Mountain South." *Appalachian Journal* 26 (Winter 1999):128–49.

————. "Put in Master's Pocket: Cotton Expansion and Interstate Slave Trading in the Mountain South." In John Inscoe, ed. *Appalachians and Race: The Mountain South from Slavery to Segregation,* 116–32. Lexington: Univ. Press of Kentucky, 2001.

Dunn, Durwood. *An Abolitionist in the Appalachian South: Ezekiel Birdseye on Slavery,*

Capitalism, and Separate Statehood in East Tennessee, 1841–1846. Knoxville: Univ. of Tennessee Press, 1997.

Dyer, Brainerd. "The Persistence of the Idea of Colonization." *Pacific Historical Review* 12 (March 1943):53–65.

Eaton, Clement. *The Freedom-of-Thought Struggle in the Old South*. Rev. ed. New York: Harper & Row, 1964; paperback ed., 1964.

———. *Henry Clay and the Art of American Politics*. Boston: Little, Brown, 1957.

———. "Slave-Hiring in the Upper South: A Step Toward Freedom." *Mississippi Valley Historical Review* 46 (March 1960):663–78.

Elkins, Stanley M. *Slavery: A Problem in American Institutional and Intellectual Life*. Chicago: Univ. of Chicago Press, 1959.

Ellis, William E., Henry Esli Everman, and Richard D. Sears. *Madison County: Two Hundred Years in Retrospect*. N.p.: Madison County Hist. Soc., 1985.

Embree, Edwin Rogers. "A Kentucky Crusader." *American Mercury* 24 (September 1931):98–107.

English, Philip Wesley. "John G. Fee: Kentucky Spokesman for Abolition and Educational Reform." Ph.D. diss., Indiana Univ., 1973.

Fairman, Charles. *Mr. Justice Miller and the Supreme Court, 1862–1890*. Cambridge: Harvard Univ. Press, 1939.

Farrelly, David G. "Harlan's Formative Period: The Years before the War." *Kentucky Law Journal* 46 (Spring 1958):367–406.

Faust, Burton. "The History of Saltpetre Mining in Mammoth Cave, Kentucky." *Filson Club History Quarterly* 41 (January 1967):5–20; (April 1967):127–40; (July 1967):227–62; (October 1967):323–52.

Faust, Drew Gilpin, ed. *The Ideology of Slavery: Proslavery Thought in the Antebellum South, 1830–1860*. Baton Rouge: Louisiana State Univ. Press, 1981.

Fields, Barbara J. *Slavery and Freedom on the Middle Ground: Maryland in the Nineteenth Century*. New Haven: Yale Univ. Press, 1985.

Fields, Carl Richmon. "Making Kentucky's Third Constitution, 1830–1850." Ph.D. diss., Univ. of Kentucky, 1951.

Finnie, Gordon E. "The Antislavery Movement in the South: Its Rise and Decline and Its Contribution to Abolitionism in the West." Ph.D. diss., Duke Univ., 1962.

———. "The Antislavery Movement in the Upper South before 1840." *Journal of Southern History* 35 (August 1969):319–42.

Fladeland, Betty. *James Gillespie Birney: Slaveholder to Abolitionist*. Ithaca: Cornell Univ. Press, 1955.

Foner, Eric. *Free Soil, Free Labor, Free Men: The Ideology of the Republican Party before the Civil War*. New York: Oxford Univ. Press, 1970.

Ford, Lacy K., Jr. *Origins of Southern Radicalism: The South Carolina Upcountry, 1800–1860*. New York: Oxford Univ. Press, 1988.

Foster, Gaines M. "Guilt over Slavery: A Historiographical Analysis." *Journal of Southern History* 56 (November 1990):665–94.

Franklin, John Hope, and Loren Schweninger. *Runaway Slaves: Rebels on the Plantation*. New York: Oxford Univ. Press, 1999.

Fredrickson, George M. *The Black Image in the White Mind: The Debate on Afro-American Character and Destiny, 1817–1914*. New York: Harper & Row, 1971.

Freehling, Alison Goodyear. *Drift toward Dissolution: The Virginia Slavery Debate of 1831–1832*. Baton Rouge: Louisiana State Univ. Press, 1982.

Freehling, William W. "The Founding Fathers and Slavery." *American Historical Review* 77 (February 1972):81–93.

———. *Prelude to Civil War: The Nullification Controversy in South Carolina, 1816–1836.* New York: Harper & Row, 1966.

———. *The Reintegration of American History: Slavery and the Civil War.* New York: Oxford Univ. Press, 1994.

———. *The Road to Disunion: Secessionists at Bay, 1776–1854.* New York: Oxford Univ. Press, 1990.

———. *The South vs. The South: How Anti-Confederate Southerners Shaped the Course of the Civil War.* New York: Oxford Univ. Press, 2001.

Friedman, Lawrence J. *Gregarious Saints: Self and Community in American Abolitionism, 1830–1870.* Cambridge: Cambridge Univ. Press, 1982.

———. *Inventors of the Promised Land.* New York: Knopf, 1975.

Gara, Larry. "The Fugitive Slave Law in the Eastern Ohio Valley." *Ohio History* 73 (April 1963):116–28.

———. *The Liberty Line: The Legend of the Underground Railroad.* Lexington: Univ. of Kentucky Press, 1961.

Genovese, Eugene D. *A Consuming Fire: The Fall of the Confederacy in the Mind of the White Christian South.* Athens: Univ. of Georgia Press, 1998.

———. *The Political Economy of Slavery: Studies in the Economy and Society of the South.* New York: Pantheon, 1965.

———. *Roll, Jordan, Roll: The World the Slaves Made.* New York: Pantheon, 1974.

———. *The Slaveholders' Dilemma: Freedom and Progress in Southern Conservative Thought, 1820–1860.* Columbia: Univ. of South Carolina Press, 1992.

———. *The World the Slaveholders Made: Two Essays in Interpretation.* New York: Pantheon, 1969.

Gilliam, Will D., Jr. "Kansas and Slavery in Two Lexington, Kentucky, Newspapers—1857." *Register of the Kentucky Historical Society* 49 (July 1951):225–30.

———. "The Lexington Press on the Compromise of 1850." *Register of the Kentucky Historical Society* 49 (January 1951):48–54.

———. "Robert J. Breckinridge: Kentucky Unionist." *Register of the Kentucky Historical Society* 69 (October 1971):362–85.

———. "Robert Jefferson Breckinridge, 1800–1871." *Register of the Kentucky Historical Society* 72 (July 1974):207–23; (October 1974):319–36.

———. "Robert Perkins Letcher: Whig Governor of Kentucky." *Filson Club History Quarterly* 24 (January 1950):6–27.

Goldin, Claudia Dale. *Urban Slavery in the American South, 1820–1860: A Quantitative History.* Chicago: Univ. of Chicago Press, 1976.

Gollar, C. Walker. "Catholic Slaves and Slaveholders in Kentucky." *Catholic Historical Review* 84 (January 1998):42–63.

Goodman, Paul. *Of One Blood: Abolitionism and the Origins of Racial Equality.* Berkeley: Univ. of California Press, 1998.

Green, Fletcher M. "Northern Missionary Activities in the South, 1846–1861." *Journal of Southern History* 21 (May 1955):147–72.

Greenberg, Kenneth S. *Masters and Statesmen: The Political Culture of American Slavery.* Baltimore: Johns Hopkins Univ. Press, 1985.

Gregory, James P. "The Question of Slavery in the Kentucky Constitution of 1849." *Filson Club History Quarterly* 23 (April 1949):89–110.

Griffin, Clifford S. "The Abolitionists and the Benevolent Societies, 1831–1861." *Journal of Negro History* 44 (July 1959):195–216.

Groves, Walter A. "Centre College—The Second Phase, 1830–1857." *Filson Club History Quarterly* 24 (October 1950):311–34.

Gutman, Herbert G. *The Black Family in Slavery and Freedom, 1750–1925.* New York: Pantheon, 1976.

Hall, Betty Jean, and Richard Allen Heckman. "Berea's First Decade." *Filson Club History Quarterly* 42 (October 1968):323–39.

Harrison, Lowell H. "The Anti-Slavery Career of Cassius M. Clay." *Register of the Kentucky Historical Society* 59 (October 1961):295–317.

———. *The Antislavery Movement in Kentucky.* Lexington: Univ. Press of Kentucky, 1978.

———. "Cassius Marcellus Clay and the *True American.*" *Filson Club History Quarterly* 22 (January 1948):30–49.

———. "Memories of Slavery Days in Kentucky." *Filson Club History Quarterly* 47 (July 1973):242–57.

Harrold, Stanley C., Jr. *The Abolitionists and the South, 1831–1861.* Lexington: Univ. Press of Kentucky, 1995.

———. "Cassius M. Clay on Slavery and Race: A Reinterpretation." *Slavery & Abolition* 9 (May 1988):42–56.

———. "The Intersectional Relationship between Cassius M. Clay and the Garrisonian Abolitionists." *Civil War History* 35 (June 1989):101–19.

———. "The Southern Strategy of the Liberty Party." *Ohio History* 87 (Winter 1978):21–36.

———. "Violence and Nonviolence in Kentucky Abolitionism." *Journal of Southern History* 57 (February 1991):15–38.

Hart, H.L.A. "Blackstone's Use of the Law of Nature." *Butterworths South African Law Review* 3 (1956):169–74.

Hesseltine, William B. "Some New Aspects of the Pro-Slavery Argument." *Journal of Negro History* 21 (January 1936):1–14.

Hickin, Patricia. "Gentle Agitator: Samuel M. Janney and the Antislavery Movement in Virginia, 1842–1851." *Journal of Southern History* 37 (May 1971):159–90.

———. "John C. Underwood and the Antislavery Movement in Virginia, 1847–1860." *Virginia Magazine of History and Biography* 73 (April 1965):156–68.

Hill, Carol A., and Duane DePaepe. "Saltpeter Mining in Kentucky Caves." *Register of the Kentucky Historical Society* 77 (Autumn 1979):247–62.

Holt, Michael. *The Political Crisis of the 1850s.* New York: Oxford Univ. Press, 1978.

Hopkins, James F. *A History of the Hemp Industry in Kentucky.* Lexington: Univ. of Kentucky Press, 1951.

Howard, Victor B. *Black Liberation in Kentucky: Emancipation and Freedom, 1862–1884.* Lexington: Univ. Press of Kentucky, 1983.

———. "The Black Testimony Controversy in Kentucky, 1866–1872." *Journal of Negro History* 58 (April 1973):140–65.

———. "The Breckinridge Family and the Negro Testimony Controversy in Kentucky, 1866–1872." *Filson Club History Quarterly* 49 (January 1975):37–56.

———. "Cassius M. Clay and the Origins of the Republican Party." *Filson Club History Quarterly* 45 (January 1971):49–71.

———. *The Evangelical War against Slavery and Caste: The Life and Times of John G. Fee.* Selinsgrove, Pa.: Susquehanna Univ. Press, 1996.

————. "James Madison Pendleton: A Southern Crusader against Slavery." *Register of the Kentucky Historical Society* 74 (July 1976):192–215.

————. "The Kentucky Presbyterians in 1849: Slavery and the Kentucky Constitution." *Register of the Kentucky Historical Society* 73 (July 1975):217–40.

————. "Robert J. Breckinridge and the Slavery Controversy in Kentucky in 1849." *Filson Club History Quarterly* 53 (October 1979):328–43.

Howe, Daniel Walker. *The Political Culture of the American Whigs.* Chicago: Univ. of Chicago Press, 1979.

Hyman, Harold M., and William M. Wiecek. *Equal Justice under Law: Constitutional Development, 1835–1875.* New York: Harper & Row, 1982.

Inscoe, John C. *Mountain Masters, Slavery, and the Sectional Crisis in Western North Carolina.* Knoxville: Univ. of Tennessee Press, 1989.

Ireland, Robert M. "Aristocrats All: The Politics of County Government in Ante-bellum Kentucky." *Review of Politics* 32 (July 1970):365–83.

————. *The County Courts in Antebellum Kentucky.* Lexington: Univ. Press of Kentucky, 1972.

Jenkins, William Sumner. *Pro-Slavery Thought in the Old South.* Chapel Hill: Univ. of North Carolina Press, 1935; reprint ed., Gloucester, Mass.: Peter Smith, 1960.

Johnson, Clifton H. "John Gregg Fee: Kentucky Abolitionist." *Crisis* 79 (March 1972):91–94.

Johnson, Michael P., and James L. Roark. *Black Masters: A Free Family of Color in the Old South.* New York: Norton, 1984.

Johnson, Paul E. *A Shopkeeper's Millennium: Society and Revivals in Rochester, New York, 1815–1837.* New York: Hill & Wang, 1978.

Johnson, Walter. *Soul by Soul: Life inside the Antebellum Slave Market.* Cambridge: Harvard Univ. Press, 1999.

Jones, Thomas B. "Henry Clay and Continental Expansion, 1820–1844." *Register of the Kentucky Historical Society* 73 (July 1975):241–62.

Julian, George W. "The First Republican National Convention." *American Historical Review* 4 (January 1899):313–22.

Keith, Jean E. "Joseph Rogers Underwood: Friend of African Colonization." *Filson Club History Quarterly* 22 (April 1948):117–32.

Kettner, James H. *The Development of American Citizenship, 1608–1870.* Chapel Hill: Univ. of North Carolina Press, 1978.

Kilby, Clyde S. *Minority of One: The Biography of Jonathan Blanchard.* Grand Rapids: Eerdmans, 1959.

Kirwan, Albert D. *John J. Crittenden: The Struggle for the Union.* Lexington: Univ. of Kentucky Press, 1962.

Klotter, James C. "The Black South and White Appalachia." *Journal of American History* 66 (March 1980):832–49.

————. *The Breckinridges of Kentucky, 1760–1981.* Lexington: Univ. Press of Kentucky, 1986.

————. "Slavery and Race: A Family Perspective." *Southern Studies* 17 (Winter 1978):375–97.

Knupfer, Peter B. *The Union as It Is: Constitutional Unionism and Sectional Compromise, 1787–1861.* Chapel Hill: Univ. of North Carolina Press, 1991.

Kohl, Lawrence F. *The Politics of Individualism: Parties and the American Character in the Jacksonian Era.* New York: Oxford Univ. Press, 1989.

Kraditor, Aileen S. *Means and Ends in American Abolitionism: Garrison and His Critics on Strategy and Tactics, 1834–1850.* New York: Pantheon, 1969.

Kuykendall, John Wells. "'Southern Enterprize': The Work of National Evangelical Societies in the Antebellum South." Ph.D. diss., Princeton Univ., 1975.

Lamb, Robert Paul. "James G. Birney and the Road to Abolitionism." *Alabama Review* 47 (April 1994):83–134.

Litwack, Leon. *North of Slavery: The Negro in the Free States, 1790–1860.* Chicago: Univ. of Chicago Press, 1961.

Long, Byron R. "Joshua Reed Giddings: A Champion of Political Freedom." *Ohio Archaeological and Historical Quarterly* 28 (January 1919):1–47.

Lucas, Marion B. "Camp Nelson, Kentucky, during the Civil War: Cradle of Liberty or Refugee Death Camp?" *Filson Club History Quarterly* 63 (October 1989):439–52.

Lucas, Marion B., and George C. Wright. *A History of Blacks in Kentucky.* 2 vols. Frankfort, Ky.: Kentucky Hist. Soc., 1992. Vol. 1: *From Slavery to Segregation, 1760–1891,* by Marion B. Lucas.

Lucas, Paul. "*Ex Parte* Sir William Blackstone, 'Plagiarist': A Note on Blackstone and the Natural Law." *American Journal of Legal History* 7 (April 1963):142–58.

Mabee, Carleton. *Black Freedom: The Nonviolent Abolitionists from 1830 through the Civil War.* New York: Macmillan, 1970.

Malberg, Edward I. "The Republican Party in Kentucky, 1856–1867." M.A. thesis, Univ. of Kentucky, 1967.

Mallalieu, William C., and Sabri M. Akural. "Kentucky Banks in the Crisis Decade: 1834–1844." *Register of the Kentucky Historical Society* 65 (October 1967):294–303.

Maness, Lonnie E. "Henry Clay and the Problem of Slavery." Ph.D. diss., Memphis State Univ., 1980.

Marsden, George M. *The Evangelical Mind and the New School Presbyterian Experience: A Case Study of Thought and Theology in Nineteenth-Century America.* New Haven: Yale Univ. Press, 1970.

Martin, Asa E. "The Anti-Slavery Movement in Kentucky Prior to 1850." *Filson Club Publications,* no. 29 (1918).

Mathews, Donald G. *Slavery and Methodism: A Chapter in American Morality, 1780–1845.* Princeton: Princeton Univ. Press, 1965; reprint ed., Westport, Conn.: Greenwood, 1978.

Mathias, Frank F. "Kentucky's Struggle for Common Schools, 1820–1850." *Register of the Kentucky Historical Society* 82 (Summer 1984):214–34.

———. "Kentucky's Third Constitution: A Restriction of Majority Rule." *Register of the Kentucky Historical Society* 75 (January 1977):1–19.

———. "Slavery, the Solvent of Kentucky Politics." *Register of the Kentucky Historical Society* 70 (January 1972):1–16.

Mayse, Edgar Caldwell. "Robert Jefferson Breckinridge: American Presbyterian Controversialist." Ph.D. diss., Union Theological Seminary, 1974.

McColley, Robert. *Slavery and Jeffersonian Virginia.* 2d ed. Urbana: Univ. of Illinois Press, 1973.

McCurry, Stephanie. *Masters of Small Worlds: Yeoman Households, Gender Relations, and the Political Culture of the Antebellum South Carolina Low Country.* New York: Oxford Univ. Press, 1995.

McDougle, Ivan E. *Slavery in Kentucky, 1792–1865.* Lancaster, Pa.: New Era, 1918; reprint ed., Westport, Conn.: Negro Univs. Press, 1970.

McGann, Agnes Geraldine. *Nativism in Kentucky to 1860.* Washington, D.C.: Catholic Univ. of America, 1944.

McKivigan, John R. "The American Baptist Free Mission Society: Abolitionist Reaction to the 1845 Baptist Schism." *Foundations* 21 (October/December 1978):340–55.

————. "The Antislavery 'Comeouter' Sects: A Neglected Dimension of the Abolitionist Movement." *Civil War History* 26 (June 1980):142–60.

————. "The Christian Anti-Slavery Convention Movement of the Northwest." *Old Northwest* 8 (Winter 1979–80):345–66.

————. "The Gospel Will Burst the Bonds of the Slave: The Abolitionists Bibles for Slaves Campaign." *Negro History Bulletin* 45 (July/August/September 1982):62–64, 77.

McPherson, James M. *The Abolitionist Legacy: From Reconstruction to the NAACP.* Princeton: Princeton Univ. Press, 1975.

————. *The Struggle for Equality: Abolitionists and the Negro in the Civil War and Reconstruction.* Princeton: Princeton Univ. Press, 1964.

Melish, Joanne Pope. *Disowning Slavery: Gradual Emancipation and "Race" in New England, 1780–1860.* Ithaca: Cornell Univ. Press, 1998.

Merrill, Walter M. *Against Wind and Tide: A Biography of William Lloyd Garrison.* Cambridge: Harvard Univ. Press, 1963.

Meyer, Leland Winfield. *Georgetown College: Its Background and a Chapter in its Early History.* Louisville: Western Recorder, 1929.

Meyers, Marvin. *The Jacksonian Persuasion: Politics and Belief.* Stanford: Stanford Univ. Press, 1957.

Middleton, Stephen. "Law and Ideology in Ohio and Kentucky: The Kidnapping of Jerry Phinney." *Filson Club History Quarterly* 67 (July 1993):347–72.

Miers, Earl Schenck, gen. ed. *Lincoln Day by Day: A Chronology, 1809–1865.* 3 vols. Washington, D.C.: Lincoln Sesquicentennial Commission, 1960. Vol. 2: *1849–1860,* by William E. Baringer.

Miller, John Chester. *The Wolf by the Ears: Thomas Jefferson and Slavery.* New York: Free Press, 1977.

Miller, Randall M., and John David Smith, eds. *Dictionary of Afro-American Slavery.* New York: Greenwood, 1988.

Miller, Rex. "John Thomas Croxton: Scholar, Lawyer, Soldier, Military Governor, Newspaperman, Diplomat and Mason." *Register of the Kentucky Historical Society* 74 (October 1976):281–99.

Moore, Edmund A. "Robert J. Breckinridge and the Slavery Aspect of the Presbyterian Schism." *Church History* 4 (December 1935):282–94.

Moore, John L., ed. *Congressional Quarterly's Guide to U.S. Elections.* 2d ed. Washington, D.C.: Congressional Quarterly, 1985.

Morrison, Toni. *Beloved.* New York: Knopf, 1987.

Morrow, Ralph E. "The Proslavery Argument Revisited." *Mississippi Valley Historical Review* 48 (June 1961):79–94.

Murphy, James B. "Slavery and Freedom in Appalachia: Kentucky as a Demographic Case Study." *Register of the Kentucky Historical Society* 80 (Spring 1982):151–69.

Nelson, Paul David. "Experiment in Interracial Education at Berea College, 1858–1908." *Journal of Negro History* 59 (January 1974):13–27.

Nelson, William E. "The Impact of the Antislavery Movement Upon Styles of Judicial Reasoning in Nineteenth Century America." *Harvard Law Review* 87 (January 1974):513–66.

Norton, Wesley. "Reaction in the Religious Press to the Campaign for Delegates to the Kentucky Constitutional Convention in 1849." *Register of the Kentucky Historical Society* 60 (April 1962):143–52.

Oakes, James. *The Ruling Race: A History of American Slaveholders.* New York: Knopf, 1982.

————. *Slavery and Freedom: An Interpretation of the Old South.* New York: Knopf, 1990.

Oates, Stephen B. *To Purge This Land with Blood: A Biography of John Brown.* New York: Harper & Row, 1970.

Paine, Christopher M. "'Kentucky Will Be the Last to Give Up the Union': Kentucky Politics, 1844–1861." Ph.D. diss., Univ. of Kentucky, 1998.

Parker, Harold M., Jr. "A New School Presbyterian Seminary in Woodford County." *Register of the Kentucky Historical Society* 74 (April 1976):99–111.

————. "The New School Synod of Kentucky." *Filson Club History Quarterly* 50, no. 2 (April 1976), 52–89.

Pease, Jane H., and William H. Pease. *Bound with Them in Chains: A Biographical History of the Antislavery Movement.* Westport, Conn.: Greenwood, 1972.

Pease, William H., and Jane H. Pease. "Antislavery Ambivalence: Immediatism, Expediency, Race." *American Quarterly* 17 (Winter 1965):682–95.

Peck, Elisabeth S., and Emily Ann Smith. *Berea's First 125 Years, 1855–1980.* Lexington: Univ. Press of Kentucky, 1982.

Perkal, M. Leon. "American Abolition Society: A Viable Alternative to the Republican Party?" *Journal of Negro History* 65 (Winter 1980):57–71.

Perry, Lewis. *Radical Abolitionism: Anarchy and the Government of God in Antislavery Thought.* Ithaca: Cornell Univ. Press, 1973.

Phillips, Ulrich Bonnell. *American Negro Slavery: A Survey of the Supply, Employment and Control of Negro Labor as Determined by the Plantation Regime.* New York: Appleton, 1918.

————. "The Central Theme of Southern History." *American Historical Review* 34 (October 1928):30–43.

Posner, Richard A. "Blackstone and Bentham." *Journal of Law and Economics* 19 (October 1976):569–606.

Post, Edward M. "Kentucky Law Concerning Emancipation or Freedom of Slaves." *Filson Club History Quarterly* 59 (July 1985):344–67.

Priest, Nancy L. "Joseph Rogers Underwood: Nineteenth Century Kentucky Orator." *Register of the Kentucky Historical Society* 75 (October 1977):286–303.

Purifoy, Lewis M., Jr. "The Methodist Episcopal Church, South, and Slavery, 1844–1865." Ph.D. diss., Univ. of North Carolina at Chapel Hill, 1965.

Ramage, Andrea S. "Bluegrass Patriarch: Robert Wickliffe and His Family in Antebellum Kentucky." M.A. thesis, Univ. of Kentucky, 1993.

————. "Love and Honor: The Robert Wickliffe Family of Antebellum Kentucky." *Register of the Kentucky Historical Society* 94 (Spring 1996):115–33.

Reilly, Timothy F. "Robert L. Stanton: Abolitionist of the Old South." *Journal of Presbyterian History* 53 (Spring 1975):33–49.

Remini, Robert V. *Henry Clay: Statesman for the Union*. New York: Norton, 1991.

Reynolds, Todd Armstrong. "The American Missionary Association's Antislavery Campaign in Kentucky, 1848 to 1860." Ph.D. diss., Ohio State Univ., 1979.

Rice, Otis K. "Eli Thayer and the Friendly Invasion of Virginia." *Journal of Southern History* 37 (November 1971):575–96.

Riddleberger, Patrick W. *George Washington Julian, Radical Republican: A Study in Nineteenth-Century Politics and Reform*. Indiana Historical Collections, vol. 45. N.p.: Indiana Hist. Bureau, 1966.

Roberts, Clarence N. "The Crusade against Secret Societies and the National Christian Association." *Journal of the Illinois State Historical Society* 64 (Winter 1971):382–400.

Rosenberg, Charles E. *The Cholera Years: The United States in 1832, 1849, and 1866*. Chicago: Univ. of Chicago Press, 1962.

Ross, Michael A. "Hill-Country Doctor: The Early Life and Career of Supreme Court Justice Samuel F. Miller in Kentucky, 1816–1849." *Filson Club History Quarterly* 71 (October 1997):430–62.

Rugoff, Milton. *The Beechers: An American Family in the Nineteenth Century*. New York: Harper & Row, 1981.

Runyon, Randolph Paul. *Delia Webster and the Underground Railroad*. Lexington: Univ. Press of Kentucky, 1996.

Sandlund, Vivien. "Robert Breckinridge: Presbyterian Antislavery Conservative." *Journal of Presbyterian History* 78 (Summer 2000):145–54.

Schwarz, Philip J. *Migrants against Slavery: Virginians and the Nation*. Charlottesville: Univ. Press of Virginia, 2001.

Sears, Richard D. *The Day of Small Things: Abolitionism in the Midst of Slavery, Berea, Kentucky, 1854–1864*. Lanham, Md.: Univ. Press of America, 1986.

———. "John G. Fee, Camp Nelson, and Kentucky Blacks, 1864–1865." *Register of the Kentucky Historical Society* 85 (Winter 1987):29–45.

———. *The Kentucky Abolitionists in the Midst of Slavery, 1854–1864: Exiles for Freedom*. Lewiston, N.Y.: Mellen, 1993.

———. *"A Practical Recognition of the Brotherhood of Man": John G. Fee and the Camp Nelson Experience*. Berea, Ky.: Berea Clg. Press, 1986.

———. *A Utopian Experiment in Kentucky: Integration and Social Equality at Berea, 1866–1904*. Westport, Conn.: Greenwood, 1996.

———. "Working Like a Slave: Views of Slavery and the Status of Women in Antebellum Kentucky." *Register of the Kentucky Historical Society* 87 (Winter 1989):1–19.

Sellers, Charles G., Jr. "The Travail of Slavery." In Charles G. Sellers, ed. *The Southerner as American*, 40–71. Chapel Hill: Univ. of North Carolina Press, 1969.

Sherwood, John C. "One Flame in the Inferno: The Legend of Marshall's 'Crosswhite Affair.'" *Michigan History* 73 (March/April 1989):40–47.

Shick, Tom W. "A Quantitative Analysis of Liberian Colonization from 1820 to 1843 with Special Reference to Mortality." *Journal of African History* 12 (1971):45–59.

Siegel, Carolyn Lee. *White Hall: The Clay Estate*. N.p., 1985.

Silverman, Jason H. "Kentucky, Canada, and Extradition: The Jesse Happy Case." *Filson Club History Quarterly* 54 (January 1980):50–60.

Sinha, Manisha. *The Counterrevolution of Slavery: Politics and Ideology in Antebellum South Carolina*. Chapel Hill: Univ. of North Carolina Press, 2000.

Skaggs, Deborah Susan. "Charles Wilkins Short: Kentucky Botanist and Physician, 1794–1863." M.A. thesis, Univ. of Louisville, 1982.

Smiley, David L. "Cassius M. Clay and John G. Fee: A Study in Southern Anti-Slavery Thought." *Journal of Negro History* 42 (July 1957):201–13.
——. "Cassius M. Clay and Southern Industrialism." *Filson Club History Quarterly* 28 (October 1954):315–27.
——. *Lion of White Hall: The Life of Cassius M. Clay.* Madison: Univ. of Wisconsin Press, 1962.
Smith, William Henry. *A Political History of Slavery: Being an Account of the Slavery Controversy from the Earliest Agitation in the Eighteenth Century to the Close of the Reconstruction Period in America.* 2 vols. New York: Putnam's, 1903.
Snay, Mitchell. *The Gospel of Disunion: Religion and Separatism in the Antebellum South.* Cambridge: Cambridge Univ. Press, 1993.
Speed, Thomas. "The Political Club, Danville, Kentucky, 1786–1790." *Filson Club Publications,* no. 9 (1894).
Sprague, Stuart Seely. "The Kentucky Pocket Plantation: Sources and Research Strategies; Mason County as a Case Study." *Filson Club History Quarterly* 71 (January 1997):69–86.
Stafford, Hanford Dozier. "Slavery in a Border City: Louisville, 1790–1860." Ph.D. diss., Univ. of Kentucky, 1982.
Staiger, C. Bruce. "Abolitionism and the Presbyterian Schism of 1837–1838." *Mississippi Valley Historical Review* 36 (December 1949):391–414.
Stampp, Kenneth M. "The Fate of the Southern Antislavery Movement." *Journal of Negro History* 28 (January 1943):10–22.
——. *The Peculiar Institution: Slavery in the Ante-Bellum South.* New York: Knopf, 1956.
——. "The Southern Refutation of the Proslavery Argument." *North Carolina Historical Review* 21 (January 1944):35–45.
——. "The Southern Road to Appomattox." In Kenneth M. Stampp. *The Imperiled Union: Essays on the Background of the Civil War,* 246–69. New York: Oxford Univ. Press, 1980.
Starobin, Robert S. *Industrial Slavery in the Old South.* New York: Oxford Univ. Press, 1970.
Staudenraus, Philip J. *The African Colonization Movement, 1816–1865.* New York: Columbia Univ. Press, 1961.
Steckel, Richard H. *The Economics of U.S. Slave and Southern White Fertility.* New York: Garland, 1985.
Steely, Will Frank. "The Antislavery Movement in Kentucky, 1850–1860." Ph.D. diss., Univ. of Rochester, 1956.
——. "The Established Churches and Slavery, 1850–1860." *Register of the Kentucky Historical Society* 55 (April 1957):97–104.
——. "William Shreve Bailey: Kentucky Abolitionist." *Filson Club History Quarterly* 31 (July 1957):274–81.
Stevenson, Brenda E. *Life in Black and White: Family and Community in the Slave South.* New York: Oxford Univ. Press, 1996.
Stewart, James B. "Evangelicalism and the Radical Strain in Southern Antislavery Thought during the 1820s." *Journal of Southern History* 39 (August 1973):379–96.
——. *Holy Warriors: The Abolitionists and American Slavery.* New York: Hill & Wang, 1976.

————. "Politics and Belief in Abolitionism: Stanley Elkins' Concept of Anti-institutionalism and Recent Interpretations of American Antislavery." *South Atlantic Quarterly* 75 (Winter 1976):74–97.

Strassweg, Elga. "The Kidnapping of Horace Bell." *Indiana History Bulletin* 46 (June 1969):105–8.

Streifford, David. "The American Colonization Society: An Application of Republican Ideology to Early Antebellum Reform." *Journal of Southern History* 45 (May 1979):201–20.

Sutch, Richard. "The Breeding of Slaves for Sale and the Westward Expansion of Slavery, 1850–1860." In Stanley L. Engerman and Eugene D. Genovese, eds. *Race and Slavery in the Western Hemisphere: Quantitative Studies,* 173–210. Princeton: Princeton Univ. Press, 1975.

Swinford, Mac. "Mr. Justice Samuel Freeman Miller (1816–1873)." *Filson Club History Quarterly* 34 (January 1960):35–44.

Tadman, Michael. *Speculators and Slaves: Masters, Traders, and Slaves in the Old South.* Madison: Univ. of Wisconsin Press, 1989.

Tallant, Harold Donald, Jr. "The Slavery Controversy in Kentucky, 1829–1859." Ph.D. diss., Duke Univ., 1986.

Talley, William. "Salt Lick Creek and Its Salt Works." *Register of the Kentucky Historical Society* 64 (April 1966):85–109.

Tapp, Hambleton. "Robert J. Breckinridge and the Year 1849." *Filson Club History Quarterly* 12 (July 1938):125–50.

————. "Robert J. Breckinridge during the Civil War." *Filson Club History Quarterly* 11 (April 1937):120–44.

————. "The Slavery Controversy between Robert Wickliffe and Robert J. Breckin-ridge Prior to the Civil War." *Filson Club History Quarterly* 19 (July 1945):156–70.

Taylor, Richard S. "Beyond Immediate Emancipation: Jonathan Blanchard, Abolitionism, and the Emergence of American Fundamentalism." *Civil War History* 27 (September 1981):260–74.

Thomas, John L. *The Liberator: William Lloyd Garrison.* Boston: Little, Brown, 1963.

Tise, Larry E. *Proslavery: A History of the Defense of Slavery in America, 1701–1840.* Athens: Univ. of Georgia Press, 1987.

Titley, Joan. "Dr. Charles Wilkins Short and the Medical Journals: 1820–1831." *Stechert-Hafner Book News* 19 (November 1964):29–31.

Tolbert, Noble J. "Daniel Worth: Tar Heel Abolitionist." *North Carolina Historical Review* 39 (July 1962):284–304.

Townsend, William H. *Lincoln and the Bluegrass: Slavery and Civil War in Kentucky.* Lexington: Univ. of Kentucky Press, 1955.

Troutman, Richard L. "The Emancipation of Slaves by Henry Clay." *Journal of Negro History* 40 (April 1955):179–81.

————. "Henry Clay and His 'Ashland' Estate." *Filson Club History Quarterly* 30 (April 1956):159–74.

Turner, Wallace B. "Abolitionism in Kentucky." *Register of the Kentucky Historical Society* 69 (October 1971):319–38.

————. "Kentucky Slavery in the Last Ante Bellum Decade." *Register of the Kentucky Historical Society* 58 (October 1960):291–307.

————. "Kentucky State Politics in the Early 1850's." *Register of the Kentucky Historical Society* 56 (April 1958):123–42.

Van Deburg, William L. "Henry Clay, the Right of Petition, and Slavery in the Nation's Capital." *Register of the Kentucky Historical Society* 68 (April 1970):132–46.

Van Deusen, Glyndon G. *The Life of Henry Clay.* Boston: Little, Brown, 1937.

Vaughan, William Hutchinson. *Robert Jefferson Breckinridge as an Educational Administrator.* Nashville: George Peabody Clg. for Teachers, 1937.

Volz, Harry August, III. "Party, State, and Nation: Kentucky and the Coming of the American Civil War." Ph.D. diss., Univ. of Virginia, 1982.

Walters, Ronald G. *The Antislavery Appeal: American Abolitionism after 1830.* Baltimore: Johns Hopkins Univ. Press, 1976.

Warford, Malcolm L. "The Making and Unmaking of a Radical Tradition: Berea College, 1855–1904." *Encounter* 38 (Spring 1977):149–61.

———. "Piety, Politics, and Pedagogy: An Evangelical Protestant Tradition in Higher Education at Lane, Oberlin, and Berea, 1834–1904." Ed.D. diss., Columbia Univ., 1973.

Wax, Darold D. "Robert Ball Anderson: A Kentucky Slave, 1843–1864." *Register of the Kentucky Historical Society* 81 (Summer 1983):255–73.

———. "Robert Ball Anderson, Ex-Slave: A Pioneer in Western Nebraska, 1884–1930." *Nebraska History* 64 (Summer 1983):163–92.

Webb, Ross A. "Francis Marion Bristow: A Study in Unionism." *Filson Club History Quarterly* 37 (April 1963):142–58.

Weeks, Louis, III. "Stuart Robinson: Kentucky Presbyterian Leader." *Filson Club History Quarterly* 54 (October 1980):360–77.

Weeks, Stephen B. "Anti-Slavery Sentiment in the South: With Unpublished Letters From John Stuart Mill and Mrs. Stowe." *Publications of the Southern History Association* 2 (April 1898):87–130.

Weisenburger, Steven. *Modern Medea: A Family Story of Slavery and Child-Murder from the Old South.* New York: Hill & Wang, 1998.

Weisert, John J. "Lewis N. Dembitz and *Onkel Tom's Hütte.*" *American-German Review* 19, no. 3 (February 1953), 7–8.

Wiecek, William M. "*Somerset:* Lord Mansfield and the Legitimacy of Slavery in the Anglo-American World." *University of Chicago Law Review* 42 (Fall 1974):86–146.

———. *The Sources of Antislavery Constitutionalism in America, 1760–1848.* Ithaca: Cornell Univ. Press, 1977.

Williams, Gary Lee. "Abraham Lincoln's Closest Friend: Joshua Fry Speed, 1814–1882." M.A. thesis, Duke Univ., 1969.

———. "James and Joshua Speed: Lincoln's Kentucky Friends." Ph.D. diss., Duke Univ., 1971.

Willis, George L., Sr. "History of Kentucky Constitutions and Constitutional Conventions." *Register of the Kentucky Historical Society* 28 (October 1930):305–29; 29 (January 1931):52–81.

Willman, Robert. "Blackstone and the 'Theoretical Perfection' of English Law in the Reign of Charles II." *Historical Journal* 26 (March 1983):39–70.

Wilson, Benjamin C. "Kentucky Kidnappers, Fugitives, and Abolitionists in Antebellum Cass County Michigan." *Michigan History* 60 (Winter 1976):339–58.

Wilson, Major L. *Space, Time, and Freedom: The Quest for Nationality and the Irrepressible Conflict, 1815–1861.* Westport, Conn.: Greenwood, 1974.

Wittke, Carl. *Against the Current: The Life of Karl Heinzen (1809–80).* Chicago: Univ. of Chicago Press, 1945.

————. *The German-Language Press in America.* Lexington: Univ. of Kentucky Press, 1957.

————. *Refugees of Revolution: The German Forty-Eighters in America.* Philadelphia: Univ. of Pennsylvania Press, 1952.

Wood, Gordon S. *The Creation of the American Republic, 1776–1787.* Chapel Hill: Univ. of North Carolina Press, 1969.

Woodman, Harold D. "The Profitability of Slavery: A Historical Perennial." *Journal of Southern History* 29 (August 1963):303–25.

Wyatt-Brown, Bertram. "The Abolitionists' Postal Campaign of 1835." *Journal of Negro History* 50 (October 1965):227–38.

————. *Lewis Tappan and the Evangelical War against Slavery.* Cleveland: Press of Case Western Reserve Univ., 1969.

————. *Southern Honor: Ethics and Behavior in the Old South.* New York: Oxford Univ. Press, 1982.

Young, Amy Lambeck. "Cellars and African-American Slave Sites: New Data from an Upland South Plantation." *Midcontinental Journal of Archaeology* 22 (Spring 1997):95–115.

————. "Risk Management Strategies among African-American Slaves at Locust Grove Plantation." *International Journal of Historical Archaeology* 1 (1997):5–37.

————. "Task and Gang Labor: Work Patterns at a Kentucky Plantation." *North American Archaeologist* 18 (1997):41–66.

Young, Amy Lambeck, Philip J. Carr, and Joseph E. Granger. "How Historical Archaeology Works: A Case Study of Slave Houses at Locust Grove." *Register of the Kentucky Historical Society* 96 (Spring 1998):167–94.

Young, Bennett H. *History and Texts of the Three Constitutions of Kentucky.* Louisville: Courier-Journal Job Printing Company, 1890.

Yzenbaard, John H. "The Crosswhite Case." *Michigan History* 53 (Summer 1969):131–43.

Zilversmit, Arthur. *The First Emancipation: The Abolition of Slavery in the North.* Chicago: Univ. of Chicago Press, 1967.

Zucker, A.E., ed. *The Forty-Eighters: Political Refugees of the German Revolution of 1848.* New York: Columbia Univ. Press, 1950.

Index

abolitionism: and antislavery conservatives, 15, 17, 38, 59–61, 98, 101–5, 110–13, 116, 120–21, 125–28, 139–40, 215; and colonization, 28, 31–32, 40–41, 45, 47, 52; and come-outerism, 174–75, 181; in Kentucky, 19, 21, 91, 96, 111, 124, 163; Lane Seminary debates, 111; mentioned, 7; and necessary-evil theory, 10–11, 21, 169, 190–91; and nonresistance, 203–4; postal campaign of, 111; racial attitudes of, 37, 178–79, 229 n. 21; southern hostility to, 15, 23–24, 44, 96, 146–47, 154; tactics of, 101–2, 193, 261 n. 18. *See also* American Missionary Association; Birney, James Gillespie; emancipation plans: immediate; Fee, John Gregg; Garrison, William Lloyd; Radical Political Abolitionists

Adams, John Quincy, 39

American Abolition Society, 196

American Anti-Slavery Society, 103, 111, 177

American Board of Commissioners for Foreign Missions (ABCFM), 233 n. 50

American Colonization Society (ACS): budget of, 29; and Cassius M. Clay, 119; divisions within, 31–32, 41–42, 54; and Henry Clay, 27; incompetence of, 16; local auxiliaries of, 28–29, 42, 45; officers and agents of, 21, 27–29, 36, 42, 48; patriotism of, 52–53, 56; program of, 31–32, 42, 45; rival programs for black removal, 30, 56, 232 n. 42. *See also* colonization; Kentucky Colonization Society

American Home Missionary Society (AHMS), 169, 172–75, 176, 181

American Missionary, 127

American Missionary Association (AMA): anticaste position of, 176–77; and antisectarianism, 176–77; antislavery position of, 176–177; Bibles for slaves campaign of, 187; colporteurs of, 184–85, 206; formation of, 176; mentioned, 209, 211, 213; schools sponsored by, 185–86, 206, 211; southern mission of, 163, 184–86. *See also* Bereans; Fee, John Gregg

American party, 256 n. 20

American Revolution: and colonization, 53; and concept of constitutional conventions, 108–9; and necessary-evil theory, 11, 224 n. 13; and nonimportation, 92; and

291

Mexican War: Cassius M. Clay's
enlistment in, 123–28, 183;
opposition of Joseph R.
Underwood to, 39, 50; and
sectional controversy, 133
Miller, Samuel Freeman, 158
Missouri Crisis, 133
Mitchell, William D., 157
mob violence: 1849 Louisville
election riot, 147–48; abandoned
by former participants, 211;
assessment of, 216–17; Bereans in
Rockcastle County, 206–8;
Cassius M. Clay at Foxtown, 147,
250 n. 26; expulsion of Bereans,
213–14, 263 n. 40; John G. Fee
and aftermath of Dripping
Springs, 195, 204–6, 261 n. 22;
John G. Fee at Dripping Springs,
194–95; John G. Fee at Lewis
Chapel, 208; John G. Fee in Estill
County, 212–13; John G. Fee in
Laurel County, 207; George
Candee in Pulaski County, 208;
impact of, 194–95, 202–10;
James S. Davis in Mason County,
212; murder of Benedict Austin,
147, 250 n. 26; *True American*,
122–23, 243 n. 15; William
Richardson at Williamsburg, 206.
See also persecution
Monroe, Benjamin, 144–45
Monroe County, Ky., 249 n. 23
Monrovia, Liberia, 54
Morehead, James T., 46, 51–52, 72,
97, 112
Muhlenberg County, Ky., 249 n. 23

National Christian Association, 256
nativism, 161
necessary-evil theory: antislavery
version of, 3, 14–15, 19–21, 38,
57, 112–13, 142–43, 225 n. 16;
and colonization, 18–19, 27–28,
38, 40–41, 46; compared with

abolitionism, 10–11, 21, 169,
190–91; compared with northern
attitudes, 8; compared with
positive-good theory, 7–8, 12, 14,
19, 23–24; at Constitutional
Convention of 1849, 157–58,
252 n. 45; decline of, 3–4, 6–7,
10, 157–58; differences among
supporters of, 19–24; dual nature
of, 14, 225 n. 16; dynamic
quality of, 17; and economics of
slavery, 8–10; effects of, xi, 3, 18–
19; historiography of, 10–11, 224
n. 13, 225 n. 16; impact of
demography and economics on,
8–10, 17, 224 nn. 8, 9; mediates
between conflicting values, 12–
14; and morality of slaveholding,
12–14, 101–2, 225 n. 15; and
nonimportation, 94, 96–97;
promotes compromise, 3–4, 14–
17, 101–2; promotes status quo,
3, 5–6, 13–15, 17–18, 38, 40–
41, 97, 112–13, 151–53, 158,
190–91, 218–19; proslavery
version of, 11, 14, 19–24, 158–
59, 225 n. 16; and racial attitudes, 3–6, 17; survival of, in
Upper South, 1–3, 7, 161–63,
168, 212, 216–18; tenets of, 1–
25. *See also* antislavery conservatives; colonization
Nelson County, Ky., 138, 249 n. 23
New Jersey, 105
Newport, Ky., 132, 134, 149, 162
Newport News, 162
New School Presbyterian Church.
See Presbyterian Church, New
School
New York, N.Y., 103, 126–27
New York (state), 20, 103, 105
Nicholas, Samuel S., 112, 139, 144
Nicholas County, Ky., 108, 249 n. 23
nonimportation: as antislavery
measure, 92–97, 112–13, 141–